The Collapse of
American Criminal Justice

The Collapse of
American Criminal
Justice

William J. Stuntz

The Belknap Press of
Harvard University Press
Cambridge, Massachusetts · London, England

First Harvard University Press paperback edition, 2013

Library of Congress Cataloging-in-Publication Data

Stuntz, William J.
The collapse of American criminal justice / William J. Stuntz.
p.   cm.
Includes bibliographical references and index.
ISBN 978-0-674-05175-1 (cloth: alk. paper)
ISBN 978-0-674-72587-4 (pbk.)
1. Crime prevention—United States.   2. Criminal justice,
Administration of—United States.   3. United States—Race relations.   I. Title.
HV7432.S78   2011
364.40973—dc22   2011006905

For Mike Klarman, Danny Richman, and Carol Steiker—
the most generous colleagues anyone could hope for

Contents

The Collapse of
American Criminal Justice

Introduction:

The Rule of Too Much Law

Little else is requisite to carry a state to the highest degree of opulence from the lowest barbarism but peace, easy taxes, and a tolerable administration of justice.

—Adam Smith, *The Wealth of Nations* (1776)

In Heaven there will be no law, and the lion will lie down with the lamb. . . .
In Hell there will be nothing but law, and due process will be meticulously observed.

—Grant Gilmore, *The Ages of American Law* (1977)

AMONG THE GREAT UNTOLD STORIES of our time is this one: the last half of the twentieth century saw America's criminal justice system unravel. This book seeks to address two questions. First, how did the unraveling happen? And second, how might our dysfunctional justice system be repaired? Answering the first question goes some distance toward answering the second.

Signs of the unraveling are everywhere. The nation's record-shattering prison population has grown out of control. Still more so the African American portion of that prison population: for black males, a term in the nearest penitentiary has become an ordinary life experience, a horrifying truth that wasn't true a mere generation ago. Ordinary life experiences are poor deterrents, one reason why massive levels of criminal punishment coexist with historically high levels of urban violence.

Outside the South, most cities' murder rates are a multiple of the rates in those same cities sixty years ago[1]—notwithstanding a large drop in violent crime in the 1990s. Within cities, crime is low in safe neighborhoods but remains a huge problem in dangerous ones, and those dangerous neighborhoods are disproportionately poor and black. Last but not least, we have built a justice system that strikes many of its targets as wildly unjust. The feeling has some evidentiary support: criminal litigation regularly makes awful mistakes, as the frequent DNA-based exonerations of convicted defendants illustrate.[2] Evidently, the criminal justice system is doing none of its jobs well: producing justice, avoiding discrimination, protecting those who most need the law's protection, keeping crime in check while maintaining reasonable limits on criminal punishment.

It was not always so. For much of American history—again, outside the South—criminal justice institutions punished sparingly, mostly avoided the worst forms of discrimination, controlled crime effectively, and, for the most part, treated those whom the system targets fairly. The justice system was always flawed, and injustices always happened. Nevertheless, one might fairly say that criminal justice worked. It doesn't anymore.

There are three keys to the system's dysfunction, each of which has deep historical roots but all of which took hold in the last sixty years. First, the rule of law collapsed. To a degree that had not been true in America's past, official discretion rather than legal doctrine or juries' judgments came to define criminal justice outcomes. Second, discrimination against both black suspects and black crime victims grew steadily worse—oddly, in an age of rising legal protection for civil rights. Today, black drug offenders are punished in great numbers, even as white drug offenders are usually ignored. (As is usually the case with respect to American crime statistics, Latinos fall in between, but generally closer to the white population than to the black one.)[3] At the same time, blacks victimized by violent felonies regularly see violence go unpunished; the story is different in most white neighborhoods. The third trend is the least familiar: a kind of pendulum justice took hold in the twentieth century's second half, as America's justice system first saw a sharp decline in the prison population—in the midst of a record-setting crime wave—then saw that population rise steeply. In the late 1960s and early 1970s, the United States had one of the most lenient justice systems in the world. By century's end, that justice system was the harshest in the history of democratic government.

Take these three trends in turn. As drivers on our highways know well, American law often means something other than what it says. Roadside signs define the speed limit, or appear to do so: 65 or 70 miles per hour on well-built highways, 25 or 30 on local roads in residential areas, something in between for local highways and main roads in business districts. But drivers who take those signs seriously are in for a surprise: drive more slowly than the posted speed limit in light traffic and other drivers will race past, often with a few choice words or an upraised middle finger for a greeting. In the United States, posted limits don't define the maximum speed of traffic; they define the *minimum* speed. So who or what determines the real speed limits, the velocity above which drivers risk traffic tickets or worse? The answer is: whatever police force patrols the relevant road. Law enforcers—state troopers and local cops—define the laws they enforce.

That power to define the law on the street allows the police to do two things they otherwise couldn't. First, state troopers can be selectively severe, handing out fines for driving at speeds no higher than most cars on the road. Second, those same state troopers can use traffic stops to investigate other crimes (assuming one can call speeding a crime), stopping cars in order to ask permission to search for illegal drugs.[4] That common practice gave birth to the phrase "racial profiling," as troopers patrolling state highways stopped black drivers in large numbers, ostensibly for violating traffic rules but actually to look for evidence of drug offenses.[5] Both enforcement patterns lead to the same bottom line. Because nearly all drivers violate traffic laws, those laws have ceased to function on the nation's highways and local roads. Too much law amounts to no law at all: when legal doctrine makes everyone an offender, the relevant offenses have no meaning independent of law enforcers' will. The formal rule of law yields the functional rule of official discretion.

So what? Arbitrary enforcement of the nation's traffic laws is hardly a national crisis. Even discriminatory traffic enforcement is a modest problem, given the far more serious forms race discrimination can and does take. Why worry about such small problems? The answer is because the character of traffic enforcement is not so different from the ways in which police officers and prosecutors in many jurisdictions battle more serious crimes. The consequence is a disorderly legal order, and a discriminatory one.

In the 1920s, Prohibition's enforcers imprisoned those who manufactured and sold alcoholic beverages, not those who bought and drank them.[6] Today, prosecutions for selling illegal drugs are unusual in many jurisdictions—instead, prosecutors charge either simple possession or "possession with intent to distribute," meaning possession of more than a few doses of the relevant drug. Those easily proved drug violations are used as cheap substitutes for distribution charges. Worse, in some places, drug possession charges have become one of the chief means of punishing violent felons. Proof of homicide, robbery, and assault is often difficult because it requires the cooperation of witnesses who agree to testify in court. If the police find drugs or an unregistered weapon on the defendant's person or in his home, those witnesses need not be called and those harder-to-prove offenses can be ignored. The drug and gun charges all but prove themselves, and those charges stand in for the uncharged felonies.

Nor is the phenomenon limited to drug cases. Convicting Martha Stewart of insider trading proved impossible, but no matter: Stewart could be punished for hiding the insider-trading-that-wasn't.[7] O. J. Simpson skated on the murder charges brought in the wake of his ex-wife's death. Again, no matter: Simpson now serves a long prison term—he will be eligible for parole nine years after he began serving his sentence—for a minor incident in which he tried to recover some stolen sports memorabilia.[8] The government rarely charges terrorism when prosecuting suspected terrorists; convicting for immigration violations is a simpler task.[9] In all these examples, criminal law does not function as law. Rather, the law defines a menu of options for police officers and prosecutors to use as they see fit.

Discretion and discrimination travel together. Ten percent of black adults use illegal drugs; 9 percent of white adults and 8 percent of Latinos do so. Blacks are nine times more likely than whites and nearly three times more likely than Latinos to serve prison sentences for drug crimes.[10] The racial composition of the dealer population might explain some of that gap but not most of it, much less all.[11] And the same system that discriminates against black drug defendants also discriminates against

black victims of criminal violence. Clearance rates for violent felonies—
the rates at which such crimes lead to suspects' arrest—are higher in small
towns and rural areas than in suburbs, higher in suburbs than in small
cities, and higher in small cities than in large ones.[12] Those relationships
correlate both with poverty and with race: the more poor people and
black people in the local population, the less likely that victims of criminal violence will see their victimizers punished.[13] Bottom line: poor black
neighborhoods see too little of the kinds of policing and criminal punishment that do the most good, and too much of the kinds that do the
most harm.

A larger measure of official discretion has also coincided with the rise
of pendulum justice. Beginning around 1950, imprisonment rates in the
Northeast and Midwest began to fall. By the mid-1960s, the decline had
accelerated and extended nationwide. The nation's imprisonment rate
fell by more than 20 percent, while the murder rate—a decent proxy for
the rate of violent felonies and felony thefts more generally—doubled.[14]
In northern cities, these trends were more extreme. Chicago's murder
rate tripled between 1950 and 1972, while Illinois's imprisonment rate
fell 44 percent. In New York City, murders more than quintupled in those
twenty-two years; the state's imprisonment rate fell by more than one-
third. Detroit saw murders multiply seven times; imprisonment in Michigan declined by 30 percent.[15] The combination of those trends meant
that the justice system was imposing vastly less punishment per unit
crime than in the past. This turn toward lenity was followed by an even
sharper turn toward severity. Between 1972 and 2000, the nation's imprisonment rate quintupled. The number of prisoner-years per murder
multiplied nine times.[16] Prisons that had housed fewer than 200,000 inmates in Richard Nixon's first years in the White House held more than
1.5 million as Barack Obama's administration began. Local jails contain
another 800,000.[17]

The criminal justice system has run off the rails. The system dis-
penses not justice according to law, but the "justice" of official discretion.
Discretionary justice too often amounts to discriminatory justice. And no
stable regulating mechanism governs the frequency or harshness of criminal punishment, which has swung wildly from excessive lenity to even
more excessive severity.

Why? Two answers stand out: one concerns law, the other democracy. As unenforced speed limits delegate power to state troopers patrolling the highways, so too American criminal law delegates power to the prosecutors who enforce it. That discretionary power is exercised differently in poor city neighborhoods than in wealthier urban and suburban communities. Far from hindering such discrimination, current law makes discriminating easy. That sad conclusion has its roots in a sad portion of America's legal history. When the Fourteenth Amendment's guarantee of the "equal protection of the laws" was enacted, one of its chief goals was to ensure that criminal law meant one law alike for blacks and whites—that both ex-slaves and ex-slaveowners would be held to the same legal standards, and that crime victims among both groups received roughly the same measure of legal protection.[18] That understanding of equal protection did not survive Reconstruction's collapse.[19] Today, the equal protection guarantee is all but meaningless when applied to criminal law enforcement, one reason why both drug enforcement and enforcement of laws banning violent felonies are so different in black communities than in white ones.

The democracy answer likewise has its roots in history: the history of American local government. In most countries, national governments or provincial governments enforce criminal law. Here, local institutions—chiefly city police forces and county prosecutors' offices—do most of the enforcing, while locally selected juries judge those criminal defendants who take their cases to trial. Likewise, in most of the world prosecutors and judges are civil servants. Here, local prosecutors—the ones who try the large majority of cases—and trial judges (appellate judges, too) are, with few exceptions, chosen by voters of the counties in which they work.[20] At least in theory, these features of the justice system give citizens in crime-ridden neighborhoods a good deal of power over criminal law enforcement in their neighborhoods.

That power is less substantial than it once was, thanks to four changes that happened gradually throughout the twentieth century. First, crime grew more concentrated in cities, and especially in poor neighborhoods within those cities.[21] Historically, crime was not an urban problem in the United States: cities' murder rates were no higher than the nation's.[22] In the last sixty years, that has changed. Poor city neighborhoods are more dangerous than they once were, and wealthier urban and suburban neighborhoods are probably safer. Today, a large fraction—often a large majority—of the population of cities and metropolitan counties live in neighborhoods where crime is an abstraction, not a problem that defines neighborhood life. This gives power over criminal justice to voters who have little stake in how the justice system operates. Second, the suburban population of metropolitan counties mushroomed. This shift in local populations matters enormously, because prosecutors and judges are usually elected at the county level. Today, counties that include major cities have a much higher percentage of suburban voters than in the past. This means suburban voters, for whom crime is usually a minor issue, exercise more power over urban criminal justice than in the past.

Third, jury trials, once common, became rare events. The overwhelming majority of criminal convictions, more than 95 percent, are by guilty plea, and most of those are the consequence of plea bargains.[23] This change shifts power from the local citizens who sit in jury boxes to the less visible assistant district attorneys who decide whom to punish, and how severely. Fourth and finally, state legislators, members of Congress, and federal judges all came to exercise more power over criminal punishment than in the past. The details are complicated; how and why this change happened is one of this book's larger stories. But the bottom line is clear enough: a locally run justice system grew less localized, more centralized.

All these changes limited the power of residents of poor city neighborhoods—the neighborhoods where levels of criminal violence are highest. Residents of those neighborhoods, most of whom are African American, have less ability than in the past to govern the police officers and prosecutors who govern them. As local democracy has faded, the rule of law has collapsed, discrimination has grown more common, and criminal punishment has become prone to extremes of lenity and severity. Here as elsewhere, correlation does not prove causation. But this coincidence seems more than coincidental. If criminal justice is to grow more just, those who bear the costs of crime and punishment alike must exercise more power over those who enforce the law and dole out punishment.

Which leads to an obvious question: How might things be set right? The solution to the system's many problems has two main ingredients.

The first is a revival of the ideal of equal protection of the laws. Criminal punishment will not control crime at acceptable cost as long as punishment is imposed and the law's protection is provided discriminatorily. The second ingredient is a large dose of the local democracy that once ruled American criminal justice. That second aspect of wise reform is already happening: the rise of community policing has made local police more responsive to the wishes of those who live with the worst crime rates. That trend needs to go farther. Plus, we need fewer guilty pleas and more jury trials in order to give local citizens—not just prosecutors— the power to decide who merits punishment and who doesn't. More jury trials in turn require a different kind of criminal law: law that looks more like the criminal law of America's past, and less like the speed limits that give state troopers unconstrained power over those who travel America's highways.

The rest of the book is organized as follows. Part One, which looks at the big picture, consists of two chapters. Chapter 1 contrasts the crime and punishment consequences of two great migrations: the waves of European immigrants who came to America's shores between the 1840s and World War I, and the black migration from the rural South to northern cities that extended over the first two-thirds of the twentieth century. Chapter 2 examines the central criminal justice problem of our time— America's enormous, disproportionately black prison population.

Part Two is the bulk of the book; the goal is to explain how the justice system came to be the arbitrary, discriminatory, and punitive beast it is. Chapter 3 covers two topics: the establishment of the constitutional rights that help to define American criminal justice, and the rise of the institutions and practices that distinguished criminal justice in the pre– Civil War North from the more privatized style of "justice" in the slave South. Chapter 4 catalogs the brief rise and swift fall of the ideal of equal protection of the laws. For a time following the Civil War, that ideal looked likely to play a large role in shaping the nation's criminal justice system, but did not do so. It still doesn't. The subject of Chapter 5 is criminal justice in the Gilded Age: roughly, the half-century between Reconstruction's end and the Great Depression's beginning. During those years, northern cities established a style of criminal justice that was more lenient, more egalitarian, and more effective than today's version. In the South, criminal justice was more punitive, more discriminatory, less stable, and less successful at controlling criminal violence. The West first resembled the South, then gradually came to adopt the North's practices.

Chapter 6 examines a particular aspect of Gilded Age criminal justice: the culture war that began with the fight against polygamy in the 1880s and ended with Prohibition's repeal in the early 1930s. In between, the justice system battled state lotteries, interstate prostitution rings, and narcotics. These battles redefined federal criminal law, and the redefinition gradually extended to the states as well. Criminal law became less a means of defining the conduct that would lead to prison or jail time, and more a means of facilitating easy convictions—and a source of ever-growing prosecutorial power. Chapter 7 discusses the pre-1960 rise of constitutional regulation of criminal justice, along with three more productive paths that regulation might have followed but didn't. Chapter 8 turns to the work of Earl Warren's Supreme Court, and the ways the Court exacerbated the inequality and instability that plagued late twentieth-century criminal justice. Chapter 9 explores four trends that have shaped the justice system in our own time: the forty-year crime wave that began in northern cities in the early 1950s and the decade-long crime drop that followed it, the sharp drop in criminal punishment that likewise began in the Northeast in the 1950s and spread to the rest of the nation in the 1960s and early 1970s, and the thirty-year explosion in the nation's inmate population that began in the mid-1970s. Crime rose and then fell, though the rise was bigger than the fall. Criminal punishment fell and then rose—and again, the rise was bigger than the fall. These trends were both symptoms and causes of the dysfunctional justice system we have today.

Part Three consists of a single chapter that turns to the future, and briefly surveys some means by which the broken machinery of American criminal justice might be repaired. The book concludes with a brief Epilogue that offers some modest reason for hope—the word *modest* merits emphasis here—that, at least in part, the repair might come to pass.

A word about intellectual method is in order. Though most of this book is about the past and a few portions of it deal with empirical data, I am neither a historian nor an empirical social scientist, as members of those guilds will quickly recognize. Good historians see understanding the past as its own end; drawing contemporary lessons from the past is "presentist," and is to be avoided like the plague. For my purposes, the history of American criminal justice serves two presentist ends: a source of cautionary tales on the one hand and of models that today's justice system could usefully follow on the other. Likewise, academic history usually emphasizes depth over breadth. This book leans the other way. The alternative is to miss the forest for the trees—and in this area, far too much of the forest has been missed.

As for the empiricists, the best ones claim only what their data sets prove. That poses a major challenge for anyone seeking to understand the justice system's past: before the 1970s, high-quality data on crime and punishment are the exception, not the rule.[24] It's always tempting to look for the car keys under the streetlight[25]—but in this instance, the best insights lie in the less well-lit spaces of the more distant past. Better to draw unconfident conclusions based on incomplete evidence than to ignore the past that has shaped the criminal justice present.

The book's conclusions are less than confident for another reason. First-rate scholars have produced substantial literature examining contemporary American crime, crime's history, contemporary criminal justice and its history, the politics of crime and *its* history. Meanwhile, scholarship on crime and criminal justice suffers from a lack of generalists. The historians, economists, sociologists, psychologists, and law professors who study those subjects have had too little to say to one another. Each piece of the elephant has been well described, but no one looks at the beast whole. Connections between past and present, law and politics, crime and criminal justice are missed. Another of this book's goals is to find some of those connections in order to understand better why our criminal justice system tolerates so much crime and produces so little justice.

I am a law professor; I have spent my working life studying the legal doctrines that govern crime and criminal law enforcement. Like all those in my line of work, I believe that legal doctrines play an important role in the sad story of American criminal justice, and they play an important role in this book. But their role is strange and widely misunderstood: law serves chiefly as a means of giving law enforcers greater discretion and more power to exercise it. Regulating the conduct of those law enforcers is mostly left to politics and politicians. This perverse partnership between law and politics has produced many of the system's worst injustices. The tendency, especially among lawyers, is to think that the chief remedy for those injustices lies in more law—especially more constitutional restrictions on the government's ability to police and punish crime. The thought has some merit: the right kind of constitutional restrictions would make for a better and fairer justice system. Even so, the more urgent need is for a better brand of politics: one that takes full account of the different harms crime and punishment do to those who suffer them—and one that gives those sufferers the power to render their neighborhoods more peaceful, and more just.

PART 1

Crime and Punishment

Two migrations and two associated crime waves largely define the history of crime and punishment in the United States. The wave of European immigrants of the late nineteenth and early twentieth centuries led to a modest rise in violence and prompted a modest response from the lenient and localized justice system of that era. The twentieth century's northward migration of southern blacks led to a wave of violent crime—which, oddly, prompted first a sharp decline in criminal punishment and then an unprecedented increase.

The consequence of those trends is an unsustainably large prison population, disproportionately composed of young African American men from poor urban neighborhoods. No democratic society can incarcerate such a large fraction of its poor population and retain the goodwill of that population, all the more so when most poor inmates belong to a different race from most of the nation's citizens. Yet a return to the crime rates of a generation ago is politically intolerable, and would represent a social catastrophe for that same poor population. The last time the number of prison inmates fell sharply—in the 1960s and early 1970s—crime rose even more sharply. Perhaps the same would happen again. That is the box in which government officials seeking to reform American criminal justice find themselves.

The box is similar to the one Thomas Jefferson imagined nearly two centuries ago. To his credit, Jefferson saw that slavery was a terrible wrong that had to end. But what horrors awaited white slaveholders upon their black captives' release? For Jefferson and his fellow masters, the answer was too awful to contemplate.

Or was it? History teaches that Jefferson's diagnosis was wrong: slavery could have been abolished much sooner and with little harm to white slaveowners. Slavery was not an unsolvable problem after all: rather, it was an expensive but eminently solvable one. The same may be true here. Perhaps America's enormous prison population can be reduced substantially without triggering another crime wave—if government officials are willing to do more than simply set prisoners free.

CHAPTER 1

Two Migrations

We are a nation of immigrants.

—Former New York Governor Herbert H. Lehman,
testifying before the House Subcommittee on
Immigration and Naturalization (1947)

The black migration was one of the largest and most rapid mass internal movements of people in history. In sheer numbers it outranks the migration of any other ethnic group . . . to this country.

—Nicholas Lemann, *The Promised Land:
The Great Black Migration and How it Changed America* (1992)

IN THE SEVENTY YEARS preceding World War I, 30 million-plus Europeans left their homelands and headed for America's shores.[1] Though a few of these immigrants settled in the South and some established farms on the midwestern prairie, the largest fraction populated the cities of the nation's industrial belt: the great swath of territory north of the Potomac and Ohio rivers and east of the Mississippi. Those cities were transformed.

Here is one sign of the transformation: in 1854, the anti-immigrant Know-Nothing Party won all but three seats in the Massachusetts legislature,[2] including nearly every Boston seat—a mark of the comprehensive Yankee domination over the Bay City a decade after the Irish potato famine had begun changing the city's demographics. Thirty years later, Boston elected its first Irish mayor; Yankee domination was a thing of the past. Another twenty years and it was the immigrants and their offspring who dominated city politics. Of the first ten mayoral elections held after 1900, seven were won by candidates of Irish ancestry: two by

John Fitzgerald, grandfather of the thirty-fifth President, and three by James Michael Curley, long the city's leading politician and most famous political rogue. (Curley later served part of his fourth term as mayor from a prison cell.)[3] Boston—ancestral home of Yankee Protestantism, dwelling of the Cabots and the Lodges—became a city run by and for Irish and Italian Catholics: Fitzgerald's city, and Curley's. Similar stories could be told of cities throughout the Northeast and Midwest.

In the first two-thirds of the twentieth century, 7 million blacks left the rural South for those same northern cities.[4] Once again, urban politics and populations were transformed. In 1910, blacks made up 6 percent of Philadelphia's population, 2 percent of Chicago's and Cleveland's, and a mere 1 percent of Detroit's. Seventy years later, those percentages were 38 percent, 40 percent, 44 percent, and 63 percent, respectively.[5] (The dramatic increases flowed partly from the northward migration of southern blacks, and partly from the parallel migration of white city-dwellers to the suburbs.) Before midcentury, white voters ran the cities of the industrial heartland; blacks had little influence on urban politics. Urban machines need votes to survive; as more blacks moved into northern cities and more whites moved out, black voters gradually became the centerpiece of those cities' governing coalitions. By the early 1980s, each of the cities just mentioned had elected black mayors: Cleveland's Carl Stokes in 1967, Detroit's Coleman Young in 1973, and both Chicagoan Harold Washington and Philadelphian Wilson Goode in 1983. Soon afterward, the first generation of big-city black police chiefs took office.[6] In the nation's largest cities, "black power" became a reality, not just a slogan.

Two Crime Waves

Both of these great migrations triggered urban crime waves. That seems natural, even inevitable. Millions of mostly poor young men uprooted from their homes and moving into crowded city slums sounds like a recipe for violence and lawlessness. Actually, given the relevant data, these crime waves should surprise. Young men in mid-nineteenth-century Ireland were a more peaceful lot than their counterparts in the United States.[7] The same was true of other European immigrant populations.[8] Based on European crime rates of the relevant time, the mass immigration of Europeans to the United States should have lowered crime rates, not raised them. The same is true of the northward movement of Southern blacks. Before about 1890, the white murder rate (meaning the rate at which whites killed, not the rate at which they were killed by others) exceeded the murder rate among blacks, in North and South alike.[9] For a century after that date, the black homicide rate rose steadily, again in North and South alike; today it is seven times the white homicide rate.[10] But when the Great Migration began, there was little reason to expect the rising black population in northern cities to prompt a large wave of criminal violence.

These surprising crime waves differed enormously: the first was short-lived and mild, the second long-lasting and severe. Regarding immigrant crime, it is useful to compare murder rates in New York and London, as the latter received vastly fewer immigrants than the former in the late nineteenth and early twentieth centuries. Table 1 shows the comparison.

At all times, New Yorkers are substantially more violent than Londoners. But the two cities' trends are broadly similar. The chief effect of New York's status as the entry point and, often, the permanent home for millions of European immigrants occurs just before and during the Civil War, when the city's murder rate briefly spiked before returning to its preimmigration level. Even during the spike, New York's murder rate was barely one-third of its twentieth-century peak. A second, milder crime increase occurs in both cities in the 1920s—though those figures may be misleadingly high. Early in the twentieth century, as Americans

Table 1. Murder rates per 100,000 population, New York and London, 1840–1925

Years	New York	London
1840–45	4.4	0.3
1860–65	10.8	0.6
1880–85	4.4	0.3
1900–05	3.5	0.4
1920–25	5.3	1.3

Note: The New York data come from Monkkonen's database. The same is true for the London data. Ted Gurr's account of London homicides paints a different picture, with a long-term decline extending to the mid-twentieth century from a level of roughly 1.5 in the 1840s. See Ted Robert Gurr, Historical Trends in Violent Crime: Europe and the United States, in Gurr, ed., Violence in America, at 21–54 (Newbury Park, CA: Sage, 1989).

learned to drive cars and as pedestrians learned to avoid them, the number of fatal traffic accidents was large. Today, deaths from traffic accidents are not counted in the data on murders and manslaughters. That was not always the case in the 1920s, when some jurisdictions treated vehicular homicides like ordinary murders and manslaughters, thereby inflating those jurisdictions' homicide numbers.[11]

Whatever the statistical role played by traffic fatalities, the larger point remains: the gap between the two cities' homicide rates was roughly 4 per 100,000 before the great wave of European immigration to the United States began, and remained roughly 4 per 100,000 after that wave of immigration had ceased. Judged purely by levels of criminal violence, the cost of Ellis Island—the price of the American melting pot—seems remarkably low.

All the more so when one considers the size and character of this great wave of immigration. Northern cities during these years were flooded with immigrants of a half-dozen different nationalities who were accustomed to making war on each other in their European homes. Most immigrants were Catholic, with a generous sprinkling of Orthodox Christians and Jews, in what had been an overwhelmingly Protestant country. Young men—the immigrants were disproportionately young and male—formed ethnic gangs that battled one another for control of city streets. All this happened in the midst of the massive social and economic dislocation that attended the Industrial Revolution, at a time when no government-funded safety net cared for the unemployed during the severe depressions that occurred every fifteen years or so. Religious and ethnic division, a surplus of young men, dramatic economic risk, and social change—these conditions bear some resemblance to the circumstances that have produced bloodbaths in Belfast and Bosnia, Beirut and Baghdad over the course of the last generation.[12] Yet violence levels in American cities in the early decades of the twentieth century bore no resemblance to the violence in those unhappy places in the decades just past. Crime was held in check. By today's standards, immigrant-dominated American cities were safe places.

They were a good deal less safe after the black migration. By the 1930s, black homicide rates in northern cities were a substantial multiple of white homicide rates.[13] So when the black share of those cities' populations began rising steeply, violent crime rose, too. Table 2 tells the story, recording

Table 2. Murder rate per 100,000 population and black share of population, selected cities, 1950–1980

City	1950		1960		1970		1980	
	Murder rate	Black share of pop.	Murder rate	Black share of pop.	Murder rate	Black share of pop.	Murder rate	Black share of pop.
Boston	1	5%	4	9%	18	16%	16	22%
Chicago	7	14%	10	23%	24	33%	29	40%
Cleveland	7	16%	10	29%	36	38%	46	44%
Detroit	6	16%	9	29%	33	44%	46	63%
New York	4	9%	5	14%	14	21%	26	25%
Philadelphia	6	18%	8	26%	18	34%	26	38%
United States	5	10%	5	11%	8	11%	11	12%

Note: City murder rates are taken from the relevant annual volumes of FBI, Uniform Crime Reports. The black percentage of city populations is taken from Campbell Gibson and Kay Jung, Historical Census Statistics on Population Totals by Race, 1790 to 1990, and by Hispanic Origin, 1970 to 1990, for Large Cities and Other Urban Places in the United States (Washington, DC: U.S. Census Bureau, Working Paper No. 76, February 2005).

the murder rate and the black percentage of city population for selected northern cities and for the nation as a whole, at ten-year intervals.

Plainly, a rising black population was not the only force driving up northern murder rates. Crime rose in all sectors of the population: notice that the nation's murder rate doubled in thirty years while the black share of its population rose modestly. As the Great Migration was nearing its end, a flood of Baby Boomers reached their late teens: prime age for male criminality. The sharp uptick in murder rates in the mid-1960s and afterward surely has something to do with the sharp rise in birthrates in the late 1940s and afterward.

Notwithstanding these qualifications, the correlation between race and urban violence in late twentieth-century America is striking. Consider the murder rates and population figures in Table 2 in the form of a scatter graph. Figure 1 covers the city data in Table 2.

The link between rising black populations and rising homicide rates might be clearer still if neighborhood-based homicide rates were widely

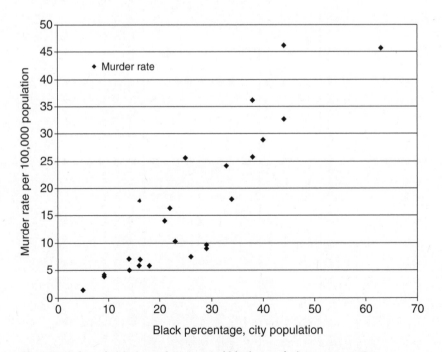

Figure 1. Selected cities' murder rates and black populations, 1950–1980

available, and the link would prove stronger if the data controlled for poverty as well as race. In Chicago's upscale, racially integrated but mostly white Hyde Park, today's homicide rate is 3 per 100,000. In neighboring Washington Park, with a poor, 98 percent black population, the rate is 78 per 100,000.[14] Not only is urban crime concentrated *demographically*, it is also concentrated *geographically*.

The demographic link made visible in Figure 1 is more controversial, but the geographic link may be more important. In 1950, northern cities' murder rates were barely higher than the murder rate for the nation as a whole. By 1970, that had ceased to be true, and it remains false today.[15] Large portions of major cities are war zones. Other large portions of those same cities, along with most of the rest of the country, are reasonably safe. More than 3 million residents of New York State live in cities or towns that saw zero nonvehicular homicides in 2007. With a combined population of a half-million, Buffalo and Rochester alone saw 104.[16] In terms of their exposure to criminal violence, Americans live in two strikingly different nations. That truth goes some distance toward defining our strange politics of crime, as voters in safe places elect the officials who shape criminal justice in dangerous ones.

Returning to demographics, as Table 2 and Figure 1 indicate, high rates of black violence in the late twentieth century are a matter of historical fact, not bigoted imagination. A large body of scholarship notes that political rhetoric about crime grew steadily more racialized as the late twentieth-century's massive crime wave picked up steam.[17] No doubt a generous measure of racism entered into the political mix—but the rhetoric wasn't all racist. Race and crime were bound up together, as immigration and crime once were, only more so. The trends reached their peak not in the land of Jim Crow but in the more civilized North, and not in the age of segregation but in the decades that saw the rise of civil rights for African Americans—and of African American control of city governments. Late twentieth-century urban violence vastly exceeded the worst of the immigrant-driven bloodshed of the late nineteenth century. Comparisons to Bosnia, Beirut, and Baghdad seem apt in this context.

If racism is not the source of the perception that black crime rose steeply, perhaps racism caused the increase. Historical causes of changes in crime are many and hard to disentangle; the notion that racism made the twentieth century's great crime wave worse will come as no surprise to anyone familiar with America's history of racial injustice. I will return to that point later. For now, suffice it to say that causation probably runs in both directions: if racism contributed to the crime wave, the crime wave also caused a kind of racism—or at least, something that looks very much like racism to its targets.

Crime victims in black neighborhoods have difficulty convincing local police to take their victimization seriously, partly because victimization is so common. At the same time, police officers are quick to treat black men as suspects in settings where white men would not be so treated. Cab drivers are quick to take on white passengers but slow to pick up black ones. Pedestrians—including, at one time, the first black president's white grandmother[18]—cross the street more readily or hold their possessions more tightly when they approach young black males on the street than when they cross paths with people from different demographic groups. All these behaviors have the same source: black crime rates that are vastly higher than white ones. Cabbies, pedestrians, and police officers alike know that the incidence of crime varies substantially across demographic groups: young black males commit, proportionally, many more violent felonies than do other portions of the population. The higher incidence of crime frightens cab drivers and pedestrians when they see young men with brown skin. Police officers presumably fear crime less than the rest of us, but they too alter their behavior because of it. Officers working in high-crime neighborhoods may find it impossible to investigate more than a small fraction of serious crimes. Safer neighborhoods have fewer crime victims who receive more police attention.[19]

Randall Kennedy captured the phenomenon best when he wrote that black men pay a "racial tax": regardless of individuals' behavior, police officers and fellow citizens alike are prone to see them first as potential criminals who need punishing, not as possible victims who need protecting.[20] Taken together, age, sex, and skin color function like Hester Prynne's scarlet letter. This demography-based suspicion is among the key social facts that define American life in the late twentieth and early twenty-first centuries. The suspicion may be more rational than racist. But to those on whom suspicion falls, it certainly *looks* racist.

Backlash

Both migrations triggered political backlashes,[21] and in both instances, the backlash had a lot to do with crime. A half-century after the influx of Irish Catholics began, a generation-long crusade against urban vice began. Urban prostitution markets were the crusaders' chief targets in the 1890s and early 1900s.[22] That phase of the anti-vice crusade reached its peak with the passage of the federal Mann Act in 1910, barring interstate transportation of women for "immoral purpose[s]."[23] The Mann Act may have emboldened the early twentieth century's culture warriors, for the next fifteen years saw that crusade's two great triumphs: the Eighteenth Amendment, which banned the manufacture and sale of alcoholic beverages, and the Immigration Act of 1924, which all but banned mass immigration to the United States.[24]

Not long after the Immigration Act was signed into law—a little more than eighty years after a diseased potato crop first drove hundreds of thousands of Irish to America's shores—immigrants and their descendants suffered their worst political defeat. New York Governor Al Smith, child of Irish immigrants and the embodiment of immigrant voters' dreams, won the Democratic nomination for president in 1928. Smith proceeded to lose the general election by one of the biggest margins in American history. Native-born Protestants apparently rejected the idea of rule by their mostly Catholic immigrant neighbors. But Smith's loss marked the end of the anti-immigrant backlash, not its peak. A few years later, Prohibition was repealed. After losing three straight presidential elections by huge margins, what had become the anti-Prohibition party won the next five.[25] Just over a century after mass European immigration began, immigrants' descendants helped elect one of their own, John F. Kennedy, to the White House.

The story of white backlash and black crime seems similar, in some respects eerily so. As the generation-long battle against urban prostitution and corner saloons disproportionately targeted immigrant communities, the generation-long drug war that began in the 1970s disproportionately targeted black communities.[26] The peak of that discriminatory drug war came in 1986, with the passage of federal legislation that punished possession of one gram of crack as much as possession of one hundred grams of cocaine powder. (Most cocaine powder defendants were white; blacks were a minority of crack users but the overwhelming majority of crack defendants.)[27] In the midst of the crack boom—just over eighty years after the Great Migration began, the same as the interval between the first great wave of Irish immigration and Al Smith's defeat—the elder George Bush won the White House after a 1988 campaign dominated by the specter of Willie Horton, a black rapist and murderer who was furloughed by the Massachusetts prison system under Governor Michael Dukakis, Bush's Democratic opponent.[28]

As with Smith's loss to Herbert Hoover, the Willie Horton election marked the beginning of the end of crime-related backlash. A few years later—in the early 1990s, about twenty years after the Great Migration ended—the twentieth century's second great crime drop began.[29] (The first began in 1934, twenty years after mass European immigration ended with the onset of World War I.)[30] After losing three consecutive presidential races by landslides, the party of the mass of black voters won the popular vote in four of the next five, and barely lost the fifth. A century after the first trainloads of southern blacks headed for homes in northern cities—roughly the same interval that separates the initial wave of famine-induced Irish immigration from Kennedy's election—the black migrants' descendants helped to elect America's first black president.

Similar as those stories sound, in one crucial respect the long-ago politics of immigrant crime and the more recent politics of black crime differed enormously. The difference is best captured not by the politicians who built their careers on backlash, but by the political careers that emerged from migrants' own communities.

The twentieth century's first half saw the steady rise of politicians whose electoral base lay in immigrant neighborhoods in large cities. David Ignatius Walsh, successor to the first Henry Cabot Lodge and predecessor to the second, won four Senate terms from Massachusetts[31] after serving for two years as his state's governor. Robert F. Wagner won four terms in one of New York's Senate seats; his son and namesake served three terms as New York City's mayor. Before his landslide loss to Herbert Hoover, Al Smith won four elections to New York's governorship in a Republican era. Wagner was born in Germany and arrived in the United States when he was nine. Walsh and Smith were the children of

Irish immigrants. All three were Catholic (Wagner converted as an adult). Walsh's father worked in a comb factory. Smith's father ran a small carting company and died when his soon-to-be-famous son was twelve, after which Smith took jobs delivering newspapers and working the counter at a small grocery to help support his family. Their stories were repeated across America's industrial belt: governors Henry Horner in Illinois and Herbert Lehman in New York, both sons of Jewish immigrants, and Connecticut Senator Brien McMahon—he changed his name from James O'Brien McMahon—were among the many examples.[32]

Few black politicians climbed so high on the political ladder. Not only is Barack Obama America's first black president, he is only the third popularly elected black Senator in American history, and neither of his predecessors serves in that body today. Taken together, those three Senators—Massachusetts's Edward Brooke and Illinois's Carol Moseley Braun are the others—won a total of four terms in office, the same number Walsh and Wagner each won himself. Only three times have black candidates won election to state governorships: Douglas Wilder in Virginia in 1989 and Deval Patrick in Massachusetts in 2006 and again in 2010. No doubt white racism helped keep those numbers small—but then, nativism and Protestant bigotry were large obstacles to Smith, Wagner, and Walsh, and to a generation of immigrant politicians like them. The size of these two migrations also played a part. By the 1920s, immigrants and their descendants constituted a large fraction of northeastern voters. Blacks occupied a comparable share of state populations only in the Deep South, where black voting was effectively barred until 1965 and where white voters remained hostile for a generation after that date. Politicians like Al Smith and David Walsh had a larger electoral base than Doug Wilder or Deval Patrick would enjoy seventy years later.

Still, numbers and racism do not tell the whole story. White fear of black crime in the late twentieth century was far worse than native-born Protestants' fear of crime by Catholic immigrants in the century's first half—unsurprisingly, since late twentieth-century urban crime rates were much higher than crime rates in immigrant-dominated cities a century earlier. In an age of skyrocketing urban violence, politicians prominently identified with major cities—white and black alike—did badly in state elections. Popular mayors of Atlanta, Los Angeles, and New York all lost campaigns for their states' governorships in the high-crime 1980s and early 1990s.[33] (It seems telling that the one who came closest to success, Los Angeles Mayor Tom Bradley, was a former police officer.) For a generation, that pattern kept black politicians firmly tied to their urban base.

A half-dozen years after the 1990s crime drop had run its course, Obama won the votes of millions of white suburbanites in his campaign for the Democratic presidential nomination, and tens of millions more in his successful general election campaign. Two decades earlier, Jesse Jackson's two presidential campaigns won the votes of fellow African Americans and few others.[34] Plainly, those two politicians have different skill sets, a fact that has a lot to do with their different levels of white support. Still, it seems more than coincidence that black politicians with Obama-like appeal to white voters did not emerge in Jackson's day. In the 1970s and 1980s, black crime was a large barrier to black politicians' ambitions. By the early twenty-first century, the barrier had crumbled. Were it not so, the Obamas might still live in Chicago's Hyde Park, not on Washington's Pennsylvania Avenue.

Explanations

Different crime patterns helped to produce different politics in the early and late twentieth century, but what produced the different crime patterns? The short answer is, no one knows. Crime trends are like the business cycle: explanations of past trends come easily, but no one seems able to predict the future—which should make one suspicious of those stories about the past. Here is the longer answer: no single factor produced the massive, racially skewed crime wave that began in northern cities in the 1950s and spread to the rest of the nation soon after, nor the much milder crime rates of the last years of the nineteenth century and the first years of the twentieth. Still, though theoretical magic bullets do not exist, at least three causes seem to have contributed to the different crime trends these two migrations spawned.

The first of these three potential causes is economic. The young men who left Europe for the United States in the nineteenth and early twentieth centuries found work, discipline, and upward mobility in American industry. The rewards for staying out of trouble with the law were high.

Not so with respect to the young black men who traveled on North-bound trains to Chicago and New York, Philadelphia and Detroit. Those young men found work at wages higher than those they could earn in their native South. But, along with their sons, they were shut out of the jobs and careers that offered hope of rising paychecks and responsibility. Crime was more attractive because its absence was less so; young black men had less to lose than their blue-collar white neighbors. Unsurprisingly, black homicides fell during both world wars, when economic opportunities for black men and women expanded—both because so many white men were in the army and because high-paying weapons manufacturers needed all the workers they could find. After the wars were done, those opportunities disappeared, and the black homicide rate resumed its upward trajectory.[35] By the time the law (finally) banned discriminatory hiring practices in 1964, the best industrial jobs were already fleeing the cities where northern blacks lived. The postindustrial hollowing out of the Rust Belt finished the work that generations of discrimination had started.[36]

That economic story seems to have a good deal of explanatory power. But economic theories of crime explain less than they seem, as a glance at the relationship between crime trends and the business cycle reveals. The last century saw two substantial, decade-long drops in violent crime: the first beginning in 1934, the second in 1992. The first of those crime drops coincided with the Great Depression's second half and a war-induced economic boom. The second crime drop coincided with a long economic expansion followed by the bursting of the dot-com bubble. The 1950s and 1960s were likewise boom times, while the 1970s saw rising inflation and unemployment plus two major recessions. The different economic circumstances of these three decades did not produce different crime trends: all three decades saw steeply rising crime across the Northeast, Midwest, and West Coast; the 1960s and early 1970s saw crime rise throughout the country. In the early 1980s, Americans experienced double-digit unemployment and the deepest recession in nearly fifty years. The murder rate fell by one-fourth. The middle and late 1980s saw rapid, low-inflation economic growth. Murders rose by more than twenty percent—then fell sharply when the 1990s saw another, longer period of low-inflation economic growth.[37] These combinations form no obvious

pattern. The performance of America's economy probably has something to do with the nation's crime trends, but the link is surprisingly
hard to discern.[38]

The historical link between crime rates and punishment patterns
seems stronger. Throughout the 1950s, 1960s, and early 1970s, northern
and western prison populations fell while crime rose; the number of prison
inmates per unit crime plummeted. In 1950, New York State housed 28
prisoners for every New York City homicide. By 1972, that number had
fallen to 3. The figures for Chicago and Detroit, Los Angeles, and Boston
are similar.[39] If punishment deters crime, as a good deal of social science
suggests,[40] its absence must work in the opposite direction: collapsing
punishment in the generation after 1950 surely contributed to skyrocketing crime in that same generation. Nothing comparable happened in the
immigrant-dominated cities of the late nineteenth and early twentieth
centuries. There, punishment per unit crime was fairly stable: declining
modestly in New York and New England, probably holding steady in
most of the old Midwest. So was the rate of urban violence: falling modestly in the latter part of the nineteenth century, rising modestly in the
early years of the twentieth.[41]

But changes in punishment levels, like changes in unemployment levels, explain less than first appears. True: imprisonment rates fell sharply
in the 1950s and 1960s while crime rose sharply, and imprisonment rates
rose in the 1990s when crime fell. But imprisonment rates skyrocketed in
the 1970s and 1980s. Outside cities, crime fell. Inside them, criminal violence kept rising. New York City's murder rate stood at 22 per 100,000
in 1972, the year the state's imprisonment rate hit its trough. By 1990, the
city's murder rate had risen to 31. The murder rates for the same years
in Chicago were the same: 22 and 31, respectively. In Los Angeles, the
analogous figures were 18 and 28. In Detroit, they were 42 and 57. (During those same years, the nation's murder rate rose from 9 per 100,000 to
11, then fell back to 9.) This was during a time when each of the relevant
states' imprisonment rates more than tripled; New York's and Illinois's
more than quadrupled.[42] If more punishment could have spared urban
black neighborhoods the crime wave that crushed many of those neighborhoods in the twentieth century's second half, that crime wave should
have crested sooner than it did.

The third explanation may be the most important. According to historian Randolph Roth, young men kill when the governments and laws that tell them to do otherwise seem unstable or otherwise unable to command loyalty.[43] According to psychologist Tom Tyler, people obey the law, when they do so, because they believe the system of law enforcement to be fair and hence worthy of their respect.[44] When the justice system seems legitimate to the young men it targets, those young men are more likely to follow the system's rules. When that justice system seems illegitimate to those same young men, crime becomes more common, and controlling it becomes more difficult.

Legitimacy sounds like a dry, academic word. The phenomenon that lies behind that word is anything but dry and is hardly the product of scholarly imaginations. Disputes about whose power is rightfully exercised are part of our cultural inheritance. Centuries of literature revolve around conflicts between the reigning king and the rightful heir to the throne; many of Shakespeare's plays explore such conflicts. Dictators' power collapses when the societies they rule come to see that power as fragile and unjustified: witness the fall of the Philippines' Ferdinand Marcos after the assassination of Marcos's opponent Benigno Aquino, or of the Shah of Iran after a year of Islamist demonstrations that he could not suppress, or of Romania's Nicolae Ceauşescu after a mass protest in Timişoara proved that Ceauşescu no longer ruled Romanian city streets. Monarchs and dictators may be especially prone to this virus, but democracies are not immune. The onset of America's Civil War, the fall of Germany's Weimar Republic, the demise of the Third and Fourth Republics in France—central to all these events was a widespread perception that the winners of the relevant elections did not truly represent those they governed. Just as Abraham Lincoln's government could not hold the allegiance of the white South, the governments of Hitler's, Pétain's, and de Gaulle's predecessors commanded neither respect nor fear in large sectors of the populations they sought to rule. Such perceptions cannot help but affect crime rates.

If that hypothesis holds true, these two very different crime waves are less puzzling than first appears. By the late nineteenth century—when crime in immigrant-dominated cities was mostly falling, not rising—working-class immigrants and their offspring largely governed the justice system that governed them. Even today, African Americans have no such power.

In northern cities in the Gilded Age, slots on police forces were patronage jobs, filled by political machines that depended on the votes of the working-class immigrants whose streets most needed patrolling.[45] Those urban machines also chose the district attorneys who prosecuted criminal cases and the judges who tried those cases. Then as now, D.A.s and trial judges were usually elected countywide; then as now, metropolitan counties included large chunks of suburban territory outside city limits. But in the late nineteenth and early twentieth centuries, those suburbs were sparsely populated. Cities contained the votes that mattered.

Urban communities exercised power in jury boxes as well as ballot boxes. Locally selected juries[46] decided a large fraction (nearly half) of serious criminal cases.[47] Those jurors were much more than prosecutorial rubber stamps. Most crimes were defined vaguely, leaving legal space for a wide range of defense arguments. The phrase "jury nullification" was unknown a century ago—not because jurors were more respectful of the law, but because the law was more respectful of arguments for lenity. The government had to prove not just that the defendant had violated the relevant criminal statute, but that he had done so with "criminal intent" or "a guilty mind" or, to use William Blackstone's more pungent phrase, "a vicious will."[48] These legal standards called for moral evaluation, not just fact-finding. Jurors were free to acquit whenever criminal punishment seemed, on balance, unfair.

Acquit they did, and frequently. More than three-quarters of turn-of-the-century Chicago homicides led to no criminal punishment—not because the perpetrator could not be identified, but because no jury would convict.[49] One historian's study of Chicago homicide cases in that period reads like a compendium of bar fights that got out of hand, nearly all of which took place in front of witnesses and most of which ended in defense victories.[50] A system in which easily identified perpetrators succeed so readily is bound to have a small prison population. Across the Northeast and Midwest, prison populations *were* small: these states incarcerated roughly one-sixth the portion of their populations that live behind bars today.[51]

Low crime rates, frequent acquittals, a small prison population—to twenty-first century Americans, this seems an impossible combination. How could a system that punished so sparingly control the violence to which rootless young men are so prone? One answer is, violence was not controlled chiefly through criminal punishment. In large measure, it was controlled through local democracy and the network of relationships that supported it. In the Gilded Age North, criminal punishment was embedded in that network of relationships. Police officers sometimes lived in the neighborhoods they patrolled, and had political ties to those neighborhoods through the ward bosses who represented their cities' political machines. Those patrols happened on foot: officers, those whom they targeted, and those whom they served knew one another. Cops, crime victims, criminals, and the jurors who judged them—these were not wholly distinct communities; they overlapped, and the overlaps could be large.[52] Rage at the depredations of criminals was tempered by empathy for defendants charged with crime: one hesitates before sending neighbors' sons to the state penitentiary. In such a system, those tempted to commit serious crimes could be reasonably confident that they would get a fair shake—which probably made the temptation less powerful. To use more contemporary terminology, the justice system of the Gilded Age relied heavily on soft power and social capital to deter crime.

One ought not romanticize that older justice system. Policing was more relational than in the late twentieth century, but it was also more brutal, more corrupt, and lazier. As one scholar puts it, officers licensed vice rather than prohibiting it, and regulated crime rather than stamping it out.[53] The justice system was vastly less harsh then than now, but lenity was, at least in part, the consequence of too few prosecutors and judges to handle the case load that urban crime generated. A large fraction, perhaps a large majority, of the jurors who judged working-class defendants came from middle-class occupations; class conflict was hard-wired into the system.[54] Still, that system—at least the version that prevailed in the nation's Northeast quarter—was more lenient, more locally democratic, less discriminatory, and more effective than today's counterpart.

Today's justice system is more centralized, more legalized, more bureaucratized—and more devoted to the use of hard power. Like the constabularies of the European empires that nineteenth-century immigrants fled, urban police forces in late twentieth- and early twenty-first-century America are professional bureaucracies, not sources of local political patronage. That fact matters more than the presence or absence of black police chiefs. Officers' relationships with residents of the communities they patrol are defined more by professional detachment than by personal engagement.[55] (The rise of community policing over the past twenty-five years has begun to reverse that trend.) Today as in the past, most urban district attorneys and trial judges are elected countywide, but the makeup of metropolitan county electorates has changed, thanks to the rising numbers of voters from suburbs and well-off city neighborhoods.

Jurors have little control over criminal justice outcomes because so few cases go to trial. Nineteen of every twenty felony convictions are obtained by guilty plea, compared with roughly two-thirds as recently as the early 1960s.[56] In the occasional trials that remain, the law gives jurors less discretion than in the past. Standards like Blackstone's "vicious will" have mostly disappeared; many of the defense arguments that carried the day in criminal trials a century ago are off limits in today's system. Defendants find it harder to claim a lack of criminal intent when that concept is defined more mechanically and much more favorably to the government. Unsurprisingly, conviction rates are higher.[57] At the same time, trial judges have less authority over sentencing; mandatory minimums and binding guidelines determine sentences that would have been governed by trial judges' discretion in the past.[58] The legal system grew more centralized: the decisions of state and national officials—especially legislators and appellate judges—came to matter much more than in the past. Local jurors' and judges' moral evaluations matter less.

Growing centralization lessened the power of the voters who bore the brunt of crime and criminal punishment alike: meaning, in the late twentieth and early twenty-first centuries, urban blacks. The consequences for America's criminal justice system have been substantial. In the 1920s and early 1930s, working-class immigrant communities battled aggressive enforcement of Prohibition—and won the battle. In the late twentieth century, drug enforcement occasioned no similar political battles, in large part because those who paid the price of aggressive drug enforcement lacked the political clout that their immigrant predecessors had.

The effects can be seen in state punishment statistics, as shown in Table 3. During the wave of European immigration—the period covered by the table's first three columns—prison populations either rose modestly, as in the Midwest and Pennsylvania, or declined substantially, as in Massachusetts and New York. In the last three quarters of the twentieth century—the last three columns of the table, the period during which the justice system responded to the crime wave that followed the black migration—imprisonment rates first rose to record-breaking highs, then fell sharply in the midst of a spike in crime, then skyrocketed. Change was the only constant.

The magnitude of the changes is hard to exaggerate. In the 1950s, 1960s, and early 1970s, in the midst of the largest crime wave in American history, prison populations fell throughout the Northeast, Midwest, and West Coast. By the early 1970s, imprisonment rates in those parts of the country were comparable to the lowest imprisonment rates in the twenty-first century Western world. In 2007, Denmark, Norway, and Sweden imprisoned 48, 55, and 55 inmates per 100,000 population, respectively; Russia's imprisonment rate stood at 513. (The European average was 116 per 100,000.)[59] In 1972, the imprisonment rates in Massachusetts, Illinois, and New York stood at 32, 50, and 64. As Table 3 shows, those same prison populations skyrocketed over the next thirty

Table 3. Imprisonment rates per 100,000 population, selected states, 1880–2000

State	1880	1904	1923	1950	1972	2000
Illinois	60	47	65	90	50	371
Massachusetts	61	65	36	78	32	252
Michigan	72	54	91	134	94	480
New York	124	71	58	107	64	383
Ohio	40	53	69	121	77	406
Pennsylvania	43	39	47	73	53	307
United States	61	69	74	118	93	469

Note: Data in the first four columns are taken from Margaret Werner Cahalan, Historical Corrections Statistics in the United States, 1850–1984, at 30, table 3-3 (Rockville, MD: Bureau of Justice Statistics, 1986). Data in the last two columns appear in 1991 Sourcebook, at 637, table 6.72, and Online Sourcebook, table 6.29.2008.

years. New York's imprisonment rate sextupled; Illinois's multiplied more than seven times while Massachusetts's rose nearly eightfold. Those staggering increases understate the degree of the change in punishment practices, because they do not take account of differences in crime rates. Nationwide, the number of prisoner-years per homicide rose more than 700 percent between the mid-1970s and the beginning of the twenty-first century.[60] In the span of a little more than three decades, Americans first embraced punishment levels lower than Sweden's, then built a justice system more punitive than Russia's.[61]

These wild gyrations in criminal punishment hit black neighborhoods hardest. Throughout the twentieth century's second half, crime grew more concentrated in cities with large black populations. When prison populations fell in the generation after World War II, they fell most in the nation's industrial belt, the states that included northern cities with large and growing black populations.[62] After the lenient turn of the 1950s, 1960s, and early 1970s came the more famous punitive turn of the century's last decades, and that trend too was disproportionately visited on black America. When prison populations turned up after 1972, the black share of those populations rose as well, from roughly 40 percent in the early 1970s to half by the mid-1990s.[63] Prison sentences became an ordinary part of male life in many black communities: a rite of passage, even a badge of honor. Today, among white men, the imprisonment rate stands just under 500 per 100,000 population: the highest in American history by a large margin. Among black men, the number tops 3,000; among black men in their twenties and thirties, the figure exceeds 7,000.[64] If present trends continue, one-third of black men with no college education will spend time in prison. Of those who do not finish high school, the figure is 60 percent.[65]

Put these extreme trends together, and the following picture emerges. In the twentieth century's third quarter, criminal punishment collapsed; high-crime black neighborhoods were abandoned to their fate. In the century's final quarter, those neighborhoods saw the mass incarceration of their young men. Near-anarchy in one generation led to authoritarianism in the next; extreme severity followed extreme lenity. In terms of the price criminals pay for their crimes, the justice system saw first a record-shattering deflation, and then an equally unprecedented inflation.

Moderation, consistency, and stable prices—characteristics not only of well-functioning financial systems, but of well-run justice systems, too— were nowhere to be found.

The pattern seems bizarre. The generation that produced the Great Society and the law of civil rights, a generation that believed in the power and beneficence of government institutions, embraced collapsing criminal punishment in the teeth of steeply rising crime: a kind of anarchism in a notably unanarchic age. Evidently, the same government that could be trusted to stamp out race discrimination and make war on poverty could not be counted on to punish crime fairly. Stranger still, the next generation—the one that embraced Reaganism and declared an end to the era of big government—created a prison bureaucracy of unprecedented size and made it the centerpiece of the government's efforts to control crime. Government regulation of markets usually does more harm than good, or so the prevailing wisdom of the twentieth century's last decades held. Yet the same blundering government bureaucracies that could accomplish little save their own preservation were thought able to suppress mass markets in illegal drugs.

What political dynamic could produce such strange outcomes? As the United States grew richer and as its nearly all-white suburbs (at midcentury, they *were* nearly all-white) mushroomed in the years following World War II, crime grew steadily more concentrated in cities, and especially in urban black neighborhoods. Thanks to sheer numbers, the political clout exercised by residents of high-crime city neighborhoods declined; the power of safer, mostly white neighborhoods in cities and suburbs alike grew. White suburbanites had little to lose from crime in black ghettoes. Throughout the 1950s and early 1960s, as violence in northern cities rose, crime remained a nonissue for suburban voters and a small matter for residents of the safer parts of those cities: their own neighborhoods were peaceful enough, and the state of other neighborhoods was no great concern. Beginning with the urban riots of the mid- and late 1960s, indifference turned to fear, then anger. The early and mid-1970s saw falling prison populations bottom out; by 1976, imprisonment was rising steeply.[66] The consequence was the most lenient criminal justice system in American history, followed by the most severe. As American criminal justice ceased to be an exercise in local self-government, stability and equilibrium disappeared. Volatility and extremism took their place.

The core reason is simple. With respect to crime and criminal punishment, residents of *all* neighborhoods, safe and dangerous alike, have two warring incentives. On the one hand, they want safe streets on which to go about their business; they want to travel to parks and schools and stores without fearing for their lives and property. On the other hand, they are loath to incarcerate their sons and brothers, neighbors and friends. The desire for order and the longing for freedom, anger at crime and empathy for the young men whom police officers arrest and prosecutors charge—both forces are powerful, and they push in opposite directions. Anyone who has been the victim of a serious crime knows the desire to see perpetrators punished that seems to be part of our nature.[67] At the same time, all those who have seen neighbors' sons behind bars, or their own, know the agony incarceration imposes on local communities.[68] Local political control over criminal justice harnesses both forces without giving precedence to either.

The balance between those dueling incentives looks different when power over criminal punishment is given to voters and officials outside the communities where crimes happen and punishments are imposed. Anger and empathy alike are weaker forces when they come from voters who see crime on the evening news than when they flow from voters' lived experience. When both forces are weak, small changes in either can produce large systemic consequences: no countervailing force checks the trend toward more or less punishment. Extreme variation becomes the norm, stable equilibrium the exception. The system oscillates not between moderate levels of mercy and retribution, but between wholesale indifference and unmitigated rage. When that happens, we see what Americans have seen over the past half-century—unfathomable lenity, followed by unimaginable severity. The cycle must be broken, and soon.

Success and Failure

The immoderate justice system of the past half-century appears to have one large victory to its credit: the dramatic drop in urban crime in the 1990s, which saw crime rates decline by a third nationwide and by as much as two-thirds in a few cities.[69] The appearance is deceptive. Crime did indeed fall after 1991—but the fall began two decades after the prison population began its steep rise. If rising punishment were the chief cause of the crime drop, crime rates should have fallen both more and sooner. And the drop in crime was much smaller than the generation-long urban crime wave that preceded it. Rates of urban violence remain a great deal higher than fifty or a hundred years ago.

New York is America's safest large city, the city that saw crime fall the most and the fastest during the 1990s and the early part of this decade. Yet New York's murder rate is 80 percent higher now than it was at the beginning of the twentieth century—notwithstanding an imprisonment rate four times higher now than then.[70] That crime gap is misleadingly *small:* thanks to advances in emergency medicine, a large fraction of those early twentieth-century homicide victims would survive their wounds today. Taking account of medical advances, New York is probably not twice as violent as a century ago, but several times more violent. At best, the crime drop must be counted a pyrrhic victory.

Sadly, in this sphere of public policy, pyrrhic victories have been the only kind on offer, and misguided reform has been the norm. The lenient turn of the mid-twentieth century was, in part, the product of judges, prosecutors, and politicians who saw criminal punishment as too harsh a remedy for ghetto violence.[71] The Supreme Court's expansion of criminal defendants' legal rights in the 1960s and after flowed from the Justices' perception that poor and black defendants were being victimized by a system run by white government officials.[72] Even the rise of harsh drug laws was in large measure the product of reformers' efforts to limit the awful costs illegal drug markets impose on poor city neighborhoods.[73] Each of these changes flowed, in large measure, from the decisions of men who saw themselves as reformers. But their reforms showed an uncanny ability to take bad situations and make them worse.

Adolf Berle and Gardiner Means would have understood why. Nearly eighty years ago, Berle and Means published one of the most important books in the history of American government.[74] The book's core claim was that ownership of business corporations had become separate from control of those corporations. Control by nonowner managers and ownership by noncontrolling shareholders gives rise to what economists call "agency cost": the managers will run the business in a manner that suits their interests, not the interests of the shareholders for whom they ostensibly work. Berle and Means saw this state of affairs as the justification for more extensive government regulation of business that would force corporate managers to serve the *public* interest—an argument reborn in contemporary debates about the proper regulation of finance and the systemic risks it poses to the economy as a whole. Contemporary scholars of corporate law tend to see the division of ownership from control as justifying efforts to align managers' incentives not with the preferences of the population as a whole but with shareholders' incentives, so that managers might better serve the needs of their firms' owners.[75]

Both arguments rest on the same insight: the interests of corporate managers should not be privileged over either shareholders or the general public. Shareholders have a moral claim to use corporations' assets to their own advantage, as private property is generally used. The public can justifiably seek to limit the power of concentrated corporate wealth to harm the society that generated the wealth. Managers can make neither of those claims. Their decisions are trustworthy only insofar as the decisionmakers are the faithful agents of someone with a larger stake in how the relevant enterprise is run.

Contemporary American criminal justice faces the same governance problem, but in worse form. After all, corporate managers have good reason to see that the businesses they run remain profitable: their jobs depend on it. The detached masters of today's urban criminal justice systems have less to lose from mismanagement. To the suburban voters, state legislators, and state and federal appellate judges whose decisions shape policing and punishment on city streets, criminal justice policies are political symbols or legal abstractions, not questions the answers to which define neighborhood life. If things go well, the benefits are felt by the residents of high-crime neighborhoods, not by the government officials who make the relevant decisions. If things go badly, the same residents of crime-ridden communities bear the cost. Decisionmakers who neither reap the benefits of good decisions nor bear the cost of bad ones tend to make bad ones. Both excessive lenity and excessive severity come

naturally to a system ruled by voters who see neither crime nor punishment up close. → people don't know all situations + factors

Is productive reform possible? Yes, but not the kinds of reforms that
twentieth-century lawyers and politicians sought. The core principle
should be the same as in the law of corporations: reduce agency cost, place
more power in the hands of residents of high-crime city neighborhoods—
for they are the ones who feel the effects of rising and falling rates of crime
and punishment, just as shareholders feel the effects of rising and falling
corporate profits. Make criminal justice more locally democratic, and justice will be more moderate, more egalitarian, and more effective at controlling crime.

Law can advance that cause, and once did so. Criminal law—the body
of legal doctrine that defines crimes—once seemed designed to ensure
that those defendants who suffer punishment deserve it in the view of
their neighbors and peers. Today, American criminal law is designed to
facilitate criminal convictions and to make plea bargaining easier for
prosecutors. Before the last half-century, the law of trial procedure made
jury trials cheap and reasonably effective, and therefore common. Today's elaborate body of procedural rules has made trials expensive, rare,
and error prone. A return to the older models of legal doctrine, both
substantive and procedural, would at least reduce the level of injustice
the justice system sees now, and might also do a better job of controlling
crime.

It is worth remembering that the Irish and Italian immigrants of a
century ago did not protect themselves against injustice through constitutional rights and procedures; constitutional law played a trivially small
role in the justice system of the Gilded Age. Nor were their interests
protected by state or national legislation. For the most part, urban crime
in immigrant-dominated cities was governed by local politics, not the
state and national kind. Voters who lived on or near crime-ridden streets
mattered; the relevant government officials had to listen to those voters
in order to keep their jobs. Black Americans have never enjoyed that
power.

America's criminal justice system is badly broken, and the consequences of the breakage can fairly be called devastating. The last wave of

criminal justice reform contributed to the problems that cry out for the next wave. Today's would-be reformers would do well to remember that, and to consider the possibility that the best models for productive change may come not from contemporary legislation or court decisions, but from a past that has largely disappeared from our consciousness. Sometimes, the best road forward faces back.

CHAPTER 2

"The Wolf by the Ear"

We have the wolf by the ear, and we can neither hold him, nor safely
let him go. Justice is in one scale, and self-preservation in the other.

—Thomas Jefferson, Letter to John Holmes (1820)

Jefferson's Prediction

Jefferson's letter is better known for another line: "this momentous question, like a fire bell in the night, awakened and filled me with terror. I
considered it at once as the knell of the union."[1] The question, of course,
was the status of black slavery.

When the letter was written, John Holmes was a Massachusetts Congressman, soon to be a Maine Senator. Maine had long been a part of
Massachusetts; in 1819, its people sought admission as a separate state. As
Holmes was among the leading political figures in that soon-to-be state,
he stood to benefit from Maine's admission. This may be why Holmes
found himself on the wrong side of the slavery debate that had divided the
country in 1820, and why he sought Jefferson's help in smoothing things
over with his constituents.

The question of Maine statehood had arisen in Congress shortly after
a would-be slave state—Missouri—also sought admission to what was
then called "the Union." A New York Representative named James Tallmadge, serving the last month of his only term in Congress, proposed an
antislavery amendment to Missouri's petition and thereby triggered a
national political crisis. Under Tallmadge's amendment, no more slaves
could be brought into the new state, and all slaves born after the date of
admission would be free on their twenty-fifth birthdays (in the unlikely

event that their masters had not already sold them to slaveholders farther South). Gradually but inevitably, Missouri would join the free North, not the slave South. By a regional vote in the northern-majority House, the amendment quickly passed. The more proslavery Senate demurred. The controversy grew more heated.[2]

Eventually, the two Houses of Congress agreed to the following deal: Missouri would be admitted as a slave state; at the same time, Maine would be admitted as a free state—thereby preserving the balance between the two sections in the Senate—and, in the remaining portion of the Louisiana Purchase, slavery would be barred north of Missouri's southern border. After a good deal of arm-twisting by Speaker Henry Clay (a slaveholding Kentuckian), barely enough Northerners swallowed this arrangement to enable its passage in the House.[3] Holmes was among Clay's most loyal supporters, one of only five Northerners who opposed Tallmadge's amendment each time it was brought to a vote.[4] Jefferson's letter was designed to help the Congressman answer charges that he was too pro-southern to merit reelection from America's northernmost state.

Knowing his audience, Jefferson made the antislavery case for slavery's expansion.[5] As long as slaves were concentrated in a small portion of the country, white masters' fear of emancipation's consequences would bar all thoughts of abolition. "Justice is in one scale, and self-preservation in the other"—notice which scale Jefferson thought weightier. The only way to avoid choosing between a permanent slave population and mass slaughter of white masters, Jefferson suggested, was to permit slavery to spread out across a larger fraction of the country so that whites might everywhere outnumber the blacks whom they so feared. By this logic, the true friends of emancipation had voted with John Holmes, not with James Tallmadge.

Jefferson's letter is often credited with great foresight: the slavery debate did indeed lead to disunion and civil war, as the "fire bell in the night" line suggested it would—though Jefferson was hardly alone in recognizing that possibility. In the midst of the Missouri debate, John Quincy Adams made the same prediction in his diary, and welcomed it. (Adams thought emancipation worth civil war: "calamitous and desolating as this course of events in its progress must be, so glorious would be its final issue, that, as God shall judge me, I dare not say that it is not to be desired.")[6] In any event, the heart of Jefferson's argument in his letter to John Holmes turned on a different forecast, and on the answer to a different question: What would happen to white masters if and when black slaves were freed? Jefferson's answer to that question was not far-sighted. On the contrary, it was provably wrong.

In the 1860s, slaves *were* freed by the Civil War (and Lincoln's war-time Emancipation Proclamation), by the Thirteenth Amendment, and by the slaves' own efforts. Save for the white soldiers whom black soldiers killed in battle, emancipation prompted no wave of violence by blacks against their former masters.[7] Instead, violence and slaughter ran in the opposite direction. During the war, black soldiers were regularly executed when Confederate forces captured them: the massacre at Fort Pillow by Nathan Bedford Forrest's soldiers and the Battle of the Crater fought in the Petersburg trenches were the most famous examples,[8] though hardly the only ones. Bloody race riots in Memphis and New Orleans, in which nearly all the dead were black and all their killers white, sped the passage and ratification of the Fourteenth Amendment to the Constitution. In the decade following the Civil War's end, more than 80 percent of the homicides in the most murderous jurisdiction in the nation—Caddo Parish, Louisiana—were committed by whites against blacks.[9] As Reconstruction collapsed in the mid-1870s, bands of white militia murdered blacks by the thousands in order to prevent them from voting and so ensure rule by white Democrats. Some of the killers became leading southern politicians. None was ever brought to justice. Across the South, state governments fell to southern whites in a series of violent coups. Overwhelmingly, blacks were the victims of that violence, not the perpetrators.

Justice and self-preservation, it turned out, were not at odds after all—certainly not for white masters. (Ex-slaves were another story: for them, self-preservation turned out to require abandoning all hope of justice.) Freedom and social peace were more compatible than Jefferson and his fellow slaveowners imagined. Slavery was an eminently solvable problem. The chief obstacle to its solution was the will of the free population, not the allegedly violent propensities of the slaves.

There are several large and obvious differences between twenty-first century America's inmate population and nineteenth-century America's slave population. The former is much smaller than the latter, both proportionally and in absolute numbers. On the eve of the Civil War, southern whites owned nearly 4 million black slaves, out of a national population of 31 million.[10] Today, the number of prison and jail inmates stands at 2.3 million, in a nation of 300 million.[11] For the vast majority of those inmates, loss of freedom is temporary—they are released when their sentences have been served. Though voluntary manumission was common practice in parts of the Upper South, most black slaves' status was permanent. The inmate population is multiracial; slaves were all of African descent. Last but certainly not least, slaves' status stemmed from their parentage; inmates are locked up because of their conduct. At least to some degree, prison and jail inmates alike earn their incarceration.[12] Slaves suffered their servitude from birth; their oppression was wholly unearned and unjustified.

Yet there are also important similarities. Incarceration is a form of slavery, as the Thirteenth Amendment's text acknowledges: "Neither slavery nor involuntary servitude, *except as a punishment for crime whereof the party shall have been duly convicted,* shall exist within the United States."[13] Like slaves, prisoners are subject to masters' rule; the essence of their condition is subjection to others' will. Like incarceration for crime, black slavery was—among its other purposes—a means of governing the poorest sector of the population: a privatized substitute for the well-functioning, appropriately sized formal justice system that the antebellum South lacked. Today, privately run prisons are increasingly common, and imprisonment is heavily concentrated among the nation's poorest members.[14] Slaves could not vote, but their presence strengthened the power of their white owners: congressional representation was based on the free population plus three-fifths of the slaves. Prisoners and ex-prisoners hold a similar status today—thanks to felon disenfranchisement laws, current and former prison inmates add to their states' and districts' representation but cannot choose their representatives.[15] The descendants of black slaves constitute roughly 40 percent of the nation's inmates though a mere 13 percent of its general population.[16] Slavery was the near-universal experience of blacks in the antebellum South; as the figures just cited show, incarceration is well shy of universal. Even so, the threat of this temporary enslavement has become part of the cultural furniture of black America.

Two more similarities are crucial. First, both slavery and imprisonment were once regarded as necessary evils, and only later seen as moral and social goods. At the time of the Founding, even slaveowners (most of them) saw slavery as an unfortunate stain on the new nation, one whose size, scope, and duration ought to be minimized if possible. Many white Southerners continued to hold such views, right up to the Civil War.[17] But in the decades before the war, a different view began to spread: John C. Calhoun's assertion that slavery was "a positive good," something to be protected and extended, not limited and restricted.[18] Likewise, at some times in America's past, imprisonment for crime was apparently seen as a sad necessity whose incidence and duration ought to be kept to a minimum.[19] In the twentieth century's last decades, that view was displaced by the notion that incarceration for crime is a positive good, even a moral obligation—but definitely not a sad necessity.

Finally, just as the specter of free blacks struck fear in southern white hearts in the early nineteenth century, so the idea of reducing the nation's enormous prison population may frighten those who live outside prison walls in the early twenty-first. Twice before in the last 75 years, America's imprisonment rate fell sharply: once during and shortly after World War II, the second time during the 1960s and early 1970s. The first time, the nation's murder rate rose nearly 30 percent; the second time, the murder rate doubled.[20] Based on these examples, ordinary citizens are not foolish to imagine that reducing the nation's swollen prison population might carry real danger, not least to the black communities that suffer the worst consequences of urban crime. Justice may compel the conclusion that far too many young black men live behind bars—but self-preservation may suggest that keeping them there is nevertheless the best of a bad set of alternatives. Jefferson's words might apply better to today's massive, racially skewed inmate population than to the slaves about whom he wrote.

Two sets of questions lie behind that massive inmate population. The first is a matter of numbers: How many prisoners are too many? Where is the relevant line, and is twenty-first-century America on the wrong side of it? The second concerns risk: Assuming today's inmate population is too large, can that population be reduced without triggering more of the very crimes that landed prisoners in their cells in the first place?

Are justice and self-preservation at odds? Though Jefferson was wrong about slavery, might his words be right when applied to crime and punishment?

Numbers

Jefferson's trade-off was between justice and self-preservation. Understanding the nature and consequences of today's enslaved population requires a different starting point: numbers and the social reality they represent.

No one knows the right number of prisoners in a given place and time, because no generally accepted yardstick exists. One's answer depends on which baseline one chooses: the point of comparison against which contemporary American punishment practices are to be measured. Three such baselines seem plausible. Today's prison population might be measured by the prison populations of America's past. Or one might compare punishment practices in the United States to the practices of other Western democracies with similar political and legal traditions. These first two baselines are the ones that dominate the relevant academic literature. Finally, the prison population might be judged relative to the incidence of serious crime—in which case the relevant figure is not the number of inmates, but the ratio between that number and the number of major crimes. That third baseline probably captures the preferences of a majority of American voters.

Take these measures in turn. By comparison to the punishment levels of America's past, today's prison population is huge. Before 1980, the highest imprisonment rate in American history came in 1939, when the nation's prisons held 137 inmates per 100,000 population. In 2008, the imprisonment rate was more than three-and-a-half times that older historical record.[21] (Save where otherwise indicated, the figures cited refer only to prison inmates, due to the limited historical data on jail populations.) The wave of incarceration that produced those numbers extended nationwide: in every region, imprisonment at least tripled in the twentieth century's second half.[22] In some jurisdictions, the increase was much larger. In 1950, 77 of every 100,000 Texans were housed in state penitentiaries; by 2000, the figure was 730. Massachusetts's imprisonment rate rose from a mere 32 in 1972 to 278 in 1997. Between 1973 and 2003, Mississippi's imprisonment rate rose from 76 to 763.[23]

The rising number of inmates was chiefly due to a rise in the number of defendants charged and convicted. Average sentences rose significantly, but not massively. In 1960, the average time served for state-court felony convictions stood at 28 months; by 1999, that figure had risen to 34 months.[24] Today's justice system does punish crime more severely than in the past—but its defining feature is that it punishes vastly more often. That proposition holds for all categories of crime. Drug cases multiplied in the late twentieth century; the rate of imprisonment for drug offenses rose tenfold in the century's last thirty years. Still, drug prisoners amount to only 20 percent of the prison population.[25] If all drug cases were removed from the statistics, America's imprisonment rate would still have quadrupled over the past thirty-five years. Drugs were a significant factor in exploding prison populations, but they are not the explosion's primary cause—and the same is true of the three-strikes laws and mandatory minimum sentences that increased punishment for various classes of nondrug crime. More inmates live in state and federal penitentiaries than in the past chiefly because prosecutors have charged and convicted more criminal defendants than in the past.

As rising crime was not evenly distributed across the population, neither were those additional criminal prosecutions, as shown in Table 4. If the general imprisonment rate is high, the rate of black incarceration can fairly be called astronomical. The black imprisonment rate for 2000

Table 4.   Black and white imprisonment rates per 100,000 population, 1950–2000

Race	1950	1960	1970	1980	1990	2000	Change, 1950–2000
Black	402	441	361	495	1,203	1,830	355%
White	86	86	64	73	177	244	184%

Note: Imprisonment rates by race for 1950, 1960, 1970, and 1980 are taken from Margaret Werner Cahalan, Historical Corrections Statistics in the United States, 1850–1984, at 65, table 3-31 (Rockville, MD: Bureau of Justice Statistics, 1986); general population data, broken down by race, are taken from the relevant volumes of the Statistical Abstract. Prison populations by race for 1990 and 2000 are taken from 1991 Sourcebook, 641, table 6.75, and from 2001 Sourcebook, 498, table 6.28, respectively. General population data, again broken down by race, for both 1990 and 2000 appear in 2001 Statistical Abstract, 13, no. 10.

exceeds by one-fourth the imprisonment rate in the Soviet Union in 1950—near the end of Stalin's reign, the time when the population of Soviet prison camps peaked. If jail inmates are included, per capita black incarceration is 80 percent higher than the rate at which Stalin's regime banished its subjects to the Gulag's many camps.[26]

The human consequences of those facts are unknown and, for now at least, unknowable. But they may prove catastrophic. Over the last thirty-five years—the period during which the nation's inmate population multiplied sevenfold—the black marriage rate fell twice as fast as its white counterpart. More than 40 percent of black men and women never marry; the large majority of black children are born out of wedlock.[27] One reason for those statistics is that a sizeable fraction of black men of marriageable age are either in prison, about to go there, or just released.[28] The black unemployment rate is more than double the unemployment rate for whites, not counting inmate populations.[29] (When inmate populations are counted, the gap increases substantially.)[30] Again, black incarceration rates contribute to that gap: even after sentences are served, the legal jobs available to former prisoners are few and unappealing.[31] That fact also explains why, in poor black neighborhoods, drug distribution networks employ large numbers of young men at low wages:[32] low-wage, labor-intensive drug dealing survives where higher-paid legal work is hard to come by. Scholars have noted the effect of poor economic opportunity on black crime,[33] but causation runs in both directions: black crime leads to black imprisonment, which reinforces the low level of economic opportunity in black neighborhoods, which in turn encourages more black crime.

The consequences of this vicious circle may be as much cultural as economic. The removal from black communities of a substantial fraction of young men and a smaller but growing fraction of young women cannot help but alter those communities' sense of identity, and the mores on which cultural identity rests. The scars may run deeper than those made by the most violent wars or the most deadly diseases. Wars sometimes carry off a neighborhood's young men—but most wars last a few years or less, and the large majority of those young men return from even the bloodiest of them. Epidemic disease may kill huge numbers—but the worst pandemic in American history, the Spanish flu that struck in 1918, claimed a smaller percentage of the population than the prison system claims in black communities today.[34] And like wars, epidemics end; they play themselves out. Mass incarceration goes on and on. Barring major changes in America's criminal justice system, the black imprisonment rate will be as high a generation from now as it is today, or nearly so. Large consequences are bound to flow from such large social facts.

As striking as the sheer size of the black inmate population is the magnitude of its rise. That population multiplied more than seven times in the last three decades of the twentieth century.[35] Change at once that rapid and that sustained has no precedent in American history. Once before—from the early 1920s to the late 1930s, the era of Prohibition and the New Deal—the United States saw a dramatic, nationwide rise in its prison population. The imprisonment rate nearly doubled, from 74 to 137 per 100,000 population. Between 1972 and 2006, the nation's imprisonment rate more than quintupled, rising from 93 to 491. The first period saw an average annual increase of just under 4 percent; in the second, the average increase topped 5 percent—and that rate of increase lasted for more than thirty years. In the Prohibition-era punishment wave, North Carolina's imprisonment rate more then tripled. In the late twentieth century, several states' imprisonment rates multiplied seven, eight, or nine times; Mississippi's rose more than tenfold.[36] The late twentieth-century run-up in America's prison population was unlike anything in America's past.

Of course, the fact that punishment levels are much higher than in the past does not prove that they are too high. Perhaps the justice system of generations past was far too lenient (true enough in the 1960s and early 1970s), or perhaps the explosion in the prison population was a logical response to changes in the character and frequency of serious crime. The black crime rate is substantially higher than its white counterpart; the difference between the two rates accounts for most—though not all—of the difference between black and white imprisonment rates.[37] The key point is that *some* explanation is called for: changes of this magnitude demand justification. Whatever else America's inmate population is, it isn't normal: not by the standards of American history.

Nor is it normal by the standards of the rest of the Western world. As of 2007, the imprisonment rate in England and Wales stood at 132 per 100,000; in Scotland, the imprisonment rate was 114. The analogous figure in the United States for the same year was 506. The British are more punitive than their Western European neighbors: the Netherlands' imprisonment rate was a mere 78; Germany's was 74, France's only 72, and Scandinavian rates were lower still. The European average was 116, thanks mostly to the former Communist states of Central and Eastern Europe. Even there, imprisonment rates are far lower than in the United States, as these figures show: Ukraine's 2007 imprisonment rate was 252; Latvia's stood at 213, and Poland's at 200. On the European continent, only Russia rivals the United States in the proportion of its citizens who are incarcerated: there, the imprisonment rate in 2007 was 513 per 100,000.[38]

When one takes account of different nations' different crime rates, the gap between American punishment practices and those of other nations grows larger still. With the large exception of homicide, most Western European nations are as crime-ridden as the United States or more so. Belgium, France, Portugal, Spain, and Great Britain all have higher rates of robbery than the United States. Austria, Denmark, the Netherlands, Spain, Sweden, Switzerland, and Great Britain have higher rates of burglary—in most instances, twice as high. Rates of auto theft are higher in France, Denmark, Sweden, and Britain.[39] If Western nations' crime rates determine the size of their prison populations, the United States should imprison roughly the same share of its citizenry as do the British or the French, the Portuguese or the Dutch—not four to seven times as many.

However one slices the data, the bottom line remains: by the standards of the rich West—the part of the world that most resembles the United States economically, politically, and legally—America's prison population is stunningly large. Even by the standards of the nations that emerged from the breakup of the Soviet Union, American imprisonment rates are surprisingly high. Either something has gone badly wrong with America's justice system in the last generation, or Russia is a better gauge of reasonable levels of criminal punishment in the United States than the richer and freer nations of Western Europe.

Justice

There is a third possibility: perhaps America's past and Europe's present are the wrong yardsticks. Instead, one might suppose, America's criminal justice system should be judged by how nearly its outcomes approximate justice. On this view, the proper standard of measurement is not prison populations past or present, foreign or domestic. Rather, the number with which America's prison population needs to be compared is the number of serious crimes that America's criminals commit.

The two reigning theories of criminal punishment taught in American law schools today embrace that yardstick. One holds that punishment for crime is a moral good because crime is a moral wrong. The other theory looks not to moral rights and wrongs but to social costs and benefits: crime is socially costly, and socially costly behavior is best reduced by raising the price paid by those who engage in such behavior. Notice that both theories—retribution and deterrence, the moral and economic justifications for imprisonment—lead to the same bottom line: the more often crime is punished, the better. To retributivists, maximizing the frequency of punishment for crime means maximizing a moral good, which must itself constitute a moral good.[40] To believers in conventional deterrence theory, the more often crime is punished, the more rare crime will be. If either of these theories is right, the appropriateness of America's prison population depends not on any of the data discussed here, but on the answer to a single question: Are the nation's prisoners, or at least a sufficiently high percentage of them, guilty of the crimes for which they were convicted and punished? Prison sentences may be a moral and social good regardless of how often they are imposed—so long as the sentences are not excessive, and so long as those punished are criminals.

Both that proposition and the theories that underlie it sound commonsensical. Surely a morally sound justice system should have no compunctions about punishing those who steal, injure, and kill for their own ends. And one might reasonably assume that the more likely murderers, rapists, and car thieves are to face punishment for their crimes, the fewer murders, rapes, and stolen cars there will be. After all, the United States experienced the worst crime wave in its history in the 1960s and 1970s, while its prison population was falling. The two largest crime drops of the twentieth century came in the 1930s and the 1990s— and both of those decades saw the prison population reach record highs.[41] In light of those propositions, the massive rise in imprisonment of the last generation may represent neither an injustice that needs remedying nor a puzzle that needs explaining, but a policy success that merits celebration.

Indeed, judged either by standard retributive principles or by conventional assumptions about deterrence, America's prison population is much too *small*. According to FBI data, 11 million violent felonies and felony thefts were reported to police in 2008.[42] If unreported crimes are added to the mix, the figure rises considerably: according to the National Victimization Survey, the true number of violent felonies and felony thefts each year is 23 million.[43] That figure does not count drug crimes. Tens of millions of Americans use illegal drugs on a regular basis; the number of dealers must be in the low seven figures. By comparison to the numbers just cited, a 1.5 million-strong prison population with something in excess of 300,000 drug prisoners seems well shy of enormous.[44] Out of tens of millions of felonies that happen each year, American prosecutors convict 1.1 million felons, roughly 700,000 of whom must serve prison sentences.[45] The world's most punitive justice system punishes a remarkably small fraction of serious crimes. What gives?

The core answer is that, like any justice system, the United States' justice system lacks the capacity to punish all major crimes—much less all crimes, period. American governments spend roughly $200 billion each year on policing, criminal adjudication, and corrections combined.[46] If even one-third of felonies were to lead to arrest, prosecution, and punishment, that annual spending figure would likely exceed $1 trillion. Policing and criminal punishment would play approximately the same role in government spending that old-age pensions and health care play today. Even a nation as wealthy as ours might reasonably conclude that the game is not worth the candle, that punishing a large fraction of serious wrongdoing is unaffordable.

That proposition would hold true even if maximizing punishment were the best means of maximizing deterrence. It isn't, for two main reasons. Criminologist Daniel Nagin captures the first:

> Evidence from perceptions-based deterrence studies . . . suggest[s] that the deterrent effect of formal sanctions arises principally from fear of the social stigma that their imposition triggers . . . If fear of stigma is a key component of the deterrence mechanism, such fear

would seem to depend on the actual meting out of the punishment being a relatively rare event. Just as the stigma of Hester Prynne's scarlet "A" depended on adultery being uncommon in Puritan America, a criminal record cannot be socially and economically isolating if it is commonplace. Policies that are effective in the short term may erode the very basis for their effectiveness over the long run if they increase the proportion of the population who are stigmatized . . . [47]

Recall the Laffer Curve, a staple of 1980s political debate.[48] Conservative economist Arthur Laffer argued that high marginal tax rates generated less tax revenue than lower marginal rates. Higher marginal rates increased the *percentage* of income the IRS takes, but lowered the *amount* of income earned by reducing the financial rewards for work. According to Laffer's theory, the second effect often overwhelms the first. The degree to which Laffer was right about tax revenues is widely disputed, but whatever the truth of the matter, a Laffer-like phenomenon plainly operates in the sphere of crime and punishment. Putting more offenders in prison cells increases the tangible price criminals pay for their crimes— but if done too often, it diminishes the intangible price by making a stay in the nearby house of corrections an ordinary life experience. The second effect can easily overwhelm the first: meaning, more punishment may yield less deterrence.

That state of affairs is especially likely given the crime numbers previously cited. Even rich, low-crime societies suffer many more crimes than the best-funded justice systems can afford to punish. Consequently, if tangible penalties are all that would-be criminals fear, the fear will not suffice to deter crime in poor neighborhoods. Absent penalties too draconian for liberal democracies to tolerate, the occasional prison sentence will inevitably be too small a disincentive. According to the FBI's figures, each year the United States sees roughly 440,000 robberies but a mere 39,000 robbery convictions.[49] If the annual Victimization Survey were used to tally the number of crimes, the ratio between those two numbers would be more lopsided still. Criminal punishment is radically selective, and is certain to remain that way. Only by preserving the value of intangible penalties can our—or any—justice system ensure that, from criminals' perspective, crime doesn't pay. That goal is hard to achieve when criminal convictions and terms in the state penitentiary are rites of passage for the young men who fill those penitentiaries.[50]

Whether or not crime pays may be the wrong question. Criminal punishment is a moral act; perhaps it is justified not by the social gain it produces but by the moral principles it honors. If punishing all serious crimes is the moral obligation of any responsible government, then the deterrent effects of such punishment are beside the point. To be sure, moral obligations that are impossible to meet—and there is good reason to believe that no free society has ever come close to meeting this one—cannot truly be obligations. Criminal punishment must be selective; absent the kinds of surveillance and draconian penalties known only in police states, there is simply no alternative. Nevertheless, a retributivist might respond, a morally conscientious government ought to strive to punish as many crimes as it can. The limit on the size of the prison population, in this view, should be determined by government budget constraints, not by any felt need to preserve the stigma associated with a term in the nearest penitentiary.

This argument is difficult to answer in the abstract. If criminal punishment is a moral imperative, today's massive prison populations may be a sign of moral responsibility. If punishment is a sometimes-necessary evil—if the exercise of mercy is as much a moral good as the imposition of punishment—those populations are a sign that American governments have lost their bearings. Which is it?

Once again, the selective nature of criminal punishment is the key to answering that question. When budget constraints drive the decisions that fill prison beds, the criminals who pay the highest price for their crimes will be those who are most cheaply caught and convicted. That dynamic inevitably produces discriminatory punishment. Drug arrests and prosecutions are much cheaper for the government in poor city neighborhoods—where drugs are sold on the street or at fixed points that the police can easily identify—than in the suburbs, where drug sales are more hidden and transactions are individually arranged.[51] There are many more poor whites than poor blacks, but the poor white population is geographically dispersed; outside the South, poor blacks are concentrated in cities.[52] Maximizing drug punishment within the limits of government budgets thus guarantees a heavily black drug prisoner population, precisely what the United States has today.

The economics of law enforcement do not always produce more punishment for the poorest criminals; sometimes, they produce the opposite. The clearance rate for violent crimes reported to the police—meaning the percentage of such crimes that lead to an arrest—varies inversely with population density. Police clear fewer crimes in large cities than in small ones, fewer in small cities than in suburbs, and fewer in suburbs than in small towns and rural areas. Gangs usually operate in densely populated areas, and where gangs operate, it is difficult for the police to find and protect the witnesses without whom violent felonies cannot be prosecuted. That is one reason why, in nearly all-white small towns, three-fifths of violent felonies lead to a suspect's arrest—while in large cities (most of which have large black populations), the analogous figure is one-third; the rate in the poorest neighborhoods is lower still.[53]

Poor black neighborhoods thus receive the worst of both worlds: too much punishment in settings where punishment does only modest good (as is probably true of imprisonment for drug crimes), and too little in cases where punishment is most needed to preserve social peace— meaning crimes of violence. That is the natural product of a retributivist justice system plagued by tight law enforcement budgets. Cash-strapped police forces put their time and attention where arrests and convictions are cheapest—low-end drug crime—and avoid more expensive-to-solve crimes: violent felonies in violence-plagued neighborhoods. If the goal is to punish as many crimes as budgets allow, as retributivism suggests, the consequence is to punish similar crimes committed in different neighborhoods differently. The moral argument for punishing as many crimes as possible runs headlong into the moral argument for treating criminals and crime victims from different demographic groups the same. Retributive justice inevitably produces discriminatory justice.

That may be why no previous generation of Americans embraced the version of retributive justice that has held sway in the United States over the past thirty years. For most of our history in most of the country, the government officials who administer the justice system, along with the voters who elect them, have behaved as though criminal punishment were sometimes necessary but always dangerous, something to be done sparingly and avoided when there is a plausible excuse for doing so. Only in the last decades of the twentieth century did most American voters and the law enforcement officials they elect conclude that punishing criminals is an unambiguous moral good. The notion that criminal punishment is a moral or social imperative—the idea that a healthy criminal justice system should punish all the criminals it can—enjoyed little currency before the 1980s.

In 1970, it ought to have been clear that America's prison population was much too small, given then-skyrocketing rates of urban violence. Today, it should be similarly clear that the nation's prison population is much too large—whether measured by the magnitude of other countries' prison populations, by the size of America's prison population over time, by the moral character of criminal punishment, or by the deterrent benefit that punishment produces. American levels of incarceration exceed the most plausible historical or comparative benchmarks by an enormous margin. Punishment's deterrent impact appears to be substantially smaller than in the past, when American prison populations were less than half of today's inflated body count. The conclusion seems inescapable: criminal punishment is both too severe and too frequent.

The optimal number of prison inmates in any society at any given time is unknowable. But whatever that number is in the United States today, the actual number of Americans living behind bars is a great deal higher. As the black imprisonment rate is now six times the record-shattering white imprisonment rate,[54] that conclusion seems especially clear when applied to the residents of urban black neighborhoods. Twenty-first-century America incarcerates too high a percentage of its population—and far too high a percentage of its black population.

Self-Preservation

All that may be true. Yet it may also be true that the enormous number of inmates in America's prisons, including the staggeringly large number of black inmates, cannot safely be reduced, at least not by much and not in the near term. Even if the deterrent benefit of many of those prison sentences is vanishingly small, their incapacitative effect may be substantial: criminals cannot commit crimes on city streets when they live behind bars. It follows that the consequences of setting those prisoners free, and of declining to prosecute large numbers of those who are similarly situated, might be both large and perverse. As Jefferson surmised, justice for those who are enslaved and self-preservation for those who do the en-slaving may cut in opposite directions. That surmise badly misjudged the slaves about whom Jefferson wrote. But today's prison inmates earned their status by committing crimes, not by their skin color. Though Jefferson was wrong then, his words may be prescient now.

There is good reason to believe otherwise. The deterrent effect of criminal punishment depends as much on punishment's quality as on its quantity: punishment deters crime only if crime, not innocence, receives punishment. The run-up in America's prison population has coincided with a decline in the effectiveness with which the justice system sepa-rates those who deserve punishment from those who don't. That sad fact gives rise to an opportunity: reducing quantity while raising quality may well enhance deterrence, not undermine it.

The explosive growth of the nation's prison population after 1970 did not coincide with an explosion in the numbers of police officers, prosecu-tors, and defense attorneys. On the contrary: while prison budgets shot up, spending on police, lawyers, and courts rose more slowly, and the number of personnel rose less still. The number of local police officers in-creased roughly 20 percent in the 1970s and 1980s, the same percentage rise as in the general population; the number of local prosecutors grew by a similar amount.[55] The number of officers patrolling most high-crime big cities—among them Boston, New York, Chicago, and Los Angeles—actually fell during those years.[56] There is no reliable measure of the number of defense lawyers, but inflation-adjusted, per-case spending on lawyers for indigent defendants fell by more than half from the late 1970s to the early 1990s. While these trends took hold, the number of felony prosecutions rose at least two-and-a-half times.[57] More so than any other aspect of American government, the prosecution and punishment of crim-inal defendants grew dramatically more efficient. The justice system became, more and more, an assembly line in which cases are processed, not adjudicated.

Assembly-line adjudication is not known for its accuracy. The greater the ratio of cases to personnel, the smaller the opportunity to examine carefully the evidence on which the government's case rests. And that opportunity was already small: even before the huge run-up in felony prosecutions, the tendency was for plea bargains to be struck early in the process, before either side had a chance to do much investigating.[58] That tendency is even stronger in today's justice system because pleading cases out quickly is a necessity, not a convenience. The upshot is that noninvestigation is the norm in American criminal litigation, careful gathering of evidence the exception.[59]

That fact sheds light on one of the justice system's most famous scandals: the abortive prosecution of three Duke lacrosse players, all white and all the children of prosperous families, for raping a black stripper at a party on Duke's Durham, North Carolina, campus in March 2006. Charges against the three defendants were ultimately dismissed, thanks in large measure to DNA evidence that indicated the victim had had sex with multiple men on the day in question, but—contrary to the victim's story—not with any of the students who attended the party. Prosecutor Mike Nifong was dismissed from the case and ultimately disbarred because he chose to believe the alleged victim, not the forensic evidence that proved the victim's story false.[60]

Nifong's conduct was outrageous. But the larger outrage is the many cases in which no forensic evidence is gathered, and in which a quick and casual police investigation leads to an equally quick and casual plea bargain between lawyers, neither of whom has the time to investigate further. Had the alleged perpetrators been poor and black, the case would have attracted much less public attention, the investigation would have been much less detailed, and the story might have had a different and sadder ending. One 1990s study found that in more than one-fourth of sexual assault cases in which the FBI crime laboratory analyzed DNA, the analysis exonerated the prime suspect: an indication of how easily innocent defendants can be convicted in cases in which no DNA is gathered and analyzed, and in which no well-funded defense lawyers are available to press the prosecution to prove its case.[61]

In the inevitably selective business of criminal punishment, selections are often made on perverse criteria. The lack of careful investigation that characterizes most felony prosecutions virtually guarantees that a significant number of innocent defendants are pressured to plead to crimes they did not commit. And within the much larger universe of guilty defendants, those who are punished most severely are often those who made the worst deals, not those who committed the worst crimes. Often, the best deals go to defendants who have the most information to sell—meaning those defendants with the most extensive histories of criminal conduct. A fairer and more functional justice system might send more powerful deterrent signals while punishing fewer defendants, by targeting the right offenders for the right reasons. For the past generation, America's justice system has emphasized the quantity of criminal punishment and not its quality. Reversing that pattern may yield a criminal justice nirvana: less punishment coupled with more effective crime control.

Our enormous prison population is no wolf held by the ear. Nor is the proper measure of justice for those inmates—along with millions more who might join them soon—at odds with self-preservation for the rest of the population. On the contrary, those two populations share a common interest in a justice system that seeks moderate punishment rather than the immoderate kind that predominates today. As was true of slavery in Jefferson's day, the solutions to this particular problem chiefly require money and political will. With the notable exception of prison budgets, those things have been in short supply in America's dysfunctional criminal justice system, at least in the recent past. But the future need not resemble the recent past. A more distant past may offer a more useful model for needed reforms.

In the wake of the Civil War, white Southerners had the opportunity to embrace more freedom for their black neighbors together with a less violent, more peaceful culture. The opportunity was missed. Today, the justice system faces a similar opportunity: more freedom and democracy in black neighborhoods, North and South alike, together with less crime in those neighborhoods. Seizing that opportunity begins with the understanding that maximizing "involuntary servitude" (to use the Thirteenth Amendment's language) is not the best means of attacking violence and other lawbreaking. Over the past few decades, Americans have forgotten that lesson. We need to learn it again—to see where it comes from, and to discover how we managed to forget something so true, and so important.

PART 2

The Past

THE FIRST CENTURY after American independence saw the emergence of two sets of legal ideals that might govern the nation's criminal justice system: James Madison's Bill of Rights, and the legal guarantees
of John Bingham's Fourteenth Amendment—especially the promise of
the "equal protection of the laws." That same century also saw the establishment of two different sets of institutional practices to govern the
justice system's day-to-day operation. In the North, local democracy did
most of the governing. In the South, democracy meant either the rule of
rich whites or the rule of white mobs.

Over the last two-thirds of the twentieth century, the justice system embraced the wrong ideals and the wrong institutional arrangements. Earl
Warren and his colleagues imposed Madison's Constitution, not Bingham's, on local police and prosecutors. And the neighborhood-level democracy that had governed criminal law enforcement in the industrial-
ized North faded, to be replaced by a more southern-style democracy in
which residents of low-crime neighborhoods establish the rules for more
crime-ridden city streets. Today, black crime is mostly governed by white
judges and white politicians, and by the white voters who elected them.

Less local democracy meant more instability. Criminal punishment
rose sharply in the twentieth century's second quarter, then fell sharply in

its third quarter—while crime skyrocketed. In the century's fourth quarter, the justice system turned more punitive, and prison populations exploded. But urban crime remained stubbornly high, even after the 1990s crime drop. The end result, in North and South alike, was a record-shattering, disproportionately black inmate population, and rates of urban violence similar to those that southern cities—but not northern ones—had known in generations past.

CHAPTER 3

Ideals and Institutions

After our Constitution got fairly into working order it really seemed as if we had invented a machine that would go of itself, and this begot a faith in our luck which even the Civil War itself but momentarily disturbed.

—James Russell Lowell, Speech to the Reform Club of New York (1888)

Our Founding Fathers, faced with perils we can scarcely imagine, drafted a charter to assure the rule of law and the rights of man . . . Those ideals still light the world, and we will not give them up for expedience's sake.

—Barack Obama, Inaugural Address (2009)

ENFORCING CRIMINAL LAW is one of government's most important tasks, yet also among the most dangerous. If crimes are punished too rarely, if violent streets are not well policed or if witnesses cannot be protected, violence and disorder can reach Hobbesian proportions. On the other hand, if crime is punished too severely—if the police behave brutally or if outsiders decree that a large fraction of the young men in some communities must live behind bars—the justice system may come to represent an engine of alien oppression in the eyes of those whose obedience it seeks to compel. Omelettes are made by breaking eggs, or so the familiar saying goes. In this sphere of governance, the omelettes must be made: no government can long survive without a working system of criminal law enforcement, and such systems are inevitably uncomfortable to those who are the targets of police officers' and prosecutors' attention. Yet to anyone who values freedom as well as safety, it will seem crucial to monitor the egg-breaking carefully, and to keep it to a minimum.

So constitutional democracies face two opposite risks: chaos or oppression, too little law enforcement or too much—and the wrong kind. Such states tend to address these twin risks in similar fashion. They create police forces and prosecutors' offices with sufficient power and personnel to keep streets safe, and craft legal rules that limit law enforcers' power by protecting individual rights of fair treatment. Put more simply, the character of criminal justice in democratic states usually depends on a set of government institutions checked by a set of legal ideals. Those legal ideals, in turn, are of a different type than the ordinary legal doctrines that govern contracts and house closings, divorces, and stock purchases. The ideals that rein in oppressive criminal law enforcement usually come from constitutional law: meaning, mere politicians cannot change or ignore them.

In twenty-first-century America, the combination of those ideals and institutions doesn't work as it should. If our criminal justice system is "a machine that would go of itself," the machinery is broken. Repairing the breakage requires discovering its source, which in turn requires understanding the justice system's institutional design, the legal ideals that allegedly protect those whom the system targets, and the historical origins of institutions and ideals alike.

Design

For most of the nation's history, the design of American criminal justice had two key features. First, as between the center and the periphery, power flowed toward the periphery: local officials, not state and national ones, managed the police forces that make most arrests and the prosecutors' offices that prosecute most cases. Second, as between civil servants and politicians, power was mostly held by the politicians: elected officials defined criminal prohibitions, prosecuted violators, and heard appeals; other elected officials supervised the local police officers who arrest most offenders. Both design features remain, but each has grown less marked with time. State and federal officials exercise more power over crime and punishment than in the past, as do the appointed, life-tenured Supreme Court Justices who sit atop the federal judiciary. In the past, local politics and local politicians reigned supreme. Today, they share power with state and national politicians, and with allegedly apolitical federal judges.

The details are easily described. Local police forces and sheriffs' offices—either headed by elected officials or directly responsible to them[1]—investigate crimes and arrest criminals. District attorneys elected at the county level prosecute criminal defendants; public defenders represent defendants too poor to hire their own lawyers. Locally elected trial judges accept guilty pleas, try criminal cases, and impose sentences on those who are convicted. State appellate judges—in most states they too are elected, either by judicial district or statewide[2]—hear and decide appeals from those convictions and sentences. State legislators define the criminal prohibitions and sentencing rules that local police officers and prosecutors enforce. That state-and-local justice system makes some 14 million arrests and prosecutes more than 1 million felony cases per year.[3]

The federal government has its own criminal justice system, less politically accountable than the state and local system but also less important, because federal officials handle few criminal cases: 7 percent of felony prosecutions, a small fraction of 1 percent of misdemeanors.[4] With roughly 12,000 agents, the FBI is the most important of the dozen or so federal police agencies that employ roughly 100,000 federal officers.[5] (By comparison, there are 620,000 full-time local police officers in the United States, and roughly one-tenth that many state troopers.)[6] Those federal agents investigate federal crimes and arrest the offenders, just as their local counterparts do. United States Attorneys and their assistants—they number 5,800, compared to roughly 27,000 local prosecutors[7]—prosecute federal cases in federal court. United States District Judges preside over those criminal cases. United States Court of Appeals judges from twelve circuits hear and decide appeals. The Supreme Court of the United States occasionally reviews those Court of Appeals decisions; the Court also defines the constitutional rules that constrain local police officers and local prosecutors. All these officials are appointed, not elected: federal judges and justices serve for life; federal agents and prosecutors serve at the pleasure of their superiors. Naturally, life-tenured federal judges have a high degree of political independence. But they are not alone: so does the FBI, and so do U.S. Attorneys, as George W. Bush's Justice Department discovered to its dismay.[8]

Two other features of these parallel justice systems bear comment. First is their funding. As the figures in the preceding paragraph show, local police and local prosecutors handle fourteen times as many felony cases as does the federal government, and several hundred times the number of misdemeanors. Yet the ratio of local cops to federal officers is only 6 to 1, and the ratio of local prosecutors to their federal counterparts is less than 5 to 1. Local law enforcement agencies tend to work at capacity. Thanks to more generous per-case funding than local governments can afford, the key actors in the federal justice system enjoy a measure of slack. For most of American history, that difference in funding had little impact on the character and quality of criminal law enforcement: policing and prosecution were cheap enough that, outside the chronically poor South, governments used as much of them as they wished. Today, its effects are huge.

The second feature concerns federal law's importance, or the lack thereof. In most areas where federal law operates, the federal government dominates the regulatory landscape; state and local governments are secondary actors. Criminal justice works differently. Murders, rapes, robberies, and burglaries—the crimes that do the most harm, and the ones that local populations care most about—are nearly always the responsibility of local police, local prosecutors, locally elected judges, and state law. The men and women who enforce federal criminal law handle more exotic but less consequential fare: high-end white-collar crime, immigration violations, crimes on federal property, plus a scattering of drug crimes and violent crimes that the state-and-local justice system usually handles. The most important effects of federal law are felt not in federal cases, but in cases prosecuted by local district attorneys under state law; the threat of harsh federal sentences can be used to extract guilty pleas in such cases. And federal law sometimes serves as a model for state law—states follow doctrinal patterns that federal courts first established. In short, federal criminal law has significant indirect effects. Its direct effects are modest.

So much for the institutions. The criminal justice system's key legal ideals come from scattered provisions of the Bill of Rights—the first ten amendments to the federal Constitution, four of which concern crime and punishment. They too are easily described. The Fourth Amendment bars "unreasonable searches and seizures" and requires that search warrants be supported by probable cause and specify the items to be seized.[9] The Fifth Amendment forbids double jeopardy: being tried twice "for the same offence"; the same prohibition renders acquittals final and unappealable.[10] The Fifth Amendment also bans compelled self-incrimination and requires the use of grand juries to indict those charged with felonies; finally, that amendment contains a catch-all provision barring the imposition of criminal punishment without "due process of law."[11] The Sixth Amendment grants defendants the rights to be informed of the charges against them, to a speedy and public jury trial on those charges at which the government's witnesses may be cross-examined and defense witnesses may be called, and at which defendants are to "have the assistance of counsel for [their] defense."[12] The Eighth Amendment bars both "excessive fines" and "cruel and unusual punishments."[13] Save for the Fifth Amendment's grand jury requirement, which applies only to federal cases, all the provisions just described apply to all levels of government: federal, state, and local.

That was not always so. The First Amendment begins with the words "Congress shall make no law"—strong evidence that the Bill of Rights was originally intended to apply to the federal government only, as it did until well into the twentieth century.[14] Yet that historical proposition is less important than it seems. The Bill's criminal justice provisions are revised versions of provisions that already appeared in many state constitutions by 1791, the year the Bill was ratified. Nearly all of the many states that joined the expanding Union after that date copied the Fourth, Fifth, Sixth, and Eighth Amendments in their own constitutions, often word for word. Long before the Supreme Court applied those amendments to state as well as federal cases (again, save for the Fifth Amendment's right to indictment by grand jury), the principles of the Bill of Rights were governing law throughout the United States.

Curiously, those legal principles made little difference before the 1960s. State constitutions included their own versions of the Bill of Rights—but for the most part, state courts interpreted that constitutional language narrowly. Whatever searches and seizures local police officers conducted were usually deemed reasonable (or, if not, remedies for illegal searches and seizures proved hard to come by).[15] Practices that led defendants to confess their crimes were almost always found to be consistent with due process and with the privilege against self-incrimination. Again for the most part, state-law versions of the Bill of Rights had little bite. That changed when Earl Warren's Supreme Court *both* imposed the federal Bill of Rights on the states, *and* reinterpreted several of the Bill's provisions to require more than state and local officials already did—a story for a later chapter.[16]

The Bill's criminal procedure provisions are iconic; they flowed from the pen of the great James Madison, history's leading constitutional author. The government institutions previously described seem a good deal less exalted. The justice system's institutional arrangements appear to be a bit slapdash, as though the relevant offices and institutions were thrown together by second-rate politicians who gave little thought to the system they were establishing—which is roughly what happened. Plus, the institutions appear to suffer from an excessive respect for the shifting winds of local politics: which, in the United States, means the low politics of urban machines. Perhaps electing county sheriffs has something to recommend it, but the notion of electing both the district attorneys who prosecute criminal cases and the judges who try those cases seems uncomfortably close to criminal conviction by local plebiscite on Court TV.

The truth is more surprising. For most of the nation's history, those grubby, politicized institutions functioned reasonably well (outside the South—an important qualification). Madison's iconic legal rights have a worse track record—they were inconsequential before the mid-twentieth century, and have been mostly perverse since. A better way to put the point might be this: America's justice system suffers from a mismatch of individual rights and criminal justice machinery, between legal ideals and political institutions. When politicians both define crimes and prosecute criminal cases, one might reasonably fear that those two sets of elected officials—state legislators and local district attorneys—will work together to achieve their common political goals. Legislators will define crimes too broadly and sentences too severely in order to make it easy for prosecutors to extract guilty pleas, which in turn permits prosecutors to punish criminal defendants on the cheap, and thereby spares legislators the need to spend more tax dollars on criminal law enforcement.[17] Constitutional law can reduce the risk of this political collusion by limiting legislators' power to criminalize and punish. The Bill of Rights did not do so. Madison's text ignores the core problem the justice system's strange institutional design poses.

Why? The answer begins with timing. The key constitutional provisions that regulate policing and prosecution came first; the institutions of American criminal justice came later. No wonder the former does a poor job of reining in the latter: ideals were not defined with the relevant institutions in mind. More broadly, both the legal ideals and the political institutions that define American criminal justice were the product of their times: more path dependency and historical accident than conscious design. Under different, easily imaginable circumstances, ideals and institutions alike would have evolved differently. The Bill of Rights might have limited the government's power to punish directly, instead of placing easily overcome procedural obstacles in prosecutors' path. Law enforcement institutions might have given control over police arrests and criminal prosecution to centralized government bureaucracies, not to local elected officials. American criminal justice might have looked like criminal justice elsewhere in the world.

A Time-Bound System

History always seems inevitable after the fact. Today, both the Bill of Rights and the large body of legal doctrine interpreting and applying it are thought to be timeless legal wisdom, unquestioned parts of the nation's constitutional heritage. Altering them is legally and politically unthinkable.

It was not always so. The principles of the Bill of Rights are less wise than they seem, and are anything but timeless. Even traditionally democratic Americans were not bound to decide that local politicians should play such a large role in governing criminal law enforcement. The story of American criminal justice has more to do with historical happenstance than with legal principle.

Begin with the Bill of Rights, the most venerated part of the world's most venerated constitution. The key criminal justice provisions of the Bill flowed not from a set of abstract principles, timeless or otherwise, but from a handful of famous cases from the seventeenth and eighteenth centuries. John Lilburne, a political gadfly who managed to offend all sides in seventeenth-century England's civil wars, was charged with seditious libel for authoring various pamphlets that treated the Cromwellian authorities with less respect than they thought appropriate. Though his authorship of the relevant documents was widely known, Lilburne wrote under a pseudonym. Under then-governing law, his words could not be pinned on him without his own testimony—which he steadfastly refused to give, claiming that no Englishman could be compelled to incriminate himself. Lilburne's claim won the day; the privilege against self-incrimination might fairly be called Lilburne's Law.[18]

A century later, agents of the Crown ransacked the homes of two other English pamphleteers and government critics, seizing their books and papers in the process. John Entick and John Wilkes (Lincoln's assassin was named for him) sued for damages and each won a considerable sum: three hundred pounds for Entick, a staggering five thousand for Wilkes. The judge who tried both cases held that such searches were contrary to the common law, a holding later enshrined in the Fourth Amendment.[19] John Peter Zenger—a disproportionate share of Anglo-American legal history has been made by men named John—was charged with libeling colonial New York's governor in his newspaper. Zenger's only defense was truth, and the relevant substantive law held that the truth of the libelous material was no bar to criminal liability. Zenger's lawyer Andrew Hamilton nevertheless sought and won an acquittal, thereby establishing the propositions that juries in criminal cases may acquit for any reason, and that no judge can overturn such decisions.[20]

Lilburne, Wilkes, Entick, and Zenger were precisely the sort of characters America's revolutionaries admired: independent-minded men who stood up to high-handed governments and lived to tell the tale. The four cases described above were likewise of a particular type. All were what we would now call First Amendment cases: efforts by government officials to punish political dissidents for their written words. But these cases arose in legal systems that knew no First Amendment. Today, crimes like seditious libel cannot exist under American law because such offenses infringe "the freedom of speech, or of the press" that the First Amendment protects. In seventeenth- and eighteenth-century England,

such offenses had long histories; there was no common-law bar to prosecuting them. Nor could there be. Seventeenth- and eighteenth-century
England was an unstable land scarred by multiple civil wars and frequent rebellions. Sharp criticism of those in power might mean nothing,
or it might be the prelude to the raising of a rebel army, as happened
seven times in the two centuries preceding American independence.[21] In
that environment, the notion that political crimes were no crimes at all
would have seemed radical indeed to the Crown and its agents, including the judges who presided over prosecutions like Lilburne's and Zenger's
or lawsuits like Entick's and Wilkes's. Yet, powerful as was the legal
concept of sedition, that same concept was also seriously problematic.
Overt disloyalty might lead to civil war, but the suppression of criticism
might produce despotic governments like those of the seventeenth-century
Stuart kings.

Creative litigants like Lilburne, creative lawyers like Hamilton, and
creative judges like Lord Camden—the presiding judge at Entick's and
Wilkes's trials—responded to these twin threats as the common law often
did: they split the difference. They also moved by indirection, using legal
procedure to right substantive wrongs without acknowledging the substantive point of their arguments. In Lilburne's case, the privilege against
self-incrimination was a roundabout and partial means of protecting Lilburne's right to dissent in a legal system that failed to recognize that right.
The same was true of Entick's and Wilkes's right to be free from unreasonable searches, and of Zenger's right to have a jury and not some government-
appointed judge decide whether he deserved punishment. These cases
have two common threads. All the defendants were charged with political
crimes. And all achieved victory through the creative use of procedure.

The Sixth Amendment right to counsel has no single historical source,
but its authors were familiar with cases like John Adams's successful defense of the British soldiers responsible for the Boston Massacre—cases
in which lawyers protected criminal defendants from what amounted to
legalized mob justice. The formal charge in that case was murder, but
because the violence began not with the soldiers but with the patriot
mob, the true charge was opposing that mob: not so different from the
political crimes charged against allegedly seditious pamphleteers and
newsmen like Lilburne and Zenger, Entick and Wilkes. The lawyer-free

criminal process that applied to most cases did a reasonably good job of protecting ordinary criminal defendants. Perhaps too good a job: eighteenth-century English lawyers and judges believed their nation's justice system faced a crisis because convictions were so rare. In politically charged cases like the Boston Massacre, the need for outside assistance was more obvious.[22]

When the Bill of Rights was written, these legal protections had little to do with ordinary criminal prosecutions. The ban on unreasonable searches and seizures barred the government from rummaging about in defendants' books and papers until it found enough to support criminal charges. That ban helped seditious pamphleteers but did little for defendants charged with assault or theft—books and papers were irrelevant in such cases. The privilege against self-incrimination protected political writers with pen names and made the prosecution of heretics all but impossible, but the privilege had no effect on run-of-the-mill criminal cases. When the Fifth Amendment was written and ratified, most criminal defendants represented themselves, and therefore had to speak in order to mount a defense. Silence was not a viable option.[23] The jury right and the associated ban on double jeopardy effectively barred the government from ordering its judges to punish its critics, because juries could defy the government and ignore judges' instructions. At the time of the Founding, criminal prosecution was chiefly a private enterprise; crime victims rather than public prosecutors decided which cases merited prosecution and which ones didn't.[24] Victims took their victimizers to court in much the same way they did in private lawsuits for money damages. The risk of a government-rigged proceeding in such cases was small. The right to counsel ensured that politically charged crimes would not yield punishment until both sides had made their strongest arguments—as long as the defendants could afford the likes of John Adams or Andrew Hamilton to represent them. The right was little comfort to criminal defendants of modest means, a category to which most defendants belonged.

The notion that these rights might serve as the legal foundation for a justice system that punished not heretics and seditious pamphleteers but murderers and rapists was foreign to the men who wrote the Bill of Rights. In large part, that was so because the criminal justice system to which the Bill's constitutional ideals apply today did not yet exist. There were no police forces or district attorneys' offices in 1791, the year the Bill of Rights was ratified. The Bill contains no provision designed to rein in the discretionary power of public prosecutors: plea bargaining and prosecutorial discretion, fundamental features of today's justice system, were unknown in the late eighteenth century. Defense lawyers like Adams and Hamilton were few and far between; the battle between opposing lawyers that dominates criminal trials today was a rare event.

By 1860, all these propositions had ceased to be true; the essential features of the criminal justice system we know today were in place. Defense lawyers and public prosecutors were common. Plea bargaining was becoming an ordinary means of disposing of criminal cases and thereby keeping a lid on crowded dockets.[25] Police officers, not private citizens, searched for evidence of crime. But these changed institutional practices came too late: the legal rights that are supposed to cabin the justice system's power were already well established. Madison and his contemporaries were not seers. Like most lawmakers, they wrote their constitutional texts with an eye toward the past they knew, not the future they had yet to see. Had that past been different or had the Bill been written a few decades later when some of that yet-unknown future had come to pass, a different list of constitutional rights would likely have emerged. The Bill was the product of its time and place.

So was the machinery of criminal justice that arose in the first half of the nineteenth century. Local police forces arose in response to the first waves of European immigration in the 1840s and 1850s. Locally elected district attorneys arose at the same time states moved from appointed to elected judges—and that change was, in part, a response to popular disgust with state legislators, leading to efforts to limit their power over the justice system.[26] I will return to these points later. For now, suffice it to say that control of criminal law enforcement by local politicians established itself at a time when such control seemed natural, perhaps the only such time in American history.

Neither of these crucial legal and political developments—the writing and ratification of the Bill of Rights, the rising power of local elected officials over criminal law enforcement—was inevitable. Timing had as much to do with them as did legal principle or political conviction. America's strange justice system, both its institutions and its key legal ideals, is partly the consequence of conscious design: by Madison and his colleagues, and by the members of the two dozen conventions that revised their states' constitutions in the mid-nineteenth century. Those designers no doubt believed they were shaping the times in which they lived and worked. But the times also shaped them. Historical accident and coincidence played large roles in the construction of America's unusual criminal justice system. Some of the accidents may be happy ones. But not all, and not the ones that enjoy the widest acceptance today.

Substance and Procedure

Two kinds of law govern crime and criminal punishment. Substantive law defines crimes and sentences: the meaning of murder and manslaughter, rape and robbery, plus the sentencing ranges that attach to particular crimes. As the name suggests, procedural law defines process: the conditions police officers must satisfy in order to get search warrants, the warnings cops must give (or not) when questioning suspects, the means by which juries are selected, the meaning of "double jeopardy" and of the right to confront opposing witnesses, the circumstances under which lawyers' errors require that convictions be reversed, and a host of similar issues. Substantive criminal law defines the rules police officers and prosecutors enforce. The law of criminal procedure defines the manner in which the enforcing is done.

Writers of constitutions agree that at least one of these bodies of law needs restraining. But which one? Should constitutions limit the government's power to define crimes and fix sentences? Are unfair procedures the greater danger? Or are the two kinds of law equally dangerous when bad rulers oppress those they rule?

Near the end of the eighteenth century, at a time when written constitutions were still a novelty, two sets of constitutional authors took a stab at answering those questions. They worked independently and almost simultaneously: James Madison introduced his draft of what would become the American Bill of Rights in June 1789; eleven weeks later, the French National Assembly adopted the Declaration of the Rights of Man and of the Citizen. To make the comparison more interesting still, Madison's friend and political mentor—Thomas Jefferson, then the United

States' Ambassador to France and soon to be George Washington's Secretary of State—may have contributed to the drafting of the French Declaration through conversations with his friend the Marquis de Lafayette, then an influential figure in the National Assembly.[27]

Notwithstanding their similar origins, these documents answered the questions previously posed differently. Here is the text of the Fourth, Fifth, Sixth, and Eighth Amendments—the portions of Madison's Bill that have to do with crime or criminal justice:

> *Amendment IV.* The right of the people to be secure in their persons, houses, papers, and effects, against unreasonable searches and seizures, shall not be violated, and no Warrants shall issue, but upon probable cause, supported by Oath or affirmation, and particularly describing the place to be searched, and the persons or things to be seized.

> *Amendment V.* No person shall be held to answer for any capital, or otherwise infamous crime, unless on a presentment or indictment of a Grand Jury, . . . nor shall any person be subject for the same offence to be twice put in jeopardy of life or limb; nor shall be compelled in any criminal case to be a witness against himself, nor be deprived of life, liberty, or property, without due process of law . . .

> *Amendment VI.* In all criminal prosecutions, the accused shall enjoy the right to a speedy and public trial, by an impartial jury of the State and district where in the crime shall have been committed, which district shall have been previously ascertained by law, and to be informed of the nature and cause of the accusation; to be confronted with the witnesses against him; to have compulsory process for obtaining witnesses in his favor, and to have the Assistance of Counsel for his defense.

> *Amendment VIII.* Excessive bail shall not be required, nor excessive fines imposed, nor cruel and unusual punishments inflicted.[28]

Procedure dominates these texts. Save for the First Amendment's protection of speech and religion, nothing in the Bill of Rights limits legislators' ability to criminalize whatever they wish. Save for the mild constraints of the Eighth Amendment, nothing in the Bill limits the severity of criminal punishment. Meanwhile, the Fourth, Fifth, and Sixth Amendments contain fifteen distinct procedural guarantees for criminal suspects and defendants—sixteen if one counts the general requirement that punishment be imposed according to "due process of law."[29] Along with the similar language that appears in state constitutions, these texts place substantive criminal law in the hands of politicians. Elected state legislators and members of Congress write criminal codes and sentencing rules. Procedure is governed by judges—not just the politician-judges who staff state courts, but the appointed, life-tenured judges and Justices who sit on the federal bench.

Now consider the text of the criminal justice-related provisions of the Declaration of the Rights of Man and of the Citizen. Five of the Declaration's seventeen Articles deal with criminal justice, in whole or in part. In English, they read as follows:

> *Article 4.* Liberty consists in the power to do anything that does not injure others; accordingly, the exercise of the natural rights of each man has no limits except those that secure to the other members of society the enjoyment of these same rights. These limits can be determined only by law.

> *Article 5.* The law has the right to forbid only such actions as are injurious to society. Nothing can be forbidden that is not interdicted by the law, and no one can be constrained to do that which it does not order.

> *Article 7.* No man can be accused, arrested, or detained, except in the cases determined by the law and according to the forms that it has prescribed. Those who procure, expedite, execute, or cause to be executed arbitrary orders ought to be punished: but every citizen summoned or seized in virtue of the law ought to render instant obedience; he makes himself guilty by resistance.

> *Article 8.* The law ought to establish only penalties that are strictly and obviously necessary, and no one can be punished except in virtue

of a law established and promulgated prior to the offence and legally applied.

Article 9. Every man being presumed innocent until he has been pronounced guilty, if it is thought indispensable to arrest him, all severity that may not be necessary to secure his person ought to be strictly suppressed by law.[30]

Roughly speaking, the Declaration is the Bill of Rights' mirror image. In the Bill, substance is governed lightly and procedure is extensively regulated. In the Declaration, procedure is governed lightly, and more wisely than in Madison's document. Substantive law is seriously constrained—or would be, had the Declaration been given binding effect.

Article 7 covers the same ground as the Fifth Amendment's due process clause, but helpfully adds that lawless behavior by law enforcers "ought to be punished." (The Bill of Rights' limits on law enforcement establish no remedy for cases in which those limits are transgressed.) Article 9 defines two useful procedural guarantees missing from the Bill of Rights: the presumption of innocence and a ban on police torture.[31] The rest of the quoted provisions deal with substance, not process. To any American lawyer, these texts are stunning—Article 4 guarantees "the freedom to do everything that does not injure others"; Article 5 declares that "[t]he law has the right to forbid only such actions as are injurious to society." This is John Stuart Mill's harm principle in action, seventy years before Mill defended that principle in his famous book, *On Liberty.* In that book, Mill argued that legal punishments should be triggered only when defendants injure others; a desire to police public morals is not a sufficient reason to incarcerate offenders.[32] Mill's idea was deemed too radical for his own legal system, and for ours. Neither Great Britain nor the United States has ever embraced it. All the more reason to marvel at the French revolutionaries who did so nearly two decades before Mill was born.

Article 8 is the Declaration's counterpart to the Eighth Amendment, which bars both "excessive fines" and "cruel and unusual punishments." But instead of banning only the most extreme criminal sanctions as American law does—the Eighth Amendment grandfathered existing punishments, including branding and whipping, by banning only "un-usual" sanctions—Article 8 rejects *all* punishments that are not "strictly and obviously necessary." As Articles 4 and 5 seem to command that doubts be resolved against criminalization, Article 8's language requires that, for those convicted of crime, doubts be resolved against severity. Freedom and lenity are to be the legal norms, criminal liability and severe punishment the carefully limited exceptions. American law knows nothing like these substantive limits on government power.

The French Revolution did not stop with the Declaration's ringing phrases about human freedom. Four years later a new list of protected rights, one that offered less constraint to the Jacobins who then ruled France, was thought to be necessary. A second, more government-friendly Declaration of the Rights of Man and of the Citizen was adopted.[33] (No accident that officials borrowed the more libertarian document's title.) Napoleon's quasi-authoritarian code followed a decade afterward, and France was launched on a different constitutional course than the one she briefly embraced in 1789. Meanwhile, the Bill of Rights, both Madison's version and the nearly identical rights protected by American state constitutions, survived and was copied as new states joined the Union and as old ones revised their basic charters. In the 1960s, Earl Warren and his colleagues extended Madison's text, making of the Fourth, Fifth, and Sixth Amendments a detailed, judicially enforced code of criminal procedure.

So when the Berlin Wall fell and both the Soviet Union and South African apartheid collapsed—events that led to a burst of constitution-writing in the twentieth century's last decade—the most visible model of a concise statement of legal rights to fair criminal justice was American, not French. Limits on police searches and seizures and a ban of compelled self-incrimination (both present in the Bill of Rights, both absent from the French Declaration) are common features of those newly democratic constitutions. So are lists of required trial procedures. One of the hot topics of today's comparative law scholarship is convergence: scholars argue that code-based justice systems like those used throughout Continental Europe and South America increasingly resemble common-law systems like those used in Great Britain and the United States. That is, code-based justice systems are becoming more proceduralized.[34] Meanwhile, Millian bans on criminalizing harmless conduct or on punishments that are less than "strictly and obviously necessary" are absent from the world's constitutions.[35]

Madison's proceduralist vision carried the day, but is it the right vision? There are two reasons to think not. First, more than substantive criminal law, criminal procedure depends on pragmatic judgments and adaptation to changing conditions. Over time, freezing procedures in place through fixed constitutional rules thus guarantees the wrong procedures. By contrast, a large portion of substantive law can and should be frozen: it rests on fixed moral principle, not changing empirics. Second, substantive criminal law is more dangerous than criminal procedure when left in the power of elected officials. Politicians can more easily use substantive law to evade unwelcome procedures than the other way around.

Roughly 60 percent of state prisoners are incarcerated for one or more of the following crimes: murder, manslaughter, rape, assault, robbery, burglary, larceny, auto theft, and fraud.[36] All the offenses just listed are universal crimes, offenses that all legal systems punish. All save auto theft were defined in volume 4 of William Blackstone's *Commentaries on the Laws of England,* published nearly two-and-a-half centuries ago.[37] Homicide excepted, Blackstone's definitions of those crimes continued to apply in most of the United States throughout the nineteenth century— and could easily apply today without disabling the justice system. The moral character of the forbidden conduct has not changed: robbers may use different weapons at some times and places than at others, but the nature of robbery and the reasons for punishing it remain the same. The character and quantity of crime changes constantly—but the *meaning* of crime is more stable, or can be if lawmakers so choose.

Criminal procedure is more changeable. In the United States, judges are mostly passive when evidence is gathered and witnesses questioned. Continental European legal systems cast judges in the more active role of supervising the investigation. Which approach leads to more accurate verdicts? Which one leaves convicted defendants convinced they have been treated fairly? These are questions of social fact, not moral truth. American law relies heavily on live witness testimony; violent street gangs in the United States do an effective job of intimidating witnesses.

Because of those two facts, gang violence is sometimes impossible for the authorities to punish directly. (That is one reason why drug punishments are so severe in neighborhoods that suffer gang violence: drug charges are used as a substitute for the violent felonies prosecutors cannot prove.) European law tends to place more weight on case files and documentary evidence, making witness intimidation a less valuable criminal skill. The relative merits of the two procedural systems depends on the truth value of the two kinds of evidence and on the different costs of producing them—which may in turn depend on the character of violent crime in the relevant place and time. Again, the key variables are social facts, not moral principles.

All of which suggests that constitutional law in the United States pays too much attention to procedure, and too little to substance. There is one more reason to embrace that conclusion. Using procedures to defeat defendant-protective substantive law is difficult, but using substantive law to evade or nullify protective procedures is remarkably easy—as is shown by the frequency with which American politicians have done it.

Take those two scenarios in turn. Imagine a robbery prosecution; imagine further that the crime is defined as the common law traditionally defined it: the intentional taking and carrying away of another's property by means of actual or threatened violence.[38] Finally, imagine that the government cannot prove some portions of that definition: perhaps the defendant's intent is unclear, or perhaps the presence of violence or intimidation is difficult to establish. How might government officials who are so inclined use procedure to convict this robbery defendant whose guilt cannot be proved? There are several familiar possibilities. Police might beat the defendant until he confesses to the crime he may not have committed. A watered-down burden of proof might allow the prosecution to skate by on weak evidence. The defendant might be denied the right to have legal counsel with the resources to investigate the facts (or hire others to do so), and consequently might be unable to mount a plausible defense. Finally, the case might be decided by a judge beholden to the government officials who want to see the defendant convicted. All of these possibilities are variations on a single theme: the proceeding might be rigged such that it can produce only one outcome. These are the methods dictators use to punish political dissidents for nonexistent crimes. Read accounts of the Soviet Union's show trials in the late 1930s, and one sees all these approaches at work.

Precisely because of their familiarity, these tactics are likely to prove hard to pull off for officials in well-functioning democracies. A few basic procedural rules resolve the problem: no coerced confessions, a high burden of proof for conviction, the right to counsel for defendants, with a corollary right to hire investigators and forensic experts, and an impartial judge (and, where applicable, an impartial jury) who is not under the thumb of the prosecutor's office. With few exceptions, democratic governments have such rules. Apply them, and procedural end-runs around substantive law are impossible.

Flip the categories, and end-runs become easy. Imagine the same robbery prosecution in a system with a panoply of pro-defendant procedures—including the basic rules just specified, plus the many procedural protections that constitutional law and the law of evidence provide in the United States. Once again, the government wants a conviction; once again, prosecutors cannot prove beyond a reasonable doubt that the defendant's conduct was intentional, or that actual or threatened violence was used to obtain the stolen money.

As before, there are several ways to skin this particular cat—but these means of evasion are both less familiar and harder to prevent than the ones previously listed. State legislators might redefine robbery: say, revise the intent term so that proof is automatic, or define "actual or threatened force" such that it is present in nearly every theft.[39] Or legislators might create a series of robbery-type offenses that vary slightly from one another: say, theft while in possession of a weapon, theft that prompts fear of injury, theft that risks harm to others, theft in public places, theft in particular institutions like banks—the list can be a long one, as a glance at any American criminal code will confirm.[40] Once these crimes are on the books, the prosecutor can charge our hypothetical defendant with several of them. (That sounds like a violation of double jeopardy, but isn't. As long as each offense requires proof of at least one fact that the others don't, the defendant could be convicted and punished separately for each crime charged, even though the charges arose from a single incident.)[41] Even if none of the charged offenses is easily proved, the odds that the government will be able to convict on at least one will usually suffice to prompt a guilty plea.

There is more. Legislators might create a series of offenses that have nothing to do with robbery or with any other serious crime; this tactic is particularly useful if the offenses are ones that a large fraction of the population commits. The prosecutor who finds a robbery charge hard to prove might discover which of these more obscure crimes the defendant has committed, and charge the defendant accordingly. If the charges pile high enough, the defendant might be punished as severely as a robber would be—without the need to prove robbery. An insidious variant on this tactic is sometimes used in federal prosecutions. If prosecutors find conviction difficult, they might investigate not the defendant but those closest to him: a spouse or lover, or perhaps a parent or child.[42]

The most common means of evasion has not yet been mentioned. Legislators might craft sentencing rules that are more severe than anyone thinks just, so that prosecutors might use the threat of those punishments to induce guilty pleas with more reasonable punishments attached. Over the course of the last generation, it has become common for prosecutors in death-penalty states to charge ordinary murder defendants with capital murder, then agree to a guilty plea with a life sentence attached.[43] The death penalty's role in such cases is not to execute murderers but to extract pleas, which avoids the need for the procedurally elaborate criminal trials the Bill of Rights guarantees.

Such tactics are not reserved for Stalinist show trials. Each of the legal moves described in the last three paragraphs is a regular feature of criminal litigation in the United States. Each renders the wide range of procedural protections American law provides irrelevant. High burdens of proof do not matter if the facts that must be proved are always present. Rights to counsel (state-paid if necessary), to an impartial judge and jury, and to appeal any conviction are worth little to defendants who are pressured into pleading guilty. The means by which procedure can be used to trump substance in criminal litigation are few and well-known. They are rare in democratic countries, including this one. The means by which substance can be used to trump procedure are many, and known only to criminal justice insiders. In the United States, their use is pervasive. Not only is substantive criminal law less bound by time, place, and circumstance than the law of criminal procedure. Substantive law is also more dangerous.

Why, then, did it not seem dangerous to the men who wrote and ratified America's key constitutional texts—which regulate criminal procedure in some detail, but leave substantive criminal law alone? There are three answers.

First, substantive law was less politicized two centuries ago than it is today. When the Constitution and Bill of Rights were written, the bulk of American criminal law consisted of the common law of England as described in Blackstone's *Commentaries*—one of the most widely owned books in the colonies. Common law comes not from the enactments of elected legislators but from judicial decisions, and eighteenth-century judges in both England and the colonies were appointed, not elected. Blackstone's four volumes were the product of centuries of judicial experience (along with some massaging by writers like Coke, Hale, and Blackstone himself). Even America's revolutionaries revered them, which is why all American states acknowledged the English common law's authority in American courts. No one in the Founding generation expected the common-law process to produce, say, the broadly defined and harshly punished drug offenses that fill American criminal codes today. Rightly so: the breadth and severity of contemporary criminal law has been the work of legislators, not judges; early American criminal law was primarily authored by judges, not legislators.

The second reason has already been mentioned: substantive criminal law was enforced differently in eighteenth-century America than it is today. Private enforcement by crime victims was the norm, government enforcement the exception.[44] Save for a few pockets like the criminal evasion of government taxes, early American criminal law was more akin to tort law— the law that governs what we now call personal injury litigation—than to contemporary criminal codes enforced by full-time, government-paid prosecutors. No one thought tort law required constitutional limits: constitutions were needed to restrain governments, not private litigants.

The last and most important reason is procedural. In the eighteenth century as today, criminal defendants enjoyed the right to trial by jury. But that right meant something quite different two centuries ago: eighteenth-century American juries had the power to decide questions of law as well as disputed facts, as Zenger's successful trial defense showed.[45] Twenty-first-century juries lack that legal power. Jurors at the time of the Founding were not the mere lie detectors that they have since become.[46] They were moral arbiters; their job was to decide *both* what the defendant did *and* whether his conduct merited punishment. Criminal law meant whatever jurors said it meant: their will trumped even Blackstone's text. With all-powerful American juries both defining crimes and applying their own definitions, the Founders had little reason to fear that legislators and prosecutors would combine to use substantive criminal law in ways that undermined American freedom. They did not anticipate that jury power would shrink, and that the scope of criminal law would expand dramatically.

The great puzzle of the Bill of Rights lies not in its wisdom or prescience. Rather, the puzzle is the Bill's survival. Lilburne and Zenger, Entick and Wilkes—these men may have been good examples of the dangers oppressive governments posed in the eighteenth century, but their cases bear little resemblance to the kinds of oppression badly run criminal justice systems visit on their targets today. The French Declaration seems almost ideally suited to limiting the power of too-powerful law enforcement agencies, and the Declaration severely limits legislatures' ability to define crimes and specify punishments as they wish. Within the realm of criminal justice, the American Bill of Rights establishes limits that police officers and prosecutors find it easy to evade, and places nearly no restrictions at all on legislative power. Barack Obama may commit himself to honoring those limits regardless of "expedience"—see the quotation at the beginning of this chapter—but the commitment is easy to make: built into the definition of the relevant rights is a good deal of leeway for law enforcement personnel to follow paths *they* find expedient.

The insubstantial character of those legal limits may be the chief source of their appeal. Late twentieth- and early twenty-first-century constitutional authors have been as eager to expand government power as to cabin it: hence the popularity of positive rights to education, health care, and employment that many contemporary constitutions include. And government officials, who have a large say in the drafting of constitutions, must prefer procedural rights that leave room for a wide range of government regulation to legal protections that limit their substantive authority in more direct ways. The Bill of Rights has not endured thanks to its success at the enterprise of constraining government power. More likely, its long legal life stems from its failure.

Machines That Go of Themselves

When longtime poet, Harvard professor, and Minister to Great Britain James Russell Lowell called the Constitution "a machine that would go of itself," he meant to mock the idea, not to give it his endorsement. Lowell's speech—delivered near the end of his life, a generation after the Civil War's end—was devoted to the proposition that the federal Constitution needed tending, that its legal and institutional machinery was less durable than Americans believed.[47]

Something similar is true of the institutional machinery that grinds out America's 1 million plus felony convictions each year. In the years before the Civil War, Northerners and Southerners established different sorts of criminal justice machinery, governed by different visions of local democracy. Soon, the processes of criminal justice became politically self-sustaining; the relevant institutions and practices became, in effect, machines that would go of themselves. In the twentieth century, those institutions and practices would evolve in ways that undermined their locally democratic character. That did not happen because lawmakers decided the institutional design of American criminal justice needed more designing. Rather, it happened because criminal justice institutions did not receive the kind of tending they needed. Even if Lowell's observation about the Constitution was wrong—some might say the Constitution's text needs following, not tending—it was abundantly right about the nation's criminal justice system.

That is a story for later chapters. For now, consider the different evolutionary paths that justice system followed in the generations between independence and civil war.

Three institutions came to define criminal justice in the North: district attorneys' offices, criminal trial courts, and urban police forces. All three institutions were and are a part of local governments—not states or provinces as in Germany and Canada, nor the national government as in Britain and France. For the past century-and-a-half, all three institutions have been headed by, composed of, or subject to politicians—again, unlike the apolitical justice systems elsewhere in the Western world. County voters elect both district attorneys and, in all but a handful of states, the judges who try criminal cases.[48] City voters elect the mayors and city council members who govern urban police forces. In metropolitan areas in the nineteenth century, city voters and county voters were the same: suburbs either were sparsely populated or did not exist.

While America's Founding generation and the generation that fought the Civil War and battled through Reconstruction crafted the nation's key constitutional texts, the generation that *preceded* the Civil War defined its key criminal justice institutions. At the time of the Founding, district attorneys, where they existed, were clerical officials appointed by state attorneys general or local judges.[49] Today's local prosecutors answer to neither judges nor state officials, and are far more than mere clerks. Again at the time of the Founding, state officials appointed the judges who heard and decided criminal cases. Those late eighteenth-century judges had more authority than late eighteenth-century district attorneys, but a good deal less authority than contemporary judges have.[50] Last but not least, urban police forces existed neither in eighteenth-century Britain—London's metropolitan police force was founded in 1829, thanks to then-Home Secretary Robert Peel (hence the name given London's officers: "bobbies")—nor in the newly independent United States. American cities were policed by a small constabulary supplemented by local residents who took turns serving as night watchmen. It would make sense to call early American criminal justice privatized—but that word assumes government control as a baseline, and eighteenth-century Americans had never known the kinds of government-run justice systems that prevail today, here and elsewhere. In the decades before the Civil War, this privately run system supervised by weak state officials grew more democratic, more powerful, and more thoroughly under the thumb of local governments.

Take these three institutions in turn. For most of the colonial era, the office of public prosecutor did not exist. Crime victims prosecuted most criminal cases, while ad hoc appointees (roughly analogous to today's special prosecutors) prosecuted the rest. In parts of the country during the course of the eighteenth century, permanent government employees gradually displaced these private citizen-prosecutors. The new public prosecutors operated at the county level, but were often chosen by state attorneys general. One more feature of early American district attorneys bears mention: they were paid by the case, sometimes by the conviction.[51]

To twenty-first-century readers, that seems scandalous. A prosecutor's job is to do justice, not to maximize punishment or to serve the interest of sometimes-vengeful crime victims. As the Supreme Court once put it, while the prosecutor "may strike hard blows, he is not at liberty to strike foul ones. It is as much his duty to refrain from improper methods calculated to produce a wrongful conviction as it is to use every legitimate means to bring about a just one."[52] Prosecutors' work is supposed to be nonpartisan: their clients are the residents of the jurisdiction they serve, including the defendants they prosecute. Paying them by the case converts otherwise even-handed public servants into heartless Javerts, eager to punish even the pettiest of crimes in order to make their living.[53] Paying them by the conviction is worse yet: that encourages prosecutors to win by any means necessary, fair and foul alike.

It did not seem so to Americans of the late eighteenth and early nineteenth centuries. The alternative to piecework pay was full-time salaries, and in many jurisdictions the job was less than a full-time job. Plus, criminal law of the time—meaning the common law of crimes, as Blackstone defined it—was not filled with the regulatory crimes and drug offenses that litter contemporary criminal codes. With few exceptions, common-law crimes were the kinds of offenses that voters in any jurisdiction at any time expect to see prosecuted when possible. Piecework pay and even payment per conviction were means of ensuring that these public officials served the public: that they did their jobs, instead of lazily collecting tax-paid salaries while ignoring the taxpayers' needs.[54]

The character of the compensation determined the character of the office. Today's salaried prosecutors exercise enormous discretionary power, choosing which criminal prohibitions to enforce and which ones to ignore, which defendants deserve punishment and which ones merit mercy. Prosecutors paid by the case have the same discretion in theory, but not in practice. Their incentive is to pursue all criminal charges brought to them, not to pick and choose among those charges. If paid by the conviction, a prosecutor's incentive is to pursue all winning cases, not to set priorities according to the seriousness of the alleged crime. Piecework pay made the job of early district attorneys ministerial, the rough equivalent of a court clerk obliged to file complaints and handle the paperwork for cases that others deem worth litigating. Or, to pick a more generous metaphor, those early district attorneys functioned like personal injury lawyers function today: like early American prosecutors, such lawyers pursue all claims they believe they can win. Failure to pursue some criminal charge did not represent a judgment that the crime in question did not merit punishment, or that some other crime deserved more attention. Those judgments were left in the hands of legislators, jurors, or perhaps judges. Depending on the circumstances, the traditional plaintiff's power to choose whether to pursue legal claims was exercised in criminal cases by crime victims or constables, grand juries or local magistrates—in short, by any-one but public prosecutors.

Had prosecutors' job remained as it was, American criminal justice might have evolved as did the criminal justice systems of Western Europe, with apolitical bureaucrats prosecuting criminal cases. Instead, two changes in institutional practice transformed criminal prosecution in the United States. First, piecework pay disappeared, replaced by fixed government salaries.[55] Second, district attorneys became elected offi-cials, each chosen by the voters of the county in which he worked.[56] The first change removed the incentive to prosecute all cases. The second change substituted for that incentive a different one: charge those crimes, and only those crimes, that local voters want to see punished. Prosecu-tion became a more powerful profession: prosecutors seeking to honor voters' preferences had to exercise judgment, not simply ratify the choices of constables or crime victims. The abandonment of piecework pay hap-pened over the course of the nineteenth century, especially the century's last sixty years. The rise of elected district attorneys happened chiefly during the last half of the 1840s and the first half of the 1850s.

Like early American district attorneys, early American trial judges were likewise chosen by state officials, usually state legislatures. In New England, appointed judiciaries remain in place today. Elsewhere, the large majority of judges—both those who try cases and those who decide appeals—are elected officials, subject to voters in the judicial district or county within which they work.[57] As with district attorneys, that institu-

tional change happened in the generation before the Civil War. Fifteen
states (out of twenty-six) rewrote their constitutions between 1844 and
1853; another five joined the Union with new state constitutions during
those years. Many of those new constitutions made judges and district
attorneys elective offices. In most other states, statutes required the same
practices.[58]

One more similarity between judges and prosecutors is worth noting.
Just as elected district attorneys exercised more power than their appointed predecessors, so too elected state judiciaries exercised more power
than *their* appointed predecessors. Partly because the United States in
the decades after independence had few lawyers, few litigants appealed
adverse court judgments. Appellate courts had little work to do: while
serving as the nation's first Chief Justice, John Jay found time to run for
New York's governorship and to negotiate a major treaty with Great Britain. Little work meant little political clout. Jay left the Supreme Court
after winning a second gubernatorial campaign, and preferred farming
his New York estate to accepting John Adams's 1801 offer of a second tour
of duty as Chief Justice.[59] (Adams's second choice was John Marshall.)

Juries' power to decide both legal and factual issues left appellate
judges scant room to shape and apply legal doctrine. That jury power
faded in the first half of the nineteenth century, while the number of appeals rose. Another number rose too: half again as many state statutes
were declared unconstitutional by state appellate courts in the 1840s as
in previous decades; that figure rose two-and-a-half times in the 1850s
and remained level through the Civil War.[60] More powerful judges corresponded with less powerful state legislators: per capita state spending
fell sharply during the 1840s, just as state constitutions were rewritten
and more aggressive state courts emerged.[61]

As state power declined, local power rose: after 1850 and for the balance of the nineteenth century save for the Civil War, local spending
doubled state spending.[62] Another force driving the rise of local governments' power was the spread of urban police forces, the first of which was
established in New York in 1845. Before that date, urban policing was
the responsibility of a small number of local constables supplemented by
a system of night watchmen: ordinary citizens who took turns walking
city streets while their neighbors slept.[63] After New York abandoned the

privatized night watch system, other cities soon followed: Baltimore's police force was established in 1847, Philadelphia's in 1850, Boston's in 1854.[64] These early urban police departments were created by state legislatures, but they soon came under the control of city governments.[65] Their creation coincided with the first great wave of European immigration, chiefly from Ireland, and with the rising urban violence that wave of immigrants spawned. The night watch system was unable to keep peace on city streets where rival ethnic gangs roamed. City police forces were designed to fill that gap.[66]

Collectively, these changes amounted to a revolution in state and local government. What accounts for this hidden revolution, and what explains its timing? The beginnings of an answer follow from this less-than-coincidental coincidence: the wave of state constitutions that produced elected judges and district attorneys followed a decade of crisis in state finance. In the wake of New York's phenomenal success with the Erie Canal, state governments undertook to build more canals, often whole networks of them, to be financed by state bonds. The strategy didn't work, mostly because the Erie Canal was better timed than its would-be imitators. Opened in 1825, the canal was an immediate success; New York quickly became the nation's leading port and the prime shipping point for midwestern farm products. A decade later, railroads began to offer a sometimes-cheaper means of shipping goods across great distances, one that did not depend on the location of lakes and rivers. Then the Panic of 1837 struck, hitting both shipping and state tax revenues especially hard. The rise of railroads and the economy's collapse made most canals built after 1835 economically unsustainable. Faced with the combination of declining revenues and steeply rising state debts, nine states—a third of the nation—defaulted. Several more came close.[67]

The political fallout was massive, as Abraham Lincoln's early career illustrates. In the late 1830s, Lincoln was the leading proponent of Illinois's elaborate plan of canal construction; that plan's passage made him the state's most prominent Whig legislator, a rising political star. Instead, it quickly became clear that the canals could not possibly pay for themselves; they were never finished. Lincoln left the Illinois legislature in 1842. Four years later, he earned a single term in the House of Representatives from Illinois's safest Whig district—which went Democratic in the next election.[68]

The voters who rejected Lincoln's canals also limited state legislators' power and created more elected offices—including locally elected district attorneys and criminal trial judges. Calls for more democracy stemmed from voters' perception that established democratic institutions had failed and needed reform. That perception applied to much more than criminal justice, but it must have been especially strong in that area. The first urban police forces were formed while Irish immigrants were driving up urban homicide rates, and while nativism was becoming a large force in American politics. (Remember the Know-Nothings and the Massachusetts legislature.) Locally elected district attorneys and trial judges probably appealed to mid-nineteenth-century voters for the same reason those voters distrusted legislators in distant state capitals—physical distance was one of the crucial facts of pre–Civil War politics.[69] Elected officials who stayed close to home could be counted on to protect the local voters who chose them. In the 1850s, that meant protecting native-born city-dwellers from immigrant crime.

If that was part of the motive behind the institutional reforms of the 1840s and 1850s, those reforms hid a deep irony. The goal may have been to protect the native-born population from young Irish men, but the long-term effect was to empower those young men and their descendants by giving immigrant communities the authority to judge their own crimes. By the nineteenth century's end, most of the cities of the Northeast and Midwest were ruled by immigrants and their children. They dominated local police forces: Irish cops decided which Irish criminals to arrest.[70] State legislators continued to have the power to define criminal prohibitions. But thanks to the constitutional changes of the 1840s and 1850s, local officials determined how, when, and against whom those criminal prohibitions were enforced. For a long time, that enforcement power mattered more than the power to define legal rules.

Antebellum Southerners created not one justice system but three: the justice of courts, the justice of masters, and the justice of the mob. The first followed the usual legal forms; the second and third operated off the books. The formal system resembled justice systems in the North, using urban police and rural sheriffs to apprehend criminals, local district attorneys to try them, and local jails and state penitentiaries to confine those found guilty. In most respects, that formal justice system was as protective of defendants' interests as those in the North—and, on some issues, more protective than today's system. Contemporary Fourth Amendment law permits arrest warrants (which justify breaking down the doors of arrestees' homes) that specify the person to be arrested but not the place where he is to be found. The Virginia Supreme Court required that the place be specified as well.[71] Today, the Fifth Amendment's double jeopardy clause permits prosecution of the same crime in multiple states. The Alabama Supreme Court held that the mere possibility that a defendant could be charged with a given crime in another state barred prosecution for that crime in Alabama.[72]

Such decisions were fairly common, and not only in cases brought against white defendants. Southern courts were sometimes used to try slaves' crimes—and in such cases defendants' rights were surprisingly well protected, even in the heavily enslaved Deep South. Historian William Freehling notes that in the generation before the Civil War, thirty-one cases of black defendants charged with murdering white victims came before the supreme courts of Mississippi, Alabama, and Louisiana. Appellate courts overturned the convictions of sixteen of those defendants.[73] In one Alabama case, the slave Bob tried to take an ax from his slave wife Dinah in order to kill her with it. In the course of the struggle, Bob killed a white child standing nearby. Some testimony suggested the killing was intentional; other testimony indicated that the child's killing was an accident, that Bob's only intended victim was Dinah. Bob was charged with and convicted of murder. Regardless of which version of the facts one believed, the murder charge seemed unassailable: killing one victim while trying to injure or kill another fell within the customary definition of murder in the mid-nineteenth century as it does today. Yet Alabama's Supreme Court reversed, holding that the evidence proved Bob guilty only of involuntary manslaughter, a less serious offense that had not been charged.[74]

Another Alabama case explains that surprising result. A state statute required that two-thirds of the jurors judging slave defendants be slaveholders. A slave's conviction for murdering a white adult was overturned because one of the jurors stood to inherit his father's slaves but had none himself; without that juror, the two-thirds requirement was not met.[75]

Slaves were valuable property, not to be destroyed save when other owners of human property thought it necessary. Protecting slave defendants
meant protecting those slaves' masters.

In a Tennessee case, the slave Elijah was convicted of murder. His lawyer, paid by his master, argued on appeal that his master should have
been permitted to testify in his defense. That claim sounds uncontroversial, but mid-nineteenth century law forbade sworn testimony by criminal defendants, by plaintiffs and defendants in civil cases, and by other
parties who stood to gain or lose from the litigation.[76] Application of that
principle should have barred Elijah's master from testifying. Nevertheless, the Tennessee Supreme Court agreed with Elijah's claim. The language in the court's opinion was as stirring as it was dishonest:

> [I]n a case like this the law . . . takes the slave out of the hands of his
> master, forgets his claims and rights of property, treats the slave as a
> rational and intelligent human being, responsible to moral, social
> and municipal duties and obligations, and gives him the benefit of all
> the forms of trial which jealousy of power and love of liberty have in-
> duced the freeman to throw around himself for his own protection.[77]

The key clause is the first one: "in a case like this . . ." Justice Reese's
rhetoric, like the court's opinions in the two Alabama cases described
previously, focuses on the rights of the slave. But the key to Elijah's case
and to both Alabama cases was the interest of slaveowners, all talk of
"tak[ing] the slave out of the hands of his master" to the contrary
notwithstanding.

Some masters needed no court to provide their slaves with something
akin to legal process. On Jefferson Davis's Mississippi plantation, slaves
were tried for alleged offenses by slave judges and slave juries; Davis's
overseer served as prosecutor and carried out the sentence if one was
imposed. (Davis gave himself the power to reduce, but not to increase,
sentences imposed by this slave court.)[78] Though Davis's system was
unusual, the idea behind it was not. This particular slaveowner fought
in the Mexican War, served in the U.S. Senate, was a member of President Pierce's cabinet, returned to the Senate, then served as President of
the Confederacy for the duration of the Civil War. For twenty years,

Davis was forced to spend most of his time on Mexican battlefields, in Washington, or in Richmond. Absent masters of large plantations—few plantation owners were absent for as long as Davis, but many spent much of their time in nearby cities, leaving others to manage their affairs—relied on paid overseers to keep their slaves in line. Those absent masters might never know the details of the whippings their overseers administered, but they would surely know about the size of this year's cotton crop. Consequently, an overseer's incentive was to worry too much about the next harvest and too little about the health of the human beings who would plant and harvest the future crops. Davis protected his slaves from too-aggressive overseers as a rancher might protect his cattle from abuse by careless employees, and for the same reason.[79]

Most masters were less generous—and it was masters' preferences, not slaves' rights, that determined the character of slave justice. That privatized justice system was often both brutal and casual, with little attention paid to anything recognizable as legal procedure. Yet justice for slaves could also be both lax and occasional: masters were forced to tolerate small offenses whose origins and perpetrators were unknown to them. At all times, two opposing incentives defined the character of masters' rule. On the one hand, slaves' health added to their owners' wealth. On the other hand, slaves were potential rebels, made more dangerous by their proximity to owners' homes and families. Masters at once trusted their slaves and were terrified of them. When fires spread through North Texas in 1859—after unusually hot, dry weather that made accidental fires a near-certainty—dozens of slaves, along with a few whites thought to be guilty of incitement, were executed as arsonists.[80] Appellate judges might talk of loving liberty and limiting power, but such talk could only be taken so far. When push came to shove, masters' power was effectively unlimited, slaves' liberty nonexistent.

Those Texas executions were examples of the third southern justice system in action: the justice of the mob, often enforced by slave patrols. In theory, these roving white gangs were the rural South's equivalent to the system of night watchmen that guarded city streets at the time of the American Revolution. As watchmen looked for would-be criminals disturbing urban peace, slave patrols looked for southern disturbers of social peace and order: chiefly runaways and other slaves traveling without their masters' permission, along with any whites who helped them. Slave-owners preferred to handle the discipline of their human property themselves, and usually did so. But slave patrols staffed by poorer whites often had their own views about the proper handling of black slaves. The result was a sizeable number of slave lynchings—how sizeable, no one knows.[81]

Over time, those slave patrols turned into enforcers of southern orthodoxy, extending their jurisdiction to include white outsiders who might be guilty of spreading dangerous ideas. John Fee, a native Kentuckian educated in antislavery Ohio, had the temerity to return to his home state and establish a network of racially integrated schools and churches. A posse of Fee's neighbors drove the young minister back to his former northern home at gunpoint—and promised to fire those guns if he crossed the Ohio River again. Two Texas Episcopal pastors named McKinney and Blunt, both of northern descent, were whipped and then driven to Indian Territory (present-day Oklahoma) with similar instructions. These churchmen got off easy: a Mississippi mob hanged three local carpenters believed to be responsible for burning a pair of cotton gins. They were among the three hundred southern *whites* lynched in the three decades before the Civil War.[82] Lynching slaves may have been more common—but even if so, such vigilante justice was not meted out lightly, for slaves were worth a considerable sum to their masters. Given the right circumstances, killing white men was a simpler matter. A coat of tar and feathers followed by northern exile was simpler still.

These instances of mob justice for southern whites who seemed insufficiently southern were both a symptom of southern violence and one of its causes. Among whites in the Deep South, antebellum murder rates were astronomical. White Floridians killed one another at an annual rate of 40–70 per 100,000, yet murder convictions were few and far between.[83] (By way of comparison, today's national murder rate is below 6 per 100,000; the murder rate in Detroit—among America's most violent large cities—stands at 34.)[84] In part, Florida's many homicides reflected the culture of honor that permeated the South; among whites, murder as a means of avenging insult was a common phenomenon before the Civil War.[85]

Those homicides also may reflect the deep fault line that ran through southern white culture. On one side were rich slaveholders, some of them fans of George Fitzhugh, the southern writer who wrote of slavery's superiority relative to the alleged "wage slavery" of the antebellum North.[86] If black slaves were better off than white workers in the North, how secure was the status of southern whites too poor to own slaves? On the other side were the mostly poor southern whites who formed Hinton Rowan Helper's target audience; Helper wrote a famous screed on slaveholders' exploitation of their nonslaveholding white neighbors.[87] If poor whites listened to the likes of Helper, how secure was southern slavery? This divide between slaveowners and poor southern whites was replicated in southern crime control. Southerners who owned human beings embodied the law on their own plantations. Nonslaveholders exercised a large measure of power over those roving slave patrols that often disciplined free whites. On both sides of the divide, the administration of "justice" regularly fell outside the bounds of the legal system.

Fear lay behind that extralegal justice. Throughout the decades leading up to the Civil War, slavery was under threat along the South's northern and western borders. Before the United States annexed it in 1845, Texas—then an independent slaveholding republic—was negotiating with an abolitionist British Empire; white Southerners worried that Texas might become a free British colony to which southern slaves could escape. By 1860, nine-tenths of Delaware's blacks and half of Maryland's were already free; Baltimore housed more than 25,000 free blacks but barely 2,000 slaves. Western Virginia was free territory in all but name. Fewer than 10 percent of Missouri's residents were slaves, and the percentage was falling.[88] Save for a brief period when Kansans could legally own slaves, Missouri's outnumbered slaveholders were surrounded on three sides by free territory. If—to antebellum Southerners, the applicable word was *when*—slavery faded in these states, the Deep South would soon become a besieged, heavily enslaved minority in an otherwise free Union: Thomas Jefferson's nightmare.

That fear led politicians from the southern borderland, always with the support of their Deep South colleagues, to seek legal guarantees for white southerners' right to determine slavery's future for themselves. Kentuckian Henry Clay orchestrated the 1820 compromise that led to Missouri's admission as a slave state. Marylander William Cost Johnson authored the gag rule that barred the House from receiving antislavery petitions in the late 1830s. In the last act of his presidency, Virginian John Tyler pushed the annexation of Texas through Congress—by joint resolution rather than by treaty, so as to avoid the need to get the votes of two-thirds of the Senate. Five years later, Virginia Senator James Mason sponsored the Fugitive Slave Act of 1850, streamlining the process by which Border South slaveowners like Mason himself could reclaim slaves who fled to the free North. Missouri's David Atchison bullied his Senate colleague Stephen Douglas into amending Douglas's Kansas-Nebraska bill in order to open Kansas to slavery, after which Atchison urged his fellow Missourians to stuff Kansas ballot boxes in order to elect proslavery territorial legislators. In his majority opinion in the *Dred Scott* case, Chief Justice Roger Taney—a Marylander who had freed his own slaves two decades earlier—opened *all* the nation's territories to slavery. Some of these men believed slavery worth preserving. Others hoped to see the institution disappear: Johnson bragged (!) that his home state of Maryland would soon be free territory, if only abolitionists would shut up and let Southerners resolve their problems free of northern interference. All agreed that southern whites must determine slavery's fate.[89]

In short, Southerners felt the insecurity of a Border South threatened by antislavery agitation from outside its bounds, of Deep South slaveowners who feared that the borderland would soon be free territory, and of nonslaveholding whites who feared subordination to black slaves. Each legal and political victory made the slave South less secure rather than more so, by producing the northern opposition white Southerners sought to preempt. In turn, that northern opposition fed southern fears, which produced the forced exiles of Fee, McKinney, Blunt, and many more like them—not to mention those three hundred lynchings of not-quite-southern-enough whites.

Those lynchings speak more loudly than any three hundred court cases could. Usually, crime and punishment are distinct enterprises; the latter is the law's price for the former. In the antebellum South, punishment was itself a crime, and law had little to do with either category's definition.

In North and South alike, law had less to do with the character of criminal justice than one might suppose. Both sections elected the judges who presided over criminal trials. In both, elected district attorneys decided whom to prosecute and for what crimes, and elected city governments reigned over those same cities' police forces. Both sections relied on local juries to decide who did and didn't merit punishment. As these different forms of democracy exerted a large influence over the justice system, legal doctrine's influence remained surprisingly modest. Even after states in both regions had enacted criminal codes, Blackstone's list of general principles largely defined substantive criminal law. The Bill of Rights—through state constitutions, not the federal one—governed criminal procedure, but the governing was light; the meaning of defendants' various procedural rights was rarely litigated. The antebellum criminal process owed more to tradition and local custom than to law. Again, these points applied to both sections: substantive law and procedure were pretty much the same in the North and in the South.

The character of the local democracy that governed criminal justice was another matter: on that score, the two sections differed dramatically. In the North, local self-government operated through both elections and jury verdicts. That sometimes happened in the South, too, but only sometimes: a large fraction of crimes was handled by slaveowners and their overseers, and a smaller but important fraction was handled by slave patrols and by local mobs. Northern criminal justice was an exercise in self-government. In the South, criminal justice usually involved the government of some by others—blacks by white slaveowners and slave patrols, dissident whites by white mobs enforcing southern orthodoxy.

CHAPTER 4

The Fourteenth Amendment's
Failed Promise

No state shall . . . deny to any person the equal protection of the laws.

—Amendment XIV, Constitution of the United States (ratified 1868)

We had to shoot negroes to get relief from the galling tyranny to which we had been subjected.

—South Carolina Senator Benjamin J. Tillman,
Speech to Reunion of the Red Shirts (1909)

THE ORIGINAL CONSTITUTION assumed a criminal justice system dominated by state governments. (Local dominance came later.) Article I, Section 8 of that document defines the power of Congress by listing the topics about which Congress may legislate. The list is a long one, with twenty-nine items, not counting the catch-all provision with which it ends: "The Congress shall have power . . . [t]o make all Laws which shall be necessary and proper for carrying into Execution the foregoing Powers." The only bodies of criminal law mentioned in that long list are counterfeiting, piracy, "offences against the law of nations," and crimes that occur within the military: a decidedly modest legal agenda. Other federal criminal prohibitions might be deemed "necessary and proper" to the execution of other powers, but Madison and his friends did not expect that category to be large, as this feature of the list shows: the clause authorizing "the Punishment of counterfeiting the Securities and current Coin of the United States" follows immediately after the clause that permits Congress to coin money.[1] The counterfeiting clause was needed only on the assumption that the power to punish counterfeiters is not implied by the "coin money" clause—which suggests that implied federal powers to criminally punish must have been few and small in the view of the Constitution's authors. Federal criminal law was meant to be narrow, and federal criminal law enforcement was meant to be rare.

Although the first of those expectations has proved wrong, the second still holds true today. Federal criminal law is broad, but it mostly covers crimes that state codes also cover: fraud, drug offenses, and some violent felonies and thefts. State and local officials handle the vast majority of those crimes, which is why the federal government accounts for a mere 6 percent of felony convictions.[2] Very little has worked out the way the Constitution's authors planned. But this has: criminal law enforcement remains, first and foremost, the job of state and local governments. The federal government is a significant player in this field, but still a small one.

Twice in American history that pattern has been disrupted, with the federal government taking on a large share of the responsibility for crime and punishment. Prohibition was the second time. Reconstruction was the first. During Prohibition, federal agents and prosecutors were the chief enforcers of the nation's alcohol laws. During Reconstruction, the Freedmen's Bureau, federal marshals, and federal prosecutors took on the responsibility for putting an end to the political and racial terrorism of the Ku Klux Klan and similar organizations. Both times, the expansion of federal power was enormous. Both times, that expansion rested on a constitutional amendment: the Fourteenth, which guaranteed ex-slaves "the equal protection of the laws," and the Eighteenth, which barred the manufacture and sale of alcoholic beverages.

Both times, expanded federal power seemed to work, at least for awhile. Thanks to the efforts of federal marshals and federal prosecutors, Klan leaders in Alabama and South Carolina were imprisoned; the level of violence against southern blacks fell.[3] Americans seemed headed for an era of racial and political peace. In the first few years after Prohibition was enacted, alcohol consumption fell sharply, as did (apparently) a range of alcohol-related misconduct.[4] The demise of the corner saloon seemed likely to usher in an age of prosperity and low crime rates. Both times, depressions—the Panic of 1873 and the Wall Street crash of 1929, both of which triggered severe, decade-long economic downturns—transformed the nation's politics. After those depressions hit, support for these two federal initiatives quickly unraveled. In 1933, four years after stocks crashed and thirteen years after the Eighteenth Amendment established Prohibition, the Twenty-First repealed it. No constitutional amendment overturned the equal protection guarantee. But the Supreme Court effectively did so in *United States v. Cruikshank* (1876),[5] three years after that era's Great Depression struck and a mere eight years after the Fourteenth Amendment was ratified.

Cruikshank read the equal protection clause in a manner that protected the Klan from federal prosecutors rather than its victims from the Klan. That judicial decision amounted to an engraved invitation to men like "Pitchfork Ben" Tillman,[6] whose words are quoted at the beginning of this chapter, to use murderous means to take back control of southern state governments and to brag about it afterward. Tillman was one of the most prominent speakers of his day on what we now call the lecture circuit, drawing large crowds of Northerners to hear his unapologetic defense of white rule over southern blacks.[7] That rule was achieved at the expense of the lives of thousands of black ex-slaves, killed to ensure that they and their friends would soon be ex-voters. So much for "the equal protection of the laws."

Reconstruction's Rise

Two carriages collided in Memphis, Tennessee, on May 1, 1866. One of the two drivers was black. This thoroughly ordinary accident triggered a three-day riot in which four dozen people were killed, several women raped, and a host of houses and businesses destroyed. Nearly all the victims of this violence were black; the perpetrators included a large fraction of the city's white police officers and firemen.[8] The following July 30, a similar riot took place in New Orleans. Louisiana's governor had called the state's Unionist constitutional convention—near the Civil War's end, that convention had drafted the state constitution that Abraham Lincoln saw as a model for a reconstructed South—back into session. New Orleans blacks were marching toward the convention center in support of black suffrage and the disenfranchisement of former Confederate officials, both of which the convention was expected to endorse. Some of the blacks were armed. When local whites threw bricks at the marchers, a few responded by firing into the white crowd. At that point, white police officers attacked the marchers, killing thirty-four blacks and wounding more than one hundred. Four whites were killed.[9]

Six weeks after the Memphis massacre and a month before the one in New Orleans, Congress voted to submit the Fourteenth Amendment to the states for ratification. Section One of the amendment reads as follows:

> All persons born or naturalized within the United States, and subject to the jurisdiction thereof, are citizens of the United States and of the State wherein they reside. No State shall make or enforce any law which shall abridge the privileges or immunities of citizens of the United States; nor shall any State deprive any person of life, liberty, or property without due process of law; nor deny to any person within its jurisdiction the equal protection of the laws.

Section Two declares that, in any state in which some adult males are denied the right to vote for reasons other than "participation in rebellion, or other crime," the number of representatives and electoral votes must be reduced in proportion to the number of voters disenfranchised. Section Three bars former state and federal officials who supported the Confederacy from holding political office, absent a congressional pardon. Section Four bars payment of Confederate war debts, and Section Five authorizes Congress "to enforce, by appropriate legislation, the provisions of this [Amendment]."[10] Sections Two and Three were the amendment's most contested provisions, but Sections One and Five turned out to matter most.

The conventional wisdom holds that Section One of the Fourteenth Amendment—source of the due process, equal protection, and privileges or immunities clauses—was designed to undo the South's Black Codes. In the Civil War's wake, ex-Confederate states enacted legislation binding ex-slaves to their employers in the manner of indentured servants. Blacks were not allowed to quit their jobs, and their employers could use physical punishments to discipline them: a form of quasi-slavery to take the place of the institution that Lincoln's proclamation abolished. In March 1866, Congress enacted the first Civil Rights Act, which did overturn the Black Codes by guaranteeing blacks and whites the same rights to make contracts and own property. Andrew Johnson vetoed the Act, after which Congress overrode his veto on April 9: three weeks before the Memphis massacre. By then, the Fourteenth Amendment was already in the works; along with many of his colleagues, the amendment's chief author—Ohio Congressman John Bingham—was concerned about the constitutionality of the Civil Rights Act. (Until that Act, the law of contract and property had been exclusively a matter for the states to decide; the Act arguably exceeded the scope of federal power.) The amendment's "privileges or immunities" and due process clauses, plus Section Five, which granted Congress the power to enforce the amendment through "appropriate legislation," were intended to render the Civil Rights Act immune to constitutional challenge.[11]

That was not, however, Section One's sole purpose. That Section's language, quoted above, accomplishes four tasks. First, it defines citizenship in a manner that includes ex-slaves, and thereby overrules Roger Taney's infamous decision in *Scott v. Sandford* (1857).[12] Second, the text overturns state laws that "abridge the privileges or immunities of citizens of the United States." Third, it extends the Fifth Amendment's guarantee of "due process of law" by making that guarantee enforceable against state and local governments.[13] Fourth and finally, the Fourteenth Amendment guarantees to all "the equal protection of the laws." By the amendment's terms, these restrictions appear to operate on government officials, not on private citizens: Section One states that "*no state* shall make or enforce any law" abridging the privileges or immunities of citizenship, and bars "*any state*" from depriving any person of life, liberty, or property without due process, and from denying any person the "equal protection of the laws." The scope and meaning of what lawyers call the "state action" requirement would prove key to the legal battle over Reconstruction.

Three of Section One's four tasks concerned the character of criminal justice. The amendment's authors believed that the "privileges or immunities" of citizenship meant, roughly, the set of legal protections listed in the Bill of Rights—including the criminal procedure rules specified in the Fourth, Fifth, and Sixth Amendments. In *Barron v. Baltimore*

(1833), John Marshall's Supreme Court had held that those protections were enforceable only against the federal government.[14] The clause governing citizens' privileges or immunities was probably meant to overrule *Barron*.[15] That mattered in a world in which southern courts could not be trusted to enforce their own state constitutions' bills of rights on ex-slaves' behalf. Before the war, some southern courts had protected slaves' rights as a means of protecting their masters' property. With no masters standing behind them, ex-slaves could hardly count on state law and state courts to guard their rights. This explains the need for the Fourteenth Amendment: the amendment could be enforced by federal legislation and in federal courts.

The due process clause decreed that criminal punishment— government-sponsored deprivations of "life, liberty, or property"— could be imposed only according to legal procedure. Before the Civil War, Republicans chafed at the summary procedures used to recapture runaway slaves, procedures that seemed to maximize the risk of misidentification and enslavement of free blacks.[16] The due process clause was meant to bar the use of such procedures when men's lives and liberty were at stake. And requiring due process as a condition of criminal punishment accomplished one more task, or seemed to do so: it forbade the system of quasi-formalized mob justice that had been the chief means of enforcing southern orthodoxy on race. Slave patrols and similar entities were functional agents of the government; accordingly, their future equivalents were subject to the clause's restrictions.[17]

The equal protection clause likewise sought to address (and redress) mob violence, but of a different sort: the kind embodied by the Memphis and New Orleans massacres. In both of those murderous incidents, police officers' job was to protect black residents of the cities they patrolled; instead of doing that job, officers killed those they were supposed to serve. Notice that the murders themselves were not the heart of the equal protection violation. The true violation was the failure to prevent those murders from happening—officers' failure to protect black victims against the violence the officers themselves perpetrated.

That guarantee of legal protection was potentially radical. Every lynching—perhaps every unsolved murder of a black victim—might be labeled a constitutional violation: the local sheriff had failed to protect the victim, and the local district attorney had failed to prosecute the killers. Even when the perpetrators were private citizens, they too participated in the constitutional violation by conspiring to deprive their victims of the needed legal protection. Thus construed, the equal protection clause might produce a federal law of homicide, theft, and assault for black crime victims, displacing the bodies of state law that traditionally governed those crimes. Federal officials—soldiers, prosecutors, and agents of the Freedmen's Bureau[18]—might supplant the local elected officials responsible for enforcing the law in southern counties. These were precisely the objections the Fourteenth Amendment's opponents raised.

The objections failed to take hold, for three reasons. First, even in 1866, the idea that lawful governments owe those they govern protection from predatory crime was an old one. As Blackstone had put the point a century before, "[T]he community should guard the rights of each individual member, and . . . (in return for the protection) each individual should submit to the laws of the community."[19] To use a leading legal historian's more compact terms, "In the shorthand of the era, allegiance is the obligation of the citizen and protection the obligation of the sovereign."[20] Second, the men who wrote and ratified the Fourteenth Amendment had grown to maturity under a justice system that satisfied the obligation the equal protection clause imposed. Private citizens supplied much of the protection themselves, through the system of night watchmen who did the job urban police forces do today. Public prosecutors supplied the rest. Until midcentury, most of them were paid either by the case or by the conviction, which gave them every incentive to offer legal protection to all: that is how they made their living. "Equal protection of the laws" seemed less than radical because Americans outside the South had seen it in action.

Third, mass murders like those in Memphis and New Orleans showed denials of equal protection at their simplest. When white police officers did the killing, there was no doubt about the government's complicity in the massacre of ex-slaves. Government officials' responsibility was less clear when private citizens were the murderers or when killers' identities were unknown. It was less clear still when, beginning in the late 1860s, pro–civil rights Republican governments took control of southern cities and towns.[21] Once that happened, southern sheriffs and police officers were less of a danger to ex-slaves' lives than when the Memphis and New Orleans police murdered dozens of their black neighbors, and local white populations more so. A congressional investigation found that from the spring of 1868 through that year's November presidential election, more than one thousand political murders—nearly all of them perpetrated by white killers against black victims—were committed in Louisiana alone. Those killings alone would have given the state an annual murder rate of 149 per 100,000 population: more than thirteen times the nation's peak twentieth-century murder rate, a staggering twenty-eight times today's figure.[22] Those thousand plus murders happened when the state and most of its parishes were governed, at least officially, by Republicans. Government officials and their allies were not the perpetrators of this crime wave. They were its victims.

The most famous Reconstruction massacre followed the same template. In the Red River valley in central Louisiana, Republicans had carved a new black-majority parish from sections of neighboring jurisdictions, naming the parish after President Grant and its capital after Grant's first vice president, Schuyler Colfax.[23] After the 1872 elections, both sides claimed control of the state and of Grant Parish. Hoping to forestall a Democratic takeover, approximately 150 black men and several dozen black women occupied the parish courthouse, along with two white men named Shaw and Register who then served as local sheriff and judge, respectively. The two whites and most of the women left the courthouse before the violence began, but not before Shaw deputized the black men who remained behind to protect parish property. These temporary deputies—agents of the lawful local government—were armed with shotguns and a few pistols. They dug a shallow trench around the courthouse for protection. Several hundred whites, armed with Enfield rifles and a cannon, took up positions near the courthouse.[24]

On April 13, 1873—Easter Sunday—the whites attacked. Cannon fire on the shallow trench drove black defenders back into the building. The whites then set the courthouse on fire and shot blacks as they fled the building. The final death toll is unknown; Charles Lane's excellent book on the massacre and its aftermath places the number of blacks killed between 62 and 81. Three white men died, two of them killed by friendly fire. Most of the black dead were murdered after surrendering or while trying to do so. Some were killed in the course of a game the killers played: lining up two or three black prisoners in a row to see how many could be executed with a single bullet. Two days after this slaughter, black bodies still littered the courthouse grounds; passengers on a nearby steamboat reported being overwhelmed by the smell of rotting flesh. Eventually, a deputy United States marshal and his assistant arrived from New Orleans and turned the trench outside the courthouse into a mass grave.[25]

Long after the massacre, the state placed a plaque at the scene of the old courthouse, stating:

> On this site occurred the Colfax Riot in which three white men and
> 150 negroes were slain. This event on April 13, 1873 marked the end
> of carpetbag misrule in the South.[26]

Like the men who did the killing, the government officials who ordered that historical marker and wrote its text were proud of the disparity between the few white corpses and the many black ones—so much so that they exaggerated the latter figure.

The killings at Colfax did not fit the simple pattern of the police riots in Memphis and New Orleans. The perpetrators were not themselves government officials—instead, they killed government officials. At a deeper level, these three murderous rampages had much in common with one another, and with Klan violence in the Reconstruction South more generally.[27] The white perpetrators of that violence were trying to deprive government officials of the ability to exercise their lawful power—so that the perpetrators might exercise that power themselves, and use it to destroy blacks' hopes of freedom and political equality. The state's historical marker captured the killers' twin goals: to put an end to "carpetbag misrule" by forcibly ejecting the rulers from office, and to return local blacks to the subservient status they held before the war. Once they seized the power of law enforcement in their respective jurisdictions, at least temporarily, the Colfax killers did precisely what the white police officers of Memphis and New Orleans had done: murdered those who most needed the law's protection.

Congress and federal prosecutors struggled to find the proper legal theory for prosecuting such cases. In February 1869, in the face of rising violence, Congress passed the Fifteenth Amendment, providing that the right to vote "shall not be denied . . . on account of race, color, or previous condition of servitude."[28] Shortly after that amendment was ratified in early 1870, Congress passed the Enforcement Act, which criminalized intimidation of would-be voters, conspiracies to deny the right to vote, and conspiracies "to hinder [the] free exercise and enjoyment of any right or privilege granted or secured . . . by the Constitution or laws of the United States."[29] Through that clause, the Enforcement Act implicitly authorized criminal prosecutions of conspiracies to deny black victims "the equal protection of the laws." With the passage of the Ku Klux Klan Act in April 1871, Congress made the authority explicit, and gave the president the power to suspend habeas corpus where Klan activity had caused a breakdown in orderly government.[30]

These statutes were quickly put to use: the remainder of 1871 and 1872 saw the indictment of hundreds of Klan leaders and members. For the most part, defendants who renounced the Klan and promised to cease their violent activities were released.[31] With respect to most of the defendants who remained, the government charged the defendants with conspiring to deprive their victims of the rights to bear arms, to be free of unreasonable seizures, and to vote, all in violation of the Enforcement Act and the Fourteenth and Fifteenth Amendments. The Bill of Rights–based theories—the idea was that Second and Fourth Amendment rights were part of the "privileges or immunities" of citizenship that the Fourteenth Amendment protected—were mostly rejected; theories based on voting achieved better results.[32]

Those theories had one glaring problem. As in the Colfax Massacre, the violence in Klan cases was usually the work of private citizens. But the Fourteenth Amendment bars "any state" from denying its residents the "equal protection of the laws," and the Fifteenth Amendment bars "the United States or any state" from denying the right to vote based on the would-be voter's race.[33] Klan defendants invariably argued that neither those amendments nor any legislation based on them could possibly apply to their behavior, because they did not exercise government power. They might be guilty of burglary and murder, arson and assault: all state-law crimes (for which they would never be prosecuted, as they well understood—among other things, Klan cases were expensive to investigate and prosecute, and sheriffs and district attorneys lacked the necessary resources). But they were innocent of the federal charges brought against them.

Federal prosecutors might have responded: Klan members may not be government officials, but exercising government power is precisely what they seek to do. Governments determine who may vote and who may not; the Klan and its allies sought to steal that responsibility wherever southern Republican officials exercised it. Likewise, governments define crimes and punishments, and decide which crimes merit prosecution and which crimes can safely be ignored. Wherever it operated, the Klan sought to appropriate those powers as well. If Klan members sought the benefits of sovereign authority, prosecutors could have argued, they should be bound by its legal restrictions.

That argument might have worked, but it wasn't tried. The argument federal prosecutors actually used was best captured by then-Circuit Judge and future Supreme Court Justice William Woods in an Alabama Klan case called *United States v. Hall* (1871):

> [T]he Fourteenth Amendment . . . prohibits the states from denying to all persons within its jurisdiction the equal protection of the laws. Denying includes inaction as well as action, and denying the equal protection of the laws includes the omission to protect . . . [T]o guard against the invasion of the citizen's fundamental rights, and to insure their adequate protection, as well against state legislation as state inaction, or incompetency, the Amendment gives Congress the power to enforce its provisions by appropriate legislation. And as it would be unseemly for Congress to interfere directly with state enactments, and as it cannot compel the activity of state officials, the only appropriate legislation it can make is that which will operate directly on offenders and offenses . . . [34]

In other words, if local officials could not stop the intimidation of black voters, the federal government could punish the intimidators. If southern blacks were victimized by violence that local authorities could neither prevent nor prosecute, federal officials could do the prosecuting. The only alternative was to have federal judges order local police to make arrests and local prosecutors to file charges—an approach too "unseemly" to contemplate in the nineteenth century.

Woods's theory prevailed in a series of Klan cases, most of them in South Carolina and Alabama. The years 1871 and 1872 saw nearly 600 convictions in federal court.[35] Those few hundred cases had large behavioral effects. Klan leaders were not like ordinary thieves and murderers; they wanted to be men of status in their society. Even a small chance of prison time was bound to be a serious deterrent to such men. Klan violence was thus a solvable problem, not like the culture wars of the twentieth century, when America's justice system sought to suppress mass markets for gambling, alcohol, and cocaine. Those fights were destined to fail; this one was winnable. South Carolina, locus of the largest number of prosecutions, was pacified for the first time since the Civil War's end. Across the South, violence levels declined.[36] Reconstruction appeared to have been a law enforcement success.

It was also a political success. The 1868 and 1870 congressional elections, held while Klan violence was effectively unchallenged by the federal government, saw Republicans lose a total of 55 seats in the House of Representatives. In 1872, after a year and a half of Klan prosecutions, Republicans gained 60 seats.[37] Democratic nominee Horatio Seymour, not Grant, probably won the majority of white votes in the 1868 presidential election; blacks gave Grant his five-percentage-point margin in the nation's popular vote.[38] (Seymour had been governor of New York during the 1863 New York Draft Riot, in which a mob of mostly Irish immigrants killed dozens of black Manhattanites. When Seymour addressed the mob, his first words were "My friends."[39] Voters had little difficulty deciding which candidate stood for protecting blacks' rights.) In 1872, Grant carried white and black voters alike; nationwide, his margin was twelve percentage points. His opponent, *New York Tribune* publisher Horace Greeley, won no state that was free territory before the Civil War. Seymour had carried New York, New Jersey, and Oregon, and nearly won Connecticut, Indiana, and California as well.[40]

These facts suggest that northern voters backed Reconstruction on the same terms as they had backed Lincoln's war. When the battle—the wartime battle to preserve the Union and end slavery, the postwar battle to protect ex-slaves' civil rights—was going well, the Republican government enjoyed broad northern support. When southern whites seemed to have the upper hand, northern voters leaned Democratic. That fit the electoral pattern of the Civil War. Republicans sustained large losses in 1862 after General McClellan's failed Peninsula campaign and the lopsided southern victory in the Second Battle of Bull Run; Democrats lost ground in 1863 after Union wins at Vicksburg and Gettysburg. Thanks to Confederate successes at the Wilderness and Cold Harbor in the summer of 1864, Lincoln assumed he would lose his bid for reelection; instead, he won decisively after Sherman captured Atlanta in September of that year.[41] The same pattern held during Reconstruction. When Klan violence was unchecked as in 1868 and 1870, Democrats gained; when the Klan suffered what looked to contemporaries like a decisive defeat, Republicans won a landslide victory in 1872. Entering Grant's second administration, the battle over Reconstruction was going well. Southern blacks seemed likely to enjoy a measure of the law's protection, backed up by federal prosecutors, federal soldiers, and northern voters.

Reconstruction's Fall

Then, the political winds shifted—thanks to the economy, not changed attitudes toward Reconstruction. Less than a month after the Colfax Massacre, Vienna's stock market collapsed; four months later, Jay Cooke & Company—Cooke had sold the bonds that financed the Civil War—went bankrupt. The American economy entered a long depression.[42] The 1874 elections changed the lopsided Republican majority in the House of Representatives to a lopsided Democratic majority: the House of Representatives elected in 1872 included 194 Republicans and 92 Democrats; the 1874 election changed those figures to 109 Republicans and 169 Democrats, plus some members who belonged to neither party.[43] (Percentagewise, a comparable swing in today's House membership would see roughly 120 seats change parties.) Democrats would control the House for the next six years, and for sixteen of the next twenty. Though it was prompted by a downturn in the nation's economy, that political sea change had little effect on economic policy. Both major parties were controlled by their "hard money" factions in the 1870s and 1880s. Consequently, both parties opposed inflation and debt relief, popular nineteenth-century remedies for an economic downturn. Samuel Tilden, the Democrats' presidential nominee in 1876 and one of the nation's wealthiest men, was called "The Great Forecloser" for his unforgiving posture toward debtors. Rutherford Hayes, Tilden's Republican opponent, devoted his administration to reestablishing the convertibility of dollars to gold, a policy that promoted deflation and hence made debtors' burden heavier.[44] On debt and government finance, the two parties occupied the same ground.

All of which elevated the political importance of Reconstruction, the key issue about which Republicans and Democrats disagreed. Following a massive shift in the partisan balance of power, Republican politicians needed to win back newly Democratic votes. Narrowing the gap between their agenda and the agenda of their Democratic opponents was a natural move. So, after the 1874 elections, Republican politicians began to suggest an end to federal control of the ex-Confederate South.[45] Republican President Hayes pulled the federal soldiers that were propping up Republican governments in Louisiana and South Carolina.[46] A depression that had nothing to do with federal policy toward the South all but destroyed southern blacks' civil rights, and changed the character of southern criminal justice for generations to come.

Changing politics affected supposedly apolitical federal courts. Klan prosecutions depended as much on legal doctrine as on congressional support. At some point, the Supreme Court—chief interpreter of federal statutes like the Enforcement and Klan Acts, and of constitutional provisions like the Fourteenth and Fifteenth Amendments—would have to weigh in on the government's legal theory in those prosecutions. "At some point" came at an unfortunate time for the government and for southern blacks: when the Justices finally addressed the Klan cases, the economy had been in depression for nearly three years, and the House of Representatives had been under Democratic management for a year and a half. Even so, while the timing was less than ideal from the government's point of view, the facts of the government's test case ought to have made up for any such deficiency. The prosecution that led to the Supreme Court's verdict on Reconstruction arose from the worst massacre in the Reconstruction South: the murders outside the parish courthouse at Colfax, Louisiana.

Following those murders, United States Attorney James Beckwith obtained ninety-eight indictments but a mere nine arrests. Most of the massacre's participants—including its ringleader, a man named Christopher Columbus Nash—evaded federal capture. Defendants were charged with thirty-two counts of intimidating black voters, denying their victims the "free exercise and enjoyment of the rights, privileges, immunities, and protection granted and secured to them . . . as citizens of the United States," denying those same victims the rights to peaceably assemble and to bear arms in self-defense, and conspiring to do the same. The case went to trial in February 1874, five months after depression had struck the United States. One defendant was acquitted; the jury hung on the other eight. A second trial in May produced five acquittals and a mere three convictions: of Bill Cruikshank, John Hadnot, and Bill Irwin, three of Nash's lieutenants.[47]

For the prosecution, the story worsened from there. Sitting as Circuit Judge, Supreme Court Justice Joseph Bradley nominally presided over the Colfax trial along with his friend Judge Woods. (Bradley was on the bench when the trial opened and again when postverdict motions were heard; in between, Woods presided alone.) Two years earlier, Bradley had written Woods a letter endorsing the position the latter would take in *United States v. Hall*.[48] Now, Bradley ruled that the three convictions in *Cruikshank* should be overturned. With respect to some of the counts, Bradley reasoned that murder and assault did not become federal crimes because they were committed by whites against southern blacks; the Fourteenth Amendment barred state action, not private action. Other counts were dismissed either because they were too vaguely worded to define a proper criminal charge or because the government had failed to allege that the violence was racially motivated. Unsurprisingly, Woods disagreed. The Supreme Court had to choose between the two.[49]

The Court followed Bradley, unanimously. Chief Justice Morrison Waite's opinion emphasized the Fourteenth Amendment's limits, not its broad scope:

> The Fourteenth Amendment prohibits a State from denying to any person within its jurisdiction the equal protection of the laws; but this provision does not . . . add any thing to the rights which one

citizen has under the Constitution against another. The equality of the rights of citizens is a principle of republicanism. Every republican government is in duty bound to protect all its citizens in the enjoyment of this principle, if within its power. That duty was originally assumed by the States; and it still remains there.[50]

The quoted passage begins with the proposition that the equal protection clause cannot support the prosecution of private citizens: "this provision does not . . . add any thing to the rights which one citizen has . . . against another." It ends with the proposition that enforcing equal protection is chiefly the obligation of the states, not of the federal government: "[t]hat duty was originally assumed by the States; and it still remains there." The first proposition made federal prosecutions in cases like the Colfax Massacre impossible. The second made such prosecutions difficult even in cases like the police riots in Memphis and New Orleans. A more complete defense victory is hard to imagine.

The same day the Chief Justice delivered that opinion, he also announced the Court's decision in *United States v. Reese* (1876).[51] The defendants in *Reese* were Kentucky election officials who refused to register a black would-be voter when he offered to pay his poll tax. They were convicted of violating the Enforcement Act by conspiring to deprive the victim of his right to vote.[52] The government's prospects in *Reese* seemed more favorable than in *Cruikshank:* the defendants were government officials, not private citizens, and the right to vote—more precisely, the right not to be deprived of that right on account of race—was expressly protected by the Fifteenth Amendment. Nevertheless, the Justices overturned the Kentucky convictions and declared the relevant parts of the Enforcement Act unconstitutional because the Act did not require proof that the defendants' conduct was racially motivated.[53]

Politics mattered as much as legal principle in these cases. Bradley's correspondence with Woods shows that at least one Justice changed his position between the time of the Klan trials of the early 1870s and *Cruikshank,* and Bradley's may have been one of several changed minds. Oral argument in *Cruikshank* happened in February 1875, a mere three months after the Democrats' massive victory in the off-year congressional elections. Both sides' arguments reflected that political timing.

Attorney General George Williams offered only a halfhearted defense of the convictions in the second Colfax trial, conceding error on most of the counts on which Cruikshank, Hadnot, and Irwin were convicted.[54] David Dudley Field, lead defense counsel in the Supreme Court—Justice Stephen Field's brother, and probably the nation's leading appellate lawyer—twice alluded to the election in his argument. Early on, Field noted that "our fellow citizens of the whole nation . . . bear us out in the assertion that the people did not suppose they were thereby changing the fundamental theory of their government" when they enacted the Fourteenth Amendment. The second reference came in response to a question from the bench about the proper means of enforcing blacks' rights. Field's answer was chilling: "If eight hundred thousand voters"—a rough estimate of the number of voting-age black males in the South—"cannot secure the rights to which they had been declared entitled, then that is the best argument that they are not worthy of them."[55] No mention was made, either by Field or by any of the Justices, of the murderous manner in which the defendants had thwarted those rights.

That dialogue would have had a different character a few years earlier, when Reconstruction appeared to be a political success. Shortly after the Civil War and pursuant to a Louisiana statute, New Orleans established a local monopoly over the business of slaughtering cattle, sheep, and pigs—downriver of the city's water supply. Three groups of butchers sued, claiming that the relevant state statute and city ordinance violated the Fourteenth Amendment by interfering with their right to make a living as (and where) they chose.[56] In 1872, the *Slaughter-House Cases* made their way to the Court, where former Justice John Campbell represented the butchers. An Alabamian who had left the Court to serve as the Confederacy's assistant secretary of war, Campbell argued that the Fourteenth Amendment protected not only blacks' right to legal protection but also whites' right to earn a living—including the right of New Orleans butchers to practice their trade.[57] Notice that Campbell, legal embodiment of the elite Confederate South, argued that the Fourteenth Amendment deserved a broad interpretation, not a narrow one. Campbell's argument lost, but only just: by a 5–4 vote, the Court held that the city's slaughterhouse monopoly was constitutional.[58] The decision was announced on April 14, 1873—the day after the massacre in Colfax.

David Dudley Field was no Southerner; he was New York's leading lawyer. Yet his *Cruikshank* argument seemed more southern than Campbell's. Where the *Slaughter-House* plaintiffs tried and failed to expand the Fourteenth Amendment's scope, the *Cruikshank* defendants tried to contract it and succeeded. Where Campbell argued that the Fourteenth Amendment upended the allocation of power between federal and state governments, Field maintained that "the people did not suppose they were . . . changing the fundamental theory of their government" when they ratified the amendment. Campbell contended that federal courts must enforce private citizens' Fourteenth Amendment rights; Field insisted that southern blacks must enforce their own rights through their votes. The gap between these two lawyers' arguments reflects the chasm that separated the politics of Reconstruction before and after the Panic of 1873—and also illustrates the manner in which changed politics produces changed law. Field's claim that southern blacks were "not worthy" of the rights the Fourteenth Amendment granted them amounted to Reconstruction's legal epitaph. The Democrats' triumph in the 1874 elections made the burial possible.

The link between legal doctrine and political currents was clearer still in *Reese*. Nineteenth-century American law often required proof of criminal defendants' intent, but almost never required proof of motive. To nineteenth-century lawyers, the distinction was fundamental. Proof of criminal intent meant proof that the defendant's conduct was not an accident. Juries could resolve that issue by examining the defendant's acts: a given defendant's conduct either was or wasn't the sort of behavior that might be done unconsciously or inadvertently. Conduct could be proved by eyewitnesses. Motive was another matter; it raised the question why the defendant behaved as he did, a question only the defendant could answer—and defendants could not be made to incriminate themselves. Government officials who denied blacks the right to vote might have done so in order to suppress Republican votes, out of animosity toward the individuals in question, or as a means of expressing their hatred of blacks as a race. Under *Reese,* only the last of those three motives made the officials' conduct impermissible. The forbidden motive was impossible to prove. It is difficult to imagine such a disabling legal holding several years earlier, when Republican supporters of Reconstruction were winning elections in the North and South alike.

Cruikshank and *Reese* meant the end of Klan prosecutions. After *Cruikshank,* there was no viable legal theory to support federal prosecution of men like Christopher Columbus Nash and his followers. They were private citizens and the Fourteenth Amendment applied only to governments; the amendment no longer "operate[d] directly on offenders and offenses," as Judge Woods had argued it should. After *Reese,* even Klan-influenced government officials were nearly unconvictable, thanks to the requirement that the omnipresent but unprovable discriminatory motive be established in every case. As the slaughter at Colfax showed, Klan violence could be stopped only by the exercise of federal power. *Cruikshank* and *Reese* left the federal government powerless to do the stopping.

The change in the nation's political tilt wrought by the depression of 1873 was temporary, as such changes always are. The legal change was permanent. The ideal of equal protection—the notion that all Americans are entitled not only to freedom from government oppression, but to a measure of freedom from private violence as well, and the *same* measure their well-to-do neighbors received—was, for all practical purposes, dead. So were thousands of southern blacks who needed that protection, and needed it badly.

Equal Protection's Alternate Path

The last civil rights legislation passed by the last pro-Reconstruction Congress[59] barred discrimination in public accommodations: railroads, inns, and the like. It provided for criminal punishment for violators, authorizing fines between $500 and $1,000—sizeable sums then—plus incarceration between thirty days and one year. Importantly, the Act also provided for civil damages for those victimized by such discrimination: $500 plus court costs for each violation.[60] Republicans in Congress sought to ensure that *this* civil rights legislation would be enforceable even without the help of federal prosecutors, because such help would not be forthcoming once a Democrat was in the White House, as seemed likely in early 1875. But these remedies could be effective only if the Act's prohibition was constitutional. The Supreme Court held otherwise in the *Civil Rights Cases* (1883). Writing for the majority, Republican Justice Joseph Bradley upheld the position he had taken as a Circuit Judge in *Cruikshank:* the Fourteenth Amendment applied only to government officials, and thus did not authorize laws barring acts of violence or discrimination by private citizens. Only Justice John Marshall Harlan, a Kentuckian and former slaveowner, dissented.[61]

Cruikshank and the *Civil Rights Cases* inaugurated a period of more than half a century during which the equal protection clause lay dormant. Throughout that period, judges saw equal protection arguments as unserious; as late as 1927, Oliver Wendell Holmes described the clause as "the last resort of constitutional arguments."[62] Discriminatory state statutes remained impermissible, but discriminatory treatment under formally neutral laws was another matter.[63] When twentieth-century southern whites were prosecuted for killing southern blacks, juries—from which southern blacks were systematically excluded—regularly found that the killers acted in self-defense, even when that finding was wildly implausible. Southern juries were less receptive to the claims of blacks who killed whites in self-defense. Formally, the law of self-defense made no distinction on account of race. In practice, the distinction was both large and obvious.[64]

Equal protection doctrine was no barrier to discrimination of that sort. Nor did the law forbid explicit racial distinctions, so long as the government's treatment of both races was formally equal. A Louisiana statute required "equal but separate" accommodations—the phrase has gone down in history with the adjectives reversed—in railway cars for white and black passengers. Over a stinging dissent by Justice Harlan, the Supreme Court upheld the statute in *Plessy v. Ferguson* (1896).[65] *Plessy* became the legal foundation for southern systems of public education, even though those systems were anything but equal. Form, not substance, was the constitutional yardstick.

In the mid-twentieth century, the National Association for the Advancement of Colored People (NAACP) mounted a legal campaign against the South's system of formally segregated public services. As part of that campaign, Thurgood Marshall and his colleagues sued state university systems that offered radically unequal services to black and white residents of the relevant states.[66] The attack succeeded; the Supreme Court ordered the integration of Southern graduate schools in *McLaurin v. Oklahoma State Regents* (1950) and law schools in *Sweatt v. Painter* (1950).[67] Based on those decisions, Marshall argued that segregated primary and secondary schools were likewise impermissible, that formal segregation and functional equality could not be reconciled. That attack likewise succeeded; in *Brown v. Board of Education* (1954), Earl Warren famously wrote that "[s]eparate educational facilities are inherently unequal."[68] Before long, what was then known as *de jure* segregation—racial separation enshrined in law—was constitutionally forbidden.

These decisions worked an enormous change in legal doctrine; the same equal protection clause that had proved useless in *Cruikshank* and the *Civil Rights Cases* was now the basis for the dismantling of legalized Jim Crow. Yet even after Marshall's victories, the core of those Reconstruction-era decisions remained good law; the equal protection clause continued to allow the worst forms of discrimination in the administration of criminal justice.[69] When Congress again barred discrimination in hotels and other public accommodations in the Civil Rights Act of 1964, congressional power rested primarily on the power to regulate interstate commerce.[70] Congress used that strategy (and federal government lawyers used the same strategy to defend the Act's constitutionality) because members feared relying on the guarantee of "equal protection of the laws." Since *Cruikshank,* the equal protection clause has forbidden discriminatory government action, not government inaction in the teeth of discriminatory acts by private individuals. The chief problem with that proposition is as clear today as in the Klan cases of the 1870s: the worst discrimination usually takes the form of private wrongs that government officials refuse to redress. Since *Reese,* the government's refusal would violate the equal protection clause only if the claimant proved that the relevant government official acted with discriminatory intent. Because such proof is hard to come by, claims of discriminatory policing and prosecution almost never succeed.

Three Supreme Court decisions from the last three decades—*McCleskey v. Kemp* (1987), *United States v. Armstrong* (1996), and *Castle Rock v. Gonzales* (2005)—show why.[71] Lawyers for Warren McCleskey, a death row inmate from Georgia, introduced evidence showing that the state's death penalty was imposed disproportionately on killers of white victims; the disproportion was especially large when the killer was black. (McCleskey, a black man, had killed a white security guard in the course of a robbery.) The Supreme Court found this evidence insufficient to prove discrimination.[72] As in all states that permit the death penalty, power over Georgia's capital murder cases was shared among dozens of prosecutors and trial judges and among hundreds of jurors. Proving that any individual prosecutor, judge, or jury acted with intent to discriminate against black killers of white victims was impossible—the number of cases handled by any one decisionmaker was too small. The system as a whole may discriminate massively, but as no single decisionmaker is responsible for more than a small fraction of the discrimination, the law holds no one accountable for it.

Armstrong involved a variation on that theme. Federal prosecutors in the Central District of California charged the defendant with conspiracy to possess and distribute crack cocaine. Defense counsel introduced evidence that, over the course of the preceding year, all twenty-four crack cases prosecuted in that district had been against black defendants. Even so, unless counsel could point to cases of white violators whom federal officials could have prosecuted but chose not to, counsel's data were not enough to justify discovery: meaning, the government could not be ordered to produce relevant information about its drug cases.[73] Without such information, defense counsel could not hope to prove that federal prosecutors had discriminated against black crack dealers like Armstrong. The bottom line was a classic legal Catch-22: Armstrong's claim couldn't win without more information, yet Armstrong could get that information only if he had a winning claim without it. Unsurprisingly given that result, successful claims of discriminatory prosecution are unheard of.

Jessica Gonzales, the plaintiff in *Castle Rock,* obtained a protective order against her sometimes-violent husband, who was barred from coming within a hundred yards of Gonzales or any of the couple's three children. In the six hours after her husband took the children in violation of the protective order, Gonzales called the Castle Rock, Colorado, police four times and drove to the police station once, pleading with officers to find her children before her husband harmed them. Despite her pleas, the police refused to intervene. Before one of those phone calls, her husband called and told Gonzales that he was with the children at an amusement park in Denver, a little more than thirty miles away. Gonzales reported this information to no avail. Ninety minutes after her last contact with the police, Gonzales's husband drove to the Castle Rock police station and sprayed it with gunfire; he was killed by return fire. The bodies of the three children, murdered minutes before the shoot-out, were discovered in his truck. Gonzales sued the Castle Rock police, claiming that their failure to protect her children violated their Fourteenth Amendment rights and hers. The Supreme Court dismissed her claim. As long as their decisions are not racially motivated—as *McCleskey* and *Armstrong* show, discriminatory motives are unprovable in this context—police officers and prosecutors have unreviewable discretion to decline to arrest or prosecute offenders.[74]

Armstrong allows police forces and prosecutors to enforce drug laws in black neighborhoods but not in white ones. *McCleskey* allows prosecutors and judges to punish crimes that victimize whites more severely than crimes that victimize blacks. *Castle Rock* allows law enforcers to ignore violent felonies for any reason or no reason at all, without fear of legal liability. All three fact patterns are paradigmatic failures to provide "the equal protection of the laws," given the meaning those words had to the men who wrote and ratified them. Yet none of those fact patterns gives rise to liability under the equal protection clause, as courts interpret that clause today. Even if Georgia's authorities are slow to punish murders of black victims, federal officials may not step in and protect those who need protection. Even if federal prosecutors in California impose tough federal drug sentences only on black drug offenders, federal judges may not order the racially disparate law enforcement to cease. Even if the Castle Rock police had no justification for failing to prevent the murders of Gonzales's three children, no federal judge can hold them responsible for the consequences of their inaction.[75]

Three decisions issued more than a century before—*Cruikshank, Reese,* and the *Civil Rights Cases*—set the law on this strange and sad path. The constitutional violations in *Cruikshank* and the *Civil Rights Cases* were the same: the failure to protect black victims from discrimination and violence. Nonprotection was likewise the relevant constitutional violation in *McCleskey* and *Castle Rock*. The earlier decisions made the later ones seem natural. The violation in *Reese* was the failure to grant the same voting rights to a black man as were granted to white men. In *Armstrong,* prosecutors charged black defendants for crimes with which white defendants were never charged. Both decisions made discrimination impossible to prove, hence impossible for courts to remedy. Reconstruction's end continues to cast a long shadow over American criminal justice.

The Absence of "Privileges or Immunities," the Emptiness of Due Process

When Ohio Representative John Bingham wrote the Fourteenth Amendment's text, he probably intended the "privileges or immunities of citizens of the United States" to include the protections listed in the Bill of Rights.[76] It didn't work out that way. A mere five years after Bingham's text was ratified, the Supreme Court decided *Slaughter-House*—and according to Justice Samuel Miller's majority opinion, the "privileges or immunities" clause has nothing to do with criminal justice; the Bill of Rights remained binding in federal cases only.

After *Slaughter-House* and *Cruikshank,* the only part of the Fourteenth Amendment that might more-than-trivially affect the criminal justice system was the clause that barred deprivations of life, liberty, and property without "due process of law." The Court first addressed *that* clause's implications for criminal litigation in *Hurtado v. California* (1884). Joseph Hurtado shot and killed a man who had been sleeping with Hurtado's wife. At the time, California law allowed prosecutors to charge even capital offenses without the vote of a grand jury. Hurtado was so charged, convicted, and sentenced to death.[77] On appeal, he argued that due process required state courts to follow the procedures specified in the federal Bill of Rights—including the Fifth Amendment right to indictment by grand jury for all "capital, or otherwise infamous crime[s]."[78] In other words, Hurtado argued that the Fourteenth Amendment's due process clause "incorporated" (the legal term) or contained within it all the prohibitions of the Bill of Rights.

The Court rejected the argument. As Justice Stanley Matthews's majority opinion emphasizes, Hurtado's argument was in tension with the relevant constitutional texts. The Fifth Amendment includes a due process clause nearly identical to the one in the Fourteenth; the chief difference is one that would interest only high-school English teachers: the former is written in the passive voice while the latter isn't. (The Fifth

Amendment's due process clause reads: "No person shall . . . be deprived of life, liberty, or property without due process of law." The Fourteenth Amendment's clause reads: "No state shall . . . deprive any person of life, liberty, or property without due process of law.")[79] Given their similar language, Matthews reasoned, the two clauses must cover similar ground. The Fifth Amendment also requires grand jury indictments in capital cases, and bans both double jeopardy and compelled self-incrimination. If, as Hurtado argued, "due process of law" meant "those procedures required by the Bill of Rights," the rest of the Fifth Amendment—for that matter, the rest of the Bill of Rights—was redundant: the Fifth Amendment's due process clause had said it all.[80]

So what did "due process of law" mean? Matthews believed the last two words of that famous phrase were the key to understanding the first two. Following due process in state-court criminal cases meant prosecuting crimes defined prospectively by state legislatures, according to procedures defined by state law. In other words—Matthews's words—criminal prosecutions should be governed by law, not by "mere will" or "act[s] of power." Matthews helpfully offered a list of examples that failed to meet that standard: "acts of attainder, bills of pains and penalties, acts of confiscation, acts reversing judgments, and acts directly transferring one man's estate to another."[81] In all those examples, legislators impose penalties on individuals instead of defining rules that govern the population as a whole. According to Matthews, the core of the due process guarantee is the promise that the same rules and procedures that apply to the rest of the population also apply to each criminal defendant. On this view, "due process of law" required not particular procedures but formal legal equality: as long as one law (nominally) applied to all, the Fourteenth Amendment would be satisfied.

Matthews's standard had one major problem: no state legislature wished to do the things the standard forbade. Private bills—legislation affecting a single individual—were common in the nineteenth century, but they nearly always involved the granting of some benefit, not the imposition of punishment. Examples include the granting of legal monopolies to particular individuals or firms, the award of medals or promotions to military personnel, and the granting of divorces to those who could not qualify under strict nineteenth-century laws governing the dissolution of marriages.

Federal and state constitutions already banned bills of attainder (legislation that ordered the criminal punishment of specified individuals) and
ex post facto laws (laws that criminalized conduct committed before the
laws were passed). No American state legislature habitually enacted legislation of the sort that made Matthews's list of unconstitutional practices
in *Hurtado.*

Consequently, Matthews's definition of due process left no room for
successful claims, as a pair of cases decided a few years after *Hurtado*
confirmed. The defendants in *Caldwell v. Texas* (1891) and *Leeper v.
Texas* (1891) complained that their indictments gave them inadequate
notice of the crimes with which they were charged, and hence violated
due process.[82] The indictments in question followed the form required
by Texas law. As Chief Justice Melville Fuller wrote for a unanimous
Court in *Leeper,* "due process is . . . secured by laws operating on all
alike":[83] as long as Texas's rules governing indictments were followed,
no federal court could grant relief. The content of those Texas rules was
irrelevant. Under such a standard, due process claims were bound to
fail. If the challenged practice violated state law, state courts would overturn the defendant's conviction on that ground; any federal due process
claim would be moot. If state courts decided that state law had been obeyed,
due process was by definition satisfied—and any federal due process claim
would be rejected. Either way, due process arguments lost. Compliance
with state law ensured compliance with the federal constitution, and state
judges had the final word on whether their own states' laws were followed. Given Stanley Matthews's reading of the Fourteenth Amendment's
due process clause, that clause required only that states enforce their own
procedures.

Legal doctrines that generate no successful claims make doctrinal
development impossible. That is why Matthews's rule-of-law definition
soon faded: before long, there were no cases in which courts could apply
that definition and flesh out its meaning. Instead, state-court criminal
defendants began to raise a different kind of due process argument: that
one or another aspect of the process that led to their punishment was
unfair, even though the process complied with all relevant state laws. In
the generation after *Hurtado,* those arguments consistently failed. Even
so, they gradually changed the meaning of "due process of law."

The story begins with *O'Neil v. Vermont* (1892). John O'Neil sold liquor in upstate New York; sales to residents of Vermont were a large fraction of his business. Vermont banned such sales, and claimed the right to enforce its ban against out-of-state suppliers. O'Neil was convicted of more than three hundred counts of shipping liquor into Vermont. His sentence was a fine of $6,600, a large sum at the time; if he could not pay it within a month, O'Neil would be sentenced to three days' incarceration for every dollar of that fine—which added up to more than fifty-four years in prison. On appeal, defense counsel argued that Vermont's exercise of jurisdiction over this New York defendant violated due process, and that O'Neil's sentence amounted to "cruel and unusual punishment" banned by the Eighth Amendment. In turn, counsel argued, the Eighth Amendment's ban applied not only to federal cases but to state cases as well, thanks to the Fourteenth Amendment's due process clause.[84]

As in *Caldwell* and *Leeper,* the Supreme Court found no issue of federal law raised by these facts. *Hurtado* still governed; because Vermont followed its own rules, the due process clause was satisfied.[85] But this time, three Justices disagreed. Stephen Field thought Vermont's claim of jurisdiction violated due process. Field, John Harlan, and David Brewer all concluded that O'Neil's sentence did so as well; the dissenters agreed with defense counsel that the Eighth Amendment applied to state court cases through the Fourteenth Amendment's due process clause.[86]

The defendant's due process claim lost again in *McKane v. Durston* (1894),[87] but the manner of the defeat was different: this time, the Court's majority defined due process more generously than in *Hurtado* and *O'Neil.* John McKane was the late nineteenth-century political boss of Coney Island. He made his living by requiring local businesses to pay protection money in order to receive police services, and through kickbacks from friends to whom he sold public land for below-market prices. The kickbacks and extortion not only lined McKane's pockets but also paid for Coney Island's police force. (One way to keep tax rates down . . .) A court order mandated the monitoring of an 1893 election in McKane's town. When the monitors showed up with the order in hand, McKane said, "Injunctions don't go here"—then ordered the monitors beaten and jailed. One of them escaped and told his story to a Brooklyn newspaper. McKane's words made national headlines. He was tried and convicted of state election law violations and sentenced to six years at Sing Sing.[88]

If McKane was the victim of any unfairness, its source was the six-year sentence. Late nineteenth-century judges rarely handed down long prison sentences; even homicide defendants routinely fared better than this crooked politician. But that fact could not help McKane in the Supreme Court: if O'Neil's fifty-four-year prison term did not violate the federal constitution, surely McKane's six-year term did not do so. So McKane's lawyers instead claimed that due process entitled him to be free on bail while his appeal was pending. New York law said otherwise. The Supreme Court unanimously rejected McKane's claim—not because New York had complied with its own laws, but because the state had treated McKane fairly. The Justices concluded that due process did not oblige New York to offer McKane appellate review of his conviction. Because the state was permitted to keep McKane in prison without the opportunity of appellate review, the state could take the lesser step of incarcerating him while his appeal went forward.[89] McKane lost—but the notion that the Fourteenth Amendment's due process clause established a federal standard of procedural fairness, enforceable on state courts, won.

Twining v. New Jersey (1908)[90] suggested that the measure of procedural fairness might be found in the Bill of Rights. Albert Twining and David Cornell were officers of a New Jersey bank charged with falsifying bank records; they were convicted and sentenced to six and four years in prison, respectively. Neither Twining nor Cornell testified in their joint criminal trial. As was common practice at the time, the trial judge noted that fact and instructed the jurors to give it whatever weight they thought appropriate—though the judge also said that, in his view, the defendants' silence deserved no weight at all: an uncommonly favorable instruction from the defendants' point of view. Twining and Cornell nevertheless argued, a bit churlishly, that the Fifth Amendment privilege against self-incrimination barred trial judges from commenting on defendants' silence when instructing juries in criminal cases, and that such judicial commentary also violated due process.[91]

Once again, the Justices rejected defendants' argument, but the rejection was less categorical than in the past. Instead of barring Bill of Rights arguments in this context as Stanley Matthews had done, Justice William

Moody's majority opinion in *Twining* says that the definition of due process might include some Bill of Rights protections—but only those protections that constitute "fundamental principle[s] of liberty and justice which inhere in the very idea of free government."[92] Ex-prosecutor Moody (best known as the man who had tried and failed to put Lizzie Borden in prison for killing her parents)[93] declined to place the right to be free of judicial comment on a defendant's silence in that exalted category. Fifty-seven years later, the Justices would decide otherwise,[94] in part because Moody's opinion left the door to such arguments open. *Hurtado*'s door had been bolted shut.

The crimes charged in these turn-of-the-century cases are telling. O'Neil sold booze; McKane rigged local elections and took bribes for selling public land; Twining and Cornell lied about their bank's assets. None of these briefly famous defendants was charged with core crimes like murder, rape, or robbery. O'Neil was the nineteenth century's equivalent to today's high-end drug dealers, at least the ones whose drug markets are reasonably peaceful—and was punished in the same wildly excessive manner. The other three were the white-collar criminals of their time. They too were punished excessively—less so than O'Neil, but then today's insider traders and corrupt politicians are punished less severely than sellers of controlled substances. Because of their lucrative lines of work, all four defendants could afford high-quality lawyers who could take advantage of all the procedural guarantees America's justice system provides. In terms of the process that led to their convictions, all received not the system's worst but its best. No wonder their claims were rejected: procedurally speaking, few criminal defendants in any era have so little cause for complaint.

Yet their claims contributed more than a little to setting the constitutional agenda for future criminal defendants, and for future Supreme Courts. Only the best appellate lawyers—the kind only the wealthiest criminal defendants could afford—would produce creative legal arguments like the ones in *O'Neil, McKane,* and *Twining.* Only defendants with no plausible grounds for procedural complaint would have need of such arguments. Legal doctrine often evolves in strange ways. Few paths are stranger than the one followed by the turn-of-the-century law of due process.

Step back from the individual trees and consider the legal forest. As late as the first decade of the twentieth century, "due process of law" remained more an argument than a doctrine. Criminal defendants raising due process claims always lost. But the nature of the claims still mattered: those failed claims would shape the law of due process when, in the middle and late twentieth century, that law grew more generous to state-court defendants. And both the nature of the claims and the rationale for rejecting them changed in the thirty years following Reconstruction's end. In *Hurtado,* the due process clause served as a guarantee that criminal punishment would be imposed according to law—good or bad, fair or oppressive—not according to legislative discretion. (Notice that prosecutors' discretion played no role in the doctrine.) In *McKane* and *Twining,* due process guaranteed fair procedures. The dissent in *O'Neil* suggested that a time was coming when fair procedures would include those procedures that the Bill of Rights required. *Twining* brought that time closer by promising to enforce the provisions of the Bill that were deemed sufficiently "fundamental."

Eventually, the last clause of the preceding sentence would fall away. The Bill of Rights would become the measure of procedural justice, the yardstick against which police officers' and prosecutors' practices were measured. Another yardstick—the ideal of "equal protection of the laws," the measure the Court rejected in *Cruikshank* and the *Civil Rights Cases*— would have made for a more just justice system. Thanks to Ben Tillman, Joseph Bradley, and many more like them, that legal measure belongs to another generation: a crucial part of Americans' legal heritage was lost and has yet to be recovered. Thanks to John McKane, Albert Twining, and a few more like *them,* constitutional law's chief concern became process, due and otherwise—not protection, equal and otherwise. We still live with the consequences.

CHAPTER 5

Criminal Justice in the Gilded Age

A wife may murder her husband in Cook County with impunity.

> —Cook County, Illinois State's Attorney Maclay Hoyne,
> commenting on Chicago juries' frequent acquittals of
> husband-killing wives (1906)

Elderly black men and women, survivors of "The Great Migration" North in the era of World War I and after, recall [Philadelphia's] justice system as essentially fair.

> —Roger Lane, "On the Social Meaning of Homicide
> Trends in America" (1989)

Our grand old Empire State HAS BEEN RAPED! . . . Hereafter, let no man reproach the South with lynch law: let him remember the unendurable provocation, and *let him say whether lynch law is not better than no law at all.*

> —Tom Watson, *The Jeffersonian,* written shortly after the
> commutation of Leo Frank's death sentence (1915)

T HE NOTION THAT LOCAL POLITICS is the best means of governing crime and criminal punishment seems strange, even a bit crazy. Americans live under the most politicized criminal justice system in the Western world, and among those who know it well, that system is hardly a point of national pride. The last half-century, with its massive drop and still more massive rise in punishment per unit crime, seems to confirm the conventional academic wisdom that politics is a poor governing tool in this area. As for the "local" aspect of local politics, Americans elect both prosecutors and most trial judges at the county level, while mayors and city councils (not governors or presidents) both supervise and fund urban police forces. If local democracy tends to produce a high quality of criminal justice, our justice system should be of higher quality than it is.

Yet that strange notion may be correct—at least in a society with legal and political traditions like ours. Notwithstanding the large role local politics plays in it, contemporary American criminal justice is more centralized, more legalized, and less locally democratic than first appears. The real test of local democracy's benefit lies not in today's justice system, but in the justice system of the Gilded Age: roughly, the half-century between the Reconstruction's end and the Great Depression. Or, rather, in the justice *systems* of the Gilded Age. What was true in the early and mid-nineteenth century remained true in the late nineteenth century and for much of the twentieth: different parts of the country employed different styles of law enforcement that rested on different visions of democracy. The South kept all blacks and many poor whites from voting; a narrow electorate governed the formal institutions of criminal justice. That formal justice system was supplemented by occasional mob rule for southern blacks, and also for white outsiders like Leo Frank, who was lynched soon after Tom Watson's editorial quoted on the preceding page. The West saw a long period in which courts, police forces, and the other institutions that mark stable governments were only sporadically effective; vigilantes sometimes did the jobs government officials did elsewhere. In the Northeast and Midwest, Gilded Age criminal justice was governed by the democracy of jury rooms and ballot boxes. Local juries and local elected officials, not local mobs, ruled.

Whether coincidentally or not, these different justice systems saw strikingly different results. Southerners lived with smaller police forces, larger prison populations, and vastly more crime than in the rest of the country. Criminal justice in the Northeast and most of the Midwest had the opposite characteristics: large urban police forces, small inmate populations, and, by today's standards, low levels of criminal violence. The West initially looked like the South, with a weak formal system of law enforcement and occasional spasms of rule by surprisingly well-organized vigilante "mobs." As the region grew more populous, the formal justice system grew stronger and vigilantism declined. Westerners adopted (some of) the practices of their neighbors in the country's northeastern quadrant, and saw western crime rates plummet. Bottom line: Where local democracy and the rule of law both operated, criminal justice was fairer and (apparently) more effective than it is today.

Northern Cities

Egalitarianism is hardly the Gilded Age's signal feature. The late nineteenth and early twentieth centuries were the era of robber barons and sweatshops, a time when the power of "the trusts" dwarfed the clout of easily crushed labor unions or ineffective government regulators.[1] In the world of legal doctrine, those fifty years were an age of constitutionalized *laissez-faire,* when conservative courts were quick to overturn legislative efforts to regulate business or to improve the lot of the poor.[2] Last but certainly not least, those years were an age when Jim Crow's strange career began, when black voting in the South all but ceased and the grip of a second slavery grew steadily tighter.[3]

Nevertheless, at least in a large portion of the country, criminal justice *was* egalitarian—at least by comparison to our own time. Women, blacks, and poor European immigrants all suffered discrimination at the hands of criminal justice officials, as blacks and (sometimes) Latinos do today. But the magnitude of the discrimination the system doled out was more modest than in the late twentieth and early twenty-first centuries. These propositions did not hold true in the South and West, and probably did not hold true everywhere in the North. But in the populous, industrializing cities of the Northeast and Midwest, policing, criminal litigation, and criminal punishment appear to have been both less discriminatory and vastly more lenient than today. Those local justice systems in the North also appear to have been more successful than their contemporary counterparts: along with modest levels of criminal punishment came what are, by today's standards, astonishingly low levels of violent crime. The question is, how did they do it? How did our predecessors at once keep crime in check, punish offenders sparingly, and do a decent job of protecting the interests of society's outcasts?

In part, the answer is criminal justice was more egalitarian than we imagine because government in general—like the society it governed— was more egalitarian than we imagine. Robber barons and sweatshops were more common than powerful labor unions. Even so, American workers earned substantially higher wages than in industrializing Europe. Government regulatory agencies often had little power, but then the same is true today, as the regulatory failures that attended the early twenty-first-century financial collapse illustrate. The more surprising truth cuts in the opposite direction. The late nineteenth and early twentieth centuries, the generations *before* FDR's New Deal, saw the creation of a large body of regulatory law, including the beginnings of the law of white-collar and financial crime: the establishment of the Interstate Commerce Commission, the passage of the Sherman Antitrust Act, legislation barring bankruptcy fraud, and the Pure Food and Drug Law—and that is only a partial list. Courts were less conservative than first appears. All the legislation just mentioned was deemed constitutional; for every judicial decision striking down some regulatory statute, several more upheld similar laws. The property rights of the rich received less protection, and government regulators' authority more, than one might suppose.[4]

Finally, in the United States at the turn of the last century, city governments were more active than state or national ones. That mattered because cities were the places where the poor and ordinary workers had the most political clout. The United States remained a mostly rural nation; at state and national levels, the countryside and small towns enjoyed enormous political power. Not so in large, industrializing cities: there, working-class neighborhoods, usually populated by recent European immigrants and their children, dominated local governing coalitions. That too mattered, because urban criminal justice was ruled by the same urban political machines that ruled those northern cities.

Begin with crime control. Generous justice systems like the one that prevailed in the Gilded Age North might be expected to produce too much generosity and too little justice; in turn, rarely punished criminals might be expected to commit too many crimes. There is reason to believe such dynamics played an important role in late twentieth-century crime, but less so with respect to the late nineteenth and early twentieth centuries. Figure 2 shows New York's murder rates in two fifty-year periods beginning in 1875 and 1950.

Gilded Age New Yorkers lived with murder rates that ranged from a low of 2 per 100,000 to a high of 6. In the twentieth century's second half, the city's lowest murder rate was 4; the highest was 31. Analogous graphs

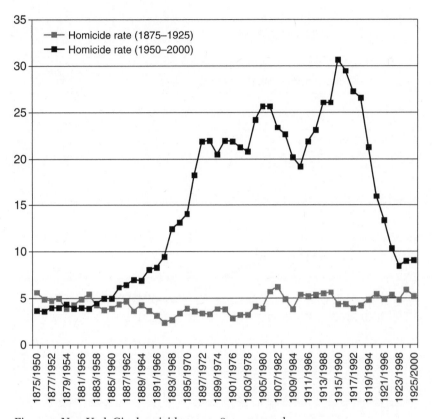

Figure 2. New York City homicide rates, 1875–1925 and 1950–2000
For New York's pre-1980 homicide rates, I use Monkkonen's data. Post-1980, I use the annual volumes of the FBI's Uniform Crime Reports, later titled Crime in the United States.

for Chicago, Philadelphia, or Boston would look similar—save that those cities saw more modest crime drops in the 1990s. The huge crime wave that took hold after 1950 has no counterpart in the nineteenth century's last decades, nor in the twentieth century's first ones.

Low rates of violence in the Gilded Age North were not the consequence of high rates of criminal punishment. More the opposite: as the murder rate fell in the late nineteenth and early twentieth centuries, New York's imprisonment rate fell with it. Figure 3 charts New York State imprisonment rates during the two periods.

New York's falling imprisonment rate is typical of northeastern states in the late nineteenth and early twentieth centuries; in the industrial Midwest, imprisonment rates rose modestly during these years.[5] In both

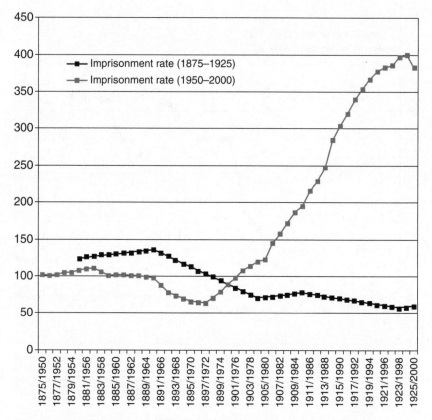

Figure 3. New York State imprisonment rates, 1880–1925 and 1950–2000
The data on Gilded Age imprisonment rates are taken from Margaret Werner
Cahalan, Historical Corrections Statistics in the United States, 1850–1984, at 30,
table 3-3 (Rockville, MD: Bureau of Justice Statistics, 1986). Imprisonment rates
are extrapolated in years for which reliable data do not exist: an accurate rendering
of the darker line in Figure 3 would show more fluctuation than the figure reveals.

regions, prison populations were fairly stable—either growing or shrink-
ing gradually—and, by contemporary standards, remarkably small. The
late twentieth century saw the opposite trends: a sharper drop in imprisonment (during a period of rising crime, so the drop is sharper than first
appears) followed by a massive rise, together with record-high rates of
violent crime. Apparently, the more stable and less punitive justice system New Yorkers used in the late nineteenth and early twentieth centuries controlled crime better than the more volatile and more punitive
system used in the 1960s and afterward.[6]

That older justice system also did a better job of avoiding discrimination against what would now be called "suspect classes"—[7] women, blacks, and immigrants—all groups that were frequent targets of discrimination a century ago, at a time when such discrimination was perfectly legal. In the early 1900s as today, domestic violence was a large problem; then as now, women victimized by such violence sometimes killed their male victimizers. Then as now, those killings sometimes happened at times of the killers' choosing, as where a battered spouse or lover lies in wait to kill her abusive husband or boyfriend. Then as now, the law of self-defense appeared to leave these victim-perpetrators high and dry: in order to prevail, defendants claiming self-defense must show that they acted in response to a threat of imminent harm, a hard showing to make unless the killer acted in the midst of a beating. After all, the victim could have called the police, or fled to a friend's apartment, or otherwise escaped the hell of frequent violence by one who claimed to love her. According to the strict terms of self-defense doctrine, abusers were treated more generously than those they abused: an abusive husband who killed his armed wife could more easily show that he was responding to a threat of imminent harm than a victim who killed her abuser between beatings.

But the strict terms of self-defense doctrine could be, and have been, made less strict than first appears. In the late twentieth century, abuse victims who killed their abusers used evidence of "battered woman's syndrome" to convince juries—sometimes—that the victims could see no alternative to striking back at their abusers, even when a phone call to the police was an available option.[8] Syndrome evidence does not guarantee an acquittal in such cases, but it does make acquittals possible, just as the vagueness of self-defense doctrine makes possible the use of syndrome evidence.

A century ago, one might suppose, the picture must have been bleaker for these unfortunate victims who lashed out at their victimizers. After all, no one had heard of "battered woman's syndrome" in the early 1900s. Outside the criminal justice system, women faced far more discrimination then than now: east of the Mississippi River at the beginning of the twentieth century, adult women could not yet vote. And the law gave them far less protection than today: among other things, abusive husbands

were free to beat or rape their wives.[9] Yet these voteless, abused women
actually fared better than their counterparts in our own time. In the Gilded
Age, more than 80 percent of Chicago women who killed their husbands
escaped punishment—among white women, the figure topped 90 percent—
thanks to what contemporaries called "the new unwritten law" granting
women broad rights of self-defense, even when no history of domestic
violence was proved.[10] Seventy years before the women's movement transformed the law of self-defense, women were achieving the results the
movement sought without the help of the legal and medical arguments
on which their late twentieth-century sisters relied.

Racial bias, though real and powerful, was likewise weaker than one
might imagine. After an exhaustive study of late nineteenth-century Philadelphia homicides, Roger Lane concluded that black murder defendants
did about as well as white ones; the Philadelphia justice system treated
the races "with remarkable evenhandedness." The picture worsened
early in the twentieth century, as racial disparities in the populations of
arrestees and convicted felons rose together with rising black populations.[11] Even then, discrimination was spotty: Jeffrey Adler's book about
turn-of-the-century Chicago homicides notes that black women were convicted far more often than white women, but that black and white men
were acquitted in similar numbers.[12] Nothing comparable to the massive
racial tilt in today's drug prisoner population existed in the Gilded Age
North.

The well-known story of Ossian Sweet captures the phenomenon.
Sweet was a black doctor who had the audacity to buy a house in a white
Detroit neighborhood in 1925. A white mob surrounded his house and
shots were fired from inside, where several of Sweet's relatives and friends
were armed. One of the shots killed a white neighbor. All eleven people
in the house, including Sweet and his wife, were charged with murder.
Clarence Darrow took the case and argued self-defense, invoking the
long history of violence against blacks by white mobs. The case was tried
twice, both times to all-white juries; in his two closing arguments, Darrow
questioned whether white jurors could fairly judge black men charged
with doing violence to a white man. The first jury hung; the second acquitted.[13] The judge in both trials was Frank Murphy, who went on to
win election as mayor of Detroit and governor of Michigan before Franklin

D. Roosevelt appointed him first to the cabinet and later to the Supreme Court. Notice that a black man was acquitted of killing a white man by an all-white jury, in a case in which the victim was unarmed and the defense all but admitted the killing. Politically speaking, the judge who presided over the case was rewarded for that outcome, not punished.[14] If that story sounds unsurprising, try to imagine Lance Ito mounting successful campaigns for Los Angeles' mayoralty and the California governorship based on his handling of O. J. Simpson's murder trial.

Black defendants like Sweet did not avoid conviction because they lived in racially enlightened times. No one would call 1920s Detroit racially enlightened: a Klan rally in a Detroit suburb in 1924 drew more than 50,000 participants.[15] Rather, black defendants fared better than their counterparts today in large part because *all* defendants fared better. A mere 22 percent of turn-of-the-century Chicago homicides led to criminal convictions; Chicago juries were quick to acquit in cases in which the killing seemed plausibly excusable. In today's justice system, felony trials are rare events, acquittals rarer still. In northern cities a century ago, both trials and acquittals were common. White women and black men achieved surprisingly good results in that older justice system because defendants as a whole achieved good results.

A large fraction of the many acquittals in this period were won by defendants from poor or working-class immigrant communities. Adler's book about violence in turn-of-the-century Chicago is a compendium of stories of homicides by that city's immigrant poor, who needed no Clarence Darrow to win their cases. As Adler notes, "generic self-defense arguments . . . nearly always persuaded jurors"[16]—abused women were not alone in winning based on borderline self-defense claims. Bar fights, disputes over card games, and drunken brawls regularly produced defense victories. Acquittals of working-class white immigrants may seem less surprising than victories by husband-killing white women and homicidal black men. But white immigrants of the late nineteenth and early twentieth centuries held a lower political status than twenty-first-century Americans might suppose. The bulk of the immigration in this period came from southern and eastern Europe; Catholics and Jews were a larger fraction of immigrants than in the past. Both groups were subject to substantial religious prejudice, a major factor in the Klan's resurgence in the 1920s.[17] The litigation success of poor immigrants is almost as remarkable as the successes enjoyed by white women and black men.

What made this low-crime, low-punishment, low-discrimination justice system work as well as it did? There are four related answers: northern police forces were large, trial procedures were simple, the legal definition of crimes was open to a wide range of defense arguments, and the demographic group that most often faced criminal punishment—working-class immigrant men—held a good deal of political power over the officials who decided when punishment would be imposed.

First, by the standards of the time, northern cities were well policed: the number of officers per unit population was two or three times as high as in southern cities. (See Table 5 for the figures.) The reasons for the three-cornered link that joins low crime rates, low punishment levels, and high levels of policing are unclear. It seems increasingly plain that such a link exists today; it probably existed a century ago as well. Consider that, in the late 1800s, one town in the Kentucky mountains suffered from a murder rate in the vicinity of 200 per 100,000 population; by comparison, New York City's murder rate was below 5 per 100,000 at the same time.[18] New York had a large police force. Functioning institutions of local government barely existed in Kentucky's portion of the Appalachian Mountains.

Obviously, other factors contributed to the gap: spread across the Appalachians were scattered counties where feuding families led to massive violence, which was less true in the urban Northeast. But then, the Northeast had rival gangs engaged in what amounted to ethnic warfare, which the eastern mountain country did not. Feuds depended on low levels of policing: in well-policed jurisdictions, the warring families and their allies would have landed in prison or jail, and a measure of peace would have returned to the countryside. Feud-ridden mountain counties slid into anarchy partly because there were too few officers to maintain even a minimal level of public order. An example makes the point: in another Kentucky county, the head of one feuding family walked into a public court proceeding and told the judge that the case before him should be dismissed. The frightened judge promptly did as he was told and dropped the charges.[19] Such transactions do not happen where well-staffed police forces or sheriff's offices protect local government institutions from violence and intimidation.

Large police forces are correlated with low crime rates today as well. Jurisdictions like New York that have seen the size of local police forces rise the most over the past two decades have also seen crime fall the farthest and prison populations rise the least. In less well-policed places, prison populations and violent crime either have risen more or fallen less. Economist and *Freakonomics* author Steven Levitt concludes that growth in the number of police officers was responsible for a significant fraction of the 1990s crime drop.[20] The available data do not allow for proof, but it seems reasonable to suppose that the link is no new thing.

Second, then-prevailing procedural rules made criminal trials cheap and therefore common. Because jury trials were more common than today, defense victories were bound to be more common as well. Alameda County, California, saw fewer than 60 percent of felony trials end in conviction; the figure dropped to 30 percent for defendants released on bail pending trial. The analogous percentages today are much higher.[21] Turn-of-the-century defendants' success rates were even better than appears from the figures just cited because far fewer criminal defendants pled guilty a century ago than today. In metropolitan counties today, 65 percent of felony cases end with a guilty plea (in most of the rest, the charges are dismissed by a judge, or the prosecutor ceases prosecution—jury acquittals are rare), and those pleas represent more than 95 percent of felony convictions.[22] In turn-of-the-century Alameda County, the analogous figures were 41 percent and 63 percent, respectively.[23] Trials and acquittals alike were far more common than today, and almost certainly more common in the Northeast than on the West Coast.[24] Because acquittals happened frequently, they were also less newsworthy than today. So, in the Gilded Age Northeast, prosecutors paid a smaller political price for acquittals and were less eager to avoid them than today. Note the logic: less elaborate trial procedures helped defendants—not the government—by making both trials and acquittals ordinary events. Prosecutors do not invest heavily in avoiding outcomes that seemed ordinary.

Third, substantive criminal law was both less clearly defined and more favorable to defendants than today's legal doctrine. Defendants rarely have occasion to challenge the application of today's bright-line criminal liability rules, in large part because those rules seem designed to fore-close defense arguments. That was not the case a century ago. Statutory conduct terms, intent standards, and affirmative defenses all invited such arguments rather than barring them. When the terms of criminal statutes were insufficiently hospitable to defense claims, courts filled the gap, as the following example illustrates. Like many of its neighbors in the years before national Prohibition, Michigan passed a local-option law banning liquor in counties that approved the ban; to discourage evasion, the legis-lature forbade not only selling alcoholic beverages but also giving them away. The Michigan Supreme Court soon established a defense for those who served liquor in their homes as an exercise of "a decent hospitality" to their guests.[25] Analogous doctrines in today's law of controlled sub-stances are unimaginable.

Such laws were everywhere in the criminal law of the Gilded Age. Another Michigan doctrine held that mutual fights in which both sides were willing participants were no crime.[26] Rape defendants were acquit-ted if their victims failed to resist coerced sex with all their might. (Today, scholars treat the narrow definition of rape that prevailed in the past as evidence of the law's misogyny.[27] They are partly right. At the same time, rape was defined more narrowly than today in part because nearly all crimes were so defined. Lenity was as much a theme of the historical law of rape as sexism.[28]) Proof of criminal intent meant proof of moral fault, not just the intent to carry out one's physical actions—the standard that usually governs today.[29] In the late twentieth century, self-defense doctrine seemed to forbid defenses for battered women who killed their batterers, save when the killing happened in the midst of a beating. The less doctrinally developed version of the defense that applied in early twentieth-century Chicago and, it seems safe to say, other northern cities awarded victory not only to abused women, but to nearly every homi-cide defendant who could offer a better reason for his—or her—crime than greed or hatred.[30]

The doctrines mentioned in the preceding paragraphs were signifi-cant not only for their lenity, but also for their vagueness. Jurors were not limited to applying bright-line rules or resolving contested questions of historical fact. Instead, they decided whether defendants behaved "rea-sonably," as the law of self-defense required (and still does), or whether those same defendants acted with an "evil-meaning mind" or a "vicious will," as the law of criminal intent required a century ago but rarely does today. In other words, jurors were called on to decide whether individual defendants deserved criminal punishment.[31] Such broad jury power made criminal trials morality plays, with jurors serving as both judge and Greek chorus. In trials-as-morality-plays, defendants could raise nearly any colorable argument in their defense—defense arguments were not much limited by the rules of criminal law, because criminal law was so un-rule-like.

The fourth answer follows naturally from the first three: political control over policing and prosecution was usually in the hands of the same groups who were most often victimized by serious crime, meaning also the same groups who were disproportionately charged with such crimes. Arrests for alcohol-related crime illustrate the point. Where political machines governed large northern cities, such arrests were few: the reigning political organizations depended on immigrant votes for their survival, and so tended to avoid strict enforcement of alcohol regulations in immigrant neighborhoods. The one major city with both a high level of machine control and a high level of alcohol arrests was Philadelphia, in which the governing political machine was Republican and relied on native-born voters, not immigrants, for its support.[32] Where immigrant communities were part of the local governing coalition, as they were in most northern cities, criminal prosecutions usually followed the preferences of those communities' residents.

Though it is hard to know for certain, the same voters who dominated urban electorates—at least the better-off members of their communities—probably enjoyed a fair measure of representation in urban jury pools. In the past as today, the common-law vicinage requirement held that the jury was to be selected from the community in which the crime happened. But that requirement meant something different in the days before widespread car ownership and elaborate city subway systems. Today, juries are usually chosen from the population of the relevant county—and because most metropolitan counties include vast suburbs, high-crime city neighborhoods have little control over the juries that try crimes committed on their streets. Evidence of jury selection practice in the late nineteenth and early twentieth centuries is sparse. That said, more localized jury selection practices must have been the norm before the rise of the automobile: would-be jurors could not easily transport themselves across large metropolitan counties to hear and decide multiday trials. More locally based juries were a practical necessity.

To be sure, the picture was not always so rosy. Many of those locally selected juries were filled with immigrants' native-born middle-class neighbors, not with immigrants or their offspring.[33] Discrimination, both ethnic and racial, was hardly unknown. Urban police forces were large but also corrupt, and policing took on a more violent cast when Irish-dominated police forces patrolled neighborhoods with more recent immigrants from southern and eastern Europe.[34] Last but not least, the law of the late nineteenth and early twentieth centuries—like today's law—offered no binding guarantee of the "equal protection of the laws." Had it done so, northern criminal justice might have avoided much of the discrimination and police misconduct that attended it.

Still, for all its complications and for all its vices, the justice system of the Gilded Age North worked better than today's more bureaucratic system, and did so without today's massive and unstable prison populations. It seems more than coincidence that northern criminal justice was also more locally democratic than its counterparts today.

The South

Two different kinds of local democracy governed criminal justice in the Gilded Age South: one formal, the other off the books. The chief characteristic of the formal justice system was its small size. In Reconstruction's wake, police forces that included sizeable numbers of black officers were both scaled back and whitened: the integrated force responsible for metropolitan New Orleans was abolished following Reconstruction's end; so was the Texas state police force, and for the same reason.[35] Table 5 lists the policing and murder rates—police officers and murders per 100,000 population—plus the number of police officers per murder in three northern and three southern cities in the mid-1930s, just after the Gilded Age's end.

Measured either per unit population or per unit crime, southern police forces were much smaller than their northern counterparts—partly

Table 5. Policing rate, murder rate, and police officers per murder in 1937, selected cities

City	Policing rate	Murder rate	Police officers per murder
Atlanta	125	39	3
Boston	292	2	183
Detroit	238	5	52
Houston	98	21	5
Memphis	93	13	7
New York	251	5	56

Note: The numbers of homicides and urban police officers are taken from Uniform Crime Reports: 1937, at 197–99, table 108; and Uniform Crime Reports: 1938, at 71, table 51, respectively. For the cities' populations, see 1941 Statistical Abstract, at 27–28, no. 30. The calculation of police officers per murder was made using a murder rate calculated to tenths, not to integers as in the table's second column.

because white Southerners had a long tradition of coupling modest-sized law enforcement agencies with occasional bursts of mob rule, and partly for a more mundane reason: before air conditioning, before civil rights, southern cities were much poorer than northern ones. All government services were underfunded by comparison to the wealthier Northeast and Midwest. That fact left southern cities with fewer police officers to contain crime than in the North, and with more crime to contain.[36]

Underfunded southern law enforcement agencies paid little attention to black neighborhoods, which led to racially skewed crime trends. One study of Mississippi homicides in the 1930s found that three-fourths of the state's murder victims were black, as were two-thirds of the killers. White killers' victims were racially mixed: 63 percent white, 37 percent black. By comparison, nineteen of every twenty black killers killed black victims.[37] One-third of those Mississippi murders led to criminal convictions, and that figure undoubtedly differed depending on the races of killers and, especially, victims. Killers of whites could expect a serious effort at arrest, prosecution, and punishment. Killers of blacks—white ones to be sure, but many black killers as well—were more likely to escape detection. That is why prison populations in the Jim Crow South were almost certainly whiter than the offender population, and sometimes whiter than the general population.[38] Black-on-white crime was rare and was punished severely. Black-on-black crime was common, and officials often ignored it.

Not only was criminal punishment discriminatory; it was also highly variable. Southern prison populations fluctuated widely, as Table 6 indicates, with turn-of-the-century imprisonment rates for two sets of four states, one northern and one southern. Notice that the lowest *and* highest imprisonment rates come from the South. Alabama's rate quintupled, and North Carolina's fell by almost two-thirds; none of the listed northern states' imprisonment rates varied by as much as 40 percent in either direction. Southern criminal justice, which was designed for inequality, produced highly variable prison populations. Inmate populations in the North were far more stable, and what little evidence we have suggests much less discrimination than in the South.[39] In the Gilded Age, variation and discrimination seemed to travel together. So did stability and equality, along with moderately lenient treatment for criminal defendants. Southern criminal justice systems had the former set of characteristics, northern justice systems the latter.

Why did the Jim Crow South have both smaller police forces than in the North and, on average, larger prison populations? There are two likely answers. The late nineteenth and early twentieth centuries saw the heavy use of convict labor in the South; prisoners' time was rented by local businesses and used in mining, farming, and a variety of construction projects.[40] Police forces always represented fiscal cost, but inmate populations were, sometimes, a fiscal benefit. That fact must have shaped law enforcement practices in the nation's poorest region. The other answer is similar: even where the feeding and housing of inmates *was* a

Table 6. Imprisonment rates per 100,000 population for selected states, 1880–1910

State	1880	1890	1904	1910
Alabama	31	72	97	158
Illinois	60	54	47	46
Michigan	72	53	54	57
North Carolina	58	88	33	32
Ohio	40	45	53	54
Pennsylvania	43	45	39	46
South Carolina	26	70	47	56
Virginia	50	70	80	104

Note: See Margaret Werner Cahalan, Historical Corrections Statistics in the United States, 1850–1984, at 30, table 3-3 (Rockville, MD: Bureau of Justice Statistics, 1986).

significant cost, that cost was borne chiefly by state governments, which paid for the building and maintenance of penitentiaries, not by the local governments that paid local sheriffs' and police officers' salaries. At the margin, local officials in the South probably preferred more punishment to more policing because the state subsidized the former but not the latter. Money was less tight in the rich North, so state subsidies and their absence probably had smaller effects on local police budgets there.

Another reason for the differences between northern and southern justice systems is the presence of an informal justice system in the South— the "justice" of lynch mobs—but not in the North. The story of lynch law's rise is intertwined with the story of democracy's decline in the South. Once Republican state and local governments were overthrown in the mid-1870s, the wholesale massacres of ex-slaves that had punctuated Reconstruction declined (though isolated lynchings increased).[41] Black voting was plainly less free than when federal troops patrolled southern polling places; even so, black voters remained common in much of the region after Reconstruction ended. Blacks continued to hold some local offices; a few held seats in the federal House of Representatives.[42] In the presidential election of 1884—seven years after Republican presidents Grant and Hayes ceased using federal soldiers to prop up Republican governments in the ex-Confederate South—Republican candidate James G. Blaine won 49 percent of Virginia's vote, 48 percent of Tennessee's, and 47 percent of North Carolina's and Florida's.[43] Had Blaine carried two of the first three of those states, he would have been elected in place of Democrat Grover Cleveland. Even a modest increase in the level of black voting, Republicans reasonably believed, would give them a solid national majority.

So, when Benjamin Harrison defeated Cleveland's 1888 bid for reelection (barely) and brought with him the first Republican Congress in eight years,[44] voting rights legislation was high on the party's agenda. That proposed legislation—Southerners called it "the Force Bill," the same name given to the statute that compelled South Carolina's nullifiers to yield to federal power sixty years earlier—would have required supervision of elections for federal office by federal marshals. Federal prosecutors were to be given the power they had briefly possessed during Reconstruction: to punish southern election officials who kept blacks off the voting rolls. The Bill passed the House on a party-line vote. It failed in the Senate only because Republican unity did not hold: Republican Senators from silver-mining states killed the bill in exchange for southern support for the inflationary Sherman Silver Purchase Act.[45] After the Force Bill's narrow defeat in 1890, the number of lynchings of southern blacks more than doubled.[46] Over the next fifty years, roughly three thousand southern blacks were murdered by southern mobs: an average of nearly 60 per year—substantially more than the number of death row inmates executed each year in today's United States.[47]

In short, lynching became again what it was in the antebellum period: a standard tool of law enforcement, southern style. Again as in the antebellum South, the "law" lynch mobs enforced was of more than one type. Victims of mob justice were often accused of homicide or rape (of white victims), crimes that could be found in the statute books. But many such victims were punished for violating the unwritten code that required black subservience toward southern whites.

After the Force Bill failed, black voters all but vanished from southern registries. The 1890s and early 1900s saw the last black Representatives lose their seats. Most of those ex-Congressmen left the region for fear of the poverty and violence that awaited them if they remained, a precursor of the Great Migration that Jim Crow spawned.[48] The number of votes cast in southern elections fell, sometimes by half or more, at a time when the voting-age population grew rapidly. Table 7 shows the contrasting northern and southern figures. Blacks account for a large fraction, but

Table 7.   Votes cast in presidential elections, selected states, 1888 and 1908

State	1888	1908	Percentage change
Alabama	175,085	105,152	−40
Illinois	747,813	1,155,254	+54
Louisiana	115,891	75,117	−35
Massachusetts	344,243	456,905	+33
Mississippi	115,786	66,904	−42
New York	1,321,170	1,638,350	+24
Ohio	839,357	1,121,552	+34
Virginia	304,087	137,065	−55

Note: The figures are taken from Presidential Elections, 1789–2008, at 141, 146 (Washington, DC: CQ Press, 2010).

not the entirety, of those declines in southern vote totals. Poll taxes, literacy and "good character" tests, and the like cut white voting by as much as half.[49]

The widespread disenfranchisement of poor whites reinforced the simultaneous rise of lynch law, just as widespread lynchings made that disenfranchisement more palatable. Poor whites deprived of power at the ballot box could exercise power, or appear to, with a rope and a tree—in much the way their predecessors on pre–Civil War slave patrols had exercised political power with a coat of tar and feathers, or worse. To be sure, poor whites did not dominate most lynch mobs, just as their predecessors did not dominate prewar slave patrols. But if the poor did not administer mob justice by themselves, neither were they excluded from it. Power over off-the-books southern justice was shared.

That off-the-books power, in turn, compensated for poor whites' powerlessness when it came to the formal justice system. Blacks and poor whites were the groups most often victimized by southern crime and most often subject to southern punishment, but blacks had no influence over southern laws or southern courts, and poor whites had little. Instead, the South's formal justice system was governed by those who least needed its services and least depended on its fairness. Lynchings were different: they were more the product of classless white democracy, one of the few spheres left in which that democracy continued to operate.[50] And lynchings were well-publicized affairs. Railroads sometimes offered reduced rates to those who sought to attend and cheer the proceedings. Spectators bought and sold souvenirs, sometimes including the victim's body parts.[51] Punishment of this sort may have been off the books, but it was hardly secret.

While the South's undemocratic democracy was putting down political roots, northern Republicans watched—and did nothing. The 1880s had seen shifting partisan control of Congress and three of the closest presidential elections in the nation's history. Neither party enjoyed a stable majority. In that environment, Republicans had good reason to try to protect the voting rights of southern blacks, and southern whites had good reason to grant a measure of protection on their own in order to fend off federal regulation. After the Force Bill failed, those incentives changed. Democrats won lopsided victories in the congressional elections of 1890 and 1892; in the second of those elections, Grover Cleveland won his second term in the White House by the biggest presidential margin in twenty years.[52] Long-term Democratic control of the federal government seemed likely, and the power of southern whites seemed safe. The number of lynchings soared, and the number of southern voters began to fall.

After depression struck in 1893, it was the Republicans' turn to win large congressional majorities—which, strangely, left white Southerners' power even safer and lynch law more secure. Beginning in 1894, Republicans controlled the House of Representatives for sixteen years and the Senate for eighteen. Republican candidates won four consecutive presidential elections, each by a bigger margin than Cleveland's in 1892.[53] This Republican era saw many of Jim Crow's worst outrages. In 1898, a white Democratic militia murdered more than a dozen black Republicans in Wilmington, North Carolina, in the course of "redeeming" that city's government. Eight years later, news reports of four assaults by black men on white women in Atlanta prompted a four-day riot that saw dozens more blacks murdered.[54] Southern politicians offered ever more brazen defenses of white violence against southern blacks. With rare exceptions, Republican politicians ignored these incidents. The votes of southern blacks were no longer needed; northern voters had given Republicans what appeared to be a permanent national majority. So Republican politicians left southern whites free to deal with their black neighbors as they chose—not because of the South's political clout in Washington, but because of its political irrelevance.

This was the third time that a nineteenth-century depression had large consequences for the character and quality of American criminal justice. The Panic of 1837 led to a wave of state defaults, after which voters took criminal law enforcement out of state governments' hands, creating a justice system governed by local politics and politicians. The Long Depression that followed 1873 led to the death of Reconstruction and to the consequent death of the ideal of "equal protection of the laws." The Panic of 1893 and the depression that followed gave Republicans a generation-long national majority without the need for southern votes, black or white. That seemingly permanent all-northern Republican majority reinforced the rise of Jim Crow, and with it the "justice" of mobs with ropes.

By the time the Democratic Party revived sufficiently to win national elections, the politics of Jim Crow were well entrenched. Southern-born

President Woodrow Wilson's southern-born cabinet members ordered the segregation of their departments,[55] a step never taken under Wilson's Democratic predecessor Grover Cleveland. Instead of fighting to protect southern blacks' rights, the generation of Republican politicians who battled Wilson's Democrats sought the votes of *white* Southerners. In an attempt to win southern support for his 1912 reelection bid, Republican President William Howard Taft named three southern Democrats, two of them ex-Confederate soldiers, to the Supreme Court.[56] White Tennesseans (few blacks were allowed to vote) chose Republican governors in 1910, 1912, and 1920; the key issue in those elections was Prohibition, not the status of southern blacks.[57] The same was true when Herbert Hoover carried half of the ex-Confederacy against Catholic Democrat Al Smith in 1928: the all-white southern electorate divided on liquor, religion, and the region's traditional loyalty to Democrats, not on racial justice.[58] Slowly, the twentieth-century South was becoming a two-party society—but white voters dominated both parties, neither of which sought to undermine the system of apartheid by which southern blacks were ruled.[59] The partial (in both senses of the word) democracy that governed southern criminal justice was unchecked, and uncontested.

Lynch law thrived in that political environment, and politicians who interfered with it did so at their peril, as Leo Frank's case shows. Frank, a New Yorker and a Jew, managed a small pencil factory in Atlanta; when a teenage girl who worked in his factory was killed, Frank was charged with the murder. In a flagrantly incorrect verdict, Frank was convicted and sentenced to death. In one of his last acts as governor of Georgia, John Slaton commuted Frank's sentence—whereupon a mob seized Frank and lynched him.[60] Slaton's political career was over; for a time, it seemed possible that the governor too would end his life hanging from a rope.[61] Onetime Congressman Tom Watson, the lynching's chief instigator, parlayed the incident into a Senate seat.[62] Such political consequences were not limited to Georgia and its Deep South neighbors: Maryland Governor Albert Ritchie lost his bid for a fifth term in office thanks to his condemnation of a 1934 lynching on that state's Eastern Shore.[63]

Victims like Frank were not executed to deter homicide more effectively, nor as a means of promoting equal justice for murder victims. Frank was a symbol, a stand-in for all the white Northerners and descendants of black slaves—the same groups subject to lynching in the pre–Civil War South—whose crimes risked undermining the South's not-entirely-legal order. Both the rules defining that order and the punishments enforcing it fell outside the realm of formal legal doctrines, part of the unofficial governance of a sadly misgoverned place. Racial oppression and a warped democracy lay at the heart of that misgovernance: Jim Crow's unwritten rules were defined and enforced by some, but the punishments were visited on others. In large measure, the same was true of the South's formal justice system, which was ruled by the votes of middle- and upper-class whites but which chiefly affected poor whites and blacks. That undemocratic democracy did a poor job of controlling crime, and an even worse job of doing justice.

The West

Initially, crime and criminal justice in the frontier West bore more than a passing resemblance to those enterprises in the South. Beginning roughly in the mid-nineteenth century—when a large chunk of what is now the western United States was acquired from Mexico by force—Westerners lived with small police forces, suffered from occasional bursts of mob rule, and endured massive rates of criminal violence. Over time, the resemblance faded. Western police forces grew: by the 1930s, those police forces were smaller than in northeastern cities but consistently larger than in southern ones. Western violence declined sharply; western murder rates grew to resemble those in the violent South less and those in the relatively calm northeast more. Vigilante justice declined too, long before southern lynch mobs ceased doing their ugly work. One distinctive feature of western criminal justice resembled neither North nor South: throughout the late nineteenth and early twentieth centuries, western states incarcerated larger percentages of their populations than states in other sections.

The dominant feature of this story is change. Every aspect of western criminal justice changed dramatically during the nineteenth century's last decades and the twentieth century's first ones. The largest change concerned rates of criminal violence. At the beginning of the Gilded Age, western violence was essentially unchecked; a famous incident captures some of the reasons why. In 1881, Wyatt Earp's brother Virgil was a deputy U.S. marshal with law enforcement responsibilities in Tombstone,

Arizona. Tombstone was also home to a pair of allied families called the McLaurys and the Clantons; a member of the latter family had stolen a horse from Wyatt. (Wyatt Earp evidently knew something about horse theft. In the early 1870s, he was appointed constable of a small town in Missouri. He left that job after he was charged with stealing twenty dollars; later, he left the Indian Territory—today's Oklahoma—in the wake of charges that he had stolen two horses. He never faced trial on either charge.) In one of the incidents that brought these two clans into conflict, the town marshal—an ally of the Earps—was trying to disarm a friend of the Clantons when the friend's gun went off, killing the deputy. Charges against the Clantons' associate were speedily dismissed.[64]

The Earps decided to take on their enemies outside the world of juries and courtrooms. To that end, Virgil Earp deputized his brothers Wyatt and Morgan, along with the family's friend and supporter Doc Holliday. After some preliminaries, the four men met the Clantons and McLaurys at the OK Corral. Holliday and Wyatt's two brothers were wounded in the ensuing gunfight, though all three survived. Tom and Frank McLaury and Billy Clanton, onetime thief of Wyatt's horse, were killed.[65]

Three aspects of this story seem telling. First, the law enforcement officers were little more than a rival gang with badges. The Earps had their own criminal history before the OK Corral; some locals believed the shootout amounted to nothing more than official murder.[66] This state of affairs was not unusual in the old West. Everyone, sheriffs and marshals included, was in business for himself; stable governments acting in the public interest were the exception rather than the rule. No wonder lawmen's authority often went unrecognized. This leads to the story's second key feature: public law enforcement in 1880s Arizona looked more than a little like private self-help—an attempt to avenge wrongs done to law enforcers and their friends. Such self-help was common, both because the law's representatives were too few to maintain order and because those few commanded so little respect. Third, one of the sources of the bad blood between these rival families was an unpunished homicide of a government official. When law enforcers and other officials can be killed without consequence, those same officials will deal with threats to their safety outside the bounds of the formal justice system. That path leads to vigilantism, a serious problem in the old West and the Jim Crow South alike.

Of course, the nineteenth-century West consisted of much more than Tombstone, Dodge City (the Earps had spent time there, too),[67] and other anarchic cow towns with an oversupply of rootless young men. Still, the level of violence in the region's southern half—the OK Corral was in Arizona—was staggeringly high, sometimes approaching 600 murders per 100,000 adults.[68] The wild West was more than a Hollywood creation.

Those supersized western homicide rates were not evenly distributed across demographic groups. Throughout the region, the most discriminated-against group both suffered the highest death toll and killed its own in the greatest numbers. Unlike other parts of the country, the identity of that group varied from place to place: Mexicans in the Southwest, Chinese immigrants in San Francisco and nearby cities, Indians and blacks in scattered locations. Just as southern blacks killed one another in ever larger numbers after Jim Crow was established, something similar happened among the Southwest's Indian and Mexican populations and in the Northwest's various Chinatowns.[69] Discrimination bred murderous violence.

Rates of violence were higher among some groups than others—but those rates were high across the board, as the life and death of onetime California Chief Justice David Terry suggests. In 1859, Terry challenged U.S. Senator and San Francisco political boss David Broderick to a duel at which Broderick was killed; Terry was tried for murder and acquitted.[70] Among those with whom Terry had a beef—it was a long list—was Stephen Field, who served with Terry on the state Supreme Court in the late 1850s and whom Abraham Lincoln later named to the U.S. Supreme Court. Thirty years after the fatal duel with Broderick, an armed Terry confronted Justice Field and was killed by Field's bodyguard. The bodyguard was tried on homicide charges and acquitted.[71] In the Northeast, lives and deaths like Terry's were nearly nonexistent. Such violent lives, lived by men who enjoyed substantial political and legal power, could happen only in a society that assumed even the most serious wrongs would be handled not by governments and legal procedures but by individuals protecting their honor.

Apparently, the assumption was well founded: even in the most violent places, criminal punishment was imposed sparingly. At the time of the shootout at the OK Corral, Arizona Territory housed a mere thirty-one prisoners out of a homicidal population of roughly 40,000:[72] fewer prisoners than the number of murders that took place in the territory each year. (Today, New York imprisons seventy times its annual number of nonvehicular homicides.)[73] A justice system that was too often unable to convict and punish even in the clearest cases led to frequent outbursts of mob rule. In the South, execution by lynch mob was a supplement to a working justice system of courtrooms and jury boxes. In the West, vigilante justice served as a substitute for a well-functioning formal justice system that did not yet exist.

Organized "vigilance committees" existed in Montana and Idaho, but the most famous instances of vigilante justice come from 1850s San Francisco, a major city that sprung up almost overnight in the wake of California's gold rush. Formal legal institutions were slow to catch up to the city's growth. The first of San Francisco's vigilance committees hanged four Australian criminals and banished two dozen others. The second committee arose in the wake of the murder of a U.S. marshal by a local gambler who was acquitted at trial—as with the Earps and David Terry, the laxity of the formal justice system seems to have prompted other, rougher forms of justice.[74]

Any similarity between San Francisco's vigilantes and the Earps ends there. The Earps and their hangers-on were a handful of transient roughnecks. San Francisco's vigilantes were a large and respectable slice of the community; the 1856 vigilance committee included some six thousand of the city's residents.[75] That oversized committee was led by local notables like Terry, leading citizens who enjoyed high levels of social status and political influence. The committee was disbanded only after ousting Senator Broderick's political machine, which catered to white working-class San Franciscans. Last but not least, the vigilantes often gave their victims trials, albeit truncated ones: participants apparently saw themselves as unofficial judges and juries, not simply as executioners.[76] Southern lynch mobs sometimes did the same. Those two groups shared one other important feature: both saw themselves as small-d democrats remedying what they believed were deficiencies in the style of democracy that governed their jurisdictions.

Although southern lynch law existed well into the mid-twentieth century, western vigilantism was largely a nineteenth-century phenomenon.

Once decent-sized urban police forces and functioning local courts existed, western prison populations waxed, and the perceived need for vigilance committees waned. To put it another way, vigilantism was a temporary feature of western criminal justice. Southern lynch mobs seemed a permanent by-product of Jim Crow.

As the twentieth century began, vigilantism receded—western crime rates fell, and western law enforcement lost its ad hoc, frontier character. By the 1890s, Oakland, California, had an eastern-style homicide rate of a mere 4 per 100,000. Even then, California criminal justice differed from its

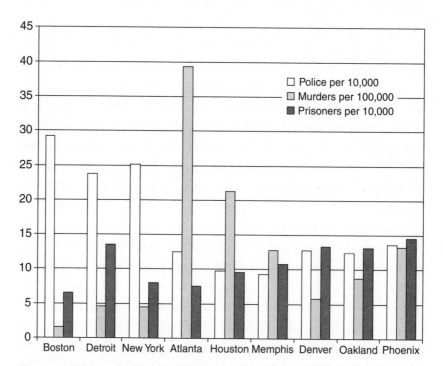

Figure 4. Policing, murder, and (state) imprisonment rates for nine U.S. cities, mid-1930s

For the numbers of homicides and police officers in individual cities, see Uniform Crime Reports: 1937, at 197–99 table 108; and Uniform Crime Reports: 1938, at 71, table 51, respectively. For the cities' populations, see Campbell Gibson and Kay Jung, Historical Census Statistics on Population Totals by Race, 1790 to 1990, and by Hispanic Origin, 1970 to 1990, for Large Cities and Other Urban Places in the United States (Washington, DC: U.S. Census Bureau, Working Paper no. 76, February 2005). For imprisonment rates, see 1940 Statistical Abstract at 3, no. 5, 4–5, no. 7, 77, no. 66.

northeastern counterparts in two key ways: western police forces were smaller, and western prison populations larger, than those in the East. Unlike northeastern cities, Oakland had a small police force in the late 1800s.[77]

Other western states did likewise; Figure 4 charts the policing, murder, and (state) imprisonment rates in the mid-1930s for nine cities—three apiece from the Northeast, the South, and the West. Large police forces defined criminal justice in northeastern cities; southern cities had markedly higher hates of homicide than elsewhere. High imprisonment rates (by early twentieth-century standards, as today's rates are much higher) were western cities' chief distinguishing feature.[78]

Step back from these details and consider the bigger picture. In the late nineteenth and early twentieth centuries, the nation's northeastern quadrant lived under a justice system with large police forces, small and stable prison populations, and low rates of criminal violence. Southern criminal justice had the opposite characteristics: small police forces, prison populations that were large on average but varied widely across time and jurisdiction, and extremely high crime rates. For most of the nineteenth century, the West mimicked the South, with southern-sized police forces and prison populations and, at least in the Southwest, southern-sized rates of homicide. By century's end, western justice systems had become more northeastern in character: police forces grew, crime rates shrank, and mob justice faded.

For the most part, these different justice systems operated under the same laws. Different states defined crimes (at least crimes that were frequently prosecuted) similarly: though each state purported to have its own rules, it makes sense to speak of an American law of rape, robbery, or murder. And where doctrinal differences existed, those differences mattered little in practice. One of the key criminal law debates in turn-of-the-century America concerned the battle between what lawyers call the "retreat rule" and what was widely known a century ago as the "true man doctrine." These dueling doctrines addressed the question whether the victim of an assault could kill his assailant even though he could have safely fled the encounter. The retreat rule held that the victim's flight was preferable to the assailant's death. The true man doctrine held otherwise: victims of assault could defend their honor whether or not they could safely retreat. Most states north of the Ohio River and east of the Mississippi required retreat. Southern and western courts found this eastern doctrine unmanly.[79] As one Missouri court put the point:

> It is true, human life is sacred, but so is human liberty. One is as dear in the eye of the law as the other, and neither is to give way and surrender its legal status in order that the other may exclusively exist . . . [No] man, because he is the physical inferior of another, . . . is . . . bound to submit to a public horsewhipping. We hold it a necessary self-defense to resist, resent, and prevent such humiliating indignity . . . and that, if nature has not provided the means for such resistance, art may; in short, a weapon may be used to effect the unavoidable necessity.[80]

Not only may victims respond to violence with violence, "a weapon may be used to effect the unavoidable necessity." Under the true man doctrine, victims may escalate—answering fists with a club, a club with a knife, or a knife with a gun—rather than suffer the indignity of retreat.

The doctrine sounds consequential, especially at a time when a large fraction of homicides arose from bar fights that spun out of control. But different self-defense standards mattered less than first appears: recall the many turn-of-the-century Chicago homicides in which defendants stood their ground and killed their assailants. "Generic self-defense arguments" were enough to win acquittals in such cases, even though Illinois law ostensibly required defendants to retreat from their assailants when possible.[81] Meanwhile, on the rare occasions when southern blacks killed whites—even when the killers plainly acted in self-defense and equally plainly had no chance to retreat—self-defense claims routinely lost. Southern whites who killed blacks and then claimed self-defense fared much better, again regardless of the presence or absence of opportunity to flee.[82] Legal doctrine had little effect on the outcomes of these cases.

What was true of the retreat rule was true more generally: local juries, not the law, decided what behavior was and wasn't appropriate for criminal defendants. The content of criminal law mattered, as law always matters. But the law's most important characteristic was its vagueness, which left room for juries and trial judges to decide cases based on their own moral intuitions. And however much influence law had on the outcomes of criminal prosecutions, Gilded Age politics had more. The chief distinction between criminal justice in the different parts of the United States lay not in the laws that allegedly governed in those jurisdictions, but in the different visions of democracy that applied and enforced those laws.

CHAPTER 6

A Culture War and Its Aftermath

This declared indifference . . . [to] the spread of slavery, I cannot but hate. I hate it because of the monstrous injustice of slavery itself. I hate it because it deprives our republican example of its just influence in the world . . .

—Abraham Lincoln, debate with Senator Stephen
A. Douglas at Ottawa, Illinois (1858)

You can make it illegal, but you can't make it unpopular.

—New Orleans Mayor Martin Behrman, on the closing of the houses
of prostitution in Storyville, the city's red-light district (1917)

Prohibition is an awful flop.
We like it.
It can't stop what it's meant to stop.
We like it.
It's left a trail of graft and slime
It don't prohibit worth a dime
It's filled our land with vice and crime,
Nevertheless, we're for it.

—Franklin Pierce Adams, *New York World* (1931)

Localism and Nationalism

There was another side to Gilded Age criminal justice, one that had little to do with homicide rates, vigilance committees, or the behavior of "true men." Between the late 1870s and 1933, America's criminal justice system fought a series of cultural battles in which criminal law—especially, federal criminal law—was a key weapon: against polygamy, state lotteries (more precisely, one state lottery), prostitution, various forms of opium, and, last but definitely not least, alcoholic drink. Taken together, these legal battles constituted a two-generation culture war, akin to the cultural battles over drug use, abortion, and gay rights in our own time. The earlier culture war transformed both the law and politics of crime.

With respect to the law, these crusades saw the rise of a new model of crime definition, embraced first by federal law and spreading to the states later in the twentieth century. The defining feature of this new and more expansive federal criminal law was its strategic character. Where constitutional limits seemed to bar exercising federal power over traditionally local issues, Congress and the courts evaded those limits. Where a straightforward definition of the conduct Congress sought to criminalize would leave federal prosecutors hard-pressed to win convictions, the relevant crimes were defined more broadly to make convictions more easily won. Curiously, these patterns were more marked in the battles against polygamy, prostitution, and opiates than in the more famous battle against liquor. Prohibition, the cultural battle that ended in the government's defeat, was also the cultural battle that was fought most transparently, with the relevant crimes defined most honestly—and with the largest measure of legal modesty. In the balance of the twentieth century, Congress and state legislatures alike used the earlier battles, not Prohibition, as their legal template. Gradually, American criminal law ceased to define the conduct and intent that prosecutors actually sought to punish, and instead treated crime definition as a means of facilitating arrests, prosecutions, and convictions.

With respect to the politics of crime, the key change has to do with the tension between localism and central control. All contested cultural battles constitute, in part, debates about the proper structure of government: one side argues that different jurisdictions should be left free to adopt different rules to suit the preferences of their local populations; the other side maintains that the nation as a whole should take a stand on matters of moral principle. Localists note that giving different states or territories the power to choose their own rules maximizes the number of people who live under rules they find congenial.[1] Nationalists answer that localism ignores the moral character of the relevant rules.

These are the positions that Stephen Douglas and Abraham Lincoln took in their iconic debates about the status of slavery in America's western territories in the 1850s. Douglas argued that settlers in those territories should decide for themselves whether to permit slavery. Lincoln maintained that the status of slavery in the territories was not a matter of personal taste but a question of right and wrong, and that the whole nation had a stake in how the question was answered. Douglas won the election campaign of which those debates were the most famous part,[2] but Lincoln won the larger argument about slavery—and about federalism. State lotteries, prostitution, and drug dealing are smaller matters than slavery; they are the sort of crimes that one might suppose should remain the job of local officials familiar with local norms. Douglas-style live-and-let-live federalism seems an appropriate approach to the issues such offenses raise. Yet there, too, Douglasite localism lost out to Lincolnian nationalism. Why?

The short answer is this: because voters care about the rules that govern people who live in other jurisdictions. Abortion opponents seek more than abortion bans in their own states; they also oppose pro-choice laws in other states. The same is true in the other direction: pro-choice voters want pro-choice laws nationwide, not just for themselves. Indeed, both groups lobby hard for policies that either increase or decrease access to abortion in other *countries*.[3] That instinct was the Achilles' heel of Stephen Douglas's defense of popular sovereignty, under which voters in territories could decide whether to allow slaveowning in their midst. Lincoln called it Douglas's "don't care" policy. Because enough voters did care, the more common reaction was Lincoln's: slavery raised questions about which many felt strongly, so the nation—not just individual states and territories—must either endorse it or place it on what Lincoln called "the course of ultimate extinction."[4]

As the vice wars of the nineteenth and twentieth centuries illustrate, that common reaction has applied to much more than slavery. A century ago on a range of issues from lotteries to liquor, from polygamy to prostitution, Lincolnian moral nationalism consistently prevailed over Douglasite federalism. Something similar is true today: federal law and national politics play large roles in the ongoing drug war; both sides in the abortion and gay rights debates have sought to nationalize those two issues.[5] Americans may be a tolerant people, but when faced with an issue of moral consequence about which many feel strongly and few are inclined to yield to their opponents, national politics and federal law enforcement quickly come into play. Moral issues go national: they migrate up the sovereignty ladder rather than holding steady on one of the lower rungs. Both the earlier culture war that focused on liquor and prostitution and the more recent one that has emphasized drugs and abortion were shaped by that political reality.

This century-old culture war was the sum of five distinct battles, each of them in large measure a fight about the character of federal criminal law. The largest and most famous of those battles was the one about liquor, which produced two constitutional amendments and a thirteen-year nationwide ban on the manufacture and sale of alcohol. Yet in some respects the smaller battles that preceded Prohibition mattered more: they set the pattern for the drug laws we have today and, to a large degree, for criminal law more generally. In the process, they changed both American law and American politics, permanently.

"Twin Relics"

In 1856, the first Republican National Convention adopted a platform condemning "those twin relics of barbarism—Polygamy, and Slavery."[6] The story of the crusade that ended the second of those "relics" is well known. The first, much less so.

Polygamy was a common practice in the early Church of Jesus Christ of Latter-Day Saints—the Mormons—and a key source of conflict between the church and the larger nation. Only a minority of Mormon adults practiced it, but its effect on Mormon culture was greater than the numbers would suggest. That was so partly because what Mormons called "plural marriage" was disproportionately practiced among church leaders, who treated it as an important aspect of their religious observance. Brigham Young, Utah's first territorial governor and the church's president and prophet, had dozens of wives; Young emphasized both the importance and the benefits of the practice for men and women alike. Like another, more famous nineteenth-century "domestic institution," polygamy led to a drawn-out conflict between local power and the federal government.[7]

As criticism of plural marriage swelled in the years after the Mormons' westward migration, the lines of political attack echoed the standard criticisms of slavery in the years before the Civil War. Antislavery politicians and publicists emphasized both the degradation slavery caused black women and the sexual corruption that it promoted among white men. Anti-polygamists did likewise, characterizing plural wives as functional slaves denied even the most basic legal protections. Men who headed multispouse households like Young's were alleged to be lazy tyrants who lived off the labor of their many wives, just as indolent southern slaveholders lived off the sweat of the blacks they owned. When Mormon Utah tried to give voting rights to women, the gesture was dismissed as an effort to grant still more power to polygamous men who supposedly controlled their wives' votes—a complaint that echoed criticism of another affront to democracy: the extra congressional representation that the pre-abolition Constitution granted slaveholders. According to their mostly Republican critics, both of these domestic institutions bred concentrated power unrestrained by law, which undermined democracy and victimized helpless women.[8]

Their first effort to bring plural marriage under the nation's legal judgment was a failure. The Morrill Act of 1862 banned plural marriage and authorized five-year prison terms for violators,[9] but without the testimony of wives and church officials, illegal marriages were unprovable. Even if proof were possible, defendants had two more-than-plausible legal arguments to fend off criminal prosecution. Article IV, Section 3 of the Constitution permits Congress to "make all needful Rules and Regulations" for American territories[10]—a clause that applied to Utah, which remained a territory until 1896. Perhaps the Morrill Act was not "needful," hence not within the scope of the power of Congress: after all, the law of marriage always had been a piece of local law, governed by the states and by territorial courts and legislatures, not by Congress.[11] The second legal argument was more straightforward: the First Amendment forbade Congress to enact legislation "prohibiting the free exercise" of religion.[12] The Morrill Act was designed to punish consensual, religiously motivated conduct, which seemed a clear violation of the free exercise clause.

Or so the defendant argued in *Reynolds v. United States* (1879).[13] When the charges against him were filed, George Reynolds was a 32-year-old man with but two wives, and was not among the church's leading figures. His conviction—the first under the Morrill Act—was a fluke:

Reynolds's second wife testified to her marriage to the defendant, evidently because she did not understand the import of her testimony.[14] In the Supreme Court, Reynolds's counsel raised both the Article IV and First Amendment arguments. A mere three years after *United States v. Cruikshank* (1876), Reynolds's legal position seemed hopeful. After all, *Cruikshank* also had involved a conflict between local and federal power—and local power had won, hands down, even in a case of mass murder of government deputies, a far greater threat to federal authority than an anonymous man with two wives. A Supreme Court that had put a stop to Reconstruction in the name of local authority seemed unlikely to embrace another national moral crusade, and one with a weaker legal justification at that.[15]

If that is what George Reynolds and his lawyers thought, the Court's decision must have come as an unwelcome surprise. Chief Justice Waite, *Cruikshank*'s author, wrote the majority opinion, all but ignoring Reynolds's argument about the limits of national power over traditionally local matters like the law of marriage. Instead, his opinion extolled monogamy's virtues and polygamy's vices before concluding: "[T]here cannot be a doubt that . . . it is within the legitimate scope of the power of every civil government to determine whether polygamy or monogamy shall be the law of social life under its dominion." "Every civil government" included the government of the United States. The opinion went on to reject Reynolds's free exercise claim, holding that the First Amendment protects religious belief and not religiously motivated actions from legal penalty. According to Waite, the alternative might legitimize such extreme practices as human sacrifice, and would "make the professed doctrines of religious belief superior to the law of the land, and . . . permit every citizen to become a law unto himself. Government could exist only in name in such circumstances."[16]

Of course, one might argue that the First Amendment explicitly made "professed doctrines of religious belief superior to the law of the land," insofar as the law sought to punish acts of religious duty. Polygamy was hardly the equivalent of homicide; absent evidence of coercion, there was no obvious reason to distinguish plural marriage from any other religious obligation. And if the existence of orderly government was at stake in *Reynolds,* the stakes must have been higher still in *Cruikshank,* where

private violence had overturned a lawful local government and murdered its supporters. No matter: polygamy was, in the Court's view, a serious moral wrong that any decent government was bound to redress, and
that was the end of the matter. Having ended the federal crusade to protect
the rights—and the lives—of black ex-slaves only three years earlier, the
Court had no trouble embracing a cheaper and more politically palatable
moral crusade.

Reynolds jump-started the campaign against polygamy. Soon after the
Court's decision, Congress enacted the Edmunds Act, which established
a new federal crime of "unlawful cohabitation": a means of punishing
plural marriage without the need of proving any marriages. Using that
new crime plus more traditional common-law offenses like adultery and
fornication, federal prosecutors targeted church leaders by the dozens
and ordinary church members by the hundreds. More than two thousand
prosecutions were brought during the 1870s and, especially, the 1880s—a
large number in a territory with a total population, children included, of
only 140,000. Many of these defendants went underground to avoid prosecution. Sometimes such evasions worked, and sometimes not: Rudger
Clawson, one of the church's twelve Apostles, was the first defendant
punished under the Edmunds Act. Sometimes wives too were subject to
criminal prosecution: hundreds of Mormon women were charged with
fornication for sharing a bed with their own husbands.[17]

Notice two key features of this story. First, the fight between the federal
government and the Mormon Church was about the federal government's
ability to control a classically local body of law: the law that defines families, and their members' rights and obligations. Whatever the strength of
anti-polygamists' moral claims, the practical effects of plural marriage
were bound to be felt where those arrangements were made and honored,
not elsewhere. If ever local power were to be respected, one might think,
it should be respected in such cases. But live-and-let-live was not a winning posture, either among politicians or in the courts. Lincoln's nationalism, not Douglas's localism, prevailed, and for the same reason it prevailed in the debate over slavery: because lawmakers and the voters who
elect them thought the relevant conduct wrong.

Second, the targets in this cultural battle included people who wished
to live law-abiding lives—a huge advantage for anti-polygamists. Ordinary

criminals may go on the lam with relative ease; few ties bind them to the kinds of life that render themselves and their affairs visible to police officers and prosecutors. So, too, criminal organizations are in the business of concealing their activities. But a church whose leaders seek to exercise power openly will find those goals hard to achieve when in hiding; the same is true of individuals who wish to run farms and pursue honest occupations. Ultimately, the Latter-Day Saints needed two related things: the ability to practice their religion in peace and a measure of political autonomy, the kind that would follow from statehood. After *Reynolds,* the federal government could deny those two needs indefinitely, unless and until the church surrendered its attachment to plural marriage. That fact goes some distance toward explaining why the church capitulated in 1890, reversing its position on polygamy once and for all.[18] The federal crusade subsided, and religious peace soon followed. Statehood for Utah followed a few years later.

Lotteries

State-sponsored lotteries have a long history in the United States. Common in the years just after independence, such lotteries became common again in the Reconstruction-era South, where Republican governments needed revenue to fund spending on education and economic development.[19] Once Democrats returned to power and slashed Republican state budgets, those southern lottery laws were quickly repealed—with one exception. The exception was Louisiana.

Louisiana's lottery was adopted in 1868; the lottery company—a private, for-profit business—was hired by the state in exchange for an annual payment of $50,000. Allegations of bribery attended the initial legislation.[20] This lottery soon operated beyond Louisiana's borders, shipping its tickets to all corners of the nation. It was not so much a means of raising money for the state from Louisianans as a means of *making* money, a bit of which went to the state, for the lottery's private owners and operators from customers scattered across the nation. Those owners and operators made out very well, as the following incident shows. In the spring of 1890, with New Orleans facing a serious flood—and with the lottery's charter up for review in the state legislature—Dr. M. A. Dauphin, the lottery company's chief executive, wrote personal checks of $50,000 to New Orleans's mayor and $100,000 to Louisiana's governor: huge sums at that time. The checks were allegedly Dauphin's contribution to flood relief efforts, but they were seen by many as bribes designed to speed the legislature's reauthorization. The mayor accepted his check; the governor refused his.[21]

Members of Congress had at least three reasons to object to Dauphin's enterprise—its inherent immorality (in the view of those who saw all gambling as immoral), the corruption that seemed to attend its establishment and growth, and the fact that a single state had foisted a national lottery on a not-necessarily-willing nation. In 1890—the year of Dauphin's large quasi-bribes, the same year that the Church of Latter-Day Saints changed its doctrine on plural marriage—Congress passed the first of two federal statutes designed to bring the lottery down: a ban on the use of the mails to transport lottery tickets. The lottery corporation answered by printing and shipping its tickets from Central America, outside the reach of the federal postal service. So, in 1895, Congress passed a similar statute with a different jurisdictional hook, this time banning the movement of lottery tickets in foreign and interstate commerce. In tandem, these two federal laws killed both the Louisiana lottery and Dr. Dauphin's finances.[22]

That victory was the least important consequence of the brief battle over the Louisiana lottery. The most important consequence was a Supreme Court decision that redefined American federalism. The decision was *Champion v. Ames* (1903).[23]

The core question in *Champion* was how to draw the line between federal authority over crime and the authority of the state and local officials who traditionally governed the nation's unsystematic criminal justice system. The most natural way to answer that question was to distinguish between different categories of offenses. Some crimes—such as evasion of federal taxes, robbing federal property, assaulting federal officials, or importing forbidden goods from abroad—plainly belonged on the federal side of the line. Others—murder, rape, robbery, and other familiar crimes—presumably fell on the side of state legislators, local police, and local prosecutors, if only because tradition had placed them there. Morals crimes like polygamy, lotteries, prostitution, and the manufacture of liquor appear to fit the second category. Some states may wish to ban lotteries; others may not. A federal ban, including prohibitions of interstate shipments or the use of the mails to distribute tickets, risks forcing those who see state lotteries as a harmless means of raising revenue to live under a moral and legal code with which they disagree. The local populations of some jurisdictions may wish to stamp out prostitution; in others, residents may prefer to limit the practice to the local red-light district. Again, federal legislation risked forcing more tolerant jurisdictions to live under laws they opposed. All of which sounds like an ideal case for Douglas-style federalism: facing serious moral disagreements, let local populations decide for themselves what rules to embrace.

That was the view held by Chief Justice Melville Fuller, author of the dissent in *Champion*. As Fuller saw it, the constitutional power to regulate "commerce with foreign nations, and among the several states" was not at stake, because the ban on the shipping of lottery tickets was a piece of morals legislation, not commercial regulation: Congress sought not to regulate the "commerce" in lottery tickets but to stamp it out. As Fuller rightly observed, the regulation of public morals was a traditional subject of state, not federal, power.[24] All of which suggested that indivisible power over this subject must belong to the states, not to Congress.

Fuller's position was probably the conventional wisdom among lawyers of his time. But it lost. Instead, the majority of the Justices held that the federal government could ban a portion of the market for lottery tickets without banning the whole—and that, morals legislation or not, the anti-lottery law fell within the scope of the Constitution's commerce clause. Those holdings continue to shape federal criminal law today. Today's federal code is littered with examples of criminal statutes that read like the second anti-lottery law: the successor to the Mann Act, which criminalizes the crossing of a state line with intent to commit an act of prostitution; the Travel Act, which bars crossing a state line with the intent to gamble in a jurisdiction in which gambling is illegal; the federal act barring the possession of a firearm by a convicted felon (case law requires that the gun must have crossed a state line)[25]—all follow the same approach to federal jurisdiction as the law challenged in *Champion*. The main federal statute punishing robbery and extortion requires proof that the relevant crime had a significant effect on interstate business, which usually means that the victim bought and sold goods that crossed state lines.[26] As these examples illustrate, much of the federal criminal code consists of crimes like those found in state criminal codes—plus a requirement that, in the course of the criminal episode, people or goods must have crossed some state border. Instead of allocating some crimes to states and others to the federal government, prohibitions like the ones just described give rise to overlapping jurisdiction.[27] States, and the local governments within their borders, remain the primary source of criminal punishment for such offenses. But the federal government enjoys a significant measure of power around the edges.

An earlier generation of political scientists called this arrangement "marble cake federalism," as distinguished from "layer cake federalism."[28] Layer cakes have distinct sections, akin to distinct powers given to different levels of government. In marble cakes, the distinctions disappear; ingredients are mixed together, such that it is hard to tell where one leaves off and another begins. Because of *Champion v. Ames,* the federalism of American criminal law has the latter character, not the former. Combine that with the defining feature of federal criminal justice—the relatively small number of federal criminal prosecutions—and the consequence is that federal law enforcers have a great deal they *can* do but very little that they *must* do. Local police and local prosecutors remained primarily responsible for enforcing their jurisdictions' vice laws, leaving federal agents and federal prosecutors free to cherry-pick politically attractive cases.

Why such a strange division of power? The answer lies neither in logic nor in constitutional design, both of which cut in Fuller's favor in *Champion.* Rather, Justice Harlan's majority opinion has the explanation: the federal ban on interstate shipment of lottery tickets had to be upheld for the same reason the federal ban on polygamy was upheld in *Reynolds*—because the underlying behavior was, in the Court's view, so obviously wrong.[29] Harlan's opinion called lotteries a "pestilence" from which ordinary citizens needed the government's protection. The need for the legislation—a need whose roots were moral, not commercial— was justification enough for the exercise of federal power. As the Mormons had discovered in the 1870s and 1880s, legal and political limits on federal power were of little moment when voters and courts entered into moral crusades. As southern blacks had learned during the same years, those limits meant a great deal more when courts decided that the time for crusading was over.

Sex, for Profit and Pleasure

The battles against polygamy and the Louisiana lottery were fought by the federal government; the point of these battles was to reverse or nullify decisions made by a territory and a state, respectively. Not so the battle against prostitution, which arose locally and migrated up the sovereignty ladder—and which was fought against criminal networks, not government-sponsored institutions.

Before the late nineteenth century, it was a one-sided battle, mostly because the enterprise of trading sex for money was so widely tolerated. The reason was not the law: the common law of crimes forbade both the running of a bordello and "disorderly conduct," the definition of which was sufficiently capacious to cover acts of prostitution. Still, police raids were rare events, partly because the officers who would carry them out were often on the houses' payroll.[30]

Later in the century, enforcement grew more aggressive, as waves of urban reformers sought to clean up vice districts. But these local crusades were usually short lived: the sheer size of the demand for prostitutes' services ensured that some means of satisfying that demand would survive.[31] Before long, a more typical equilibrium returned: low-level enforcement aimed at street solicitation—in Chicago, police focused their attention on "naked girls leaning out of windows to advertise their charms"—along with a large measure of tolerance for more orderly and discreet forms of the business. Sometimes, those tolerant equilibria were sustained by tax revenue. In St. Paul, Minnesota, the leading brothels paid the city treasury several thousands of dollars per year. In some parts of the West, taxes from bordellos funded public schools and other government services. Elsewhere, graft was more the norm: in late nineteenth-century Atlanta, one of the police commissioners owned several of the city's houses of prostitution.[32]

The most common means of accommodating the world's oldest profession was a form of urban zoning, with prostitution restricted to designated areas of the relevant city. Within such districts, prostitutes were permitted to conduct business more or less freely; outside them, they were subject to police raids and criminal punishment. New Orleans offered the most famous example. In 1897, a local businessman named Sidney Story proposed limiting prostitution to a twenty-block area of the city—a territory soon known as Storyville. Seven hundred fifty prostitutes plied their trade there, in a city with a population of fewer than 300,000. (In Manhattan, the number of prostitutes topped 10,000.) At its peak, Storyville's various houses made profits of $1 million per month; the neighborhood became not just a Mecca for vice but the birthplace of jazz and ragtime—Jelly Roll Morton played the piano in one of the neighborhood's bordellos. The district was shut down only after the United States entered World War I: New Orleans was a shipping point for a large number of soldiers and sailors, many of whom contracted venereal diseases from the local working women.[33]

Restricting the business to red-light districts, limiting raids to streetwalkers and window advertisers, using established houses as sources of revenue for city budgets or for officials' personal enrichment—these may have been the dominant means of regulating urban prostitution, but they were not the only means. Reformers still sought to close such businesses. Theodore Roosevelt, president of New York City's police commission in the mid-1890s, briefly became the scourge of the city's vice markets before moving on to military glory in the Spanish-American War and, soon after, to higher political office. But Roosevelt and others like him faced obstacles well beyond public demand for the services they sought to stamp out. Sometimes, the laws that urban reformers sought to use undermined the reformers' own goals.

That happened in New York with respect to one of Roosevelt's chief enforcement priorities: the Sunday closing laws, which barred the operation of the city's many corner saloons on the Christian Sabbath. The state legislature ordered saloons closed on Sundays, but hotels with ten or more rooms were exempt from the order; such institutions could serve liquor as long as they also served meals to their hotel guests. Saloons quickly converted themselves into small hotels, offering rooms and meals to their "guests" and hence preserving their liquor business. Soon, these "hotels" became bases of operation for local prostitutes[34]—in effect, one-stop vice shops. Such unintended consequences were a common problem with the use of criminal punishment to regulate vice. The relevant transactions were consensual; no victim reported the offense. All concerned had an interest in avoiding police attention. The markets in question were sustained by a large public demand, which meant that raids and crackdowns were bound to be, at best, only incomplete successes. And proving the requisite crimes was often difficult absent "stings" or strategically defined crimes.

There the intermittent quasi-crusade against prostitution might have remained had Congress not chosen to embrace that crusade and to give it a different cast. An international agreement on curbing the sex traffic in young women led Chicago Congressman James Robert Mann to introduce the Act that bore his name, better known at the time as the White Slave Traffic Act.[35] (As with the battle against polygamy, the crusade against prostitution was thick with talk of white women enslaved.) The stated goal of the Mann Act was to punish the international and interstate trafficking in women coerced into prostitution. But the Act's language went much farther, authorizing punishment for "any person who shall knowingly transport or cause to be transported . . . in interstate or foreign commerce, . . . any woman or girl for the purpose of prostitution *or debauchery, or for any other immoral purpose* . . ."[36] The italicized phrases proved as broad as they sounded. The Act led to the conviction of an engaged couple who, in search of work, traveled from Pennsylvania to Alabama, living as husband and wife along the way. An unmarried New Jersey couple was convicted for taking a ten-day vacation in Miami.[37] The government tried to prosecute Jack Johnson, the first black heavyweight boxing champion, for traveling and sleeping with his white girlfriend, whom he later married.[38]

In *Caminetti v. United States* (1917), the Supreme Court upheld a Mann Act conviction on similarly innocuous facts. Caminetti was charged with no acts of prostitution but with taking a train from Sacramento, California, to Reno, Nevada, along with his mistress, with whom he intended to have sex.[39] As in *Champion v. Ames,* the defendant argued, plausibly, that his conduct bore no relationship to "commerce" as that term is ordinarily understood, because he sought no pecuniary gain from the relationship: Caminetti was his mistress's lover, not her pimp. Consequently, any "immoral purpose" was of a different character than the immorality associated with prostitution, coerced and otherwise. As in *Reynolds v. United States,* Caminetti maintained that the Constitution left the regulation of public morals to state and local governments.

If anything, these arguments were stronger in *Caminetti* than in *Reynolds* and *Champion.* In *Reynolds,* the Court could rely on the federal government's broad power over federal territories, but not so in *Caminetti.* The lottery law at issue in *Champion* barred the shipment of tickets, which seems a paradigmatically commercial transaction—again unlike *Caminetti,* where the relevant transaction was purely sexual. Nevertheless, the result was the same as in the earlier two cases. The requirement that Congress restrict criminal statutes' scope to foreign and interstate commerce was formal, not functional. So long as something or someone had crossed a state or national border, federal power to punish crime was essentially automatic. The relationship between the border crossing and the alleged evil that the criminal statute aimed to prohibit can be wholly arbitrary—Caminetti could as easily have journeyed to San Francisco for sex; the engaged couple previously mentioned might have traveled from Philadelphia to Pittsburgh in their quest for jobs—without changing that conclusion.

That much followed naturally from *Champion.* In another crucial respect, *Caminetti* went farther. The issue concerned the law of statutory interpretation, the often-arcane legal doctrine that determines how narrowly or broadly courts read the text of statutes (here, criminal statutes). *Caminetti*'s dissenters—the vote was five to three—argued that the phrase "any other immoral purpose" should be read in light of the statute's central goal: the suppression of coerced prostitution. At the very least, the dissenters maintained, the government should be required to prove that Mann Act defendants acted with the goal of making money, not merely with the goal of having sex.[40] That argument was true to the statute's history, though the law's language offered little support for it. The central question the case posed was whether a statute's purpose, together with sound criminal justice policy, trumped its text.

Today, the answer is clearly "no." Statutory purposes are not binding law; statutory texts are. A century ago, the answer was less clear.[41] American criminal codes were less code-like than other bodies of legislation:

often, criminal statutes simply repeated the common-law definition of the relevant class of criminal conduct, leaving both definition and development to the courts. A host of criminal statutes made no mention of criminal intent; courts nevertheless developed intent standards that were imposed in cases in which no statutory language invited the imposition. The same was true of defenses like duress, insanity, entrapment, and self-defense: all arose from judicial lawmaking, not the legislative kind. The making of American criminal law was a joint exercise; judges exercised as much lawmaking power as did legislators, possibly more. The notion that a broadly worded criminal statute like the Mann Act must be read precisely as written was, for most of American history, a foreign notion.

Caminetti helped to change that state of affairs. Not all at once: common-law development continued, in federal and (especially) state cases alike. But the trend toward greater deference to statutes' language, even when that language seemed to produce odd and harsh results, gradually captured first federal criminal law and then, over the balance of the twentieth century, state criminal law as well. *Caminetti* proved a harbinger of things to come.

That trend has had large consequences for American criminal law. In other fields, legislation is about tradeoffs and compromises. When writing and enacting criminal prohibitions, legislators usually ignore tradeoffs and rarely need to compromise. Save for law enforcement lobbies, few organized, well-funded interest groups take an interest in criminal statutes; criminal defendants' interests nearly always go unrepresented in legislative hallways. Legislators thus have little reason to focus carefully on the consequences of the prohibitions they write. That makes criminal legislation more a bidding war than an exercise in horse-trading, as a famous piece of narcotics legislation illustrates. In 1986, Congress enacted a statute fixing the sentence for possession of a single gram of crack cocaine at the level used to punish possession of a hundred grams of cocaine powder. In congressional debates preceding passage of the bill, one member proposed a weight/sentencing ratio of twenty to one; another suggested fifty to one. One hundred to one, the ratio finally enacted, was the highest anyone proposed.[42] Crack-powder legislation was the product of an auction, not a political compromise.

In such a system, laws like the Mann Act are natural. Judge-made law is different. Judges hear arguments from both sides, and they make law in the context of concrete cases in which the more-than-symbolic consequences of legal rules are clearer than in the abstract world of legislative drafting. *Caminetti* marked the beginning of the long decline of common-law crime definition. For the same reason, the case marked the rise of criminal prohibitions like the Mann Act itself: laws that criminalized far more conduct and authorized punishment of far more people than Congress's purposes could plausibly justify. A ban on coerced prostitution morphed into a ban on extramarital sex—as, later, bans on drug manufacture and distribution would morph into prohibitions of drug use and possession.

Narcotics

The chief drug war of the early twentieth century concerned alcohol, not any of the range of narcotics that so obsessed the late twentieth-century legal system. But early twentieth-century America had its own battle with several of those drugs, and that battle cast a long legal shadow: the character of today's drug law stems in large part from judicial decisions in that first fight against the evils of opium, cocaine, and their offshoots.

The legislation that defined that early drug war was the Harrison Act, passed in 1914. In part, the Act was a piece of domestic politics, as criminal prohibitions nearly always are. Voters on the West Coast increasingly feared the consequences of opium dens in Chinese neighborhoods; there was a good deal of political talk about the drug's tendency to enslave young white women.[43] (Once again, women's slavery was a rhetorical theme of turn-of-the-century culture wars.) At the same time, southern whites feared the allegedly widespread use of cocaine by southern blacks, which seemed to put Jim Crow's elaborate system of racial oppression at risk: coked-up blacks might refuse to submit to that degrading system.[44] One of these phenomena—the opium dens—was real enough; widespread cocaine use by blacks was more myth than fact. Myth or not, both phenomena made a federal drug ban politically possible.

International politics also played a role in the Act's passage. In the wake of the Spanish-American War, American military forces conquered the Philippines, leaving the United States responsible for that territory's thriving opium market. The United States was thereby drawn into international negotiations that sought to cabin the trade in opium and its derivatives, both in Asia and in the West.[45] Those negotiations, in turn, put pressure on Western governments to establish bans on the relevant drugs.

In other countries, enacting nationwide drug bans was a simple matter. Not so in the United States, where direct federal prohibition of the manufacture and sale of the relevant drugs was assumed to be unconstitutional. The vast majority of drug transactions occurred within the bounds of a single state; federal power to regulate interstate commerce did not extend to the regulation of intrastate manufacture and sale, even of dangerous goods like heroin and cocaine.[46] The fight against Mormon polygamy was not a useful model; Congress could more easily substitute its preferred law of domestic relations for that of Utah's territorial legislature than it could rewrite the law of marriage followed by dozens of *state* legislatures. Nor did federal anti-lottery laws offer a template for drug regulation. If lottery tickets could not be shipped by mail or train, the Louisiana lottery could not operate. Drugs crossed national and international borders through more varied means and were a good deal harder to identify, so bans on interstate shipment would accomplish little. Prostitutes conducted their business locally; they were not regularly crossing state borders. Consequently, the Mann Act forbade only a tiny fraction of transactions involving prostitution—again, an unhelpful precedent for federal drug law. Another regulatory approach was needed.

So Congress used its power to tax. Section One of the Harrison Act stated that all those who sell or distribute the relevant drugs "shall register with the collector of internal revenue of the [relevant] district," and required all such registrants to pay an annual tax of one dollar. Section Two was the Act's key provision; it specified that, some classes of government officials aside, only doctors acting "in the course of [their] professional practice" could prescribe such drugs, and pharmacies could sell them only pursuant to such prescriptions.[47] In other words, Section One stated that all sellers must register with the government and pay a modest tax, while Section Two decreed that few legal sellers could exist. The tax was a fig leaf—not a means of raising money but a cover for a bill that barred drug dealers, sellers of patent medicine, and most pharmacies from distributing opium and cocaine, and forbade doctors to do so absent medical necessity. By a 5–4 vote, the Supreme Court declared this ruse constitutional, finding that tax legislation "cannot be invalidated because of the supposed motives which induced it."[48] Form, not substance, controlled.

Two other legal challenges to the Harrison Act were more far reaching. The defendant in *United States v. Balint* (1922) claimed he could not be convicted of violating the Act when he did not know the character of the drugs he distributed.[49] The defendant in *United States v. Behrman* (1922) was a doctor who claimed that he acted in good faith when prescribing drugs for an addict.[50] The Act itself specified that criminal punishment was not to be imposed on doctors issuing prescriptions in the course of their medical practice. According to Behrman, that provision described his conduct precisely.

Balint's and Behrman's claims were legally strong. In *Balint*, Chief Justice Taft noted that "the general rule at common law was that scienter"—meaning criminal intent—"was a necessary element in the indictment and proof of every crime." Taft acknowledged that Balint had no such intent.[51] As for *Behrman*, Oliver Wendell Holmes's dissent in that case stated that denying Behrman's defense amounted to "constru[ing] the statute as creating a crime . . . without a word of warning."[52] That absence of fair warning is the key to both judicial decisions. One might suppose that a central condition of a free society is the ability to stay out of prison—to avoid trouble with the authorities if one is willing to comply with society's laws. *Balint* and *Behrman* made honest mistakes a precursor to prison terms, meaning that even those who *try* to comply with the law might face serious criminal punishment: hardly the mark of a just criminal justice system.

Why, then, did these two related claims lose? The answer was the same as in the polygamy and lottery cases: public necessity. Acknowledging the general requirement of proof of culpable intent, Chief Justice Taft's opinion in *Balint* went on to state that the requirement is suspended if its operation is sufficiently inconvenient to the government:

> While the general rule at common law was that [criminal intent] was
> a necessary element in the indictment and proof of every crime, . . .
> there has been a modification of this view in respect to prosecutions

under statutes the purpose of which would be obstructed by such a requirement.[53]

Such obstructed purposes were particularly common, Taft went on to note, "where the emphasis of the statute is evidently upon achievement of some social betterment rather than the punishment of the [relevant] crimes."[54] Notice the irony. When the government seeks to punish morally heinous conduct, it must prove that defendants acted intentionally. When the punished conduct is morally neutral—before the Harrison Act, sales of cocaine and opium were both legal and common—the government may dispense with proving intent on grounds of social need. It is precisely in cases in which criminal statutes seek "social betterment" that defendants are likeliest to commit crimes through innocent mistake. *That very likelihood,* Taft's Court held, justified the conviction and punishment of such defendants. The Harrison Act, the Justices concluded, was not a piece of ordinary criminal law; it was a species of public health regulation to which the principles that limit criminal punishment did not apply. The only limits that did apply were those that suited the government's convenience.

The government's convenience or, in the law's terms, public necessity—attacking the relevant conduct was important, so all legal steps to that end must be permissible—was the defining principle of the pre-Prohibition federal law of vice. Necessity in turn bred opacity. Federal criminal law increasingly became a game of bait and switch, with some federal powers used to evade restrictions on others, and with some defendants punished in order to ease the punishment of the relevant statutes' real targets. Shipping regulations were used to shut down the Louisiana lottery. The Mann Act used the power to regulate interstate travel as a means of criminally punishing immoral sex, and used the punishment of immoral sex as a substitute for punishing forced prostitution, which was the Act's real purpose. Congress having found that polygamy prosecutions were unwinnable, the Edmunds Act used unlawful cohabitation as a means of punishing plural marriage without the inconvenience of proving any marriages. In the most transparent dodge of all, the Harrison Act used

Congress's tax power to enact a federal ban on distribution of the covered drugs. The same Act dispensed with proof of culpable intent, and criminalized even good-faith mistakes by doctors if they fell outside Congress's or the courts' vision of medical necessity.[55]

Thanks to the manipulation of federal powers, as in the lottery laws and the Harrison Act, federal authority over drugs, gambling, and illicit sex—classically local issues all—was well established long before Franklin D. Roosevelt and the New Deal gave us a larger and more powerful federal government. The more important manipulation involved the definitions of the relevant crimes. The Edmunds Act, the Mann Act, the Harrison Act: all these pieces of federal legislation extended criminal liability beyond the conduct Congress sought to target, presumably to make punishing the targeted behavior a simpler task. Hard-to-prove crimes need not be a problem; the crimes could simply be redefined to make proof easier. If some undeserving defendants fell within the justice system's grasp, well, that was the price of effective legal regulation. There was all too little legal virtue in America's long battle against vice.

Prohibition

Prohibition is best known as the great disaster of American criminal justice: the "noble experiment"—Herbert Hoover's famous phrase[56]—that failed miserably, the metaphorical drug war that the nation not only lost but in which it surrendered the field. The story is familiar: omnipresent speakeasies and the federal agents who tried unsuccessfully to shut them down (Izzy Einstein and Moe Smith were the most famous at the time), Eliot Ness and his "untouchables" (better known today, thanks to Brian De Palma's movie), Al Capone and the St. Valentine's Day Massacre, the rise of Mafia-style organized crime, mass contempt for the law and ever-rising criminal violence. These were Prohibition's progeny, a legacy of crime and disrespect for legal institutions that scarred American government for a generation.

Much of that familiar story is wrong. Prohibition enjoyed more success than the standard line allows. Alcohol consumption fell dramatically in the early 1920s, and while it rebounded later that decade and in the early 1930s, even after Repeal consumption remained much lower than before the ban was enacted. Social workers observed sharp declines in domestic violence and abuse and substantial improvements in public health.[57] Factory workers drinking their weekly pay envelopes and starving their families became a less common phenomenon than before, partly because corner saloons were fewer and partly because the price of drinking was sharply higher. Before Prohibition, quarts of beer, gin, and whiskey cost 10¢, 95¢, and $1.60, respectively. According to one study, after the ban was in place those prices rose to 80¢, $5.90, and $4.00.[58] No wonder consumption fell.

The chief evidence for a Prohibition-induced rise in violent crime is an increase in the homicide rate in the 1920s and early 1930s, which was at least partly the consequence of the rising use of automobiles. Once vehicular homicide became a separate legal and statistical category, the rate of homicides by other means—the basis for today's homicide rate—returned to its previous level and declined further from there. Odds are, Prohibition was associated with some increase in criminal violence, but the increase was more modest than the conventional wisdom would have it. And violence against women and children went down, not up.[59]

As for growing disrespect for the law, that phenomenon was real, as a host of contemporary witnesses testified, but there is another side to the story. More so than any of the other vice wars of American history, past or present, Prohibition's legal design and enforcement *honored* the rule of law. For all the justified claims of enforcement bias, it bears emphasizing that the criminal law of alcohol was enforced, and seriously—especially by the federal government, which accounted for the largest share of the nation's prison population in history. In the mid-1920s, federal prosecutors charged a few hundred Mann Act cases per year and about the same number of regulatory crimes (violations of the Interstate Commerce Act, the Pure Food and Drug Law, and similar statutes). Federal prosecutors charged between 40,000 and 56,000 Prohibition cases per year, rising to nearly 66,000 by 1932. This constituted roughly two-thirds of federal criminal cases—both a larger absolute number, notwithstanding a tripling of the nation's population, and a larger share of federal criminal cases than drug cases occupy today.[60]

Federal law contained no legal ruses designed to establish federal power over traditionally local issues, as was true of the Harrison Act's

dollar-a-year tax on the distribution of opiates. A constitutional amendment explicitly vested concurrent power over the trade in alcoholic
beverages in state and federal governments. Nor did the Volstead Act,
the key federal statute on the subject, establish strategic crimes akin to the
Edmunds Act's offense of cohabitation, a more easily proved substitute
for multiple marriages. The law of Prohibition may have been foolish, but
it was also transparent, free of the game-playing that had characterized
the federal law of vice in the past.

Begin with the experiment's legal source. The Eighteenth Amendment banned "the manufacture, sale, or transportation of intoxicating
liquors within, the importation thereof into, or the exportation thereof
from the United States."[61] Notice what is missing: there is no provision
banning the possession or consumption of alcoholic beverages; only manufacture, sale, and transport (an adjunct to sale) are forbidden. Save for
provisions governing the use of alcohol as something other than a bev-
erage, the same was true of the Volstead Act, as the Supreme Court
unanimously held in a rare case brought for an allegedly illegal purchase.[62] The Act expressly exempted from its coverage the possession
and use of alcohol in private homes and its provision to "bona fide
guests." One more Volstead Act provision is worth noting here: doctors
were expressly allowed to prescribe alcohol as part of a treatment program for alcoholics.[63]

Today, simple possession of marijuana, cocaine, heroin, or any of a
long list of controlled substances can lead to a term in a nearby correctional facility, and there are no exemptions for home use, much less the
serving of illegal drugs to guests. In the 1920s, federal drug laws barred
prescribing narcotics for addicts.[64] Today's drug law is broader, barring
the prescription of marijuana to combat the nausea that attends most
cancer treatments.[65] In all these respects, federal legislation banning
alcohol—and most state legislation as well—was far more generous.

To use the terminology of the day, the Volstead Act was "bone dry" in
one important sense, but not in another. The Act criminalized the sale of
beer and wine as well as liquor; the ban applied to all products that contained more than a half-percent of alcohol, a small fraction of the percentage used in ordinary beer.[66] But the Act exempted simple possession, purchase, home use, medicinal use, and the use of alcohol in religious

worship. Likewise, the law of Prohibition showed greater respect for individual privacy than did, say, the Mann Act or than does contemporary drug law. As with all laws barring the sale or purchase of intoxicants, Prohibition could be enforced only through intrusive forms of police searches and seizures. Yet the intrusions were more limited than in contemporary drug cases, thanks to the Volstead Act's exemptions for purchase and home use, and thanks also to the broad exemption for medical treatment, which left a large range of doctor-patient interactions free from state scrutiny.

At a distance of eighty years it is impossible to be certain, but these doctrines likely had large political effects. Addicts and casual drinkers were not transformed into criminals, as are their counterparts in drug cases today. One could seek medical care for addiction without risking criminal punishment; likewise, one could take a drink from time to time without rendering oneself an outlaw, hence outside the range of legitimate public discussion. All of which made public debate freer and more open than debates about drug policy in our own time. In the last generation, the highest ranking public official to call for drug legalization was Baltimore Mayor Kurt Schmoke.[67] During the 1920s, leading national politicians like governors Al Smith of New York and Albert Ritchie of Maryland openly called for Prohibition's repeal.[68] Smith and Ritchie were both leading contenders for the Democratic presidential nomination in the 1920s and early 1930s; Smith won that nomination in 1928. No opponent of drug criminalization could have won a major-party presidential nomination in the 1980s or 1990s, at the height of the drug war. The robust debate about Prohibition's merits that Americans conducted in the 1920s and early 1930s has no counterpart in public discussion of drug policy over the past few decades.

It has few counterparts in American history. The ban on alcohol began with a constitutional amendment ratified by forty-six states, the product of a long-running national debate over the policy's merits.[69] Thirteen years later, another such debate led to another amendment repealing the earlier one—this time with thirty-eight states ratifying[70]—and returning power over the regulation of alcoholic beverages to state and local governments. Legal change was highlighted, not hidden. Public discussion was encouraged, not suppressed. Not since Reconstruction, and perhaps not even then, had Americans so openly debated the merits of criminal laws and punishments—and Reconstruction ended with a pair of Supreme Court decisions (*Cruikshank* and *Reese*), not with a democratically ratified constitutional amendment. Note the irony: Prohibition unraveled in part because the crime was defined more narrowly and because public debate about it was conducted more openly than with other anti-vice crusades. The crusade that was conducted with the greatest respect for its opponents is the one that failed most completely. Other, less respectful crusades have had much more staying power.

Open public debate, honest legal doctrine, and serious levels of enforcement were Prohibition's biggest virtues. But with serious enforcement came serious problems. In some jurisdictions, local law enforcement agencies initially played the largest role: in one nine-month period, the New York Police Department alone made 10,000 arrests for Prohibition violations[71]—at the time, considerably more than the total number of inmates imprisoned on Prohibition charges nationwide. That level of enforcement was self-defeating. Neither local nor federal justice systems were equipped to handle such large and sudden increases in criminal dockets: most defendants pled guilty and were let off with small fines or a few months in local jails. The consequence was that, through the mid-1920s, inmates incarcerated on alcohol charges were primarily found in local jails (40 per 100,000 population), not in state or federal prisons (3 or 4 per 100,000), and more than three-quarters of the prisoners were held by the states, not by the federal government. Later in the decade, as enforcement shifted from local police to federal agents and as federal sentences rose, those imprisoned on alcohol violations would rise to 14 per 100,000—two-thirds of them imprisoned on federal charges.[72] In much of the country, enforcement by state and local agencies all but ceased; New York, once so aggressive in enforcing the liquor ban, repealed its state enforcement statute in 1923.[73] More and more, Prohibition became what its supporters had strived to avoid: the job of federal officials, not the joint responsibility of all levels of government.

Inevitably, enforcement was biased. The Wickersham Commission, appointed by Hoover to study and report on Prohibition's progress, had this to say about the different treatment afforded upscale and downscale markets for alcohol:

> In the nature of things it is easier to shut up the open drinking places and stop the sale of beer, which was drunk chiefly by working men, than to prevent the wealthy from having and using liquor . . . in their clubs . . . [W]hen the industrial benefits of prohibition are pointed out, laboring men resent the insistence of employers who drink that their employees be kept from temptation . . .[74]

The best evidence suggests that beer consumption fell by more than two-thirds during the 1920s. Consumption of liquor fell substantially less.[75] If only because of the respective prices, beer was the working-class drink of choice; more upscale consumers drank cocktails. Beer's larger volume and lower price required larger physical plants, more elaborate transport, and more readily identified points of sale. Because liquor had the opposite characteristics, its sellers could afford—meaning, its wealthier customers would pay for—less easily detected forms of manufacture, transport, and sale. The market in which poor customers participated attracted a good deal of law enforcement attention. The market used by wealthier drinkers, much less so.

This class bias was no new phenomenon; it was and is a common feature of vice markets: wealthier customers pay for more discreet forms of the relevant vices and hence bear less risk of arrest and prosecution than their poorer counterparts. High-end call girls do business through individually arranged meetings; street hookers solicit customers in public. At the height of the late twentieth-century boom in crack cocaine, that drug was usually sold at fixed street corners in poor city neighborhoods. Cocaine powder was much more expensive, partly because its sales were individualized and took place at varied locations. The poorer portions of these markets inevitably see more arrests and prosecutions than do more upscale markets. At first blush, that is no bad thing. Poverty, violence, addiction, domestic abuse—all are the common side effects of lower-class vice markets. Such collateral damage is less prevalent among upper-class consumers, whose wealth gives them a greater margin for error, a capacity to live dissipated lives without disastrous consequences. If crack markets caused more social harm than markets for cocaine powder, one might suppose, those who trade in the more dangerous drug market should be punished more consistently and more severely than participants in the more benign market. If working-class consumption of alcohol caused more deprivation and violence than upscale consumption, punishing the former while giving the latter a pass seems more an instance of wise social policy than discriminatory enforcement.[76]

But that policy is, and was, at war with itself. Prohibition could succeed only if those who were its targets, or at least a sufficiently large fraction of them, agreed that buying and selling alcoholic beverages was wrong.[77] Enforcing the law only when the trade in alcohol led to collateral social harm sent the signal that the trade was wrong only when it caused such harm. Which, in turn, meant that drinking was wrong only when working-class consumers did it—hardly a credible moral message from those consumers' point of view.

Class bias has long infected the criminal law of prostitution, yet neither that body of law nor the federal Mann Act collapsed in response to public criticism of inconsistent enforcement. Similar persistent bias occurred with respect to the contemporary enforcement of drug laws where, in the 1990s and early 2000s, blacks constituted a minority of regular users of crack cocaine but more than 80 percent of crack defendants.[78] And by the 1920s, the enforcement of federal criminal law already involved a huge measure of selectivity. Think of the federal mail-fraud statute, enacted during Reconstruction, which criminalized all frauds in which the mails were used, and which defined "fraud" much more broadly than did the common law. Given the ease of proving use of the mails, federal mail fraud functioned as a generic federal fraud offense—an all-purpose white-collar crime—much as it does today. Yet fewer than 4 percent of early twentieth-century federal charges were for mail fraud; then as now, the overwhelming majority of frauds either were ignored or were left to local law enforcement.[79] There was no popular movement to undo the law of mail fraud due to its spotty enforcement.

Why was Prohibition different? Partly for the obvious reason: alcohol had long been an important part of both lower- and upper-class culture. Given that circumstance, large-scale opposition to the alcohol ban, even in the face of supermajority support for it, was a near certainty. But that was not the only reason—for it was Prohibition's supporters, not its opponents, who produced Repeal. The key moment came in the 1932 presidential election, an election dominated by two issues: the Great Depression, then nearing its bleakest period, and the status of Prohibition. In the battle for the 1932 Democratic presidential nomination, the leading "dry" candidate was New York Governor Franklin D. Roosevelt; his chief rival, 1928 nominee Al Smith, was the leading "wet." Roosevelt's base of support lay in the dry West and South. Smith's base was the wet Northeast. The convention that nominated Roosevelt by a two-thirds margin also voted overwhelmingly for Repeal.[80] In the general election against pro-Prohibition Herbert Hoover, Roosevelt switched sides and ran as the wet candidate—and defeated Hoover by a more than two-to-one margin in the West and South.[81] Repeal won because the large majority of dry America accepted it: in the Democratic convention, again in the general election, and yet again in the process by which thirty-eight states endorsed Prohibition's end. Evidently, a critical mass of dry voters preferred abandoning the national ban on alcoholic beverages to enforcing that ban in a manner that seemed at odds with the rule of law—a degree of commitment to equal justice that is, to put it charitably, lacking in our own time. Biased enforcement led not to long-term equilibrium, as with late twentieth-century drug enforcement, but to the undoing of the alcohol ban.

All of which makes Prohibition something other than the unmitigated disaster it is usually said to be. It seems closer to the truth to say that Prohibition was America's good culture war, one fought by democratic means with reasonably fair and open legal rules. Its enforcement was tilted both by class and by ethnicity—blacks were disproportionately targeted in the South, Italians in the North[82]—but no more so than drug enforcement is today, and with less severe sentences imposed on those who were convicted. Best of all, its resolution was more democratic and hence politically healthier than the outcomes of other culture wars, past and present alike. The battle over abortion has been resolved, for now at least, by judicial fiat: abortion became not a crime but a constitutional right because the Supreme Court said so in *Roe v. Wade* (1973).[83] The one-sided battle over drug law and enforcement has been resolved by tacit compromise: we have tough drug laws that are enforced aggressively in some neighborhoods and barely enforced at all in others. The battle over Prohibition was resolved by public persuasion: Americans saw the consequences of the dry experiment and changed their minds about its merits. Because they did so—because the crusade against alcoholic beverages failed—no such crusades would be fought by similar rules again. That was the noble experiment's saddest legacy.

After Repeal

Prohibition's defeat posed a serious problem for the pro–New Deal Democrats who controlled Congress, the White House, and most state governments in the 1930s, along with the progressive Republicans who were their sometime allies. Even after Repeal, crime remained a major political issue: this was an era of celebrity crimes (the Lindbergh baby's kidnapping) and celebrity criminals (John Dillinger, Baby Face Nelson, Bonnie Parker and Clyde Barrow, and the list goes on). Nominal homicide rates were high: more than 9 per 100,000 at the time of Repeal, comparable to the rates in the 1970s and early 1990s. As unions expanded in the wake of the Wagner Act, so did concern with labor violence and respect for private property. Frank Murphy, former Detroit mayor and the judge in the Ossian Sweet case, lost his 1938 bid for reelection as Michigan's governor because he was seen as too soft on sit-down strikers who occupied the factories where they worked.[84]

The New Dealers' response to other political issues was to centralize power in Washington. If ever there were a time when the federal government might have taken over the day-to-day work of criminal law enforcement, the 1930s was that time. But the takeover didn't happen. The federal government already *had* taken over the primary work of enforcing Prohibition, and the effort had not produced the desired results. By the time of the New Deal, centralized control had acquired a bad name in the realm of criminal justice; New Deal–era politicians had no stomach for another effort to nationalize street-level law enforcement. At the same time, those politicians did want to find ways to capitalize on public concern about crime. Reconciling those two preferences was not easy. How might one claim political credit for fighting crime without bearing responsibility if the fight fails? A pair of young men on the rise—FBI Director J. Edgar Hoover and Manhattan District Attorney Thomas E. Dewey—answered that question in the same manner at about the same time. Thus was born the modern politics of crime.

The solution was to go after not crimes but criminals: pick a few high-profile bad guys, then take them down as publicly as possible. Eventually, Hoover's FBI institutionalized that strategy with its Ten Most Wanted list, which became a fixture in American post offices and thereby in American culture.[85] (Hoover could have made a fortune in advertising.) Dewey was more successful still. An ambitious young lawyer on the make, he became America's first celebrity prosecutor—Rudy Giuliani, only bigger—by charging and convicting Richard Whitney, the disgraced head of the New York Stock Exchange, and Lucky Luciano, then New York's leading Mafia don. Those convictions made Dewey a national hero: *Time* put him on its cover in early 1937. By the summer of 1939—Dewey was then a 37-year-old local prosecutor who had never won an election outside Manhattan—he was the leading candidate to succeed Franklin D. Roosevelt in the White House, more popular than FDR himself.[86] But for Adolf Hitler, Whitney's and Luciano's convictions might have made Dewey president, eight years before his upset loss to Harry Truman. Dewey went on to serve three terms as New York's governor, win two Republican presidential nominations, and play a large role in winning another such nomination for his political ally Dwight Eisenhower.[87]

Other politicians noticed. In the late 1930s, William O. Douglas was an obscure academic (a redundancy) before Franklin Roosevelt made him chair of the Securities and Exchange Commission, a job Douglas used to undertake a very public crusade against alleged Wall Street speculators.[88] In 1950, Estes Kefauver was a first-term Senator from Tennessee known chiefly for his interest in antitrust policy. The Senate's Democratic leadership chose Kefauver to chair an investigation into links between organized crime and big-city Democratic machines, hoping to keep that investigation as low profile as possible. The leadership was sorely disappointed: the Kefauver Committee's hearings drew more television viewers than the World Series.[89] Wisconsin's Joe McCarthy was another unknown first-term Senator in search of an issue when he gave his February 1950 speech accusing the Truman State Department of employing dozens of Communist spies: a false charge that McCarthy made repeatedly, each time reaping another crop of national news headlines.[90] Before the hearings conducted by the Senate Rackets Committee in 1959, Robert Kennedy was an anonymous Senate staffer, best known as the younger brother of the junior Senator from Massachusetts. As the committee's lead counsel, Kennedy used those hearings to build a reputation as the dogged investigator who exposed Jimmy Hoffa and his mobbed-up Teamsters union.[91]

These practitioners of the symbolic politics of crime were Dewey's descendants, Hoover's heirs. Douglas and McCarthy, Kefauver and Kennedy won fame and power not by fighting crime but by talking about it. Politically, the tactic worked. Douglas became the youngest Supreme Court justice since Joseph Story and was nearly chosen as FDR's running mate in 1944, and hence nearly became president when FDR died the next year.[92] In the 1952 New Hampshire primary, Kefauver beat the man who did succeed FDR, knocking incumbent Harry Truman out of that year's presidential race. Kennedy became Attorney General in his brother's administration partly thanks to the reputation he made in the Hoffa hearings.[93] McCarthy, a dissolute drunk, was for a few years among the most powerful men in the United States.

Taken together, these creative politicians changed the governance of America's justice system. Before Hoover and Dewey, the politics of crime mostly resembled the politics of fixing potholes: local voters governed local officials who administered the relevant government services locally. State legislators and members of Congress were small players: with few exceptions, substantive criminal law was not the subject of high-profile legislation. The vice crusades of the late nineteenth and early twentieth centuries began to change that state of affairs. After Prohibition's end, the phenomenon grew more widespread, extending to crimes that had nothing to do with polygamy and prostitution, lotteries and liquor. Hoover's and Dewey's political progeny helped to nationalize the politics of crime.

Kefauver's hearings were the most obvious example. Kefauver took his committee on the road, visiting fourteen cities. The hearings exposed some sordid stories. In Kansas City, home of the old Pendergast machine that had launched President Truman's political career, the committee explored the murder of Charles Binaggio, a mobster who had helped bankroll Missouri Governor Forrest Smith, only to have Smith turn on him once in office. Prosecutors were closing in on Binaggio when he was gunned down by rivals.[94] In Chicago, too, a badly timed murder attracted public attention: a former city detective who planned to testify was killed just as the victim was placed under federal protection. One witness who *did* testify was Chicago's Democratic candidate for sheriff. A career investigator for the state's attorney's office, his net worth was over $300,000, a very large sum in those days. Implausibly, he claimed to have made his money speculating on grain futures.[95]

The New York hearings attracted the most attention. The star witness was Frank Costello, then the head of the Gambino "family." Costello had placed a condition on his testimony: the cameras had to stay away from his face. It was a poor deal for Costello. The TV cameras focused on his hands; the result was, as one writer puts it, "superb theater: tense dialogue accompanied by clenched hands, fingers drumming the table top" and "nervous hands ripping sheets of paper to shreds."[96] When the questioning got tougher than Costello had expected, he walked out— while 30 million Americans watched.[97] Former New York City Mayor Bill O'Dwyer testified about his decisions to appoint Costello's friends to key city boards and about the influence Costello's money bought. One incident attracted particular notice: in the early 1940s, when O'Dwyer had been Brooklyn's district attorney, a key witness in one of his murder investigations, Abe Reles, fell (or was pushed) to his death from his hotel room. All six of the police officers assigned to protect Reles claimed to have fallen asleep.[98]

Even in the cities in which it was most active, the Mob was a small issue for most residents. Nevertheless, mobsters like Costello and his political allies like O'Dwyer captivated the public that tuned in to Kefauver's hearings. Political context likely had more than a little to do with that public reaction. Seven months before the hearings began, China had fallen to Mao's Communists. Three months later, Joe McCarthy accused the State Department of harboring dozens of Communist agents. One month after Kefauver's hearings began, the North Korean army invaded South Korea. Over the course of the next year, the public learned that Merl Young, a Truman friend who worked for the Reconstruction Finance Corporation, had received a mink coat for his wife with money paid him for arranging an RFC loan to a friendly business. Soon after the Young story broke, viewers watched Costello and O'Dwyer testify. These stories reinforced one another, blended together in the public mind. All were about misplaced loyalty—to mobsters, to foreign powers and ideologies, to government officials' own financial well-being. In a political atmosphere like that, Kefauver's hearings resonated.

As Kefauver's career shows, members of the government's executive branch were not the only politicians eager to use symbols to capitalize on public interest in crime. Legislators played the same game. The 1932 Lindbergh kidnapping prompted a federal kidnapping statute, just as the rise of celebrity gangsters led to the Anti-Racketeering Act barring extortion and the National Firearms Act banning possession of machine guns, both enacted in 1934.[99] (Notice that, though the Firearms Act was designed to punish gangsters who *used* such weapons to commit their crimes, the Act criminalized mere possession.) The Kefauver hearings prompted passage of a federal statute banning the possession of machines used for gambling where the machines had crossed state lines. A few years later, Congress enacted the Travel Act, barring (among other things) crossing state lines with the mere intent to violate state gambling prohibitions.[100] These pieces of federal legislation were not designed to stamp out kidnapping or gambling or to regulate the firearms trade; rather, they were tools used to exploit the publicity surrounding famous crimes like Bruno Hauptmann's—convicted of kidnapping and killing the Lindberghs' infant son—and famous criminals like John Dillinger and Frank Costello.

Over time, state legislators came to embrace the same practice, as shown by the wave of anti-carjacking laws that followed a famous Maryland crime in the early 1990s.[101] Carjacking consisted of a combination of auto theft, kidnapping, and sometimes murder—all of which were crimes in every state before Pamela Basu's death. Anti-carjacking statutes were not a means of defining some new crime; the crimes were old ones and were already on the books. Rather, those statutes were designed to permit the legislators who enacted them to take credit for doing something about salient crimes like Basu's murder.

Sometimes such laws turn out to be purely symbolic: three years after it was enacted, the federal Violence Against Women Act of 1994 produced zero criminal prosecutions nationwide.[102] Whatever is true of the *law* of domestic violence, *enforcement* of that body of law remains a matter for state and local officials. Often, though, symbolic politics produces more than political symbols. New criminal prohibitions, even ones that overlap existing laws, give prosecutors more cards to play in plea bargaining sessions, and thereby give jurors fewer opportunities to exercise the discretion that characterized criminal justice during the Gilded Age. As those things happened ever more often beginning in the 1930s, power over American criminal justice—at least the power to manipulate political symbols—gradually shifted from the local communities where crimes took place, to the voters who elected the legislators who enacted these not-quite-symbolic criminal prohibitions.

Geography

To put the point another way, Hoover, Dewey, Kefauver, and their many imitators helped to change crime's political geography. Most crimes belong to the neighborhoods where they happen; outsiders to those neighborhoods have little stake in the relevant case outcomes. Politically speaking, criminal charges brought against high-profile defendants like Bruno Hauptmann and Frank Costello—or, more recently, O. J. Simpson and Bernard Madoff—belong to everyone. The vice wars of the late nineteenth and early twentieth centuries made for more such cases, and thereby invited voters in America's small towns and countryside to weigh in on the character and consequences of crime outside their own jurisdictions, chiefly in America's cities. State and national politicians learned a crucial lesson: they could win votes in some places by attacking crime in others. State legislators and members of Congress, governors and even presidents— soon after Robert Kennedy's brother won the White House, the new administration announced its legislative agenda on crime[103]—increasingly took political ownership of crime and punishment.

As the geography of crime's politics grew more expansive, the geography of crime itself grew more concentrated. For most of American history, New York City's homicide rate was lower than the rate for the nation as a whole. Beginning in the 1950s, that ceased to be so; by 1980, New York's rate was two-and-a-half times the nation's, even though the national rate had more than doubled in twenty years. More and more, violent crime was becoming an urban phenomenon. (Today, the opposite trend has taken hold; in many metropolitan areas, high rates of violent crime have spread to working-class suburbs.) Crime was concentrated *within* cities as well: by midcentury, the black homicide rate had reached ten times the rate among whites, meaning that the growing black neighborhoods in northern cities were much more crime ridden than the wealthier and whiter neighborhoods in those cities.[104]

As their share of urban crime grew, those same black neighborhoods' power over urban law enforcement remained modest at best. Beginning in the 1940s, as the black population of northern and some southern cities was exploding, so was the population of the white suburbs surrounding those cities. Both local district attorneys and trial judges are elected countywide in the United States; metropolitan counties typically include both cities and close-in suburbs. The suburban share of those counties' populations rose sharply in the generation after the war—and cities' share declined. In 1940, Chicagoans were 70 percent of the population of the Chicago metropolitan area; by 1960 their share had fallen to 57 percent, by 1980 to 42 percent. During the same years, Cleveland's percentage of its metropolitan population fell from 69 to 49, then to 30. Detroit's fell from 68 to 44, then to 28.[105] Wherever counties included both urban and suburban voters, the mix of those two categories changed: suburban voters grew more numerous, and city voters less so.[106] White suburbanites' power over local prosecutors and trial judges grew, even as those officials focused a larger share of their attention on crime in urban black communities.

Even in cities that are independent entities—cities that do not belong to the same county as neighboring suburbs—a version of the same phenomenon happened, as the crime gap between poor black neighborhoods and rich white ones grew ever larger. (Recall Chicago's Hyde Park and Washington Park: the latter's homicide rate is 26 times the former's.) Criminal law enforcement is redistributive; its benefits go disproportionately to the poor but are paid for disproportionately by the rich. At a time when middle- and upper-class whites were already heading for the suburbs, cash-strapped cities could not afford to give them greater incentives to do so. Low-crime white neighborhoods in cities thus enjoyed more political power than numbers alone would have given them. Black neighborhoods enjoyed less, and still do.

Of course, white residents of metropolitan areas had always governed their black neighbors, even in the North: recall that Ossian Sweet was freed by a white lawyer, white jurors, and a white judge. Before the mid–twentieth century, though, that fact had smaller effects on northern criminal justice than one might suppose. Black neighborhoods accounted for a small fraction of northern cities' populations. The neighborhoods that dominated urban crime—working-class white neighborhoods, mostly European immigrants and their offspring—also governed urban policing and, to a large degree, urban criminal justice generally. The lenient doctrines and practices used in blue-collar white neighborhoods spilled over to urban blacks. The growth of large, high-crime black neighborhoods in northern cities, along with the coincident explosion of white suburbs surrounding those cities, made that egalitarian equilibrium impossible to maintain.

Two signs of that changed reality were the swift rise in the nation's prison population in the years after Repeal—on top of a steep rise during Prohibition—and a steady increase in the black percentage of that prison population. Figure 5 shows the first trend. The increase peaked in 1939, the year World War II began; Congress enacted a draft the next year. As the number of young men in the custody of the army grew, the imprisonment rate fell—then, after the war's end, resumed its rise more slowly. And as the number of prisoners grew, the black share of the prison population grew with it. Between 1923 and 1960, while whites' imprisonment rates rose by 20 percent, the black imprisonment rate more than doubled.[107] The lenient and modestly egalitarian justice system of the Gilded Age was at an end.

Not coincidentally, so was neighborhood control over urban criminal justice. Even as national politicians were absorbing a larger share of crime's political oxygen, white suburbanites' power grew at the expense of black city-dwellers, thereby changing the *local* politics of crime. In a low-crime era—nationally, the years following World War II saw the lowest homicide rates in American history—voters in safe white urban and suburban neighborhoods paid little attention to local criminal law enforcement. Less voter interest meant that, for a time, the localized justice system that governed most criminal cases increasingly fell outside politicians' field of vision. The day-to-day work of policing and prosecution came to be the job of technocrats. Police forces grew less politicized and more professionalized.[108] Local prosecutors and judges (at least the less

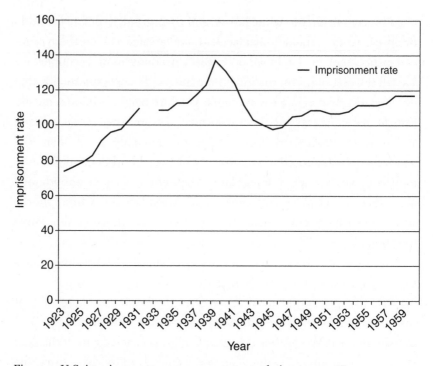

Figure 5. U.S. imprisonment rate per 100,000 population, 1923–1960
Online Sourcebook, table 6.28.2009.

politically entrepreneurial ones) paid less attention to local voters, and more to the norms of the legal profession to which they belonged. Legislators revising state criminal codes listened less to their constituents, who weren't saying much, and more to academic law reformers—experts in criminal justice who drafted a model criminal code designed to replace messier, inexpertly drafted state codes.

These professionals and experts changed the justice system almost entirely for the worse. Professionalized police forces grew detached from the neighborhoods they patrolled, especially so as foot patrols were replaced by officers in cars. By the 1960s, enough northern prosecutors and judges doubted the legitimacy or effectiveness of criminal punishment to cause their states' prison populations to shrink significantly even as crime spiraled upward.[109] The law professors who wrote the Model Penal Code helped to replace a system of legal doctrine that worked with one that didn't; the same is true of the Supreme Court Justices who crafted a new body of federal constitutional law to govern criminal procedure. Just as Prohibition had given centralized control of criminal justice a bad name, so too the apolitical, expert-based criminal justice of mid–twentieth century America gave expertise a bad name—a lesson voters would remember when, beginning in the late 1960s, an angrier style of politics seized control of the system.

CHAPTER 7

Constitutional Law's Rise:
Three Roads Not Taken

> The State is free to regulate the procedure of its courts in accordance
> with its own conceptions of policy, unless in doing so it offends some
> principle of justice so rooted in the traditions and conscience of our
> people as to be ranked as fundamental.
>
> —Chief Justice Charles Evans Hughes, writing
> in *Brown v. Mississippi* (1936)

IN THE WAKE OF AMERICA'S FIRST GREAT CULTURE WAR, another
legal trend took hold: the rise of the law of constitutional criminal
procedure. That body of constitutional law was different than the body
of law that produced Supreme Court decisions like *Reynolds v. United
States* or *Champion v. Ames*—cases that posed the question whether Congress could legitimately criminalize defendants' behavior. Twentieth-
century constitutional law posed another question: May the government
investigate, try, and punish crime *in this manner?* The focus was on procedure, not substance—on the ways in which local police officers, prosecutors, and trial judges did their jobs, not on the character of the conduct
those local officials sought to punish.

The rise of that proceduralist body of constitutional law had a long
and slow history, composed of two distinct threads. First came a series
of federal cases elaborating on the Fourth Amendment's ban on "unreasonable searches and seizures"—then applicable only to federal agents,
not to state and local police.[1] These cases offered broad protection for

targets of police attention so long as the police in question worked for the federal government. The second thread arose from the Jim Crow South, where midcentury state courts sometimes allowed legal processes that amounted to little more than judicially sanctioned lynchings. The Supreme Court tried but largely failed to put a stop to those instances of thinly veiled mob rule. In the process, the Court made a small but significant body of due process doctrine that applied to local police and prosecutors and to state courts, including officials and courts outside the South. In the 1960s, the two threads merged: the Supreme Court crafted a series of (mostly) Bill of Rights–based rules that applied to state and local officials, not just federal ones.

Federal Procedure

The federal cases began in 1886 with *Boyd v. United States*.[2] Boyd was a dishonest importer of glass to be used in some federal government buildings; his contract allowed him to bring some of the glass into the country tax-free. According to Boyd, early shipments suffered a lot of breakage—which, if true, entitled him to skip paying taxes on later shipments. The relevant government officials disbelieved Boyd's claim. So the government moved to seize a batch of recently imported glass; in order to make its forfeiture case, the government subpoenaed invoices on an earlier batch. Boyd complained that the subpoena was an unreasonable search in violation of the Fourth Amendment and amounted to compelled self-incrimination in violation of the Fifth. The lower court rejected the claim and ordered Boyd to produce the invoices, which supported the government's fraud claim. Notwithstanding Boyd's fraud and in a ringing opinion about the need to protect "the sanctity of a man's home and the privacies of life," the Supreme Court reversed.[3] Because the invoices were papers and because they belonged to Boyd, federal officers were not allowed even to see them, much less to seize them.

Notice the nature of the Court's decision. The point was not to protect innocents from unmerited punishment—Boyd was a tax cheat. Technically, the case against him was not even criminal; the government sought to take possession of the allegedly broken glass, not to put Boyd in prison for lying about it. Nor was the Court's goal to see to it that Boyd was treated fairly, that he was represented by counsel and given an adequate opportunity to defend himself. Rather, the point of the decision was to protect Boyd's privacy.

The protection was stunningly broad. Had the Court's decision survived intact, searches for and orders to produce documents would have been barred almost across the board. The twentieth-century rise of the federal regulatory state, including much of the New Deal, would have been impossible given such a doctrine. So the same Court that issued the decision later cabined it. In *Hale v. Henkel* (1906), the Justices held that *Boyd*'s protection did not extend to corporations or corporate documents, and that the government's subpoena power was a good deal broader than *Boyd* suggested.[4] In *Marron v. United States* (1927), the Court held that *Boyd*'s ban did not apply to materials used to commit crimes, including in that case a ledger with accounts receivable for an illegal liquor business.[5] *Shapiro v. United States* (1948) allowed the government to obtain records that the law required one to keep.[6] Boyd's claim would have lost had it arisen after *Marron* and *Shapiro* instead of before.

And that was not all: in *Olmstead v. United States* (1928) the Court decided, over strong dissents by Justices Holmes and Brandeis, that wiretaps did not constitute "searches" under the Fourth Amendment.[7] Under *Olmstead,* one's conversations received less constitutional protection than one's papers. So long as they could install the relevant devices without trespassing on suspects' property, federal agents could tap suspects' phone lines whenever they wished—a legal proposition that remained true until the late 1960s.[8]

Hale, Marron, Shapiro, and *Olmstead* have fooled some legal scholars (I was one of them)[9] into thinking that pre-1960s federal law offered only modest protection against aggressive police search tactics. The truth is otherwise. Even given these decisions, Fourth Amendment regulation of federal policing was both extensive and more than modestly protective of search targets.[10] Here are a few examples: *Weeks v. United States* (1914) established what became known as the "exclusionary rule"—the doctrine that evidence obtained in violation of the Fourth Amendment cannot be used in criminal prosecutions of suspects who were illegally searched.[11] In *Gouled v. United States* (1921), the Court barred searches for "mere evidence": unless the evidence in question was either contraband or was used to commit the relevant crime, the police were not permitted to look for it.[12] In *Gouled,* that meant incriminating documents could not be used against the defendant in a fraud case—even though documents are often the key evidence in fraud cases.

Weeks meant that federal criminal litigation would uneasily balance two quite different agendas: determining whether the defendant committed the crime charged, and judging whether the federal agents who investigated that crime behaved properly. *Gouled* meant that, where Fourth Amendment law applied, those federal agents would operate under serious restrictions. Oddly, *Olmstead* shows just how serious: had the wiretap in that case been deemed a Fourth Amendment "search," it would have been forbidden even if the search had been justified by probable cause and preceded by a warrant. The conversations the agents recorded were "mere evidence," hence not proper targets of police searches.[13] *All* electronic surveillance, however well justified, would have been barred. This helps explain the Court's ruling in *Olmstead:* as between banning and permitting all such surveillance, the ban must have seemed dangerous, even for a Court that was generally protective of civil liberties.

And the Court *was* protective of civil liberties: *Weeks* and *Gouled* were not alone, as a trio of cases from Prohibition's last days suggest. Since colonial times, officers have had the power to search the defendant's person and the place where he was arrested, including his home if that was the site of the arrest.[14] *United States v. Lefkowitz* (1932) sharply limited that power. Lefkowitz, a middleman in a liquor distribution system, was arrested in his office. Federal agents searched closed desk drawers, and seized books and papers found in them. The Supreme Court held that the search-incident-to-arrest went too far.[15] In *Grau v. United States* (1932), federal agents searched for and seized evidence of large-scale manufacture of whiskey in the defendant's home.[16] Federal legislation held that searches of private homes were permissible only where the police were seeking evidence of sale, not just manufacture. The lower court held that the quantities involved made it clear that the manufacture in *Grau* was done for the purpose of sale, not for private consumption. The Supreme Court reversed: evidence of manufacture was not an adequate basis for the search, regardless of the size of the manufacturing operation.[17]

Sgro v. United States (1932) was the most telling of these three Prohibition-era decisions because the alleged constitutional violation was so minor. In *Sgro*, a warrant was issued to search a hotel bar operated by the defendant; the warrant specified that the search must happen within ten days of its issuance. Three weeks later, not having conducted the search, officers returned to the federal commissioner (today he would be called a magistrate) who signed the warrant; the commissioner reissued the warrant under a new date. Not good enough, the Supreme Court held: the commissioner should have explicitly found that the supporting affidavits still justified the search, instead of so finding implicitly. Even if those affidavits *did* justify the later search, that search was invalid.[18]

Taken together, the cases offer surprisingly broad protection against allegedly unreasonable searches by federal officials. One leading scholar of the period calls Prohibition enforcement "repressive,"[19] a word that captures the conventional wisdom fairly well. But the conventional wisdom gets it wrong; enforcement was both more restrictive and more respectful of the privacy of search targets than is enforcement of contemporary drug laws—partly because Fourth Amendment standards were, for the most part, stricter then than now. *Olmstead* was the exception; *Lefkowitz, Grau,* and *Sgro* the norm.

Three more propositions about these Prohibition-era federal search and seizure cases seem clear. First, the defendants in several of these cases were a good deal wealthier than typical criminal defendants. Olmstead ran a $2 million a year liquor business, and Grau's home was large enough to accommodate a major manufacturing operation.[20] Few defendants have such resources. Second, the cases bore little resemblance to ordinary criminal cases. There were no murders, rapes, or robberies among them, naturally, as local police and local prosecutors were responsible for investigating those crimes and prosecuting the offenders. Federal criminal cases offered more exotic fare. Third, the Prohibition cases involved a crime that would soon be repealed.[21] If the law of search and seizure made it difficult to enforce the Volstead Act, that was no big deal—soon there would be no Volstead Act to enforce.

All of which means the stakes in these cases were small. Whether federal agents and prosecutors were able to punish a modest number of well-off defendants charged with liquor offenses mattered little even while Prohibition lasted. It mattered not at all once Prohibition fell. And the cases were poor proxies for the kinds of prosecutions that did matter. Violent felonies and felony thefts raise different issues than liquor cases; the police use different tactics when investigating these very different crimes. It would constitute the sheerest chance if legal rules that had been made for a few unusual alcohol cases worked well in the mass of more ordinary criminal investigations—conducted by local police, not by federal agents.

The Constitution and Jim Crow

The second line of cases was very different from the first. Instead of federal cases of white-collar crime or alcohol violations, these were rape or murder cases decided, in the first instance, in state courts. Not just any state courts: these were cases from the South, and they captured the kind of justice early- to mid-twentieth-century southern courts afforded southern blacks. Four of the five cases to be discussed yielded Supreme Court decisions that regulated state-court criminal justice on behalf of southern black defendants. The fifth involved not a black defendant but a black crime victim; the Supreme Court never saw the case. All five showed the national court system's ineffective responses (or lack thereof) to claims by blacks seeking protection from Jim Crow justice. In each, the legal system came close, sometimes tantalizingly so, to offering something larger and better. In each, the opportunity was missed—hence the pressure on Earl Warren's Supreme Court to embrace more aggressive reforms.

The first case arose in Phillips County, Arkansas, site of one of the deadliest episodes of racial violence in American history. Legal historian Michael Klarman tells the story:

> [B]lack tenant farmers and sharecroppers . . . tried to organize a union and to hire white lawyers to sue planters for [the tacit enslavement of black farm workers]. Local whites cracked down with a vengeance. When whites shot into a church where black unionists were meeting, blacks returned the gunfire. A white man was killed. Mayhem quickly ensued. Marauding whites . . . supported by federal

troops ostensibly dispatched to quell the [disturbance] went on a rampage. They tracked down blacks throughout the countryside and killed dozens of them. Seventy-nine blacks, and no whites, were prosecuted and convicted for their actions during this "race riot," and twelve received the death penalty . . . Huge mobs of angry whites surrounded the courthouse, menacing the defendants and the jurors and threatening a lynching.[22]

The defendants in the Phillips County case rightly argued that the threatened lynching turned the trial into the functional equivalent of a real lynching, with a thin veneer of legal procedure to hide the injustice: a criminal trial as Potemkin village.[23] Arkansas state courts rejected the argument.

When the case made its way to the Supreme Court in *Moore v. Dempsey* (1923), the Justices agreed with the defendants. Oliver Wendell Holmes's majority opinion noted that "mere mistakes of law" in state-court cases were not for the Supreme Court to correct. But, in Holmes's words, "if . . . the whole proceeding is a mask—[if] counsel, jury and judge were swept to the fatal end by an irresistible wave of public passion," the resulting trial violated due process.[24] Elsewhere in his opinion, Holmes noted that the trial lasted forty-five minutes, and that the jury returned its guilty verdict after fewer than five minutes' deliberation. Defense counsel was assigned the same day as the trial; counsel had no opportunity to meet with the defendants, called no defense witnesses, and made no motion for change of venue: all signs of a rigged legal process.[25] Yet the winning argument in *Moore* rested on none of these procedural failings. Instead, the winning claim rested largely on what happened outside the courtroom, where a lynch mob stood ready to take justice in its own hands in the unlikely event of an acquittal or a hung jury.

The decades after *Moore* saw more mob-dominated southern trials, but few *Moore*-like appellate reversals. *Moore* evolved into a modest requirement that, in cases that raised a sufficiently strong public outcry, trial courts should grant defense motions for change of venue—a requirement that applied only intermittently in the South, where such motions were most needed.[26] The Supreme Court's decision in *Moore* failed even to put an end to proceedings like the one in *Moore,* much less usher in any deeper change in appellate review of criminal convictions.

The Court's two decisions in the famous Scottsboro Boys cases had larger legal effects but similarly small practical ones. The defendants were nine black youths charged with raping two white women, both suspected prostitutes, on a freight train that carried them from Tennessee to Alabama. The government's evidence consisted mainly of the alleged victims' testimony, which one of the two women recanted after the first round of trials. (Both had good reason to lie: otherwise, they might face federal Mann Act charges for crossing a state line with the intent to commit acts of prostitution.) One defendant's case ended in a mistrial—a portion of the jury insisted on a death sentence, even though the prosecutor had not asked for one. The rest were convicted and sentenced to death. As in *Moore,* a lynch mob surrounded the courthouse. Also as in *Moore,* defense counsel was assigned on the morning when the trials began; counsel was given no opportunity to prepare a defense before the defendants were tried.[27]

Twice, the Supreme Court overturned the convictions and death sentences. In *Powell v. Alabama* (1932), the Justices held that the same-day provision of counsel in a capital case violated due process.[28] After another round of convictions and death sentences—and after one of the complaining witnesses, Ruby Bates, disavowed her earlier testimony—the Court reversed again in *Norris v. Alabama* (1935), this time on the ground that blacks had been excluded from the pool of local residents from which the juries were chosen.[29] Throughout this saga, the Scottsboro cases attracted international publicity. By the time the decision in *Norris* was handed down, public opinion outside the South held, almost certainly correctly, that the defendants were innocent.[30] Even so, Alabama prosecutors stubbornly continued to prosecute, Alabama juries stubbornly continued to convict, and Alabama appellate courts stubbornly continued to affirm the inevitable convictions. All the defendants who were initially sentenced to death were spared execution—but all served substantial prison terms.[31]

Like *Moore* only more clearly so, *Powell* and *Norris* turned cases of clear substantive injustice into vehicles for the vindication of procedural rights. Also like *Moore,* the procedural rights in question seemed designed to ensure fairer and more accurate adjudication: trials dominated by lynch mobs are unlikely to quibble over the defendants' guilt; trial outcomes are not to be trusted where the defense counsel lack time to prepare their case; juries stacked against defendants are prone to deliver unfair guilty verdicts. Even so, the procedures in question were not enough to remedy the injustice that prompted them. The Scottsboro Boys got higher quality and better prepared counsel in their retrials, but better lawyers were no obstacle to a second and third round of convictions.[32] Just as *Moore* did not put a stop to mob-dominated trials, neither did *Norris* end the selection of all-white juries, which remained near-universal in the Deep South for a generation longer and common for a generation after that.[33]

The proceduralism of *Powell* and *Norris* barely touched the racism that dominated the Scottsboro trials. *Powell*'s right-to-counsel ruling had an abstract quality; it seemed disconnected from the racial injustice that must have prompted the Supreme Court to hear the case. *Norris* was better on that score, for the decision rested squarely on race discrimination in jury selection. But that was a small part of the racism that underpinned the Scottsboro Boys' guilty verdicts. Only black men charged with raping white women were convicted on the alleged victims' say-so, and only they faced the death penalty for sexual assault,[34] two propositions that played no role in either of the Court's Scottsboro decisions. Judicial review in the Scottsboro cases was a sterile, formal exercise.

But if *Powell* and *Norris* lacked a sense of substantive justice, they had one key advantage, an advantage that gave them a measure of legal staying power. *Powell* and *Norris* enforced guarantees that appear in the federal Bill of Rights. Were the Bill enforced in state courts, as it soon would be, the two decisions could easily have been grounded in the Sixth Amendment's guarantees of "the assistance of counsel" and of trial by a fairly selected jury.[35] The Scottsboro cases were precursors of the 1960s decisions applying an expanded version of the Bill of Rights to state and local governments.

The fourth case in the progression was *Brown v. Mississippi* (1936).[36] Along with two fellow sharecroppers, Ed Brown was charged with killing his white landlord. The local deputy sheriff beat the defendants until they confessed to the crime; in the state-court proceedings, the deputy admitted the beatings, noting only that they were "not too much for a Negro." The confessions were the key evidence against the defendants. Though torture-induced confessions had led the Mississippi Supreme Court to overturn convictions of blacks for killing whites in the past, that court affirmed the defendants' convictions. The federal Supreme Court reversed, holding that the admission into evidence of involuntary confessions violates the Fourteenth Amendment's due process clause.[37] (The Justices might have used the Fifth Amendment's ban on compelled self-incrimination instead, but that provision had been held not to apply to the states, and a long legal tradition held that the privilege against self-incrimination applied to in-court proceedings, not to police questioning.)[38]

Brown was an easy case. It was also unusually productive: over the next thirty years, the Supreme Court reversed dozens of convictions in response to claims that the defendant's confession was obtained by force rather than by persuasion—a far larger body of case law than *Moore, Powell,* or *Norris* spawned over the same time period.[39] Yet cases like *Brown* persisted because the application of *Brown*'s rule depended on a measure of honesty from the police officers who behaved coercively and from the state court judges who, in the first instance, passed judgment on the officers' interrogation tactics. Had the deputy in *Brown* denied torturing the defendants and had the trial judge purported to believe the denial, the Supreme Court would have been effectively barred from intervening. Absent better evidence than the testimony of the key actors, *Brown*'s application boiled down to swearing contests between criminal defendants and the officers who apprehend them. The police tended to win such contests, and still do.

Two more features of *Brown* are worth noting here. First, the Court's standard called on trial judges to consider all relevant circumstances: anything that bore on the question whether the defendant voluntarily confessed was relevant to the defendants' claim. *Brown* fell far short of a guarantee of fair treatment by the police, but the decision seemed to point in that direction. Second, though Ed Brown and his codefendants may well have been innocent—certainly their confessions do not prove otherwise, given the manner in which those confessions were obtained— the Supreme Court's ruling applied regardless of defendants' guilt.

Brown did not require that confessions produced by physical force (later, the Court would add psychological pressure to the list of forbidden interrogation tactics, if the pressure was sufficient to overbear the suspect's will)[40] be barred from evidence absent strong corroboration. Such confessions were barred, period. In *Brown,* this was a meaningless distinction: such brutal treatment was bound to elicit false confessions. In later years, as *Brown*'s ban of coerced confessions extended to more subtle forms of coercion, it would not be so.

The fifth case did not lead to any appellate rulings. It began with a violation of the South's unwritten racial code by one who did not understand that code. It ended with a mutilated corpse, an acquittal, and a magazine article.

On July 25, 1955, Emmett Till turned fourteen.[41] He lived in Chicago with his mother; three weeks after his birthday, she put him on a train to Memphis so that he could visit his cousins in rural Mississippi while she took a vacation. Till was not tall—five feet four or five inches—but he was stocky, weighing in at 160 pounds; his size probably made him appear older than he was. He talked older, too, and a great deal more boldly than the black population of Mississippi was accustomed to. On August 24, a Saturday, he and some friends were hanging around outside Bryant's Grocery and Meat Market in the inaptly named small town of Money, Mississippi. A young white couple named Roy and Carolyn Bryant ran the store. That evening, Carolyn and Juanita Milam, Roy's half-brother's wife, were minding the store.

Till had been engaged in some teenage male bragging when his cousins and friends (there were nine in all) dared him to go inside the door and talk to Carolyn Bryant. Unfamiliar with Mississippi norms, he took the dare. According to Bryant's later testimony, Till grabbed her hand and asked her for a date; when she moved away from him, he blocked her, put his hands on her waist and said, "Don't be afraid of me, baby. I ain't gonna hurt you. I been with white girls before." Horrified, one of Till's cousins grabbed him and pulled him outside the store. Before he and his cousins and friends drove away, Till whistled at Carolyn Bryant.

When Roy Bryant and J. W. Milam found out what had happened at the store, they decided to teach Emmett Till a lesson. Initially, they planned only to beat him. But Till's response to the beating apparently surprised them: he didn't cry, he didn't beg, and he continued to tell the two white men about the white girls he knew in Chicago. Enraged, Bryant and Milam beat Till more savagely, then shot him, tied a heavy fan to his neck, and threw his body into the Tallahatchie River.[42]

In the sad world of the Jim Crow South, that was not enough to make Till's murder national news. The rest of the story was. First came the discovery of Till's body. His face was crushed; clearly, the murder had been preceded by an almost unimaginably brutal assault. Till's mother made sure the world saw—she persuaded Mississippi officials to send Emmett's body north to Chicago for burial, where she had it displayed just as Bryant and Milam had mutilated it.[43] Bryant and Milam were arrested and tried for the killing; despite a strong case, they were acquitted by an all-white jury. Four months later, an article in *Look* magazine appeared in which Bryant and Milam confessed and told the whole ugly story. Protected by double jeopardy against a second murder prosecution, they were free and clear.[44]

It was as if, forty-one years later, O. J. Simpson had told the world he'd killed his ex-wife and Ronald Goldman, told how, and said he was glad he'd done it. Only worse: Simpson was in no sense the agent of his state and local governments—Bryant and Milam were. The episode began with a violation of the South's racial code, and it ended when the two killers imposed the penalty. They held no formal public office, but as surely as Emmett Till had been murdered, his murderers were Jim Crow's police officers, its district attorneys—and its hangmen.

The Till murder and its aftermath captured two key aspects of the latter days of Jim Crow criminal justice. First, the legal process remained thoroughly white dominated. Bryant and Milam's trial was an exercise not in local self-government but in local *white* self-government. Indeed, the surprise was that the state's key witness was a black man: Moses Wright, Till's host, who pleaded with the defendants to leave Till alone when they came to get him, hours before his death.[45] (Another surprise was that the two defendants were prosecuted: a sign that even in Mississippi, older Jim Crow norms were beginning to fade.) Second, as had long been true, southern courts, southern officials, and all-white southern juries devalued the interests of black crime victims, especially those who suffered at the hands of white victimizers. Courts and juries, police and prosecutors existed to provide Bryant and Milam with the "protection of the laws." No one protected Emmett Till.

That last proposition was crucial. Once Bryant and Milam won their acquittal, no politician or set of appellate judges could overturn the verdict—not even when the two perpetrators admitted their crime. The same was true in the many cases in which crimes against black victims yielded no prosecution. Once a local district attorney decided not to file charges, the case was closed; decisions not to file charges were and are unreviewable by any court.[46] Such decisions were not only committed to prosecutors' discretion, they were also invisible to the appellate judges who police compliance with the law. In Till's case, the entire saga played out before a national audience: anyone who read a daily newspaper knew of Till's murder and the killers' acquittal. But that level of publicity was rare, and remains so. As a general matter, appellate judges (Supreme Court Justices included) know about the small slice of litigated cases that appear before their courts, not about the much larger portion of cases that never climb the appellate ladder.[47] And, with rare exceptions, no court sees any of the many crimes for which no one is arrested and prosecuted. That is one reason why Supreme Court–driven constitutional regulation would aim to protect criminal *defendants'* rights. To the Supreme Court Justices who would soon reshape the law of criminal procedure, crime victims like Till remained all but invisible.

Entering the 1960s, the constitutional law of criminal justice seemed unsatisfying at best. Tough rules—meaning tough on the police—like those applied in Prohibition-era search and seizure cases governed federal officials, but only those officials. Local police officers and prosecutors were subject to the gentler restrictions of cases like *Moore, Powell, Norris,* and *Brown.*

And southern "justice" seemed in need of a major overhaul. Day-of-trial appointment of counsel for indigent defendants in capital cases, as in *Moore* and *Powell,* no longer happened. But in large parts of the South, appointed counsel in noncapital cases was distressingly rare, and again the federal Constitution had little to say about the practice. Lawyers representing black defendants often faced ostracism or worse if they defended their clients' interests aggressively.[48] Decades after *Norris v. Alabama,* all-white juries remained the norm throughout the South and probably in much of the North as well, thanks to prosecutors' strategic use of peremptory challenges. (Peremptory challenges allow each side to strike a certain number of potential jurors without offering any justification for the strikes. Prosecutors often used such challenges to eliminate blacks from the jury pool, a tactic that remained legal until 1986.)[49] Confessions produced by *Brown v. Mississippi*–style beatings were rarer than in the past, thanks mostly to more professionalized and better trained police forces.[50] But other forms of arm-twisting and coercion remained common, in North and South alike.

That was not all. Many jurisdictions were in the habit of handing out months of jail time based on amorphous crimes like vagrancy or "disorderly conduct," which appeared to mean, roughly, displeasing the authorities. In some jurisdictions, such noncrimes were used to justify dragnet-type arrests based on unsupported suspicion of more serious offenses.[51] Defendants could be required to pay for the production of trial transcripts, which effectively barred poor defendants from appealing their criminal convictions. As of 1960, all but the last of these practices were constitutionally permissible; the provision of free transcripts to indigent defendants was mandated in 1956.[52]

State law already addressed some of these problems, but not all of them, not sufficiently, and not in the South. To federal judges and Justices who wished to right some of these wrongs, federal constitutional law— meaning, as a practical matter, legal doctrine based on some combination of three sources: the Fourteenth Amendment's due process and equal protection clauses and the various provisions of the Bill of Rights—was the most obvious means of legal reform.

Three Roads Not Taken

What shape would reform take? That question divided into three others. Substance or process: would the Court limit legislators' ability to define crimes as they wished, or would the Justices focus on procedure, as does the Constitution's text? Equal protection or due process: would the Justices craft new antidiscrimination rules, or would the Court address the merits of the relevant procedures without respect to their effects on poor and black defendants? Last but not least, Bill of Rights–based rules or due process–based standards: would Warren's Court turn to the rules used in federal cases, rules based on the Fourth, Fifth, and Sixth Amendments, or would it expand on the looser due process standards applied in cases like *Moore v. Dempsey* and *Brown v. Mississippi*? The answers the Warren Court gave—the Court would focus on procedure, largely ignore equal protection, and embrace Bill of Rights–based rules—all seem obvious in retrospect. They were not obvious at the time.

The Court did not settle on those answers right away. Three Warren-era decisions—*Lambert v. California* (1957), *Robinson v. California* (1962), and *Griswold v. Connecticut* (1965)—suggested that substance might win out over process. In *Lambert*, the defendant violated a local ordinance requiring convicted felons to register with the police; the defendant failed to register because she didn't know about the ordinance that directed her to do so. The Court overturned her conviction because she lacked fair notice of the crime for which she was punished.[53] *Robinson* invalidated a state statute criminalizing drug addiction, reasoning that addiction is a status, not voluntarily chosen conduct.[54] *Griswold*, the most famous of the three cases, struck down a Connecticut statute criminalizing the sale or use of contraceptives.[55] Later, the case would spawn a right of privacy that now includes a (limited) right to abortion and a (once again limited) right to have sex with consenting adults, free of official punishment.[56]

Lambert might have developed into a ban on surprising criminal liability, of which there is a great deal given the capacious nature of contemporary criminal codes. *Robinson* might have severely limited liability for drug purchase or drug possession, thereby remaking the criminal law of drugs in Prohibition's image.[57] *Griswold* might have evolved into a constitutional none-of-your-business principle, barring criminal punishment for private behavior in the ordinary sense of the word "private," or for conduct within one's home that causes no direct injury to anyone else. None of these things happened.[58] Instead, the Court made the constitutional law of criminal *justice* into something narrower and less useful: a constitutional law of criminal *procedure*.

So too with respect to the other legal roads not taken. *Griffin v. Illinois* (1956) used the equal protection clause to require the free provision of trial transcripts to indigent defendants appealing their convictions.[59] *Douglas v. California* (1963) used the clause to mandate state-paid counsel for the same set of defendants.[60] These decisions might have formed the foundation of a strong bar on practices that disadvantage poor criminal defendants. That body of law does not exist. Today, in state courts throughout the country, criminal defendants are confined prior to their trials for failure to make bail—meaning, they are confined for their inability to pay a sum of money said to be needed to assure their appearance in court. The discriminatory bail system survives even though defendants who cannot make bail are more likely to be convicted at trial than defendants who can.[61] Race discrimination claims fared even less well. The jury pool in *Swain v. Alabama* (1965) included six blacks, all of whom were struck by the prosecutor's use of peremptory challenges. In a case in which a black defendant was charged with raping a white woman, trial by the resulting all-white jury was deemed no violation of the equal protection clause.[62] Warren Court criminal procedure doctrine would be grounded in due process, not equal protection.

And that due process doctrine would in turn flow from the Bill of Rights, which the Supreme Court of the 1960s and after has seen as "incorporated" in the Fourteenth Amendment's due process clause.[63] Consequently, the law of criminal procedure contains many bright-line rules like the famous warnings required by *Miranda v. Arizona* (1966).[64] Consider-all-the-circumstances standards like the ones applied in *Moore v. Dempsey* and *Brown v. Mississippi* are less common.[65] *Moore* and *Brown* might have been the template for a general requirement that defendants be treated fairly, and not just in the police station. That requirement did not emerge from the due process cases. Instead, *Miranda* did.

Why did the Justices decline to follow these alternate paths toward constitutional regulation of state-court criminal justice? With respect to aggressive substantive review—the kind of law that *Lambert, Robinson,* and *Griswold* might have made—there is no good answer. Those three cases prove that a constitutional law of substance, in place of the detailed law of procedure we have, was legally possible. That it didn't happen probably has more to do with the Constitution's text—the second word of the due process clause is "process," and the Bill of Rights' clear focus is procedure—than with anything else. The Constitution is not written with substantive criminal law in mind. More's the pity.

With respect to the other two roads not taken, the story is more complicated, and perhaps also more interesting. Consider due process doctrine in the style of *Moore* and *Brown* first. The requirement that, as a matter of due process, confessions be inadmissible unless they were voluntary seemed both vague and empty, at least once one got beyond cases of physical torture like *Brown*. That is one reason why the Court changed course, replacing the old voluntariness standard with the set of rules mandated by *Miranda*. But the alleged emptiness of voluntariness was a function of the evidence used to apply the legal standard: chiefly the testimony of the defendant and the interrogating officers. Better evidence would make for more accurate fact finding, which in turn would mean better application of the legal doctrine. That happy progression was entirely possible. All that was needed was a requirement that interrogation sessions be taped so that judges could see (or at least hear) for themselves how the relevant actors behaved. *Miranda* rests on the premise that rules were needed to regulate police interrogation properly. In truth, more facts were needed—and *Miranda* left the facts as muddy as ever.

Something similar was true of the equal protection doctrine that did not emerge in the 1960s, but might have. The point is well captured by the story of one of the Warren Court's last criminal procedure decisions: *Duncan v. Louisiana* (1968).[66] In the fall of 1966, Gary Duncan was a nineteen-year-old black man with a family and a full-time job.[67] He lived in Plaquemines Parish, Louisiana, where Duncan's nephew and cousin, both twelve years old, attended a newly integrated local public school. Duncan drove by the two boys walking home from school when four white classmates of roughly the same age crossed the street to confront them; an uneven fight was clearly in the offing. Duncan stopped his car and told his nephew and cousin to get inside. Herman Landry, one of the four white boys, told Duncan, "You must think you're tough," whereupon Duncan either touched or slapped Landry's elbow—to anyone who has seen young males fight, "touched" seems more likely—and told him to go home. Having prevented the fight, Duncan drove off with his nephew and his cousin in his car.[68]

The alleged slap left no mark. Nevertheless, Duncan was charged with "simple battery," defined as "a battery, without the consent of the victim, committed without a dangerous weapon."[69] In turn, Louisiana law traditionally defined "battery" as "the intentional use of force or violence"—notice: *or,* not *and*—"upon the person of another."[70] The crime carried a sentence of up to two years in prison, plus a fine of up to $300.

On *Duncan*'s facts, the charge seemed absurd. No reasonable prosecutor would so much as consider filing battery charges based on a touch or mild slap on the alleged victim's arm. The district attorney's office was seeking to punish Duncan not for injuring Herman Landry but for telling a white boy what he should do, for helping two black boys escape a beating, and for his black relatives' presence in what had been an all-white public school. Yet preposterous though it seemed, the battery charge was legally plausible. Duncan evidently intended to touch Landry's arm. And while that touch was well shy of violent, it might have constituted a peculiarly mild form of the use of force. A nineteen-year-old was directing a twelve-year-old to calm down and go home—which, if accompanied by any physical contact, might be deemed forcible enough to qualify under Louisiana's battery statute, especially when the force was applied by a black man to a white child. Given such a broadly defined crime, the chief problem with the charge was not its legal insufficiency. Rather, the problem was that the district attorney was using a purely technical crime to punish Duncan for behavior that would be ignored if done by a white man. Emmett Till's killers could go free, but Gary Duncan had to pay for telling a white boy to go home, and for daring to touch him while doing so.

Duncan's lawyer asked for a jury trial, but his motion was denied. In Louisiana, juries were available only in felony cases, and battery was a misdemeanor. Duncan instead had a bench trial that ended in conviction; he was sentenced to two months in jail plus a $150 fine. The Louisiana Supreme Court declined to review Duncan's conviction.[71]

The case then made its way to the federal Supreme Court, where the Justices reversed. Justice White's majority opinion concluded that the Sixth Amendment right to a jury trial applied in state courts as well as federal courts, and that the right entitled Duncan, and anyone else facing charges with a potential sentence of more than six months' incarceration, to a jury. But Duncan would not get his jury: soon after the High Court's ruling, the Louisiana legislature revised the battery statute to cap potential sentences at six months' jail time, so the district attorney could retry Duncan before a compliant state trial judge.[72]

Plainly, a better legal remedy was needed. And one was available, at least in theory: it seemed utterly obvious that no white man in similar circumstances would be treated as Duncan was. But seeming utterly obvious is different from finding provable facts. Absent detailed records of other battery cases and their fact patterns, either in Plaquemines Parish or elsewhere in Louisiana—the kind of records no jurisdiction kept in the 1970s and few keep today—the size of the gap between the treatment blacks and whites received would remain a matter of educated guesswork. Judicial intuition was a thin reed on which to rest a binding constitutional judgment, especially one with such major implications.

The absence of evidence was a solvable problem and still is. Courts could require state or local governments to keep records of cases in which criminal charges are filed, including not only the formal charges but also the facts on which those charges were based. Such records would make it possible to prove what was plainly true in *Duncan:* that the defendant's conduct differed from the conduct that produced other battery convictions. Absent such records, equal protection claims in such cases were bound to be nonstarters.

That may be why Warren's Court did not rest on equal protection, either in *Duncan* or in most of its other criminal procedure cases. Ever since the 1960s, legal conservatives have criticized the Court of that decade for its radicalism, and for resting its decisions on nothing more than the Justices' own preferences. Both criticisms miss the mark. The Warren Court's work looked as it did partly because the other approaches to constitutional reform seemed less legally grounded, more intuitive than lawlike—and partly because the Justices were a good deal less radical than the conventional wisdom of the time had it. An equal protection ruling in *Duncan* would have been far more innovative than the Supreme Court's decision in that case. Such a ruling also had the potential to accomplish more than the Supreme Court's decision accomplished— notice how easily the Louisiana legislature dodged the Court's ruling; no similar dodge would have been possible had the Court found that

Duncan had been denied the "equal protection of the laws." The Court's decision accomplished little precisely because it was so conservative, relying on the traditional jury right rather than on more legally inventive forms of judicial review. A different style of lawmaking might have proved more effective. As in the first Reconstruction, so it was in the second: the law seemed to promise an end to discriminatory criminal justice, but the promise remained unfulfilled.

CHAPTER 8

Earl Warren's Errors

If some can beat the rap, all must beat the rap.

—Attorney General Nicholas Katzenbach, characterizing and
criticizing the idea of giving state-paid lawyers to indigent
defendants under police interrogation (1965)

Why do you say we should not encourage [the criminal suspect] to
have a lawyer? Are lawyers a menace?

—Chief Justice Earl Warren, questions asked during oral argument
in *Miranda v. Arizona* (1966)

Our cities are jungle paths after dark.

—Ronald Reagan, speech given during first campaign for
California's governorship (1966)

I T IS ONE OF HISTORY'S STRANGER IRONIES that Earl Warren—a
progressive Republican who won both parties' nominations while governor of California,[1] later the Chief Justice who devoted his judicial tenure to protecting civil rights for black Americans and expanding civil
liberties for all Americans—helped usher in the harsh politics of crime
that characterized the twentieth century's last decades. Warren and his
fellow Justices sought to make the nation's criminal justice system *less*
politicized, and more protective of the rights and interests of criminal
defendants. Expanded constitutional rights were supposed to guard defendants against the kind of politics that victimized the poor and blacks
while guarding the interests of middle- and upper-class whites. But in
criminal justice as elsewhere, unintended consequences often swamp
the intended kind.

The swamping was partly due to bad timing.[2] In a series of landmark decisions issued between 1961 and 1969, Warren's Supreme Court imposed a new set of procedural limits on state and local law enforcement—in Judge Henry Friendly's apt words, the Court crafted a new constitutional code of criminal procedure.[3] By 1961, prison populations were already falling in the Northeast and Midwest; violent crime was already on the rise in those regions' cities. By the middle of the decade, those trends had spread to the rest of the nation. In the short run, the Court's rulings made criminal law enforcement and litigation more expensive, which meant even less criminal punishment—when the price of anything rises, its incidence falls—and (probably) still more crime. Plus, the procedure-focused character of the Court's decisions made them easy to attack once voters demanded tougher law enforcement practices: it is one thing to overturn convictions of defendants who may well be innocent, quite another to reverse otherwise valid convictions based on one or another procedural error. And the timing of those decisions made rising voter criticism inevitable. If anything invites a political backlash, expanding criminal defendants' rights in a period of steeply rising crime and rapidly falling punishment does so. The upshot was a nationalized and punitive politics of street crime that lasted a generation. This in turn opened the door to political entrepreneurs like another, very different California Republican: Ronald Reagan. Thus did Warren-style legal doctrine wind up promoting Reaganite politics.

Still, the problems with the work of Warren's Court went beyond the coincidence of new procedural protections, rising rates of violent crime, and falling rates of imprisonment. The Warren Court's criminal procedure doctrine purported to accomplish two main tasks. First, the Court expanded the rights of poor defendants to receive the assistance of counsel at state expense: at the police station, at trial, and on appeal.[4] Second, Warren and his colleagues gave those defense lawyers a new role: not challenging the state's case or advancing defenses to the relevant criminal charges, but enforcing the Court's new procedural rights. Some of those rights seemed designed to help the justice system do a better job of separating guilty defendants from innocent ones,[5] but only some. The Court's two most consequential criminal procedure decisions, *Mapp v. Ohio* (1961) and *Miranda v. Arizona* (1966), followed a different path.

Mapp barred the use of evidence obtained through illegal searches, a rule that had applied only in federal court but was now the law in all criminal cases.[6] *Miranda* gave suspects a right to the assistance of counsel during police questioning[7]—a time when the counsel's primary job is to keep her client's mouth shut. The defense lawyers who enforced those rights were not bringing forward evidence of their clients' innocence but suppressing evidence of their guilt. Whatever their other merits, such practices were bound to make the justice system do a worse job of separating those defendants who deserve punishment from those who don't—its central task. This was criminal procedure as defined by James Madison's Bill of Rights, not by John Bingham's Fourteenth Amendment.

Decisions like *Mapp* and (especially) *Miranda* were supposed to have one large compensating advantage: they were supposed to promote equality among rich and poor. As the wealthy can use legal counsel to help them deal with police investigations, poor suspects should have the same privileges—the view mocked by then–Attorney General Nicholas Katzenbach in his quote at the beginning of this chapter. But Katzenbach did not know the half of it. By making defense lawyers more central to criminal litigation than they already were and by dramatically enlarging the range of legal claims they could raise on their clients' behalf, Warren's Court *increased* the gap between rich and poor defendants—and, given the racial distribution of poverty in midcentury America, between black and white defendants as well. Because the time and quality of defense counsel mattered more than before, those defendants who could buy better quality attorneys and pay them to work more hours were more advantaged than before. Relatively speaking, their poorer counterparts grew more disadvantaged. The justice system grew less egalitarian through the Supreme Court's efforts to make it more so.

The Path the Court Chose

The core ideas of the Warren Court's criminal procedure doctrine had to do with evidence: the manner in which police officers could gather it, and the types that could be used against the defendant in court. For the most part, those ideas came from the Bill of Rights: the Fourth Amendment's ban on "unreasonable searches and seizures," the Fifth Amendment's prohibition of compelled self-incrimination, and the Sixth Amendment's guarantees of "the assistance of counsel" and the right to confront opposing witnesses.[8]

There is something more than a little strange about that state of affairs. Involuntary confession cases aside, the law of evidence had not been the Court's chief focus before the 1960s, and there is no obvious reason why that proposition had to change. Moreover, the core problems the justice system faced entering the 1960s—discriminatory justice in the South, failure to provide the "protection of the laws" to poor and black crime victims in the North, the strategic use of "crimes" like vagrancy and loitering in all parts of the country, the low quality of justice available to poor defendants—bore little relation to the Bill of Rights' legal agenda. The law of criminal procedure came to be based on the Bill not because of the Bill's merits, but because the Fourth, Fifth, and Sixth Amendments seemed to promise legal rules with bite, unlike the supposedly empty standards used in cases like *Moore* and *Brown*. The content of the rules seemed an afterthought.

The story begins with Dolly Mapp, a black woman who ran a boarding house in Cleveland. The police suspected her of complicity in an illegal gambling operation. They also suspected her of hiding the perpetrator of a recent bombing, part of an ongoing battle between rival bookmakers. When the local police showed up to search her boarding house, one of the officers showed Mapp what purported to be a search warrant. Mapp grabbed the piece of paper and stuck it in her blouse, after which the officer reached in and grabbed it back. The "warrant" never surfaced in the subsequent litigation. The odds are that it never existed.[9]

The police proceeded to search the house, finding neither gambling paraphernalia nor the alleged bomber. They did find three dirty books in a trunk in the basement, so Mapp was charged with and convicted of possession of obscene material. When the case made it to the Supreme Court, the issue the lawyers briefed and argued was whether states could, consistent with the First Amendment, prohibit the possession of obscene books in one's own home. The Justices would rule for Mapp's side of that debate—eight years later and in another case. In *Mapp v. Ohio*

(1961), the Court took a different tack, applying the Fourth Amendment's exclusionary rule to state and local police.[10] Because the police should have gotten a warrant to search Dolly Mapp's boarding house but didn't, they had violated the Fourth Amendment. And because of that violation, the pornographic books were inadmissible, leaving Mapp's conviction unsupportable.

Mapp had two large effects. First, it guaranteed that a large fraction of criminal litigation would have to do with the conduct of police officers, not the behavior of criminal defendants. That changed the character of criminal litigation, and not for the better. The depth of the change became evident only over time. In the 1960s, when the number of criminal prosecutions was probably falling substantially,[11] the justice system was not operating at capacity, meaning that the system could absorb new tasks at limited cost. When the number of prosecutions began rising steeply in the mid-1970s, that would cease to be true. In a justice system in which all the key actors—police officers, prosecutors, and defense attorneys—*do* operate at capacity, more attention paid to enforcing Fourth Amendment doctrine means less attention paid to other, more important issues, including the defendant's conduct and intent. Even were that not so, suppression of illegally seized evidence is a particularly poor sanction to apply to the police, because police officers lose nothing when evidence is excluded at defendants' trials. Most criminal litigation is like a relay race: police identify and investigate the suspect, make the arrest, and then hand off the case to prosecutors. The exclusionary rule penalizes the anchor in this race; prosecutors and the public suffer for police officers' mistakes.

The Court might have done well to choose another remedy for police misconduct, and a few years later, a different and better remedy was readily apparent: institutional injunctions—orders compelling police departments whose officers frequently violate search and seizure law to adopt better procedures. That is akin to the approach the Court took when it began to enforce school desegregation orders in the late 1960s and orders requiring improved prison conditions in the 1970s and 1980s.[12] In those cases, the Justices, and federal judges more generally, did not penalize individual government *officials;* rather, the goal was to force the offending government *institutions* to adopt needed reforms. Judicial orders required

largely segregated school districts to adopt busing plans so that black
and white children might attend the same schools in larger numbers.
Prison officials were told to build bigger facilities in order to relieve over-
crowding. Similar orders might have been issued to misbehaving local
police forces. If officers were too trigger-happy, more extensive training
in the use of deadly force might be ordered; if street stops focused disproportionately on blacks or Latinos, better training and supervision of
the selection of suspects might be required. But the possibility of such
institutional injunctions wasn't on the Court's radar screen in 1961. *Mapp*
came a decade too soon.

Mapp's second consequence goes to the character of the law that governs local police officers. Because of *Mapp*, doctrines like *Gouled*'s "mere
evidence" rule, *Lefkowitz*'s restrictions on searches incident to arrest,
and *Sgro*'s bar on the reissuance of warrants—doctrines that once bound
only federal agents—now applied to ordinary searches by local police.
The law of search and seizure had played a small role in local policing
before *Mapp*, but not so afterward. And the Court went farther. In *Beck
v. Ohio* (1964)—like *Mapp*, the case arose from a gambling investigation
in Cleveland—the Court applied the exclusionary rule not only to illegal
searches but to illegal arrests as well.[13] Even if the illegality was a close
call, the product of nearly all searches conducted after an invalid arrest
was inadmissible. Overturning *Olmstead, Katz v. United States* (1967)
found that an eavesdropping device placed on a public telephone constituted a Fourth Amendment "search" for which probable cause and a
warrant were required.[14] *Katz* meant that even searches that involved no
physical trespass might violate citizens' Fourth Amendment rights. *Terry
v. Ohio* (1968) (yet another Cleveland case) held that a brief street stop
was permissible only if the police had reasonable grounds to believe the
suspect was engaged in criminal activity, and that a frisk of the suspect's
outer clothing was permissible only given similarly reasonable grounds
to believe the suspect had a weapon.[15] *Terry* spawned a large body of law
regulating police-citizen street encounters that had previously gone unregulated.[16] Taken together, *Beck* and *Terry* constituted a large expansion in
Fourth Amendment regulation of arrests and searches by state and local
police. *Katz* amounted to expanded regulation of searches by federal, state,
and local officials alike.

These decisions could work only if suspects had lawyers who could file the requisite motions to suppress illegally seized evidence, and who could appeal later convictions if those motions were incorrectly denied. The Court obliged by dramatically expanding the right to state-appointed counsel. *Gideon v. Wainwright* (1963) gave poor defendants a right to appointed counsel in felony cases, later expanded to felonies plus misdemeanors that might lead to a term of incarceration.[17] *Gideon* mattered chiefly in the South; elsewhere, appointed counsel in such cases was already routine. Another decision issued the same day mattered more: *Douglas v. California* (1963), which gave indigent criminal defendants the right to state-paid counsel on appeal.[18] *Mapp*'s exclusionary rule made defense lawyers enforcers of the increasingly stringent search and seizure standards by which local police were bound. *Gideon* and *Douglas* ensured that those defense lawyers would be available to do the enforcing.

The expanding right to counsel did not stop there. In a series of police interrogation cases, Earl Warren's Supreme Court brought the right to counsel into the police station, making defense lawyers, at least in theory, the chief regulators of the propriety of police interrogation. *Massiah v. United States* (1964) held that a criminal defendant who had been formally charged had a right to have counsel present during any questioning by the police, including surreptitious "questioning" by undercover agents.[19] *Escobedo v. Illinois* (1964) held that this right applied to a defendant under arrest but not yet charged, if the defendant asked to speak with a lawyer.[20] Last but not least, *Miranda v. Arizona* (1966) gave defendants a right to counsel during any police questioning that took place while the defendant was in police custody.

Miranda was by far the most important of these decisions. Its core holding was captured by the four famous warnings that Warren's majority opinion required police officers to deliver before questioning, that the suspect

> has the right to remain silent, that anything he says can be used against him in a court of law, that he has the right to the presence of an attorney, and that if he cannot afford an attorney one will be appointed for him prior to any questioning if he so desires.[21]

Those warnings seem designed to persuade suspects that talking is fool-ish and that, if they want help keeping quiet, they need only ask and help will be supplied, if necessary at state expense. The rules governing waiver of these rights likewise seemed stacked against the government. In order to introduce any incriminating statements, the government bore the "heavy burden" of proving that the suspect had heard these warnings and nevertheless made a voluntary, knowing, and intelligent waiver of his rights. If the suspect asked for a lawyer, questioning must cease and (the Court later held) could not start again save at the suspect's instigation.[22] Any waiver of such expansive rights would seem, by definition, some-thing less than knowing and intelligent.[23] Putting defense counsel in police interrogation rooms sealed the point. Defense counsel's sole job in that setting is to put a stop to police questioning, to see to it that any incriminating statements her client offers are paid for in the coin of re-duced charges or a more favorable sentence, not given away for free— and only prosecutors, not the police, can make such deals.[24] Introducing defense lawyers into police interrogation seemed more a means of banning police interrogation than a means of regulating it.

Even for the reformist Supreme Court of the 1960s, banning police interrogation was a bridge too far. So, unsurprisingly, *Miranda*'s protec-tions proved less expansive than Warren's majority opinion suggested they would be. Or, rather, those protections proved expansive only for a favored class of suspects. For those savvy or well-informed enough to say *Miranda*'s magic words—"I want to see a lawyer"—when the police de-liver the required warnings, the Court's decision amounted to a right to opt out of police questioning entirely. To those savvy suspects, Earl Warren's opinion did abolish police interrogation. But they constitute only 20 to 25 percent of the suspects police seek to question. For the other three-quarters, the state could prove waiver simply by showing that the suspect heard the warnings and proceeded to talk to the police. With respect to them, *Miranda* changed little. After *Miranda,* the police were as free to induce suspects to waive their rights as they had been to "per-suade, trick, or cajole" suspects into talking before *Miranda*.[25]

This bottom line was at odds with *Miranda*'s ideological justifica-tion, best explained by a Yale Kamisar essay that anticipated the Court's decision by a year. Kamisar's essay was titled "Equal Justice in the

Gatehouses and Mansions of American Criminal Procedure."[26] The gatehouses in that title are America's police stations; the mansions are its courtrooms. During criminal trials in those courtrooms, defendants testify only with the advice of counsel and under the supervision of a judge. In police stations, any such testimony comes outside public view and outside the presence of judges and lawyers. Kamisar argued that equality requires extending at least the basic protections of the court-room to the police station: the view that then–Attorney General Nicholas Katzenbach characterized as "if some can beat the rap, all must beat the rap." Earl Warren may have believed in Kamisar's vision, but the subse-quent case law has not followed it. Instead, *Miranda* doctrine gives so-phisticated suspects—chiefly recidivists and white-collar defendants[27]—the right to avoid police questioning altogether, while giving most suspects nearly nothing at all. That makes for even less equality than in Kamisar's gatehouses and mansions.

That *Miranda* did not lead to a more egalitarian criminal justice sys-tem should not surprise. The Bill of Rights (*Miranda* was based on the Fifth Amendment privilege against self-incrimination) was not written with equality in mind, least of all equality across race and class: its chief authors were white slaveholders.[28] Nor was it a surprise that application of the Bill of Rights led to a less accurate system of criminal adjudication. Accuracy was not the point of excluding illegally obtained confessions and physical evidence. On the contrary, by mandating the suppression of relevant evidence of defendants' guilt, decisions like *Mapp* and *Miranda* made adjudication less accurate, not more so.

What *was* the point of those decisions? For *Miranda,* the most likely answer is the advancement of Kamisar-style equality of result: if, with the help of skilled lawyers, wealthy and sophisticated suspects could game the system, the poor and unsophisticated must be given the same opportunity. As things turned out, *Miranda*'s effects were precisely the opposite: the sophisticated were better off than before; their less savvy counterparts were not. With respect to *Mapp,* the underlying goal of the Court's decision is less clear. The Justices surely intended to enforce the Fourth Amendment's warrant requirement more effectively—but why was that goal so important? Search warrants are issued by magistrates based on police affidavits and a few minutes' conversation; neither the search target nor his counsel plays any role in the process. Unsurprisingly, this one-sided process leads to one-sided results: the overwhelming majority of search warrant applications are granted. It is unclear why anyone would want the scope of police authority to be defined by such a process.[29] *Mapp* was designed not to advance some vision of the law of police evidence-gathering but simply to enforce the relevant rules—regardless of those rules' rationales.

The observation applies to more than just *Mapp*. When the Supreme Court enforces the Fourteenth Amendment's due process and equal protection clauses, the Justices must decide what due process is about and what "equal protection" means. When the Court enforces one or another provision of the Bill of Rights, there is less intellectual work to be done. The question is whether the defendant did or didn't receive "the assistance of counsel" or a jury trial, whether the police did or didn't obtain a valid search warrant, or the like. One needs no theory of the relevant right to decide such issues; unsurprisingly, the rights in question lack clear theories. The point of these procedures is usually beside the point.[30] For the most part, criminal procedure based on the Bill of Rights is a set of rules divorced from reasons. So, as the Court applied one after another Bill of Rights provision to state and local police officers, prosecutors, and judges, the relationship between rules and reasons—more precisely, the relationship between the law of criminal procedure and a more just criminal justice system—grew ever more indistinct. The law was its own justification.

That mattered a great deal, for the Supreme Court of the 1960s used the Bill of Rights to remake the law of criminal procedure. The Fourth Amendment's warrant requirement and ban on unreasonable searches and seizures,[31] the Fifth Amendment privilege against self-incrimination and ban on double jeopardy,[32] the Sixth Amendment rights to counsel,[33] to a trial by an impartial jury,[34] "to be confronted with the witnesses against" the defendant,[35] and "to have compulsory process for obtaining witnesses in [the defendant's] favor"[36]—the Court deemed each of these rights "incorporated" into the meaning of due process, and the Fourteenth Amendment's due process clause applied to state and local officials. Consequently, each of these rights applied to those officials, not just to federal agents and prosecutors.

By themselves, these decisions did not transform state-court criminal processes. All the procedures just mentioned already existed; indeed, most had existed for centuries, which explains their inclusion in the Bill of Rights. But a different kind of transformation happened: Warren-era criminal procedure decisions raised the level of legal uncertainty that attached to the relevant doctrines. The boundaries of rights that had been long settled became hotly contested. Contested legal doctrine attracts litigation and creates opportunities for able defense lawyers. Increasingly, the chief subject of criminal litigation became the definition of procedures based on the Bill of Rights.

This process extended well beyond the 1960s; in fact, it continues today. The Sixth Amendment right to counsel led, in the 1970s and 1980s, to the emergence of the right to the "effective assistance" of counsel.[37] *Duncan*'s right to a jury trial soon produced elaborate bodies of law governing jury selection; in the last decade, it has produced an even more elaborate body of law governing jury power over criminal sentencing.[38] These developments have led to massive amounts of litigation. Most important of all is the aftermath of *Pointer v. Texas* (1965). The defendant in *Pointer* was charged with robbery. The victim and key government witness testified at the defendant's preliminary hearing; at that hearing, the defendant was not represented by counsel and lacked the skill to cross-examine that witness himself. By the time of Pointer's trial, the witness had moved to California; instead of bringing him back to Texas to testify, the government was allowed to read the witness's preliminary hearing testimony into the trial record. The Court held that this process violated the defendant's Sixth Amendment right "to be confronted with the witnesses against him."[39]

Forty-five years later, *Pointer* has morphed into a ban on introducing a wide range of out-of-court testimony in criminal trials, even if the witness is unavailable to testify. *Giles v. California* (2008) shows this rule's breadth. The defendant in *Giles* was charged with murdering his ex-girlfriend. Noting that the victim was unavailable to testify at trial because of the defendant's crime, the government introduced statements the victim had made to a police officer after an earlier instance of domestic violence. The Supreme Court found this procedure a violation of the confrontation clause.[40] A year later in *Melendez-Diaz v. Massachusetts*

(2009), the Court ruled that reports from state crime laboratories must be introduced into evidence through the live, in-court testimony of the officials who produced the reports—without such testimony, the reports themselves are inadmissible.[41] Notice that it matters not that the ex-girlfriend's statements in *Giles* were reliable evidence of the defendant's pattern of violence, nor that the report in *Melendez-Diaz* was better evidence of the defendant's drug possession than any live testimony could be. Reliability, the Court emphasized, is not the point. The confrontation clause does not aim to promote the use of reliable evidence. Rather, its point is to promote confrontation—and the clause rests on no theory of why confrontation advances any rational policy goal.[42]

Decisions like *Giles* and *Melendez-Diaz* reinforce one of the traditional features of American criminal trials: their reliance on live witness testimony rather than on the case files that play such a large role in criminal litigation in continental Europe. Live witness testimony may have been the best possible means of proving guilt in the eighteenth century, when the confrontation clause was written and ratified. It hardly follows that it is the best possible means today. On the contrary, the greatest advance in criminal procedure of the past generation—the increasing range and accuracy of forensic evidence, including DNA—depends on the scientific analysis of physical evidence, not on live testimony. *Melendez-Diaz* undermines that advance. Forcing crime laboratory technicians to double as courtroom witnesses raises the cost to the laboratories of performing the technical analysis that is their raison d'être. Unless the laws of supply and demand have been repealed, higher costs mean less analysis, and hence a less accurate adjudication system. This is the natural consequence of anchoring the nation's criminal justice system to a set of procedures defined by eighteenth-century English law—procedures whose rationales have been largely lost in time—not by the system's contemporary needs and capacities.

Warren's Errors

The first, and perhaps the worst, error Warren's Court made was to do that anchoring—to tie the law of criminal procedure to the federal Bill of Rights instead of using that body of law to advance some coherent vision of fair and equal criminal justice. Two other mistakes were especially important. Warren and his colleagues continued and exacerbated a long-term trend: they proceduralized criminal litigation, siphoning the time of attorneys and judges away from the question of the defendant's guilt or innocence and toward the process by which the defendant was arrested, tried, and convicted. And the Justices of the 1960s showed poor timing: the Court chose to ramp up the level of constitutional regulation of state and local criminal justice at a time when crime was rising sharply and criminal punishment was falling substantially, first in the country's Northeast quadrant and later in the nation as a whole. That combination was bound to produce a backlash, both political and legal—and soon did so. The upshot was that the law of criminal procedure made arrests and prosecutions more expensive when there were too few of them and, strangely, cheaper when there were too many.

Consider these errors in turn. The level of procedural regulation, both of policing and prosecution, was already on the rise when the 1960s began: state appellate courts were rapidly adopting protective procedures like the exclusionary rule and state-appointed lawyers before the Supreme Court required them to do so.[43] The Court accelerated that process, beginning in 1961 with *Mapp*. Procedural claims mushroomed. One 1980s study of litigation by state-appointed defense lawyers captures the effect. Its authors found that the attorneys visited the crime scene in 12 percent of homicide cases (4 percent for other felonies) and interviewed witnesses in 21 percent of homicide cases and, again, 4 percent of other felony cases. Use of experts was similarly rare, occurring in 17 percent of homicide cases and only 2 percent of other felony cases. Written motions were filed, meanwhile, in approximately 26 percent of homicide cases and 11 percent of other felony cases.[44] Criminal trials were and are rarer still. As these numbers show, the norm in criminal litigation is little activity of any sort. But what activity there is, at least on the defense side, is primarily procedural: motions practice, not factual investigation.

That motions practice is quite different from the kind one finds in civil cases. There, pretrial litigation focuses on two sets of motions: the defendant's motion to dismiss, accompanied by an argument that the plaintiff has not stated a legally valid claim, and both parties' motions for summary judgment, in which the two sides offer evidence suggesting the case at hand is easy on its facts, hence one for which trial would be a waste of time. In criminal cases, pretrial litigation focuses on whether the government has jumped through the proper procedural hoops: whether prosecutors have produced the legally required discovery, whether probable cause justified the relevant police searches, whether the defendant was given *Miranda* warnings before he was questioned, and the like.

A civil defendant's success in a motion to dismiss or in a motion for summary judgment indicates that the defendant has a strong claim on the merits: that an accurate adjudication based on all the available evidence would produce a defense victory. A criminal defendant's success on a motion to suppress a confession or physical evidence suggests the defendant has a *weak* claim on the merits: otherwise, there would be no incriminating evidence to suppress. In civil and criminal cases alike, the most favorable settlements go to those litigants who would fare best if the litigation continues. But in criminal cases, the class of favored litigants is upside down: often, the guiltiest do best.

That affects the manner in which defense attorneys spend their time. Interviewing witnesses and visiting crime scenes takes considerable effort. Filing boilerplate motions to suppress physical evidence or to compel discovery is easier. A system in which defense lawyers operate at capacity—another study showed that court-appointed lawyers in one jurisdiction represented 400 felony defendants or 1,000 misdemeanor defendants per year[45]—puts pressure on those lawyers to substitute cheaper forms of litigation for the more expensive kind. By generating more procedural litigation, Warren Court decisions produced less litigation of the merits of criminal charges: whether the defendant committed the relevant crime, acted with the requisite intent, or had some available defense. That cannot help the justice system do its core job of separating those who deserve criminal punishment from those who do not.

The point applies even to procedural rights that are designed to promote *better* sorting, like the right to the effective assistance of counsel or the government's obligation to disclose exculpatory evidence to the defense.[46] Trials with effective defense counsel are more likely to reach accurate guilty verdicts; the same is true of trials that happen after the government has turned over evidence favorable to the defendant. But enforcement of these rights focuses not on the accuracy of the defendant's conviction; rather, the focus is on the rights themselves. The goal is not to identify possibly innocent defendants who lacked quality counsel or were unaware of some piece of useful evidence. Instead, these rights protect *all* defendants harmed by the relevant procedural errors. At best, appellate review of this sort gets at accuracy indirectly. Better simply to ask whether the government proved its case than whether defense counsel behaved properly or whether the prosecutor handed over the appropriate evidence.

The Court's other error—bad timing—requires some explanation. As seen in Table 8, the available nationwide data show fairly stable crime and punishment through the 1950s and early 1960s: not the sort of environment in which a procedural revolution would be expected to generate a backlash. But the nationwide data hide stark regional differences. In the major cities of the Northeast and Midwest, homicide rates were rising throughout the relevant period. Prison populations were either stable or falling—meaning that the amount of punishment per unit crime was falling substantially. In the South, the opposite was true: homicide rates fell substantially while imprisonment rates rose. After 1963, homicide rates rose and per-crime punishment fell everywhere, though both trends were more extreme in the North than in the South.

Take those southern trends first. Two forms of discriminatory justice plagued the Jim Crow South: the failure to protect black crime victims like Emmett Till, and the punishment of black defendants like Gary Duncan—especially those who had allegedly victimized whites—on weak evidence or trumped-up charges. Because the South was changing in the mid-twentieth century, the mix of these two types of discriminatory justice was changing as well. The nonprotection of victims like Till was becoming less common, as is illustrated by the fact that local prosecutors brought Till's killers to trial. Discriminatory prosecutions like Duncan's (and worse) probably grew more common, as white southerners increasingly substituted courts and lawyers for private threats and lynch mobs.[47]

The available imprisonment data show both trends at work. South Carolina's imprisonment rate almost tripled during the 1940s and 1950s; North Carolina's rate doubled, and Virginia's nearly did as well.[48] The largely privatized system of law enforcement by mob that had long ignored

Table 8. Homicide and imprisonment rates per 100,000 population, selected jurisdictions, 1950–1972

City	1950		1963		1972	
	Homicide rate	Imprisonment rate	Homicide rate	Imprisonment rate	Homicide rate	Imprisonment rate
Atlanta	31	131	18	174	55	174
Boston	1	54	7	39	17	32
Chicago	7	90	10	85	22	50
Detroit	6	134	8	103	42	94
Houston	15	77	10	118	23	136
Memphis	10	82	8	87	20	82
New Orleans	11	94	10	116	28	92
New York	4	102	7	101	22	64
United States	5	109	5	114	9	93

Note: Save for the nationwide data at the bottom of the table, homicide rates are calculated by city, imprisonment rates by state. For New York's homicide rates and for the nation's, I use Erik Monkkonen's data; for other cities, the homicide rate is based on data in the annual volumes of the FBI's Uniform Crime Reports. Imprisonment rates are based on data in the annual volumes of the Statistical Abstract of the United States.

crimes against black victims was dying, and increasingly populous southern prisons were a sign of its demise. Less discriminatory law enforcement meant more punishment for crimes victimizing blacks, which in turn meant rising levels of black incarceration—since, in the mid-twentieth-century South as elsewhere, most crime was intraracial. Between 1937 and 1964, the number of blacks annually admitted to state prisons rose 79 percent in North Carolina, 43 percent in South Carolina, and 58 percent in Texas. Between the 1940 and 1960 censuses, the black population rose 14 percent in North Carolina, 2 percent in South Carolina, and 28 percent in Texas.[49] Better protection of black victims made for more frequent punishment of black criminals.[50] So the rising number of blacks in prison was evidence of better law enforcement in cases with black victims—though it probably also meant more punishment imposed on bogus charges such as those Duncan had faced.

The North was another story. There, punishment was falling while crime rose, the opposite of southern trends in the 1950s and early 1960s. Massachusetts and Michigan saw their imprisonment rates drop by roughly a quarter between 1950 and 1963; during those same years, Boston's murder rate more than quadrupled while Detroit's rose by one-fourth. Georgia, Texas, and Louisiana all saw substantial *increases* in imprisonment; the murder rates in Atlanta, Houston, and New Orleans all fell.[51] southern cities remained more homicidal than their northern counterparts, but the two were converging. After 1963, homicide rates rose steeply in all parts of the country. But the North and West saw another trend as well: sharply declining prison populations in the midst of a wave of criminal violence. New York's imprisonment rate fell by more than a third between 1963 and 1972; Illinois's and California's fell 41 percent and 44 percent, respectively. In Chicago and Los Angeles, murders more than doubled; New York's murder rate more than tripled. Even as crime spiraled ever higher, criminal punishment appeared to be collapsing.

The collapse affected urban black neighborhoods most of all. The 1960s saw embattled, nearly all-white urban police forces respond to complaints about their style of law enforcement by pulling back from black neighborhoods, leaving some of those neighborhoods in a state of near anarchy. According to the FBI's urban arrest data, the rate of black arrests fell 14 percent between 1960 and 1968; the white arrest rate rose slightly during the same period.[52] The available evidence suggests that the South saw increases in the numbers of blacks arrested, prosecuted, convicted, and punished, while the North saw those numbers decline significantly—in the midst of a massive crime wave.

These various trends were not equally visible to appellate judges like those who sat on the Supreme Court. In the South, the region to which the Court paid the most attention—the Court's revolution in criminal procedure followed its decision to ban school segregation by only a few years—punishment of blacks was on the rise. A rising number of southern prison sentences coincided with rising numbers of lawyers able and willing to take cases like Gary Duncan's and to carry them up the appellate ladder, which in turn meant more such cases on the Supreme Court's docket. The southern crime trend the Justices were likeliest to notice was the frequent victimization of blacks and whites who lobbied for or exercised civil rights. (Recall that Duncan attracted official hostility partly because his nephew and cousin attended a newly integrated school.) From the Justices' point of view, it must have seemed an ideal time to do something about the excessive punishment of black suspects and defendants by southern sheriffs and district attorneys.

The more populous North saw a different kind of excess: an excess of lenity, not severity, especially in high-crime black neighborhoods.[53] But those trends were largely invisible. Unlike the twentieth century's last decades, crime data of all sorts were not widely publicized, accurate data even less so, and punishment data less still. Thus, the slow collapse in criminal punishment that began around 1950 and accelerated in the 1960s was not widely reported. And appellate courts—including the Court that sits atop America's judicial pyramid—could not see arrests and prosecutions that never happened, nor prison sentences that were never imposed. In short, the southern trend that appeared to require the most attention was *Duncan*-style discriminatory prosecution, which the Justices could see. The failure to provide the "protection of the laws" to black crime victims, a declining problem in the South but a growing problem in the North, remained hidden.[54]

Early in the 1960s, rising levels of northern crime may have been hidden as well. They did not remain so—in part because of the round of

234 of THE PAST

urban riots that began in Harlem in 1964 and continued in black neighborhoods in major cities for the next four summers. These riots were
bloody: 34 were killed in Los Angeles in 1965, 43 in Detroit in 1967, another 23 in Newark that same year.[55] These riots changed the politics of
what 1960s politicians called "law and order"—a political catchphrase
long before it was the name of a popular television franchise. Barry Goldwater, the 1964 Republican nominee, tried to make crime an issue in that
year's presidential campaign. Goldwater was trounced, receiving a mere
38 percent of the vote. In 1968, Republican nominee Richard Nixon and
independent candidate George Wallace copied Goldwater but with more
success: between them, Nixon and Wallace got 57 percent of that year's
popular vote.[56] Rising crime—especially in northern cities, and especially in those cities' black neighborhoods—and several "long, hot summers" (another 1960s catchphrase) explain much of the difference.

At the least, issuing decisions like *Miranda* in the midst of rising murder rates and spreading race riots was a political error of the first order. It
also proved to be an error in legal tactics. The Warren Court's decisions
made arrests and prosecutions, hence also prison sentences, more expensive; that is the natural consequence of adding new restrictions on police
evidence-gathering and new procedural claims to criminal litigation.
More expensive law enforcement inevitably meant less law enforcement,
at a time when punishment per unit crime was falling by 60 percent nationwide.[57] Pendulums that swing in one direction tend to swing back.
The very doctrines that raised the cost of policing and prosecution created pressure on judges to reduce those costs. And the form that Warren
Court doctrines took made cost reduction an easy matter. The consequence
was a more streamlined criminal process—one designed to yield the most
convictions at the least cost—than the one that existed before Earl Warren and his colleagues crafted their constitutional revolution.

To understand that strange consequence, it helps to think of the relevant procedural rules as a legal tax on police officers and prosecutors.
The legal tax consisted almost entirely of procedural rights exercised by
individual suspects and defendants. In American law, individuals who
hold such rights may use them as they wish: rights are almost always
waivable at rightholders' discretion, like property interests that may be
sold when and to whom their owners choose. Cutting Warren's proce-

dural taxes was easy: one need only establish generous waiver rules, and help police and prosecutors to induce as many waivers as possible. After 1970, Warren's successors did just that.[58] Police officers and prosecutors reaped the benefit: dramatic rises in rates of arrest, prosecution, and imprisonment.

Fourth Amendment law bars intrusive searches without probable cause and, sometimes, a warrant. If the target of the search consents to it, however, the warrant and probable cause requirements disappear. Post-1970 Supreme Court decisions make obtaining consent easy: police need only ask; if the circumstances suggest that police requests are the functional equivalent of commands, so much the better.[59] Fifth Amendment law bars the interrogation of arrested suspects without a voluntary, knowing, and intelligent waiver of the suspects' rights to remain silent and to the assistance of counsel. Most suspects are easily induced to waive those rights, given the generous *Miranda* waiver doctrines the post-*Miranda* Court has crafted.[60] The various trial rights the Constitution guarantees apply only to defendants who take their cases to trial. Guilty pleas waive those rights, and the state is free to use even extortionate threats to induce pleas.[61]

In all these areas, constitutional law establishes procedural hurdles the state must clear—but also creates cheap alternatives if clearing those hurdles seems too costly. The net result is to make searches, interrogations, and criminal prosecutions cheaper, not more expensive. Louis Michael Seidman captured the dynamic in a brilliant article about *Miranda* doctrine in the early 1990s. Before *Miranda*, courts reviewed police interrogation under a voluntariness standard that, at least sometimes, had real teeth. Since that decision, judges have relied on *Miranda*'s warnings and invocation rules to ensure that confessions are the product of suspects' free choice, with little examination of the character of police questioning. Consequently, Seidman notes, confessions that might have been suppressed before *Miranda* are routinely admitted today.[62]

Before *Mapp v. Ohio,* the probable cause requirement applied to local police searches but was not rigorously enforced because of the absence of a binding exclusionary rule. In the age of consent searches, probable cause rarely applies—police need *no* cause once they have consent, and, today, they usually have consent.[63] Before the 1960s, criminal trials were more casual than today, but still common: something like one-third to one-fourth of felony charges led to trials. Today, the analogous figure is one-twentieth: the Warren Court made criminal trials more elaborate but also rarer.[64] Fourth Amendment searches, police station confessions, and criminal convictions alike are probably cheaper now, from the government's point of view, than before Warren and his colleagues crafted their procedural code. The law of criminal procedure raised the cost of policing and prosecution when that cost was already too high, and lowered it when the cost was already too low. The consequence was to make *both* the punishment drop of the 1960s *and* the punishment rise of the following three decades larger and more destructive.

The Politics of Backlash

Before the 1960s, conservative politicians were either indifferent toward crime or mildly libertarian in their attitudes toward criminal defendants. Conservative Republican President William Howard Taft opposed Prohibition; his son Robert criticized the Nuremberg prosecutions. Save for the father's fondness for trust-busting and the son's late-career flirtation with McCarthyism, neither Taft ever sought to make political hay from crime.[65] For political conservatives, that stance was natural. Criminal punishment is an especially intrusive form of government regulation. Spending on criminal justice—including prison spending—is redistributive: money spent to warehouse poor criminals comes disproportionately from rich taxpayers' pockets. Conservative politicians dislike government regulation and redistributive spending.

Two conservative governors in the liberal 1960s—George Wallace and Ronald Reagan—upended that tradition.[66] Before Wallace, southern politicians' chief goal with respect to crime was to keep the federal government away from it.[67] Wallace sought to keep the federal government away from civil rights—but with respect to crime, he focused not on states' rights but on black criminals, and (even more) on the liberal white judges who allegedly protected them. His 1968 stump speech included these lines: "If you walk out of this [hall] tonight and someone knocks you on the head, he'll be out of jail before you're out of the hospital, and on Monday morning they'll try the policeman instead of the criminal."

As race riots struck many American cities, Wallace bragged about Alabama's version of social peace: "They start a riot down here, first one of 'em to pick up a brick gets a bullet in the brain." Such racially charged rhetoric worked: Wallace ran strong races in three Democratic presidential primaries in 1964; four years later, he carried five states and won 13 percent of the popular vote on a third-party ticket.[68]

Reagan was more subtle—instead of rhetorical bullets to the head, Reagan noted sadly that "[o]ur city streets are jungle paths after dark" (the jungle reference was a clear piece of racial code: Reagan wasn't *that* subtle)—and also more effective. In his 1966 campaign for California's governorship, Reagan took Wallace-style tough-on-crime rhetoric, made it more respectable, and used it to draw blue-collar Democrats across the partisan aisle in huge numbers: enough to win by a million-vote margin against a seemingly unbeatable opponent.[69] One of his key tactics was to link urban rioting with disorder on college campuses—a largely white crime problem. That move helped him appeal to white racists without identifying himself as one of them.[70] By so doing, Reagan married two political constituencies that his contemporaries thought were incompatible: economic conservatives who had opposed the New Deal and white union members who had formed its core base of support.

Partisan politics was transformed. To northern and western politicians of the 1950s and early 1960s, blacks and pro–civil rights whites were the swing voters for whose allegiance the two parties competed. Dwight Eisenhower won 40 percent of the black vote in 1956; Richard Nixon won nearly a third in 1960.[71] With the support of every Republican Senator, the Republican Eisenhower administration pushed for major civil rights legislation in 1957; though the bill was watered down by Senate Democrats, Eisenhower ultimately signed the first such legislation enacted since Reconstruction.[72] While blacks were the object of partisan competition, blue-collar whites were generally seen as a core part of the Democratic base.[73] Reagan intuited that, thanks to the Kennedy and Johnson administrations' support for civil rights, blacks and white liberals were now solidly Democratic; yesterday's swing voters didn't swing anymore. Rising crime, falling punishment, and liberal Supreme Court decisions protecting criminal defendants' procedural rights had created a new set of swing voters: blue-collar whites. That changed electoral configuration gave conservative Republicans the opportunity to build a national majority, just when that opportunity seemed most distant.

The Warren Court's criminal procedure decisions were crucial to that process, in three respects. First, those decisions allowed politicians to attack black crime indirectly by condemning the white judges who protected black criminals, not the criminals themselves. That gave conservative politicians like Reagan a chance to appeal to more than racist whites. Second, the Court made street crime—violent felonies and felony thefts: classic state-law crimes—a national political issue for the first time since Reconstruction. One reason crime played a larger role in national politics in the last decades of the twentieth century than ever before[74] is that, in the midst of a frightening crime wave, national politicians could talk about the kinds of crime that voters feared most. Instead of Mafia corruption of local governments and labor unions, the crimes that made Estes Kefauver's and Robert Kennedy's careers,[75] the combination of the Supreme Court's decisions and 1960s crime trends made robbery and burglary, murder, and rape national issues. Earlier generations had assumed that only local officials concerned themselves with such crimes. Earl Warren helped change that political equation. Third, because the Court was the Court, crime talk was cheap talk: politicians couldn't change the constitutional rulings that prompted so much controversy, so their criticisms were unburdened by the need to exercise governing responsibility.

Reagan and Wallace exemplified that last point. California's imprisonment rate fell by nearly half during Reagan's two terms in Sacramento. Alabama's imprisonment rate did likewise under Wallace.[76] Neither of these tough-on-crime governors managed to reverse those trends. Their tough rhetoric was just that: rhetoric. Like Kefauver's hearings and Hoover's Ten Most Wanted list, the conservative politics of crime was an exercise in political symbolism that seemed to have no substantive consequences.

But symbols do not remain purely symbolic for long; substantive consequences have a way of catching up to them. When conservatives like Reagan, Wallace, and Richard Nixon[77] won blue-collar white votes by attacking soft judges and (indirectly) black criminals, liberal politicians were forced to respond. Liberal Democratic President Lyndon Johnson supported and signed legislation that funneled money to local police and purported to overrule *Miranda v. Arizona:* the Omnibus Crime Control and Safe Streets Act of 1968, the first of what became a long series of federal crime bills targeting urban street crime.[78] Liberal Democratic presidential candidate Robert Kennedy made tough measures against urban disorder a centerpiece of his campaign for his party's nomination. Jimmy Carter—embodiment of the southern Left in the early 1970s— presided over a 40 percent increase in Georgia's imprisonment rate, while neighboring Alabama's prison population stagnated. Liberal Republican Governor Nelson Rockefeller proposed ramped-up penalties for heroin offenders; the so-called Rockefeller laws became the model for the next wave of tough state drug statutes. The same year Rockefeller signed those laws, New York's imprisonment rate turned up after fifteen years of decline.[79]

For the balance of the 1970s—as liberal Democrats controlled Congress, most state legislatures and governorships, and nearly all big-city mayoralties—prison populations rose steadily.[80] America's punitive turn did not come from the political right, at least not initially. Rather, the rise in punishment came from the left's response to the right's rhetoric.[81] That response soon bred its own response. Once liberal politicians like Johnson and Kennedy embraced punitive politics, the right's bluff had been called. Conservative politicians had two choices: they could back down, cede the crime issue to their liberal opponents, and admit that their tough rhetoric was cheap talk. Or they could follow suit and ramp up punishment still more.

They followed suit. Reagan was once again a key player, the model for his party and for his ideological camp. As governor, he had specialized in combining tough talk with soft policy or no policy at all. As president, his walk matched his talk: he signed into law the most draconian piece of drug legislation to date; partly as a consequence, the federal imprisonment rate doubled in the 1980s. In an increasingly conservative age, state prison populations saw similar trends.[82] The conservative politics of crime remained symbolic at its core—but the symbolism worked only if conservatives were seen as tougher than liberals. What began as a political bluff had become a bidding war.

The bidding war continued through the 1990s, as liberal Democrats faced the same problem that conservative Republicans had faced under Reagan and embraced the same solution. Overall, late twentieth-century states with Republican legislatures and governors increased prison populations faster than states ruled by Democrats—but there were plenty of exceptions. Ann Richards served as the Democratic governor of Texas from 1991 to 1995; she followed Republican Bill Clements and was replaced by Republican George W. Bush. Under Clements and Bush, Texas's imprisonment rate rose 29 percent and 5 percent, respectively; under Richards, it rose 128 percent. Democrat Mel Carnahan replaced Republican John Ashcroft as Missouri's governor in 1993. In Ashcroft's two terms in office, Missouri's prison population grew more slowly than the nation's; in Carnahan's two terms, the number of Missouri prison inmates grew almost twice as fast as the national average. Democrat Douglas Wilder's four years in the Virginia statehouse saw that state's imprisonment rate increase 45 percent. Under Wilder's Republican replacement—George Allen, who campaigned on a promise of ending parole—imprisonment *fell* 2 percent.[83]

The moment that best captured both the liberals' dilemma and their response to it came shortly before the New Hampshire primary in 1992. Then-Governor Bill Clinton, falling in the polls, returned to Arkansas to supervise the execution of a mentally disabled black inmate named Ricky Ray Rector.[84] It worked: Clinton finished a close second in New Hampshire, was hailed as "the Comeback Kid," and went on to win the White House. The Rector execution was Clinton's gruesome answer to the elder George Bush's use of Willie Horton to defeat Michael Dukakis four years earlier. The character of the answer captures the relevant political dynamic. This was no philosophical argument between opposing sides; rather, it was a war of images in which both sides sought to send the same message. As the Horton and Rector incidents illustrated, the politics of crime had devolved into a game of can-you-top-this.

Bush probably found Lee Atwater's Horton ad distasteful,[85] and Clinton may have felt similarly about Rector's execution. If so, the two presidents' distaste highlights an important feature of late twentieth-century politics: right and left alike supported criminal justice policies that, in principle, they found repugnant. The Reaganite right opposed big government yet helped create a prison system of unprecedented scope and size. The Clintonian left opposed racially discriminatory punishment yet reinforced and expanded the most racially skewed prison population in American history. The source of this conflict between politics and principle was the same on both sides. Crime policy was not a means of addressing crime—and the policy's consequences for the poor blacks who were both victimized by crime and punished for it were, politically speaking, irrelevant. Each side supported punitive policies because the other side had done so, and because changing course seemed politically risky.

Such political stances worked because the votes that mattered most— the votes for which the two parties competed, the ones most likely to switch sides if the other side's crime posture seemed more attractive— were not the votes of crime victims and their friends and neighbors, much less of criminal defendants and *their* friends and neighbors. They were the votes of those for whom crime was at once frightening and distant, those who read about open-air drug markets and the latest gang shootings in the morning paper. Neighborhood democracy faded, and was replaced by a democracy of angry neighbors. The consequence was much more criminal punishment, distributed much less equally.

The Supreme Court was hardly responsible for all this. Homicide rates were rising in most of the nation before the 1960s—meaning that rising crime cannot have been caused by Warren Court's decisions issued during that decade. Large social, political, and economic forces lay behind the riots and rising crime that were concentrated in urban black neighborhoods. Likewise, prison populations started falling in the Northeast and Midwest several years before *Mapp v. Ohio* inaugurated the legal revolution in criminal procedure. After *Mapp*, prison populations fell more and faster than police arrests, though the Supreme Court regulated the police more aggressively than it regulated criminal trials.[86] Plus, not all state prison populations fell; some rose even during the 1960s.[87] These facts suggest that local prosecutors, not the police and not the Supreme Court, were the chief force driving inmate populations down during those increasingly violent years. (Just as local prosecutors have been the chief force driving those populations up since 1973.) The Court's decisions probably exacerbated both crime and punishment trends, but the trends themselves had other causes. No doubt the strange combination of a crime wave and a punishment collapse would have produced a backlash with or without the cooperation of Warren's Court.

But if the Justices did not cause the backlash, they made a large contribution to it. Just as the culture wars of the late nineteenth and early twentieth centuries nationalized the politics of vice, just as Estes Kefauver's hearings and Robert Kennedy's Teamsters investigation nationalized the politics of organized crime, decisions like *Mapp* and *Miranda* extended the trend to cover crime in general. The Supreme Court became fodder for the 1968 presidential campaign, while crime was the nation's top domestic issue during that campaign.[88] And nationalized politics was made more perverse by the perversity of the Court's decisions. Had the Court acted to protect against punishment for trumped-up "crimes" like Gary Duncan's or Dolly Mapp's, the public reaction might have been more positive. Had the Court taken steps to give the likes of Emmett Till—along with the many black crime victims in northern cities whose victimization the justice system ignored—a greater measure of "protection of the laws," voters might have seen and approved the justice of the Justices' approach. But the proceduralized law that the Court made seemed designed to protect the guiltiest suspects and defendants. That was not a pattern likely to appeal to ordinary voters.

The true surprise about the Warren Court's criminal procedure decisions is that they *did* attract public support, at least over time. *Miranda* is a good example. Immediately after the Court's decision in the summer of 1966, most surveys showed substantial public disapproval—enough so that in 1968 Congress passed and Lyndon Johnson signed a statute purporting to repeal *Miranda* in federal cases.[89] Then the issue faded. *Miranda* seemed not to cost the police much: the large majority of suspects talked in spite of the famous warnings. After a while, even the police weren't exercised about the decision. When, in 2000, the Supreme Court voted 8 to 1 to uphold *Miranda* and invalidate the 1968 repeal—the majority opinion was authored by conservative Chief Justice William Rehnquist[90]—the move produced no serious public opposition. Supreme Court criminal procedure cases came to seem invisible to the public: the backlash outlasted its causes. A 1989 case striking down legal bans on flag burning[91] attracted far more public attention than even the most consequential criminal procedure decisions. Warren's Court had changed the criminal justice system, and the changes had become permanent.

Those changes were far from inevitable. *Mapp* and *Miranda* were both decided by one-vote margins,[92] and the majority in each case included a pair of Dwight Eisenhower appointees—Warren and Brennan—whose votes surprised their nominators. Brennan was appointed in a presidential election year, 1956, as a means of appealing to Catholic Democrats,[93] hardly a move likely to spawn a pro-defendant revolution in the law of criminal procedure. Like Thomas E. Dewey, who turned down the Chief Justice position that Warren accepted, Warren was a tough ex-prosecutor[94]—not an appointee who seemed likely to author opinions expanding the rights of criminal suspects and defendants. In large part because of his stance toward criminal justice, Dewey came to refer to Warren as "the big dumb Swede." For his part, Brennan "just changed on us," as Dewey (who advised Eisenhower on Supreme Court appointments) later noted.[95] Had either of these two surprising votes proved less surprising, the Court might have adopted the stance Dewey himself probably would have taken had he held Warren's job: pro–civil rights in race cases but tough on criminal defendants.

It was not to be. For the second time in a generation—the judicial attack on the New Deal in the mid-1930s was the first—the Court put itself at odds with most ordinary voters on issues about which those voters cared. One result was nicely captured by the title of Fred Graham's book on the legal revolution of the 1960s: it was a "self-inflicted wound" on the Court.[96] It was also a wound on the nation's politics, and one that has not yet healed.

CHAPTER 9

The Rise and Fall of Crime, the Fall and Rise of Criminal Punishment

In this, our age of infamy
Man's choice is but to be
A tyrant, traitor, prisoner:
No other choice has he.

—Aleksandr Pushkin (1820s), quoted in Alexander Solzhenitsyn,
Cancer Ward, trans. Rebecca Frank (1968)

Don't snitch!

—Popular T-shirt in African American neighborhoods (early 2000s)

Crime's decline is one of the great mysteries of the 1990s . . . No one predicted [it], and the usual theories—better policing, tougher sentences, lower unemployment—don't seem to explain it fully.

—Robert Samuelson, *Newsweek* (1999)

THE TWO GREAT STORIES of late twentieth-century crime and criminal justice were a massive punishment wave and a less than massive but still substantial crime drop. A few numbers capture the importance of these two stories. America's imprisonment rate rose from fewer than 100 per 100,000 population in the early 1970s to more than 500 today. Before 1980, the nation's historical record was 137. In the 1990s and early 2000s, America's rate of violent crime fell by more than a third.[1] We live in a safer country than the one our predecessors knew in the 1970s and 1980s. We also live in a more punitive country—by a huge margin—than at any time in American history.

In broad outline, those stories are familiar. Two other stories are less well known. Before the generation-long punitive turn of the late twentieth century came a generation-long lenient turn, starting in the Northeast and expanding to the West and South. Prison populations fell, and punishment per unit crime plummeted—the number of prisoners per homicide fell 60 percent nationwide, and considerably more than that in the large cities of the Northeast and Midwest.[2] As the explosion in the nation's prison population was unprecedented, so was the collapse in criminal punishment that preceded it. As for the 1990s crime drop, that positive trend followed several decades of bad news about crime, especially urban crime, and especially urban crime in poor black neighborhoods. Rising levels of criminal violence began in the Northeast, Midwest, and West in the early 1950s; the South joined the trend beginning in the mid-1960s. Nationwide, the homicide rate doubled. In most major cities, it tripled, quadrupled, or more. New York's murder rate sextupled; Detroit's multiplied eight times.[3] Beginning in the early 1970s, the two-decade-long rise in crime was followed by a nearly two-decade-long plateau: crime fell modestly in the nation as a whole, but rose modestly—on top of the huge increases of the 1960s—in the nation's cities.[4] The decade-long crime drop of the 1990s followed a nearly two-generation-long crime wave.

So crime rose and then fell, while criminal punishment fell and then rose—precisely what is supposed to happen if punishment deters crime as it should. But the trends do not match up so neatly. The rise in criminal punishment lasted more than thirty years; the crime drop lasted only ten. If more punishment drove urban crime down—it probably helped, but only to a limited degree—the medicine took a surprisingly long time to take effect. Not only was the timing of crime and punishment trends out of sync; so were their respective magnitudes. Punishment levels rose much more than crime fell. Today, our cities are considerably more violent than before the great crime wave of the twentieth century's second half, yet the nation's imprisonment rate is quintuple the rate before that crime wave began. If punishment deters crime, we seem to be getting much less deterrent bang for the imprisonment buck than we once did.

Add it all up, and the picture is quite different than the conventional wisdom allows. We do indeed have a massive, bloated prison population, the criminal justice crisis of our age. But the justice system that produced that population is not hard-wired to punish excessively—or if it is, it became so only recently. A mere forty years ago, America's justice system seemed hard-wired to avoid criminal punishment, not to impose it. In the age of pendulum justice, American criminal justice seems prone to excess in *both* directions. Likewise, the crime drop of the 1990s is not evidence that the system works as it should. More the opposite: even after that crime drop, the nation's bloated prison population coincides with rates of urban violence that, a half-century ago, would have seemed intolerable outside the South.

Instability

The current conventional wisdom holds that the justice system's defining feature is its punitive character. Given the size of the nation's prison population, the point is hard to dispute. But a single generation ago, one might equally plausibly have said that the system's defining feature was its lenient character, the rarity with which criminal punishment was imposed. If one takes a still longer view, it appears that neither severity nor lenity defines the justice system. Instability does.

The figures in Tables 9 and 10 confirm that proposition. Table 9 covers the U.S. murder rate per 100,000 population, imprisonment rate by the same measure, and prisoner-years per murder—the latter figure is a rough index of the relative price criminals pay for their crimes—in 1910 and at ten-year intervals beginning in 1923. Table 10 covers the same information, this time using New York State's imprisonment rate and New York City's murder rate to form the relevant ratio. (Imprisonment data are kept at the state level, not at the local level, and state-level homicide rates are not available before the last few decades. But New York City constitutes a sufficiently large fraction of the state's population that the ratio of state prisoners to city homicides is a decent proxy for the punitiveness of the state's justice system.)

Notice the third column in both tables. In the twentieth century's first quarter, punishment per unit crime was both low and fairly stable. After

Table 9. Murder and imprisonment rates and prisoner-years per murder, United States, 1910–2003

Year	Murder rate per 100,000 pop.	Imprisonment rate per 100,000 pop.	Prisoner-years per murder[a]
1910	8	75	10
1923	9	74	8
1933	10	109	11
1943	5	103	20
1953	5	108	23
1963	5	114	25
1973	10	96	10
1983	9	179	21
1993	10	359	38
2003	6	482	85

Note: The nation's murder rate through 1973 is taken from Monkkonen's data; after that date, the annual volumes of the FBI's Uniform Crime Reports supply the relevant data. The imprisonment rates for 1910 and 1923 are taken from Margaret Werner Cahalan, Historical Corrections Statistics in the United States, 1850–1984, at 30, table 3-3 (Rockville, MD: Bureau of Justice Statistics, 1986); later imprisonment rates appear in Online Sourcebook, table 6.28.2009.

a. In Tables 9 and 10, the numbers of prisoner-years per murder are calculated using murder rates that are rounded to the nearest tenth, not to the nearest integer as in the table's first column.

Table 10. Murder and imprisonment rates and prisoner-years per murder, New York, 1910–2003

Year	Murder rate per 100,000 pop.	Imprisonment rate per 100,000 pop.	Prisoner-years per murder
1910	5	78	14
1923	5	58	12
1933	7	74	10
1943	3	111	41
1953	4	105	26
1963	7	101	14
1973	22	71	3
1983	23	172	8
1993	27	354	13
2003	7	339	46

Note: Through 1973, New York murder rates are taken from Monkkonen's data; after 1973, the data come from the annual volumes of the FBI's Uniform Crime Reports. Imprisonment rates from 1910 and 1923 appear in Margaret Werner Cahalan, Historical Corrections Statistics in the United States, 1850–1984, at 30, table 3-3 (Rockville, MD: Bureau of Justice Statistics, 1986). Between 1923 and 1973, imprisonment rates are taken from the data in the annual volumes of the Statistical Abstract. From 1973 on, imprisonment rates appear in 1991 Sourcebook, 637, table 6.72, and Online Sourcebook, table 6.29.2008.

Prohibition's end, punishment levels fluctuated wildly, like a pendulum that swings ever larger distances rather than smaller ones. In the nation as a whole, the number of prisoner-years per murder rose 123 percent in the thirty years after Repeal; then, in a single decade, that ratio fell by substantially more than half. In the century's last thirty years, the ratio multiplied more than eight times. In New York, the fluctuations were more extreme still. Prisoner-years per murder quadrupled in the decade after Repeal, then fell more than 90 percent in the next thirty years, then multiplied fifteen times in the thirty years after that. These huge swings would be moderated somewhat if we used reliable state homicide data, which do not exist for most of the relevant period—but only somewhat. Since the 1930s, criminal punishment has oscillated between extremes of severity *and* lenity. The pendulum swings both ways.

Whatever else such a system is, it isn't stable. Which is why the hypothesis advanced by the late Senator Daniel Patrick Moynihan—that the rising crime rates of the late twentieth century caused Americans to "define deviancy down"—is either wrong or seriously incomplete. In a famous article published in *The American Spectator* in 1993, Moynihan maintained that criminal punishment was, in practice, neither a necessary evil nor a moral and social good, but a constant that remains unchanged in the face of large changes in crime. In this view, rising levels of deviant behavior prompt not more punishment but redefined deviancy: conduct that would have been condemned in a world with low crime rates is tolerated when those rates rise.[5] Crime rates may vary, but if Moynihan was right, the level of criminal punishment—the amount of deviant behavior a given society is willing to condemn—should tend to hold steady.

That proposition is demonstrably false: in the United States as a whole, criminal punishment has varied more than crime, not less. In the century covered by Table 9, the nation's murder rate varied by a ratio of two to one, the imprisonment rate by a ratio of seven to one, and the number of prisoner-years per murder by a ratio of more than ten to one. Far from punishing some fixed quantity of deviant behavior, twentieth-century Americans tested the limits of criminal punishment in both directions. How little punishment can a functioning criminal justice system dole out in the midst of steeply rising crime? How many criminals can such a system incarcerate when crime is falling? In the 1960s and early 1970s, the justice system answered the first question. In the 1990s and the first decade of the twenty-first century, it has answered the second. Both times, the system overshot the mark. Punishment fell dramatically, then rose stratospherically. Moynihan-style constancy is the characteristic the justice system most plainly lacks.

It may also be the characteristic the justice system most desperately needs. Price stability is a feature not only of healthy economies but of healthy criminal justice systems as well. Stable prices for serious crimes are to time what the rule of law is to place: as the rule of law should guarantee that offenders from different neighborhoods face the same penalty for the same crime, stable prices (meaning the odds of punishment times its severity) should ensure that penalties do not change radically from one year to the next—or, for that matter, from one generation to the next. Change as radical as the United States has experienced over the past eighty years, in both directions, suggests that criminal punishment is based more on political fad or caprice than on the moral quality of the defendant's conduct.

The rise of unstable criminal punishment coincides with the rise of black populations in northern cities, and also with the rise of a more nationalized politics of crime. Outside the South, criminal justice became increasingly about the management of urban black populations: in the Northeast in the early 1950s, 5 percent of the general population but almost 30 percent of the prison population was African American.[6] But those populations did not, and still do not, exercise the kind of power that high-crime immigrant communities exercised a half-century earlier. At the peak of the great wave of European immigration and for at least a generation after, immigrants and their children dominated urban police forces. Slots on those forces were the objects of political patronage; officers answered to ward bosses and were personally involved in local politics. By the mid-twentieth century, those police forces were both more professional and more insulated from local political winds. Even as black crime became the central issue northern city governments faced, black officers constituted fewer than ten percent—usually many fewer—of those cities' police forces.[7]

The evidence is more sparse, but it seems likely that local prosecutors likewise grew more politically insulated. District attorneys still ran for election in the mid-twentieth century, as they do today. But they were be-coming more the creatures of the bureaucracies—and the legal profession—to which they belonged than of the voters whom they represented.[8] (One sign of the change: voters began to treat local district attorneys as some-thing akin to civil servants, routinely reelecting them in high- and low-crime times alike: in the sixty-eight years after Thomas E. Dewey left the office, a grand total of three men served as Manhattan's District Attor-ney. One served less than a single year; the other two—Frank Hogan and Robert Morgenthau—won, between them, seventeen terms in that of-fice.) And the legal profession's ideological slant had changed. In the late nineteenth century, elite opinion held that prosecutors were too lenient, too quick to dismiss winnable cases or bargain away serious charges.[9] In the course of the twentieth century's first half, that state of affairs changed. The early 1920s saw Harvard Law School Dean Roscoe Pound and then-Professor (later Supreme Court Justice) Felix Frankfurter publish a study of criminal prosecution in Cleveland that seemed to show local prosecu-tors were too quick to prosecute and punish, not too slow.[10] By the 1960s, the Pound-Frankfurter view was the professional norm. Many judges and prosecutors had qualms about the efficacy of criminal punishment in general.[11] In the United States, those qualms applied with special force to the punishments imposed on black offenders.

The change in elite opinion extended to politicians. Vice president and Democratic presidential nominee Hubert Humphrey captured the mind-set in the course of the 1968 campaign: "You're not going to make this a better America just because you build more jails. What this coun-try needs are more decent neighborhoods, more educated people, better homes . . . I do not believe repression alone can bring a better society."[12] Notice the equation of repression and criminal punishment. No wonder a generation of local prosecutors and judges, at least in the North and West, drove prison populations down even as crime rose.

This was not the first time democracy had ceased to restrain criminal law enforcement, producing a system that swung wildly between exces-sive lenity and still more excessive severity. Recall the punishment sta-tistics of the late nineteenth- and early twentieth-century South, home of both the nation's smallest prison populations and its largest ones. Blacks and poor whites, the justice system's chief targets (and also its chief beneficiaries), were either barred from voting or seriously restricted in their exercise of the franchise. This partial democracy of upscale whites produced small police forces and unstable prison populations; it also coincided with much higher levels of violence than elsewhere in the nation. In the last two-thirds of the twentieth century, a different kind of partial democracy took shape in northern cities, with voters outside those cities exercising more power, and voters within them—especially the ones who suffered the most from rising crime—exercising less. Prison populations grew more volatile, criminal violence grew more geographically concentrated, and urban crime rates came to resemble those previously known only in the South.

Notice that the decline of local democratic control over criminal justice did not inevitably produce more punishment, nor did it inevitably produce less. As in the early twentieth-century South, it produced both: first much less punishment, then vastly more. The crucial regulating mechanisms that governed northern cities' justice systems in the Gilded Age—frequent jury trials, prosecutors elected by voters in poor and working-class city neighborhoods (because more upscale city neighborhoods and suburbs were more thinly populated than today), and police forces ruled by urban machines that depended on working-class immigrant votes for their survival—faded. Bureaucratic detachment, legal procedure, and symbolic politics took their place. The consequences were poor crime control, rapidly changing punishment practices, and massive inequality.

A Punishment Tsunami

The mid-twentieth century's lenient turn was the product of more detached police, more liberal prosecutors, and a political disconnect between a justice system that served one set of voters but was governed by another. Yet for all that, the justice system's sharp turn toward lenity remains a puzzle. There was no obvious policy reason why prison populations should have fallen in the teeth of rising crime, as they did in the North in the 1950s and throughout the country in the late 1960s and early 1970s. Nor was there any obvious political advantage to be gained by reducing criminal punishment, again in the midst of steeply rising levels of criminal violence. Lenity was partly the consequence of suburbanites' indifference to rising urban crime. Still, by definition, indifference is less than passionate; it is hard to believe there were large political returns to be had for politicians who pushed the number of inmates in their jurisdictions downward. It seems safe to say that, had the mid-century drop in America's prison population never happened, no one would be surprised.

The punitive turn was different: it had both an obvious policy justification and carried the equally obvious promise of political benefit. The size of the increase in late twentieth-century prison populations may surprise, but the fact and timing of the increase should not.

The policy justification was simple: by the early 1970s, punishment per unit crime had fallen massively, and crime had risen massively, especially in increasingly violent cities. Recovering the justice system's ability and willingness to punish serious crimes was a legitimate goal, even a social necessity. Proof is impossible, but the low and falling prison populations of the 1960s and early 1970s probably contributed to rising levels of serious crime during those years—even though comparably low prison populations in the early 1900s seem not to have had a similar effect. The small number of inmates in the later period coincided with high and rising crime rates: much higher than anything northern cities saw in the twentieth century's early years. By the late 1960s, the moderately lenient justice system of a century ago had become something much more extreme. Wherever the line is between a merciful justice system and one that abandons all serious effort at crime control, the nation had crossed it. A turn toward more punishment was natural.

As for politics, the punitive turn was partly the consequence of the trends that preceded it. Simultaneously rising crime and falling punishment were bound to create a backlash, and the backlash was bound to result in rising prison populations. By providing focal points for public anger, the coincidence of urban race riots and pro-defendant Warren Court decisions like *Mapp* and *Miranda* helped to nationalize the backlash and made it more extreme when it came. Entrepreneurial politicians like George Wallace, Ronald Reagan, and Richard Nixon on the right and Lyndon Johnson, Robert Kennedy, and Nelson Rockefeller on the left tapped into that backlash and added to its force. None of this should come as a surprise. Unlike the lenient turn of the 1950s and 1960s, the punitive turn that followed was inevitable.

Its scope and size *weren't* inevitable. Imprisonment rates did not just rise sharply in the late twentieth century; those rates quintupled. African American imprisonment rates came to exceed the rate at which Stalin's Soviet Union incarcerated its citizens. Residents of black neighborhoods increasingly believed, with reason, that their life choices were limited to those Pushkin identified two centuries ago: they could ally themselves with their prison-bound young men or with the system that bound them. Tyrants, traitors, prisoners—none were good options. No wonder black neighborhoods in the early twenty-first century, when imprisonment rates were reaching their peak, spawned a "don't snitch" movement.[13]

Why, then, did the punitive turn amount to a turn toward extremism and excess? We have explored two reasons: a political backlash that led to a partisan bidding war, and the rise of procedural rights crafted by the Supreme Court and the subsequent rise of rules governing the all-too-easy waiver of those rights. Four more reasons stand out. First, the punitive turn was so punitive because it was so long-lasting—and it lasted so long in large part because the crime wave that prompted it lasted even longer. Second, the allocation of budget authority—state and federal governments fund the prisons, and local governments pay for their own policing—made imprisonment cheap for local officials, who proceeded to impose far too much of it—which is why the populations of our cities are not only overpunished but also underpoliced. Third, the law of guilty pleas made such pleas easy for prosecutors to extract, which allowed the justice system to increase dramatically the ratio of convicted felons to prosecutors and defense lawyers. Fourth and finally, substantive criminal law changed in ways that likewise encouraged more guilty pleas and fewer jury trials. The law once gave juries and judges the power to decide whether the defendant had behaved badly enough to justify criminal punishment. Today's substantive law leaves that power in prosecutors' hands.

Take these points in turn. If the punitive turn went too far, it did so because it lasted for more than a generation, not a decade or two. The 1920s and 1930s also saw imprisonment rates rise sharply; the end of that period witnessed a crime drop comparable with the one in the 1990s. Both times, punishment and crime rose in tandem while the justice system fought a drug war. Both times, after an extended period of failure, crime turned down sharply. Both times, the imprisonment rate kept rising for several years after crime began to fall. In the first period, the average annual rate of increase in the nation's imprisonment rate was 4 percent; in the second period, the rate of increase was 5 percent—higher, but not dramatically so. But the first period saw imprisonment rise for sixteen years; the latter period saw prison populations rise for twice that length of time. That fact, plus the harsh drug sentences of the late twentieth- and early twenty-first centuries (which had no counterpart in the Prohibition era), explains why imprisonment rose 85 percent in the 1920s and 1930s but more than 400 percent in the thirty years after 1972.[14]

In other words, America's inmate population rose so *high* because it rose for so *long*—and the wave of incarceration that swept over the country beginning in the mid-1970s lasted so long in large part because the crime wave that prompted it lasted even longer. Crime began rising in the Northeast in the early 1950s, spreading to the rest of the nation in the 1960s. After 1973, crime fell modestly in the nation as a whole, but the trends were different in high-crime cities, where crime continued to rise for the balance of the 1970s and again in the late 1980s. Depending on where in the country one lived, one saw either a thirty- or forty-year-long wave of violent crime. A thirty-year run-up in the prison population was a natural consequence. Instead of rising punishment driving crime rates down, rising urban crime drove punishment ever higher.[15] Causation was running in the wrong direction.

The second cause has to do with the politics of budgets, which gave local prosecutors every incentive to send as many defendants as possible to the ever-more-swollen state penitentiaries. States pay for those penitentiaries, but local officials—chiefly prosecutors and trial judges—make the decisions that fill them. To the local voters who elect those officials, and hence to the officials they elect, prison sentences are nearly a free good. Meanwhile, local governments, not states, pay more than 90 percent of the tab for the local police forces that are responsible for the overwhelming majority of street-level law enforcement.[16] Policing and imprisonment are substitutes: they are the two main ways governments spend money to battle crime, and historically, more of one tends to mean less of the other. One of these alternatives is heavily subsidized; the other isn't. No wonder the number of urban police officers per unit population held steady in the 1970s and 1980s, while the imprisonment rate more than tripled. The upshot is a radically different justice system than America once had: in 1970, there were more than twice as many local police officers as prison inmates; today, there are more than twice as many prisoners as local cops.[17]

The point is not that this allocation of power and budget responsibility dictated a huge run-up in the prison population. Authority over prisons and policing was allocated in the same way in the 1960s and early 1970s, when prison populations were low and falling. Rather, the point is that once political pressure was brought to bear on local prosecutors to ramp up criminal punishment, as happened beginning in the mid-1970s, no force pushed in the opposite direction. Once the punitive turn got rolling, it kept rolling; there was nothing to stop it. The justice system became the rough equivalent of a vessel with no one at the wheel, its course and speed set by forces that were opaque even to the government officials who were subject to them.

The consequence was a failure of democratic governance. Where state and local officials alike were responsible for rising levels of imprisonment, neither was truly responsible. Prosecutors sent more and more defendants to state prisons in part because state legislators kept building more prison cells: a classic application of the *Field of Dreams* principle— if you build it, they will come. For their part, the legislators kept adding to their states' stock of prison beds because local prosecutors kept sending defendants to state prisons: if they're coming, you must build it. Neither set of officials fully controlled the process by which those prison beds were made and filled, so neither was able to slow or reverse that process. And the voters with the largest stake in that process—chiefly African American residents of high-crime city neighborhoods—had the smallest voice in the relevant decisions.

These claims run counter to the growing academic conventional wisdom that politicians consciously used the criminal justice system as an alternative means of governing the nation's poor.[18] That conventional wisdom gives too much credit to the politicians, whose conduct offers little evidence that they were seeking to create a justice system like the one we have today. And if the politicians did consciously choose the system we have, their predecessors in the 1960s and early 1970s must have chosen the justice system *they* had: a justice system dominated by lenity, not severity. Absent a theory that explains why politicians' and voters' preferences changed so radically in such a brief period of time, it seems more likely that the various actors in the system did what came naturally. They followed their own preferences when the voters allowed, and made choices that conformed to short-term political incentives when the voters insisted on a different tack. Cumulatively, those choices changed the justice system radically: first in one direction, then the other. But neither the officials in charge of criminal justice—from Supreme Court Justices to state legislators, from prosecutors to police chiefs—nor the voters planned on such radical change, in either direction.

The need to rein in criminal justice budgets might have placed limits on the rise of the prison population had that need existed. It didn't, because those budgets were too small. In fiscal year 2005—after the run-up in imprisonment—corrections budgets amounted to a mere 2.6 percent of state spending nationwide. That is one-fifth of state expenditures on education, barely half what state governments spend on health care or highways. Cities' and counties' spending on local jails amounted to even less: only 1.6 percent of local budgets. Federal spending on federal prisons was smaller still: less than three-tenths of 1 percent of overall federal spending, and that was before federal spending took a huge upward turn in the wake of the 2008 financial crisis.[19] These figures were simply too small to exert much pressure on government budgets, especially during the boom years of the 1980s and 1990s when government revenues rose steadily and steeply.[20]

Plus, as governments discovered during the twentieth century's last decades, sharp increases in corrections spending need not be accompanied by proportionate increases in spending on courts, lawyers, and police officers. Prisoners might be expensive to incarcerate, but they were cheap to arrest and convict. Arrests per police officer rose by one-third between 1976 and 1989.[21] Felony prosecutions per prosecutor doubled between 1974 and 1990.[22] Per-case spending on lawyers for indigent defendants fell by half between 1979 and 1990.[23] These data all point to the same conclusion: as imprisonment ramped up through the 1970s and 1980s, America's criminal justice system grew much more efficient—fewer personnel were needed to send more inmates to the nation's prisons and jails.

The punitive turn's third and fourth causes have to do with legal doctrine, and require more explanation. The presence of more than 1.3 million inmates in state prisons, using only 60 percent more prosecutors than had been used to incarcerate 200,000, required a justice system that tried many fewer cases and pled out many more.[24] That justice system in turn required a body of law governing guilty pleas that did little governing, leaving prosecutors free to extract such pleas by any means that suited them. The generation after 1970 saw the emergence of that body of law. The second legal change was more far-reaching. Guilty pleas are easily induced when the law that defines crime is both broad and specific, leaving little room for defense arguments that might lead to jury acquittals. Historically, American criminal law was at once narrow and vague. Both features changed gradually over the course of the twentieth century—but the change was especially stark in the decades that saw America's inmate population explode.

The late twentieth-century law of guilty pleas is nicely captured by *Bordenkircher v. Hayes* (1978).[25] Paul Hayes stole a check belonging to the Brown Machine Works, a local business in Lexington, Kentucky. Hayes made out the check to the Pic Pac grocery for $88.30 and forged the signature. In January 1973, he was charged with "uttering a forged instrument," a crime that carried a sentence of two to ten years in prison. That is not the sort of case one wants to take to trial because there is no good way to explain why Hayes was signing a check that wasn't his. So Hayes was, predictably, looking for a plea bargain. But he had a record: two felony convictions, one for robbery and one for "detaining a female" (plea bargained down from a sexual assault charge). So his prosecutor, Glen Bagby, offered Hayes a plea on the forged check charge with a recommended sentence of five years. If Hayes declined to take the deal, Bagby threatened to charge him under Kentucky's three-strikes law, which carried a mandatory life sentence. Hayes refused the offer, Bagby filed the three-strikes charge, whereupon Hayes was convicted and sentenced to life in prison.[26]

A decade or two earlier, Hayes probably would have been charged with stealing the check, pled guilty, and gone to prison for two years, the low end of the statutory sentencing range. By the time *Bordenkircher* arose—Hayes was convicted in 1973—local prosecutors like Bagby were beginning to take a tougher stance toward repeat offenders like Hayes, hence the five-year offer. Bagby had not wanted to send Hayes away for life: the habitual criminal law was a means of getting Hayes to accept Bagby's offer, nothing more. Were it otherwise, Bagby would not have been willing to let Hayes plead and receive a mere five years in prison. But once Hayes declined the offer, Bagby had little choice but to go ahead and file the habitual criminal charge. Plea bargaining is what academics call a "repeat-play" game; the same lawyers negotiate pleas again and again. A prosecutor who becomes known as a pushover will be taken advantage of, not once but many times. So while Bagby's threat to use Kentucky's three-strikes law was probably unfair even in Bagby's eyes, once the threat was made, it had to be carried out.

The central issue before the Supreme Court in *Bordenkircher* was whether Bagby's threat was permissible. The Court held that both threat and charge were indeed permissible—whether or not anyone with Hayes's record had been charged under the three-strikes law, and whether or not Bagby himself believed the life sentence was harsher than Hayes deserved. The fairness of the charge was irrelevant. The only question, in the Court's view, was its formal legality: as long as the three-strikes law was constitutionally valid (it was), and as long as its terms applied to Hayes (they did), Bagby's threat raised no legal problems.

The Court's decision allowed the government to do two things that, in combination, were hard to pull off: raise the guilty plea rate and raise average sentences, *at the same time*. Plea bargains involve compromise— the defendant agrees not to take his case to trial; the prosecution agrees to less severe punishment than the law might allow. More guilty pleas mean more such compromises, which in turn should mean lower average sentences. But if the law allows for punishment more severe than even prosecutors wish—as it did in *Bordenkircher,* and as it did increasingly often in the twentieth century's last years—those "compromises" are easy ones for prosecutors to make. Bagby evidently thought a five-year sentence was a fair result. The small amount of the stolen check might have suggested a more lenient sentence would be fairer; on the other hand, Hayes's criminal record counseled in favor of severity. How these dueling arguments might have played out in bargaining and before a sentencing judge is anyone's guess. But Bagby did not need to guess, nor to run the risk that a contested sentencing hearing might yield a result more to Hayes's liking than the five-year offer. The three-strikes law meant that Bagby could, in effect, guarantee that Hayes would receive no less than five years.

So what? If the Kentucky legislature believed someone with Hayes's record deserved life in prison, what could possibly be wrong with an offer to let the defendant plead on more generous terms? The answer is this: the legislature may have believed no such thing. The three-strikes law was mandatory with respect to sentencing judges—once convicted under that law, Hayes had to receive a life sentence—not with respect to prosecutors like Bagby. (Even were it otherwise, Bagby easily could have evaded the law by charging Hayes with some form of misdemeanor theft, thereby eliminating the third felony conviction. Most sentencing rules are like this: in practice, they bind judges, not prosecutors.) The legislators who enacted the law knew full well that prosecutors would exercise discretion when enforcing it—meaning that some defendants with three felony convictions would receive much lighter sentences than the law contemplated. But the legislature opted not to choose which defendants would be so blessed. Instead, prosecutors could choose. Bagby was free to use the three-strikes law not as a means of imposing just sentences on repeat offenders, but as a means of extracting plea bargains without the need for any real bargaining. After *Bordenkircher,* offers like Bagby's would be accepted, and quickly.

The rules on which such offers were based became common in the century's last few decades. Recidivist sentencing laws like Kentucky's, mandatory minimum sentences for illegal weapons possession or for possession of more than some specified amount of various illegal drugs—these and similar laws granted prosecutors the power to threaten sentences that neither the enacting legislators nor the prosecutors themselves wished to apply, all as a means of inducing guilty pleas with prosecutors' preferred sentences attached. The predictable consequence was more easily induced guilty pleas *and* harsher sentences.

Bordenkircher was followed by lower court decisions that extended even farther. When Jonathan Pollard was prosecuted for spying for Israel, the government induced him to plead guilty by threatening to incarcerate his sick wife for the balance of her life.[27] Another defendant pled guilty after the government threatened to imprison his parents for trying to help him evade capture[28]—an offense that is almost never enforced against anyone, much less against suspects' families. A host of murder defendants plead guilty and receive life sentences rather than go to trial and see prosecutors seek the death penalty. (This gives prosecutors an incentive to charge capital murder in cases in which they have no desire actually to impose the death penalty. Capital punishment's largest consequence is not the few dozen executions that happen each year in the United States but the many life sentences imposed after plea bargains designed to avoid death sentences.)[29] Outside the plea bargaining process, such threats would be deemed extortionate. Within that process, such threats were par for the course. That made guilty pleas, with harsh sentences attached, dramatically easier for the government to obtain.

Change in the character of substantive criminal law—the body of law that defines crimes—had the same effect. Three mutually reinforcing changes were key: criminal liability rules grew broader, the number of overlapping criminal offenses mushroomed, and the definition of crimes grew more specific. These changes rested on a larger change in criminal lawmaking: legislators, not appellate judges, became the system's chief lawmakers. Instead of restating the common law of crimes, American criminal codes have become more code-like and more expansive. Each of these shifts in substantive criminal law made it possible for prosecutors to prosecute more defendants, and each made it easier for prosecutors to induce a larger share of those defendants to plead guilty.

The most important change may have come in what lawyers call the law of *mens rea,* the law of criminal intent. Traditionally, that body of law required proof that the defendant acted with a state of mind that was worthy of moral blame. Some vestiges of that earlier state of affairs still exist in American law; the law of homicide is the clearest example.[30] But for the most part, the concept of wrongful intent—the idea that the state must prove the defendant acted with a "guilty mind," the English translation for the Latin *mens rea*—has gone by the boards. Criminal intent has become a modest requirement at best, meaningless at worst.

The older state of affairs is nicely captured by Justice Robert Jackson's opinion in *Morissette v. United States* (1952).[31] The defendant took spent bomb casings—metal tubes used by military pilots in practice bombing runs—from government land and sold them for scrap, realizing some $80 in the transaction. Because these events happened in 1948, when military bases filled with unused equipment dotted the countryside, Joe Morissette was charged with theft of government property.[32] Morissette evidently knew what the casings were and clearly knew they were found on government land. Save for the fact that anyone might care to prosecute him, there was no pertinent fact about which he could plausibly claim mistake. Jackson nevertheless overturned Morissette's conviction, reasoning that no jury had found "criminal intent . . . *wrongfully* to deprive another of possession of property."[33] The word "wrongfully"—which appears nowhere in the relevant statute—does all the work in that phrase: the kind of intent Morissette lacked was not cognitive or motive-based; it was moral. In *Morissette,* proof of criminal intent meant, roughly, proof of the kind and level of moral fault that one ordinarily associates with theft.

Compare *Morissette* with a California decision called *People v. Stark* (1994).[34] Stark was a general contractor on the edge of insolvency. While building some doctors' offices, Stark took payments received from the doctors who hired him and used them to pay off debts to subcontractors who had worked on earlier jobs. His still-unpaid current subcontractors complained, as did the doctors. Stark was charged under California's diversion of funds statute, which forbids the use of money intended for one job to pay for another.[35] There was no evidence that Stark sought to stiff either the doctors or his current subcontractors; he maintained, plausibly, that he planned to perform all his contracted work and to pay all his debtors. At most, he was guilty of borrowing without his lenders' permission. His true offense was going bankrupt. Nevertheless, the court found, Stark had the "general intent" required for conviction under the California's statute because he intended to do what he did: use money from one set of clients to pay subcontractors who had worked on other clients' jobs.[36]

The distance from *Morissette* to *Stark* captures the change in the law of criminal intent. *Morissette* required that, as a condition of criminal conviction, a jury find that the defendant knew he was doing something wrong. Not so in *Stark:* the general intent standard used in that case, the standard that applies in the large majority of criminal cases, includes no requirement that the defendant intend to harm someone, to do wrong, or to break the law.[37] Blackstone's classic dictum that criminal intent requires a "vicious will" forms no part of that standard. The defendant is guilty if he intended his physical acts and if those physical acts violate the conduct terms of a criminal statute. But save only for those too intoxicated to know what they are doing, everyone intends his physical acts—and, under the governing law, intoxicated defendants are usually judged as if they were sober.[38] The upshot is that, in most cases, findings of criminal intent are automatic. The law of intent no longer serves the function it served in *Morissette:* a means of ensuring that only those who understand that they are engaged in serious misconduct can be criminally punished.

The phenomenon is not limited to intent. Robbery requires theft by force or threat of force. But threatened force turns out to mean little more than theft in the presence of others: the threat to do what is necessary to keep the stolen money or goods is implied by the defendant's conduct.[39] Burglary once required proof of violent entry into a building or separately secured structure. Now, entry into any room, even through an open doorway, with intent to commit a crime once inside counts as the offense.[40] Thefts that once had to be charged as larceny, a lesser offense that carried more modest penalties, can now be punished as burglaries and robberies, which lead to more substantial sentences. The definition of larceny or simple theft has likewise expanded; it now includes cases that once would have produced only civil suits for breach of contract.[41] Fraud once required proof of a false statement of fact upon which the victim relied to his detriment, thereby causing him to lose some amount of money or some piece of property. Today, no identifiable victim need suffer any tangible loss; it is enough if the defendant defrauded her victim of "the intangible right of honest services."[42] And the government need not prove a false statement of fact: false promises and passive deceit— meaning nondisclosure, not false disclosure—are good enough.[43]

All these doctrines make guilty pleas easier to extract by eliminating issues that might otherwise lead to jury trials. The broader criminal liability is, the less likely the defendant can raise any colorable defense to the charges against him, and the more likely the defendant will agree to plead guilty. And the steeply rising number of guilty pleas was crucial to the massive increase in America's prison population.

The rise of criminal codes with many highly specified overlapping crimes accomplished the same end. American law contains no requirement that a single criminal incident be charged as a single offense. Prosecutors may charge as many distinct crimes as the law supports—and the defendant may be punished separately for each one so long as each offense requires proof of at least one fact that the others don't.[44] By substituting a list of overlapping offenses for a single crime, legislators offer prosecutors two ways to induce defendants to plead guilty. The first has to do with specificity—the more specifically defined crimes are, the more likely the result of any criminal trial will be clear, leaving little reason for the defendant not to plead the case out. The second means of inducing pleas is charge stacking. Charging a series of overlapping crimes raises the odds that the defendant will be convicted of *something,* and often allows a prosecutor to threaten a harsher sentence than would attach to any single offense. Both effects raise defendants' incentive to plead guilty.

A host of criminal statutes fit the description just offered; here are two examples. Sections 922 and 924 of Title 18 of the U.S. Code define the chief federal gun crimes: mostly violations of registration requirements, illegal gun possession, and the use of guns when committing other crimes. Fifty-two distinct offenses are defined by those sections. A century ago, the law of sexual assault contained three offenses: rape (sex by force), assault with intent to commit rape, and statutory rape (sex with an underage victim).[45] Rape was defined narrowly: the government had to prove not only physical force and the absence of consent, but also that the victim had resisted the sex act to the limits of her ability. Today, the resistance requirement has been eliminated, and the degree of force required for conviction is substantially lower than in the past.[46] These changes in the law of rape have received a great deal of scholarly attention. Another change has occasioned less comment: the law of rape has been replaced with a much broader law of sexual assault, with state codes defining a series of different types of coercive sexual contact. California's penal code defines seven forms of rape, three versions of statutory rape—including a

criminal bar on consensual sex with a partner under the age of 18—
and six versions of what the code calls "sexual battery": sixteen offenses
in all.[47]

The reform of the law of rape is usually credited to the work of
feminist scholars like Susan Brownmiller, Susan Estrich, and Catherine
MacKinnon.[48] These scholars rightly called the older law of rape mi-
sogynist for its protectiveness of perpetrators rather than victims. Their
work spawned a rape reform movement; the dropping of the old resistance rule and the expansion of the meaning of forcible sex are widely
seen as the consequence of that movement—and are likewise widely seen
as victories for the women's right to sexual autonomy.[49] But it may not
have been women's autonomy that lawmakers sought to protect. After
all, there was no large-scale social or intellectual movement to reform the
law of theft or fraud, yet those areas likewise saw dramatic expansions in
the scope of criminal liability. Such expansion has been the norm over the
course of the last generation, not the exception. Were it otherwise, the
guilty plea rate in felony cases could not have reached 96 percent, and
without that high guilty plea rate, the prison population could not have
reached a million and a half.[50]

The combination of these two related trends—expanding criminal liability and a rising number of guilty pleas—meant that, as the *quantity* of
criminal punishment grew, its *quality* declined. Thanks to broader criminal liability rules, the status of convicted felon no longer means what it
once did: offenders acquire that status having committed offenses much
less severe than the ones that traditionally led to felony convictions and
prison terms. Thanks to more easily induced guilty pleas, criminal litigation does a worse job than it once did of separating those who have committed the crimes charged from those who haven't. Not only have Americans chosen, at least tacitly, to punish millions more criminal defendants
than in past generations, we have also chosen to do the punishing with
less justification and with sloppier procedures.

Changes in substantive criminal law contributed substantially to the
punitive turn, but what prompted the changes in substantive criminal
law? In part, legal change flowed from the long backlash that followed in
the wake of the rising crime and falling criminal punishment of the
1960s. Expansive crime definition allowed legislators to be seen as tough

on crime.[51] The Supreme Court decisions that reshaped the law of criminal procedure helped the process along: broader and more specific substantive law was a means of inducing guilty pleas, which were in turn a means of evading the otherwise costly procedural rights that Earl Warren's Court created.

But those were not the only forces pushing toward the kind of criminal law under which Americans live today. Legal theory—the world of ideas—also played an important part. One of the large trends of late twentieth-century legal thought was the rise of textualism: the theory that statutory and constitutional texts mean what they say and nothing more. That proposition sounds obvious; in truth, it is anything but. Much of American law has its origin as common law: law made by judges in the course of resolving individual cases. Over time, statutes have displaced much of that common law, but the displacement is not total: courts continue to fill in gaps in statutory language, and sometimes add exceptions and extensions that legislators did not themselves enact. Textualists look askance at judicial lawmaking of this sort. In their view, the judicial interpretation of statutes is no dialogue between legislators and judges, to use a common academic metaphor. Rather, it is a monologue in which legislators speak and judges follow orders. The theory is most often associated with its leading judicial proponent, Justice Antonin Scalia, who wrote a famous article justifying his views titled "The Rule of Law as a Law of Rules."[52] The title is telling. Textualism is not simply a theory of deference to legislators (though it is that); it is also a theory that renders law more rule-like, less vague and flexible, because judges are not permitted to read exceptions and defenses into statutes.

Historically, criminal law was far from a textualist field. Long after states enacted criminal codes, as they did during the course of the nineteenth century, appellate courts continued to define many of the field's key doctrines. The (older) law of criminal intent and the law of defenses—self-defense, duress, insanity, and the like—were almost entirely the product of court decisions, not statutes. So when textualism struck criminal law, it did so with special force.

An example makes the point. The federal false statements statute criminalizes falsehoods made "on any matter within the jurisdiction . . . of the Government of the United States."[53] Exceptions are made for some proceedings in federal courts and before Congress; otherwise, the text allows for no exemptions from criminal liability. Nevertheless, over the course of several decades, a number of federal courts held that an "exculpatory no"—a false denial of guilt without more—would not yield liability under the false statements statute.[54] The idea was that anyone caught off guard in a weak moment might refuse to own up to embarrassing behavior (the false denial need not have involved illegality). Such a refusal seemed too innocuous to trigger federal criminal liability.

In *Brogan v. United States* (1998),[55] the Supreme Court faced the question whether the exculpatory no exception should survive. Brogan was a labor union official whom the government suspected of labor racketeering—basically, taking bribes from employers to sell out the workers he represented. But the FBI agents investigating Brogan were uncertain that they could prove the charge; some of the alleged payments had happened long enough ago that the statute of limitations had run, and other payments might fall within one or another exception in the labor racketeering statute. So the agents went to Brogan's home and asked him whether he had taken money from the relevant employer. Brogan said no; the agents already knew the correct answer was yes. After Brogan spoke, the agents told him he had violated the false statements statute. In effect, the agents used the statute to establish a fallback charge in case the more serious racketeering allegations didn't pan out. Brogan argued that his denial fell within the exculpatory no doctrine. Notwithstanding the shadiness of the government's tactics, the Supreme Court rejected Brogan's argument and invalidated the doctrine on the ground that the statute's text didn't authorize it.[56] Scalia wrote the majority opinion. Before the last generation, doctrines like the one that once governed exculpatory no's were common, and decisions like *Brogan* were rare. Today, those two propositions have been reversed.

Scalia's opinion in *Brogan* did not cite the Model Penal Code (MPC), a draft criminal code issued by the American Law Institute in 1962 and largely authored by longtime Columbia law professor Herbert Wechsler.[57] But *Brogan* was as much Wechsler's handiwork as Scalia's. When drafting the MPC, Wechsler's goal was to rationalize criminal law, to replace vague common-law standards that Wechsler thought meaningless—like the longstanding requirement that murders be committed with "malice aforethought"[58]—with more precise legislative rules. (*Stark*, not *Morissette*, represented something akin to Wechsler's preferred *mens rea* analysis.) In the three decades after its issuance, a majority of state legislatures extensively revised their criminal codes and Congress debated revising the federal criminal code. The MPC proved influential in that process. This was not because of the content of its rules: most MPC provisions turned out not to matter much; outside a few pockets such as the law of criminal attempts, few legislatures adopted them.[59] But the MPC's method—resolve as many issues as possible with legislative text, leaving little room for judicial lawmaking—caught hold. Before the MPC, courts often asked what intent standard seemed appropriate for the criminal statute in question: *Morissette* was the model. After the MPC, such questions were more often treated as a matter of interpreting statutory texts, as the exculpatory no issue was treated in *Brogan*. The MPC made the rise of Scalia-style textualism swifter and more complete, and made criminal law more vulnerable to it.

The upshot was a body of criminal law defined almost wholly by legislatures, not jointly by legislators and appellate judges. The difference matters. When arguing in court, prosecutors and defense attorneys alike have the chance to justify their preferred legal outcomes. Potential criminal defendants are not exactly a powerful lobby in legislative hallways, so legislators tend to hear from only one side—the government's side. Making American criminal law a more legislative field inevitably meant both broader and more specific criminal liability rules. As criminal law grew more textualist, it also grew more tilted in the government's favor. One result was more decisions like *Brogan*. Another result was more inmates in prison cells.

Drugs (and Violence)

Nowhere have the consequences of expanded criminal liability been greater than in the criminal law of drugs. Recall the criminal law of alcohol during Prohibition: possession of liquor was not a crime, and would-be defendants were permitted to serve alcohol to guests in their homes. No such limits apply to today's drug crimes, as *United States v. Hunte* (1999)[60] illustrates. Cheryl Hunte had the poor judgment to have a boyfriend, Joseph Richards, who was a "known drug dealer." Hunte joined Richards and one of his colleagues for a road trip during which Richards picked up several thousand dollars' worth of marijuana. Hunte made none of the plans, participated in neither the relevant negotiations nor the drugs' packaging, and, save for smoking one joint, did not handle the drugs. Most important of all, Hunte neither funded the drugs' purchase nor stood to gain from their sale. She was simply along for the ride. Even so, a panel of judges from the United States Court of Appeals for the Seventh Circuit affirmed her conviction for possession of marijuana with intent to distribute and conspiracy to do the same, on the ground that there was "some nexus between the defendant and the drugs."[61]

Hunte captures the character of contemporary drug law. Distribution is proved by proving possession of more than user quantity, and (as Cheryl Hunte learned to her dismay) possession need not depend on whether the defendant has actually handled the merchandise. Worse, drug law—state and federal alike—assigns punishment based on the weight of the drugs found in the defendants' possession. That principle leads to decisions like *Whitaker v. People* (2002),[62] in which the Colorado Supreme Court affirmed the twenty-year prison sentence of a "mule" carrying a suitcase full of methamphetamine on a Greyhound bus. David Whitaker was charged with importing methamphetamine into the state and with possession with intent to distribute the drug. The government was not required to prove that Whitaker knew how much methamphetamine he carried, nor that he knowingly crossed a state border, nor that he stood to make a large profit from his errand.[63] (Major dealers rarely travel on Greyhound buses.) As in *Hunte*, both liability and punishment rested on the drugs and on the defendant's proximity to them.

Drug laws like those at issue in *Hunte* and *Whitaker* make both convictions and draconian prison sentences nearly automatic. All plausible mitigating arguments—I was traveling with my boyfriend; I had no idea how much I was carrying; at worst, I'm a small player in a large criminal enterprise—are deemed out of bounds. No wonder the rate of imprisonment for drug crime has multiplied tenfold since the early 1970s; today's rate exceeds the total imprisonment rate in 1975.[64] Nothing remotely comparable happened during Prohibition, in large part because the law of Prohibition made mass imprisonment for alcohol violations impossible. With respect to drug crime, the law makes mass imprisonment easy.

This has given rise to another phenomenon that has fueled the rise of American prison populations: the use of easily proved drug offenses to punish harder to prove violent felonies. Consider a recent story about a Boston gang bust:

> Authorities said yesterday they are keeping a promise to prosecute 25 members of a violent street gang they hold responsible for 57 shootings and six slayings in Dorchester and Mattapan in two years.
>
> The Lucerne Street Doggz, who authorities said have about 40 members ranging in age from 18 to 28, now face federal and state gun and drug trafficking charges that could keep some jailed for up to 40 years.
>
> "We told them we wanted them to put their guns down," Police Commissioner Edward F. Davis said at a press conference . . . "The ones that continued are being prosecuted today," Davis said. "We are following through on the warning that was issued" . . .
>
> Seeking to break the gang's grip and improve the quality of life for residents, authorities said, they held two meetings last year involving gang members, police, job training groups, members of the 10 Point Coalition, and law enforcement.
>
> During the meetings, dubbed Operation Ceasefire, authorities detailed the prison sentences that courts can impose for crimes involving guns and drugs, according to an affidavit by Boston police Sergeant John J. Ford . . . [65]

The reason for the bust was the spate of shootings for which the Lucerne gang is responsible. But the crimes charged are selling drugs, and buying and selling unregistered guns.

That story is not unusual, and not limited to Boston. For the past generation, punishing drug and gun crime (by "gun crime," I mean offenses involving gun registration and licensing, not the use of guns to commit violent felonies) have been used as means of battling violent crime. Even when the drug in question is marijuana, prosecutors regularly justify drug prosecutions as surrogates for violent crime charges.[66] The pattern is especially clear in the federal system. Bill Clinton instructed the FBI to treat gangs like the Lucerne Street Doggz as it had treated the Mafia, and charging proxy crimes was a key means of taking down Mafia families, dating back to Robert Kennedy's tenure in the Justice Department.[67] The Lucerne story illustrates the degree to which the pattern has taken hold in local prosecutors' offices as well.

The historical norm was very different. During Prohibition, unrelated charges like the tax charge that sent Al Capone to prison were sometimes used to target bootleggers, but alcohol charges were not used to target more traditional crimes. The other vices that federal and state law have forbidden over the years were used strategically against high-profile mobsters such as Lucky Luciano or the various Mafia defendants, who faced federal gambling charges—but Mob cases were rare, and nearly all of them were federal. With few exceptions, laws banning violent felonies were enforced straight up, as is proved by the high acquittal rates in homicide cases that were common a century ago. Charges like those in the Lucerne case were unknown. Why did that state of affairs change?

There are three answers: historical coincidence, a changed political structure, and law enforcement necessity. Mass markets for illegal drugs arose just after the wave of violence that swamped northern cities, and just when political pressure was forcing big-city prosecutors to ramp up criminal punishment. For urban police looking to increase their arrest numbers and urban prosecutors seeking higher conviction rates, drug cases were a godsend. As for political structure, local electorates seem to like transparent charging practices—meaning that the crimes charged are the reasons for criminal punishment. That is probably why drug sentences are so much more severe in urban black neighborhoods than in wealthier and whiter suburbs.[68] Suburban drug cases are prosecuted directly, not as a substitute for other crimes. In most suburbs, criminal justice remains a locally democratic enterprise. In high-crime cities that enterprise has changed, and not for the better.

The third reason—law enforcement necessity—requires explanation. Police clearance rates in violent crime cases were high in the past because the cases were easy. Killings tended to follow a few simple fact patterns; identifying the killer was not hard. As Roger Lane has noted, that state of affairs changed beginning in the mid-twentieth century: both stranger killings and robbery-murders rose, and the friends-and-family killings that had dominated homicide statistics in the past declined sharply.[69] Clearance rates fell.[70]

As evidence-gathering in violent crime cases grew more difficult, the law of criminal procedure placed more restrictions on it. Confessions and eyewitness testimony are crucial to the prosecution of many violent felonies. Thanks to *Miranda,* confessions grew harder for the police to obtain in the 1960s,[71] especially from suspects savvy enough to understand the value of their procedural rights. As for eyewitness testimony, criminal violence is frightening, not only to its victims but to those who see and hear it as well; witnesses fear becoming victims themselves if they testify. The rise of violent urban gangs in the last generation is partly attributable to the gangs' skill at silencing would-be witnesses.[72] Both the rise of police interrogation doctrine and the rise of urban gangs made violent crime cases harder to build and harder to win—especially in high-crime city neighborhoods.

In earlier generations, these problems might have produced procedural reforms designed to make policing and prosecution of violent offenses easier. But constitutional law bars the most obvious reforms. *Miranda* grants sophisticated suspects the right to be free from all police questioning, not merely the coercive kind—and that right cannot be undone by mere politicians. The same is true of the right to confront the state's witnesses, which forces American prosecutors to build cases on live testimony rather than the written case files European prosecutors use.[73] Drug law seemed to offer a ready solution to these problems. Physical evidence—the drugs themselves, the paraphernalia used to consume them, the cash used to buy them—is omnipresent in drug cases, making eyewitness testimony either peripheral or needless. Police investigation is cheap: a single street stop or buy-and-bust might produce multiple arrests, with many fewer man-hours than in a robbery or homicide investigation. And drug markets in poor city neighborhoods were and are associated with high rates of violence in those neighborhoods.[74] For all these reasons, the substitution of drug prosecutions for violent felony cases was natural.

Drug laws passed in the 1970s, 1980s, and 1990s facilitated that substitution. Draconian sentences far beyond anything attached to vice crimes in the past were attached to possession of even small quantities of selected drugs—and the drugs selected for such severe treatment were those used and sold in poor black neighborhoods.[75] As *Hunte* illustrates, the definitions of the relevant crimes were mechanical; no open-ended defenses or intent arguments were made available to the unlucky defendants charged with drug offenses. Late twentieth-century drug statutes, state and federal alike, did what the Mann Act had done three-quarters of a century earlier: instead of defining the prohibited conduct, they aimed to make punishment for other conduct easier.[76]

That proposition makes sense of several otherwise puzzling features of drug enforcement and drug politics. Both the timing and demographics of drug punishment track violent crime, not drug crime. The thirty years after 1960 saw an unprecedented explosion in criminal violence. The thirty years after 1970 saw an unprecedented explosion in drug punishment. As for demographics, blacks are imprisoned for drug crime at nine times the rate of whites. Rates of illegal drug use vary little across the races. Rates of criminal violence vary much more: in 2006, the murder rate among whites stood at 3 per 100,000; among blacks, the analogous figure was 24.[77]

The link between drug enforcement and violent crime also explains the absence of large-scale political opposition to contemporary drug laws, despite the draconian punishments those laws impose on drug offenders. Much milder punishments for other vices prompted much more political opposition in the late nineteenth and early twentieth centuries. That earlier age was more moralist than ours: early twentieth-century Americans criminalized all forms of extramarital sex; twenty-first-century Americans make adult consensual sex a constitutional right.[78] Yet Prohibition proved politically unsustainable, while the drug war is politically untouchable. If drug enforcement *isn't* a response to criminal violence, these political facts seem inexplicable.

There is more. Politicians and judges alike worried obsessively about the chronically inconsistent enforcement of the Eighteenth Amendment, and about what those enforcement patterns said about the rule of law in America.[79] Drug enforcement has been plagued by inconsistency and discrimination far worse than anything Prohibition produced, yet the drug war's supporters still refuse to abandon their cause. Everything about the war on drugs and the politics associated with it makes sense only on the assumption that drugs were not the war's primary target. Violence was.

So, in the many cases in which direct punishment for violence was impossible, drug laws have made indirect punishment easy. That increased both the size and the racially disproportionate character of state prison populations in two mutually reinforcing ways. First, the use of drug charges as a substitute for violent felony charges increased sentences for *non*violent drug crimes. Drug crimes were not solely proxy crimes; a large fraction of incarcerated drug offenders, like Hunte and Whitaker, were suspected of drug crimes and nothing else. But the laws authorizing their punishment were designed with violent offenders in mind. So nonviolent drug offenders were, in effect, punished both for the crimes they committed and for the violence of the drug markets in which they participated. Because poor city neighborhoods had the most violent drug markets, residents of those neighborhoods received the most severe drug sentences. The use of drug crime as a (partial) proxy for violence amounted to a sentencing enhancement, and a dramatic one at that, for black drug crime.

Second, because drug punishment was and is a poor tool for deterring violence, violence levels remained high even as drug punishment escalated, which reinforced political support for tough drug punishment in a vicious circle. Recall the Lucerne Street bust. The gun and drug charges filed in that case may track gang members' history of criminal violence, but only in the aggregate. The gang was targeted because of the many acts of violence its members committed, and (at least in part) because of the many acts of violence members of other Boston gangs committed. But no gang member knows which particular acts of violence prompt such targeting. From the point of view of any individual offender, the odds that any particular shooting will lead to a later drug trafficking prosecution must be very low. Meanwhile, the gains from the shooting, or at least a large share of them—vengeance, status within the gang, a reputation for toughness— are captured by the perpetrator. One reason why violence by drug-dealing gangs remains high is that, from the point of view of the perpetrators, it pays.

The consequence is massive drug punishment that deters neither violence nor drug crime. Its dominant incentive effect has more to do with

politics than with crime. From its inception, the drug war has been fueled
by violence in urban black neighborhoods. Continued violence means a
continuing supply of the symbols on which the symbolic politics of crime
feeds. Politically speaking, the drug war is self-sustaining as long as it
continues to create casualties. Tragically, those are never in short supply.

The Great Crime Drop

By the early 1990s, an ever-rising level of urban violence seemed a permanent feature of American life. Predictions of even higher crime rates, fueled by the coming of age of Baby Boomers' children, were common.[80] As
the generation-long crime wave that began in the 1950s took everyone by
surprise, so too did the crime wave's end. No one expected crime to fall.

But it did fall, and considerably. Beginning in 1992, crime of all sorts
began to decline; the decline was especially steep in major cities, which
had borne the brunt of the preceding crime wave. Unsurprisingly, falling crime had large political effects, three of which were key. First, the
crime drop seemed to vindicate the course the justice system had followed, including the massive rise in imprisonment that began in the
mid-1970s and continued through the century's end. That made the imprisonment rise harder to stop and reverse than it might have been otherwise. Second, as crime fell, it became a less salient political issue, especially for state and national politicians. That made large-scale criminal
justice reforms harder to enact. The third effect cut the other way: to the
extent that politicians did pay attention to crime and criminal justice,
the attention was less one-sided than before. Legal changes that favored
suspects and defendants became thinkable. Political space for criminal
justice reform opened up.

The crime drop's political and legal effects have occasioned surprisingly little comment, but a large literature debates the drop's causes. A
host of factors have been credited with falling crime: the growing economy of the 1990s, the end of the boom in crack cocaine, rising imprisonment levels, rising numbers of urban police officers, changes in police
tactics, even changes in abortion rates.[81] Obviously, the potential causes
with the largest implications for criminal justice policy involve imprisonment and policing. Increased numbers of both inmates and police of-

ficers probably contributed to the crime drop, and the former may have contributed more than the latter. Even so, putting more police boots on violent urban street corners proved more cost effective than putting more young men in prison cells.

Begin with the crime drop's magnitude. According to the FBI's data, felony thefts fell 30 percent between 1991 and 2000. Violent felonies fell by a third, homicides by more than 40 percent.[82] As Table 11 shows, some large, high-crime cities saw even larger declines. Notice that, large though it was, the crime drop was small by comparison with the huge, decades-long rise in urban crime that preceded it. The average drop in the murder rate in the nine cities listed in Table 11 was just under half. The average *rise* in the murder rate from 1950 to 2000 in those same cities was 220 percent. Even after the 1990s, urban crime rates remained vastly higher than in the early 1950s. The one major exception was the South, where cities like Atlanta and Houston saw a reversion to something close to their midcentury murder rates. In 1950, only southern cities saw double-digit murder rates; fifty years later, southern-style levels of criminal violence were common in cities nationwide. Even in New York, where crime fell more than in any other major city, the murder rate was—and remains[83]—substantially higher than a half-century before.

Table 11.   Murder rate per 100,000 population, selected cities, 1950–2000

City	1950	1991	2000	Percentage change, 1991–2000	Percentage change, 1950–2000
Atlanta	31	51	32	−38	+4
Boston	1	20	7	−65	+386
Chicago	7	33	22	−33	+208
Denver	4	18	6	−67	+67
Detroit	6	59	41	−31	+567
Houston	15	36	12	−67	−22
Los Angeles	3	29	15	−49	+363
New York	4	29	9	−70	+135
Philadelphia	5	28	22	−20	+273
Median	5	29	15	−49	+200

Note: See Uniform Crime Reports: 1950, at 94–101, table 35; Uniform Crime Reports: 1991, at 108–56, table 8; Crime in the United States: 2000, at 115–57, table 8. The last two columns in the table are calculated based on murder rates rounded to the nearest tenth, not to the nearest integer as in the table's first three columns.

Crime rates leveled off after 2000. The median murder rate in the nine cities listed in Table 11 rose slightly between 2000 and 2008; the nation's murder rate fell slightly. In five of the nine cities listed in Table 11, murders fell; in the other four, murders rose. Nationwide, violent felonies and felony thefts continued to decline, but modestly: by about 10 percent, not by one-third as in the 1990s.[84] The crime drop of the twentieth century's last decade became a crime plateau in the new century's first decade.

In the short run, the crime drop reinforced the political status quo. By the time crime began to fall, America's prison population had been rising steeply for two decades. Had crime remained at 1991 levels, rising inmate populations might have been seen, correctly, as an expensive policy failure. Instead, tougher and more frequent punishment seemed a policy success—one the voters demanded more of. For some years after crime rates began to fall, *New York Times* crime reporter Fox Butterfield filed stories about the anomaly of rising imprisonment in the midst of falling crime.[85] Conservative commentators have mocked this supposed anomaly, claiming instead that rising imprisonment *produced* falling crime rates.[86] The clear implication is that prison populations should rise still more so that crime might fall still more.

In the medium to long term, the crime drop produced at least the potential for substantial political change. As late as 1995, the Gallup poll placed crime as the nation's number one domestic political issue. By the beginning of the new century, the issue had faded considerably.[87] In 1994, Congress passed and President Clinton signed legislation offering significant federal subsidies for the hiring and training of more police officers. By the early 2000s, that money was diverted to homeland security; the idea that the federal government would pay for another 100,000 cops on city streets (as Clinton had promised) was politically dead and remains so today.[88] That too is part of the crime drop's legacy.

Falling crime has produced more positive changes as well. In 1994, in the same legislation that subsidized local police hiring, Congress authorized federal court injunctions against police forces with a pattern of violating citizens' constitutional rights.[89] In 2000, a Republican governor of Illinois ordered a moratorium on executions in that state due to doubts about the guilt of some of the state's death row prisoners[90] (and as a means of distracting voters from the governor's own legal problems). In the last years of the twentieth century and the first years of the twenty-first, some two dozen state legislatures enacted laws limiting or banning racial profiling, and requiring the keeping of records of traffic stops so that the bans might be enforced. Some of those same legislatures adopted measures designed to reduce their states' prison populations.[91] These were the actions of savvy politicians, not academic law reformers. They would have been politically impossible in, say, the late 1980s, when crack markets were booming and murder rates were rising. For a generation, the state and national politics of crime all but foreclosed moves that might benefit criminal suspects or defendants. Thankfully, that generation is over.

The list of causes assigned to the crime drop is as varied as its political consequences. The destruction of the crack boom in the last half of the 1980s led the younger brothers of warring dealers to follow different paths, lest they wind up dead or in prison as their older brothers did. The growing economy of the 1990s gave would-be criminals better options for earning a living legally. Tougher gun control laws made gun crimes more costly, hence less common. *Weaker* gun control laws made it easier for potential crime victims to protect themselves against predatory crime, thereby deterring such crime. Changes in the abortion rate in the 1970s led to fewer young men available to commit crimes in the 1990s. The rise of community policing led to more effective police work, which in turn produced lower crime rates. The expansion of urban police forces increased the police presence in high-crime city neighborhoods, producing less crime in those neighborhoods. The vast increase in the nation's inmate population reduced crime both by incapacitating hard-core offenders and by deterring others who wished to avoid long prison terms. Last but not least, "cyclical forces that are not the result of crime policy changes, population trends, or the economy" might account for a large fraction of the crime drop.[92]

Some of these theories have been effectively debunked; others plainly hold at least a germ of truth. Neither the growing economy nor gun control laws—in either direction—contributed substantially to the 1990s crime drop.[93] The end of the crack boom probably did so, as did changes in the abortion rate as part of a larger change in fertility among teenage girls.[94] (Just as more young men in the population meant more crime in the 1960s, fewer young men helped produce falling crime rates thirty years later.) And given broadly similar crime trends elsewhere in the Western world, "cyclical forces" surely played a significant role in America's crime decline.

The important question is whether changes in policing and imprisonment, or either of them, are responsible for a substantial share of the crime drop. If so, 1990s crime trends may amount to an argument for still more imprisonment, for the institutionalization of new police tactics, and/or for more increases in the size of urban police forces. With respect to imprisonment, the leading work has been done by economist Steven Levitt and by sociologist Bruce Western. Levitt estimates that about one-third of the drop in violent crime—roughly, a drop of 12 percent—was due to increased imprisonment. Western's estimate is a good deal lower: about a tenth of the decline in crime, meaning a drop of 2 percent to 5 percent.[95] Notice that even if Levitt's estimate is closer to the mark than Western's, the effect is small given the magnitude of the rise in imprisonment. The 1990s saw imprisonment rise by more than half, on top of huge increases in the preceding two decades. By itself, that 50 percent increase was greater than the entire prison population in 1982—and that year saw what was then the highest imprisonment rate in American history.[96]

As Levitt notes, his relatively high estimate of the value of increased imprisonment does not take full account of declining marginal utility: each additional increment of criminal punishment is worth a little less than the one before. Even if, in the aggregate, increased imprisonment accounted for a substantial fraction of the 1990s crime drop, the value of the last portion of the increase may approach zero or may even be negative— as Western emphasizes.[97] Of course, the marginal utility of all things declines; imprisonment is not special in that respect. But given the magnitude of the late twentieth-century increases in the prison population, the odds are high that the value of additional increments of punishment *now* is trivially small, and possibly perverse.

Compare the figures cited above with Levitt's estimate of the effect increased police hiring had on crime in the 1990s: between one-fifth and one-tenth of the crime drop, or a 5 percent to 6 percent crime decline overall. That sounds modest, but the increase in policing was modest, too: the number of local police officers per unit population grew by a mere 10 percent during the 1990s, compared with a 58 percent rise in imprisonment during that decade—on top of an already record-high prison population.[98] If Levitt's estimated crime consequences are right, it took between $700 million and $840 million in additional police spending to produce a 1 percent drop in crime. The analogous amount of spending on prisons and jails was $1.6 billion. Using Western's lower estimate of the benefits of increased incarceration, the additional corrections spending needed to produce a 1 percent crime drop was between $3.9 billion and $9.6 billion.[99] The lesson of the 1990s is that, given our already swollen prison population, the more cost-effective crime-fighting strategy is putting more police boots on violent city ground, not putting more criminals in prison cells.

And these per-dollar crime benefits dramatically understate the benefits of policing relative to imprisonment. For the most part, the cost of a rising prison population is not felt in corrections budgets. The bulk of that cost takes the form of broken lives, jobs never held, and marriages and families never formed. The collateral costs of more policing are much lower—indeed, they are more benefit than cost, given the other major policing trend of the 1990s: the rise of a style of policing that focused more on crime prevention and less on criminal punishment.

Consider that trend. An increase in the number of urban police officers did not produce an increase in the number of arrests. Instead, as the number of officers rose, the urban arrest rate fell (by 22 percent), and the rate of arrests of black suspects fell even more (by nearly one-third).[100] After a generation of rising efficiency in American criminal justice—more arrests, convictions, and prison sentences per police officer or prosecutor—urban policing grew dramatically *less* efficient. For the most part, the additional officers were not used to staff new SWAT teams or to make more undercover drug buys. Rather, higher levels of policing led to a greater police presence on high-crime city streets before crimes happened, not afterward. That increased police "footprint" in turn made possible the parallel increase in police interactions with the local population, the core idea behind community policing, which has become urban America's reigning philosophy of police work. High-crime neighborhoods could begin to see urban police forces as means of keeping young men out of trouble, not tools used to put ever more of those young men behind bars.[101]

So the 1990s saw governments employ two very different crime-fighting strategies, one of which was a good deal more successful than the other. One was to ramp up punishment from already stunning levels. The other was to ramp up policing more modestly; the latter strategy coincided with a change in policing style that focused more on prevention and less on punishment—more on improving relationships with residents of local communities and less on maximizing arrests. These two anticrime strategies flowed from decisions by different levels of government. More punishment stemmed partly from the decisions of local prosecutors, partly from tougher sentencing laws, and partly from procedures and substantive rules that facilitated easy convictions through guilty pleas. State and federal appellate judges, state legislators, and members of Congress produced those legal rules. The increase in policing was partly due to congressional subsidies, but was mostly the product of local decisions: cities paid for the majority of the increase in the size of their police forces, and continued to pay for more than 90 percent of their police budgets.[102] And the rise of preventive, community-oriented policing was almost entirely the product of local decision making. In short, the "soft" strategy was more locally democratic, the "tough" strategy more the product of decisions by state and national judges and politicians. The soft strategy succeeded better, while the tough strategy was far more expensive. Centralized power has a poor track record in American criminal justice.

But the softer of these two strategies soon fell victim to bad economic trends. The recessions that followed the bursting of the dot-com bubble and the September 11 attacks led to significant cuts in the size of urban police forces. Roughly half of the 1990s increase in the size of urban police forces has been undone. Meanwhile, the prison population continued to grow, albeit more slowly than before.[103] So far, the crime-fighting strategy that depended most on state budgets has prevailed over the one funded by even more cash-strapped cities. That was true even before the financial crash that struck in the fall of 2008. It may prove still more true after.

The greatness of the great crime drop of the twentieth century's last decade is yet undetermined. The drop's size was substantial: a major social achievement, at least in the short run. Its long-term consequences are less clear. If, a couple of decades hence, the crime drop appears only to have reinforced the criminal justice status quo, if American prisons remain overstuffed and American cities underpoliced, it will amount to little more than a missed opportunity. On the other hand, if the crime drop creates the political space in which large-scale reforms can happen, it may be at once the best and most consequential trend in the long and troubled history of American criminal justice. The range of future possibilities is large.

The massive decline in criminal punishment that began in the Northeast in the 1950s and spread to the rest of the nation in the 1960s and early 1970s was a social catastrophe; it contributed to disastrous levels of urban violence and disorder and made a destructive backlash inevitable. The still more massive increase in criminal punishment that followed was likewise catastrophic, inflicting deep wounds on the neighborhoods where crime and punishment are concentrated. Now the need is for something more than (not less than) another swing of the pendulum. The justice system has seen enough extremism and excess. Justice and moderation, not alternating periods of lenity and severity, must be the system's lodestars now. How to find and follow those better paths is the subject of the next chapter.

PART 3

The Future

For the past half-century, American criminal justice has experimented with rule by centralized law and partly centralized politics. The experiment failed. The justice system suffers from the rule of too much law, and from the rule of the wrong kind of politics.

The keys to useful reform are decentralization, local democracy, and—last but definitely not least—money. Local neighborhoods should exercise more power over the administration of justice within their bounds, as they once did. State and federal governments should exercise less, as *they* once did. One of the keys to making those things happen is more jury trials, with juries drawn from neighborhoods, not metropolitan counties. In turn, those trials will happen only if both substantive law and procedure change—the changes need not be radical—to make guilty pleas more costly. Local governments should pay more for the prison beds they use, and less for the police officers they employ, which would make for fewer prisoners and more cops.

It would be too optimistic to call these changes probable. But they are possible, with the right legal vision and with a large enough measure of political will. Discrimination, excess, and injustice are the frequent products of the nation's failed justice system. It need not be so, and perhaps one day, will not be so.

CHAPTER 10

Fixing a Broken System

The decision as to what kind of conduct by African Americans ought to be punished is better made by African Americans . . . than by the traditional criminal justice process, which is controlled by white lawmakers and white law enforcers.

—Paul Butler, *Harper's Magazine* (1995)

Butler's Argument

In the magazine article just quoted, former prosecutor and later law professor Paul Butler famously—some would say infamously—argued for "the subversion of American criminal justice."[1] Butler, a black man himself, maintained that far too many young black men were being sent to prison for nonviolent drug offenses, and urged black jurors to respond by refusing to convict black defendants in drug cases, regardless of the governing law and the evidence. That is, Butler argued for jury nullification. The argument was not well received: even the liberal *New York Times*,[2] not to mention a bevy of academic opponents,[3] criticized Butler for making it. Butler's own words explain why. Jury nullification is "subversion"; it undermines the rule of law.[4] If black jurors will not convict black drug defendants, the law of controlled substances will differ for blacks and whites. Race-based substantive law seems a poor response to criminal justice racism.

Yet Butler's argument is both less radical and more attractive than first appears. For most of American history, white jurors exercised the power that Butler suggested black jurors exercise: the power to acquit despite proof of intentional criminal conduct—defining both criminal conduct and intent as those terms would be defined today. The label "nullification" did not attach to that power. On the contrary, substantive criminal law invited the discretionary judgments that Butler's critics call lawless. Extralegal mercy was not extralegal; it was part and parcel of the way crimes were defined. Butler's critics ignore that fact, and also this one: the legal doctrines that invited jurors to exercise mercy in the past have all but disappeared. Jury nullification became a much-debated topic in the 1990s not because jurors grew less respectful of the law, but because the law grew less respectful of arguments that might prompt the exercise of mercy.

As the law that defines crimes and sentences grew harsher, the power to exercise mercy did not vanish. Rather, it migrated and changed form. Instead of juries and trial judges deciding whether this or that defendant merits punishing, prosecutors decide who deserves a trip to the nearest penitentiary. Thanks to substantive law that makes convictions easy to obtain and acquittals much harder, prosecutors' decisions tend to stick. More broadly and specifically defined crimes have helped to reinforce the rule of discretion, not the rule of law. It sounds strange but remains true: embracing Butler's defense of jury nullification would be a step in the direction of a better past, one that honored law more and official discretion less. So much for subversion.

Butler's argument highlights the crisis of legitimacy that the criminal justice system faces. A system that locks up a large fraction of young black men might prompt resistance even if black men and women chose whom to imprison and for how long. If those choices are made by outsiders, residents of the communities where mass incarceration hits hardest, or at least many of them, are bound to see the justice system as an alien force that does not have those communities' best interests at heart. Once that happens, criminal punishment is, at best, a weak deterrent. In this case, the nation's swollen prison population is not just a disaster, but a pointless disaster. One way or another, that crisis must be addressed, and addressing it requires reducing the prison population substantially.

At the same time, crime must be held in check. Even after the 1990s crime drop, urban homicide rates outside the South remain at historically high levels. Historical data with respect to other violent felonies and felony thefts are harder to come by, but the same is probably true of those offenses. Today's high crime rates carry a huge social cost. Were a sharp drop in the prison population to push crime rates even higher, as likely happened in the 1960s and early 1970s, that cost would be still higher. The goal must not be fewer prisoners alone, but fewer prisoners *and* less crime—along with a justice system that seems more legitimate to residents of high-crime, mostly black city neighborhoods.

How are those goals to be reached? The short answer is by making today's style of criminal justice more democratic. Local, state, and national governments might change the allocation of budgetary responsibility for criminal justice: in particular, who pays how much for local policing and state prisons. The right changes could produce fewer prisoners and more cops, which would push crime rates down even while reinforcing the trend toward neighborhood-friendly styles of policing. Prosecutors' incentives might be better aligned with the interests of those who live where crime and punishment loom largest. Without radical change in either substantive law or procedure, the number of jury trials might be increased substantially, and jurors might be given a larger role in resolving tried cases. Jury selection might be altered so that juries better represent the neighborhoods where crimes happen—the chief means by which today's justice system can be made more locally democratic, and hence more legitimate in the eyes of those whom the system targets.

The point of these changes is to alter the allocation of power over criminal punishment in the United States in a way that legal conservatives as well as Butler-style liberals might approve. Criminal law enforcement was once governed locally; the residents of the neighborhoods most affected by it had a large say in its size and character. Today's justice system is more centralized: state and federal officials, along with suburban and small-town voters, have more power over urban criminal justice than in the past, and residents of high-crime cities have less. If anything about American criminal justice needs changing, that does.

Policing and Punishment

For the better part of a century in the Northeast and Midwest, the ratio of police officers to prison inmates stood, roughly, at two to one. In the

South and West, it was closer to one to one. Today, nationwide, that ratio stands at less than one to two.[5]

More than any other statistic, that one captures what is most wrong with American criminal justice. Police officers facilitate criminal punishment: they arrest the offenders whom prosecutors convict and prison wardens punish. But in the aggregate, large police forces have the opposite effect. More cops on city street corners tend to mean fewer inmates in prison cells. The lenient style of criminal justice in northern cities a century ago used large police forces; the more severe South was much less well policed. The link between more cops and fewer prisoners remains strong today—as does the link between those two characteristics and lower crime rates. The city with the biggest increase in the size of its police force during the 1990s was New York. The same city saw the biggest drop in urban crime during the 1990s. And the state that saw one of the smallest rises in its imprisonment rate in that decade and the biggest imprisonment drop since is again New York.[6] States that saw both higher than average increases in the number of local police officers and lower than average increases in prison populations saw an average drop in violent crime of 31 percent. States in the opposite categories saw violent crime fall an average of only 2 percent.[7] Putting more police officers on city streets belongs on a very short list of policy moves that should reduce *both* crime *and* the number of prisoners.

Increasing the number of police officers would have two other good results. Putting more officers on urban street corners means investing in the institutions that are most responsive to the people who call those street corners home. Thanks to the rise of community policing, urban police meet with, consult with, and listen to residents of high-crime city neighborhoods to a degree that no one else in the justice system does. More money for urban police forces thus amounts to an injection of local democracy into a system that badly needs the medicine. The second good result concerns the allocation of police time and personnel across crimes. Laws banning violent felonies are underenforced in poor black neighborhoods; drug crimes in those same neighborhoods are punished too frequently and too harshly. Increasing the police-to-population ratio would address both problems. New York's experience in the 1990s supports that hypothesis: the city's policing rate rose by more than a third, clearance rates for nondrug felonies also rose sharply, and felony drug arrests fell.[8] That combination is natural: massive levels of drug punishment exist in part as a cheaper substitute for direct enforcement of violent crimes. More personnel make direct enforcement affordable, and thereby also make the indirect kind less attractive.

How can the ratio of police officers to prisoners be changed? One answer is by changing who pays for local police forces and state prisons. As things stand now, cities and counties pay nearly all of local police budgets, while state governments pay for building and running state penitentiaries. That allocation of budget responsibility makes it easy for local governments to impose too many prison sentences while hiring too few police officers.[9] The incentives would change for the better if states, or state and federal governments taken together, paid half the bill for local policing (the charge would come to about $34 billion per year), while local governments paid half the cost of the prison beds they used (roughly $21 billion per year).[10] Both cost-shifting measures are important, but the first is more so. Long ago, state and federal governments assumed a large share of the responsibility for paying for urban public schools, though the evidence that more money means better school performance is thin. The evidence that hiring more police officers improves crime control—without ramping up prison populations—is more robust.[11] Yet cash-strapped cities are left to fund their police forces on their own. The predictable result is underpoliced city streets.

There are two large political obstacles to changing that state of affairs. The first has to do with private-sector police: security guards, privately funded neighborhood patrols, and the like. For most of the twentieth century, the use of private police declined as the number of public police officers rose: crime control and order maintenance increasingly became the responsibility of governments, not private entities. By the late 1960s, public police officers substantially outnumbered private ones. By the century's end, the ratio of public officers to private security guards was two to three, and the disparity was growing—and that ratio does not take account of the roughly 100,000 private investigators and store detectives.[12] Increasingly, public police patrol is limited to those areas whose residents and business owners cannot pay for their own security. Inevitably, that fact reduces the incentive for wealthy taxpayers to pay for more police officers.

The second obstacle is more serious. The financial crash of 2008 and its aftermath initially prompted a huge wave of federal spending, a tiny portion of which helped cities minimize cuts in their police forces—there was too little money to prompt increases in force size.[13] In the medium-to-long term, the crash has created enormous pressure to cut government budgets of all kinds to bring revenues and expenditures into some semblance of balance. New spending initiatives are suspect and will remain so. As in the nineteenth century—recall the Panic of 1837 that led to elected judges and prosecutors, or the Long Depression of the 1870s that killed Reconstruction, or the depression of the 1890s that reinforced Jim Crow's rise—so, perhaps, in the twenty-first: hard economic times may shape the character of criminal justice long after the hard times end. If so, the effect will be very much for the worse.

But while the politics of policing seems unpromising, it is not an insurmountable obstacle to better policy. Federal and state aid for local law enforcement means more jobs, and in a time of high unemployment, job creation remains a political imperative, huge deficits notwithstanding. There is precedent for that kind of aid, at least at the federal level. The federal government has invested in local police twice before: in 1968, when Congress established the Law Enforcement Assistance Administration, and again in 1994, when Congress passed the Violent Crime Control and Law Enforcement Act. Both times, federal money spurred a sharp rise in the number of urban police officers per unit population.[14] But the federal subsidies were too modest. Bill Clinton promised to put another 100,000 cops on city streets; in the end, the federal government paid for something in the vicinity of one-sixth that number, and only for a few years.[15] Clinton's original number is a reasonable goal: had it been achieved, Americans would have roughly 310 police officers per 100,000 population; by comparison, the analogous figure in EU countries is 351.[16] The cost of an additional 100,000 police officers is not trivial, but neither is it prohibitive. Total spending for local police stands at $68 billion per year; a one-sixth increase in the number of officers (that is, roughly, what 100,000 more local police officers represent) might be expected to cost as much as $15 billion per year. By comparison, total government spending on criminal justice stood at $214 billion in 2006.[17]

If political incentives make re-creating the Clinton proposal hard, a reformed body of constitutional law might help the politicians along. For a brief time during Reconstruction, the Fourteenth Amendment's guarantee of "equal protection of the laws" meant roughly what it said: all citizens had the same right to the law's protection. Ex-slaves terrorized by Klan members were entitled to a government that did its best to stop the terrorism. If local officials couldn't or wouldn't fulfill their constitutional obligation to protect the local population—*all* of that population, rich and poor, black and white—the federal government was obliged to offer some protection of its own. *United States v. Cruikshank* (1876) ended that constitutional obligation, and with it Reconstruction.[18] More than a century later, *McCleskey v. Kemp* (1987) and *Castle Rock v. Gonzales* (2005) confirmed the ending: *McCleskey* made discrimination impossible to prove, and *Castle Rock* gave the government unfettered discretion to choose when to enforce the law and when to ignore it.[19] But *Cruikshank, McCleskey,* and *Castle Rock* are at odds with the original understanding of the Fourteenth Amendment. In a better, healthier constitutional order, those decisions would fall. If they did—if the older vision of equal protection were revived—the underpolicing of violent neighborhoods, along with the consequent underenforcement of violent felonies in those neighborhoods, would be more than a policy failure. It would be a constitutional violation, one that governments at all levels would be obliged to remedy.

Return to the inverse relationship between the size of urban police forces and the number of prison inmates. That inverse relationship between levels of policing and punishment is especially strong today, thanks to changes in the prevailing style of policing. Before the 1990s, conventional wisdom on policing emphasized police officers' role as the first step in the process that leads to criminal punishment. In order to catch more offenders and hence make more arrests, doctrine stressed speed and surprise. Urban police forces invested in reducing their response time to 911 calls, and in high-speed, violent SWAT teams—the policing equivalent of "shock and awe"—that could roll into crime scenes with overwhelming force, make arrests, and roll out. The goal was more efficient punishment, and that goal was reached: the number of arrests per officer rose steadily through the 1970s and 1980s. But greater efficiency didn't produce the desired outcomes. On city streets, "shock and awe" generates shock and anger, plus sympathy for the young men the police are targeting. Violent, in-and-out raids and quick street stop-and-frisks are bound to have a high error rate, meaning that innocent residents of high-crime neighborhoods pay a large price for efforts to catch guilty ones.[20] And no matter how quickly the police respond to 911 calls, the response is never quick enough: five minutes is four minutes too long; the crime has happened, and the perpetrators have left the scene.

Hence the change in conventional policing wisdom since the 1980s. Policing scholar Herman Goldstein captured its essence when he advocated a style of police work that seeks to solve problems rather than rack up arrests.[21] James Q. Wilson and George Kelling captured an important part of the payoff from changed tactics when they wrote about the tendency of graffiti and broken windows to spread if left untended. Such public markers of disorder, Wilson and Kelling argued, send the message that criminals own the streets; over time, the message becomes a self-fulfilling prophecy. More and better police patrols allow a larger slice of the local population to walk the streets in comfort, which in turn means fewer signs that those streets have been abandoned to their fate.[22]

A good picture of that dynamic in action comes from an odd place: the long-running war in Iraq. Consider the following excerpt from a *New York Times* story in the fall of 2006 about a military operation in a violent part of Baghdad. The first name you will read was a member of the local municipal council:

> Like others in the area, [Mr. Jabouri] raved about being able to sleep again on his roof, away from the sweltering indoor heat. He said some of the families who had fled the violence seemed to be returning, and that the Iraqis and Americans who searched his home were respectful and seemed sincerely interested in improving the neighborhood . . . Sections of the neighborhood have been assigned to the same squads so that residents and officers can become better acquainted.
>
> The United States military has also allotted $5 million to [the neighborhood], with much of the current outlay going to Iraqis who pick up trash . . . The results were hard to miss. Piles of rancid gar-

bage behind the market had been cleared, and workers elsewhere tossed more into trucks. Iraqi police cars and American humvees lined the streets.[23]

Notice three things the soldiers did. First, they lined up with their humvees on the street, out in the open. That sends the message that the streets are safe. Second, they hired Iraqis to pick up the trash—which made it possible to go outside, wander through the market, sleep on rooftops. Soldiers made the streets both safer and more pleasant, which led to more people on the streets. The bigger the local population's street presence, in turn, the harder it is for militias and insurgent gangs to operate. The third move was most important of all: they built relationships with the local population.

These counterinsurgency tactics could have been taken from a community policing manual.[24] Today's policing conventional wisdom emphasizes the same three moves: a more public police street presence in the most violent areas, a problem-solving approach to local blights like garbage on the streets or gang signs on local buildings, and, most important of all, the building of relationships between police officers and local neighborhood residents. In some cities, the relationship building extends to local churches: Chicago police helped residents of one high-crime neighborhood hold a prayer vigil aimed at ending youth violence. In some, the relationships extend even to members of local gangs, who are both encouraged to put a stop to their own gangs' violence and threatened with imprisonment if they refuse.[25]

Notice how remarkable this is. Government agencies—which is what urban police forces are—have submitted themselves and their conduct to the scrutiny of a constituency that has limited power over them. That is hardly a common course of action among government officials. Because it *is* remarkable, no one should be surprised that the trend is partial and incomplete. Community policing is a capacious term, and while urban police forces across the country have adopted the label, the measure of tactical reform varies widely.[26] The tendency to maximize arrests instead of Goldstein-style problem-solving remains strong. Drug arrests by violent SWAT teams remain common in some places. Distrust of police in African American communities remains common as well.

Yet there is less to that distrust than meets the eye. Given the sheer size of the increase in black incarceration over the past forty years, the *absence* of bad feeling toward the justice system would be more remarkable than its presence. Local police officers are the representatives of that system with whom ordinary citizens—black, white, and otherwise—have the most contact. So they are the most natural targets of any ill will. Phenomena like the "don't snitch" movement may be prompted by patterns of prosecution and sentencing, neither of which police officers control. Even so, such phenomena inevitably strike at the police, who are on the streets, rather than assistant district attorneys, who are not. The true surprise is that, judging by polling data, the level of black distrust of the police is essentially unchanged over the past forty years—a time when the black imprisonment rate more than quadrupled.[27]

Progress may not show up in Gallup's numbers, but it is both real and striking: on the whole, urban police forces are more attentive to local preferences than a generation ago, and far more attentive than urban prosecutors are today. Spending more on urban policing thus means more funds for the law enforcement entity that pays the most attention to the views of residents of high-crime neighborhoods. That makes criminal law enforcement more locally democratic. And more spending means more personnel, which in turn reinforces changed tactics: relationship building requires more officers than buy-and-busts and SWAT teams. Better styles of policing and less cash-strapped urban police forces are mutually reinforcing. Together, both more money and better tactics make for more democratic policing, more nearly equal justice, and—best of all—more effective crime control.

Reducing America's swollen prison population will require more than fatter police budgets; changes in the law and practice of criminal sentencing are also key. Three aspects of sentencing most need changing. The first is its severity. America's inmate population is infamously massive. Average sentences are vastly higher than in other Western countries, and significantly higher than in previous periods in this country.[28] Second comes racial disparity: black inmates outnumber white ones by a large margin, though blacks constitute only 13 percent of the general population and non-Hispanic whites more than two-thirds.[29] Most of that disparity is the consequence of different crime rates among different demographic groups—but some of it is the consequence of discrimination, and that discrimination needs attacking. Third is excessive prosecutorial power. Over the course of the past few decades, prosecutors have replaced judges as the system's key sentencing decisionmakers, exercising their power chiefly through plea bargaining. That prosecutorial power is unchecked by law and, given its invisibility, barely checked by politics.

Promising legal moves to reduce the severity of criminal sentences are already happening. Hawaii is experimenting with certain but brief jail sentences for probation violations. (The norm is for violators to return to prison to serve the balance of their original sentences, which can be considerable.) Because probation violations account for a sizeable chunk of the prison population, that move, if widely embraced, might reduce that population significantly. Some jurisdictions have tried battling street gangs by issuing injunctions that make it hard for gangs to meet; violators can be charged with contempt and sentenced to several months in local jails. Both the injunctions and the jail sentences disrupt gangs' activities, making it harder for them to operate—and do so without re-creating the same gangs in state penitentiaries, as long prison sentences sometimes do.[30]

The most promising and far-reaching move comes from the law of federal sentencing. Before 2005, that body of law was famously detailed and even more famously severe. Federal sentencing was based on a combination of the defendant's criminal history and a set of factual findings related to the defendant's crime. That combination yielded a grid with 258 distinct sentencing ranges.[31] Federal judges had little discretion to sentence offenders outside the grid; the overwhelming majority of federal sentences were, in effect, dictated by the grid that was in turn dictated by the Federal Sentencing Guidelines. And Guidelines-based sentences were, as a general matter, more severe than sentences in any state. All that changed with *United States v. Booker* (2005).[32] In *Booker*, the Court declared much of the Guidelines unconstitutional because they required judges rather than juries to find, by a preponderance of the evidence rather than beyond a reasonable doubt, the facts on which sentences were based. But instead of simply invalidating the Guidelines, the Supreme Court rendered them "advisory": they carry legal weight but are not legally binding—meaning that juries need not find the relevant facts, and the beyond-a-reasonable-doubt standard no longer applies.[33] Pre-*Booker,* federal sentencing was rule-based. Today, it is based on a combination of rules and discretion, and the discretion is as important as the rules.

Without quite saying so, federal judges since *Booker* have treated sentencing discretion differently in cases in which the judges sentence below the Guidelines levels than in cases in which sentences are (even) harsher than the Guidelines would suggest. In practice, discretion is asymmetric: judges exercise the freedom to offer federal offenders a measure of mercy, but are more constrained when it comes to more severe sentences. In effect, the Guidelines have become sentencing ceilings rather than sentencing rules: below the ceilings, federal sentencing is largely discretionary so long as judges explain their decisions in some reasonable fashion.[34] That state of affairs offers a useful model for a kind of sentencing law that might push prison populations down rather than up. Were states to follow the federal model (as a few already have), severe sentences for the most violent offenders might remain as they are; sentences in other cases might fall. Sentencing levels might return to those of America's past, when our justice system was less harsh than it is today.

The huge racial disparity in America's inmate population is a harder nut to crack. A substantial portion of that disparity will and should remain: crime rates among blacks are much higher than among the rest of the population,[35] so, at least in part, the prison population should reflect that truth. But there is no explaining the massive racial tilt in the drug prisoner population in terms of different crime rates: what evidence we have on the subject suggests that blacks, whites, and Latinos violate the drug laws at similar rates.[36] How might the size and scope of that racial tilt be reduced?

Changes in sentencing law, such as those previously discussed, would help; bigger budgets for local police would help more. Increased spending for lawyers and courts would be another goal: as things stand now, severe docket pressure pushes prosecutors to focus their attention on indigent defendants who can be induced to plead guilty without much effort, and the pool of indigent defendants is disproportionately black.

A system in which docket pressure and budget constraints play a smaller role in criminal justice outcomes would be a less discriminatory system than ours is. But even with all these moves, a large measure of discrimination would likely remain.

Two other moves would address, and in part redress, that discrimination; both derive from the underused concept of "equal protection of the laws." The first is straightforward. Courts should entertain claims that criminal sentences for defendants belonging to different racial and ethnic groups differ, even when the crimes charged are similar. Notice that this comprises similar crimes, not just identical ones—sentences assigned for possession of crack cocaine (usually imposed on black defendants) should be brought in line with cocaine powder sentences (usually imposed on whites), as many scholars have argued. (At long last, Congress has made substantial progress toward this goal, though more remains to be done.)[37] Punishment for crimes that victimize blacks and crimes that victimize whites should likewise be aligned, once relevant differences in fact patterns are accounted for. Both *McCleskey v. Kemp* (1987), which all but bars claims of discrimination against black crime victims, and *United States v. Armstrong* (1996), which does the same for claims of discrimination against black defendants,[38] should be overturned.

The other legal move is less familiar but no less important. For all sentences of incarceration over some minimal level—say, three or six months—prosecutors should be required to show that sentences at least as severe have been imposed some minimum number of times for the same crime in the same state on similar facts. A recent Supreme Court decision offers a useful model. In *Graham v. Florida* (2010), the Justices held that sentences of life without possibility of parole for juvenile defendants violate the Eighth Amendment's ban on "cruel and unusual punishments."[39] To show that such sentences are unusual, Justice Kennedy's majority opinion noted the number of prisoners serving such sentences nationwide: 123, of which 77 were in Florida.[40] Given the huge number of serious, nonhomicide crimes for which juvenile defendants are convicted each year, that number—outside Florida, an average of one prisoner per state—proves that life-without-parole sentences for juvenile defendants are exceedingly rare. They are so rare that one cannot claim with a straight face that those sentences are imposed systematically, in lawlike fashion.

When a given sentence for a given crime in a given state is likewise imposed less than systematically, its imposition should be deemed a violation of equal protection: different laws are being applied to similarly situated offenders. Over time, as databases grow, the government could be required to show that at least equally severe sentences are imposed for the same crime on similar facts in different parts of the state: a means of reducing the gap between sentences for black defendants and sentences for white ones. Obviously, the requirement cannot apply to crimes or fact patterns that occur only very rarely. But most crimes and fact patterns happen often. When that is so, as it usually is, it seems reasonable to require some evidence that the government treats similar cases from different communities similarly. When it comes to criminal sentencing, the government should have to show that it adheres to the rule of law, not to the rule of prosecutors.

Over time, strong antidiscrimination rules together with rule-of-law protection would moderate sentencing levels. Legislators could still craft symbolic sentencing rules—but those rules would be *purely* symbolic, mere expressions of outrage with no practical consequence. With respect to more consequential rules, this approach gives legislators information they too often lack about the price of substantive rules. In an age of constrained budgets, legislators often choose lenity when the price of severity is made clear.[41] Banning discrimination and requiring systematic enforcement would make the price of severity a great deal clearer than it is now.

Prosecution

As the numbers of police officers and prison inmates need to change, so do the numbers of prosecutors and public defenders. Because there are too few lawyers available to try criminal cases, too few cases are tried, and far too many are resolved by low-visibility plea bargains. The conduct of local prosecutors needs to change as well. Two changes are crucial: criminal prosecutions need to become more transparent, and they also must be made more locally democratic. The former change is a necessary condition of the latter: democracy is impossible when voters cannot tell why the system punishes when and whom it does.

Numbers first. In 1974, 17,000 local prosecutors were responsible for some 300,000 felony prosecutions each year. Thirty years later, the number of local prosecutors had grown to 27,000—but the annual number of felony prosecutions had exploded, topping 1 million. In the earlier year, the percentage of felony convictions obtained by guilty plea stood at roughly 80 percent. In the later year, that percentage had reached 96 percent.[42] Reliable data on the number of lawyers available to represent indigent criminal defendants—and on the number of defendants too poor to hire counsel for themselves—do not exist, but there is good reason to believe the numbers on the defense side are more extreme still. Docket pressure defines the professional lives of those who litigate criminal cases in American courts. If the number of guilty pleas is to fall, as it must in a system that punishes less promiscuously than ours does, the number of lawyers doing the litigating—and the amount of public money spent on criminal litigation—must rise, and substantially.

How is that to happen? One possible answer comes from the body of Sixth Amendment law that allegedly guarantees defendants the "effective assistance of counsel." To date, that body of law has regulated the quality of lawyering criminal defendants receive (and the regulating has been done poorly). The quantity of defense lawyering is largely unregulated.[43] This gets it backward. Ensuring a reasonable level of attorney quality is probably beyond the law's grasp because, extreme cases aside, no one knows how to distinguish good attorney tactics from bad ones. However, ensuring an adequate quantity of representation is an achievable goal—and raising quantity tends to raise quality as well: more and better funded lawyers prepare their cases better, which would make for more reliable outcomes both in cases that plead out and in cases that go to trial.

Judges could simply order states and localities to spend more on lawyers for indigent defendants; the Sixth Amendment right to "the assistance of counsel" arguably requires as much. But better funding need not involve judges setting budget lines. Appellate courts could instead establish a default rule designed to prompt legislative action: say, in all jurisdictions that set up expert commissions to recommend appropriate funding for indigent criminal defense and then follow those recommendations, effective-assistance-of-counsel doctrine will not apply. Elsewhere, effective assistance standards will be ratcheted up sharply. If this default rule applied, state legislators would have an incentive to establish sensible processes for fixing budgets for indigent defense, and room to experiment with different funding patterns—more money for defense lawyers in some jurisdictions, more money for investigators or defense crime labs in others. Over time, we would see which experiments worked best. Instead of aiming to dictate outcomes, the constitutional law of criminal procedure might aim to improve incentives, leaving politicians in charge of outcomes.

Adequate funding for criminal defense would have large side benefits. Prosecutors' offices are likewise grossly underfunded. If budgets for defense attorneys rose, states would be compelled, as a practical matter, to increase prosecutors' budgets in order not to lose too many criminal cases. Higher budgets would allow for more careful investigation of criminal cases, which would (one hopes) spare some innocent defendants punishment. Higher budgets would also bring down the guilty plea rate from current astronomically high levels. Guilty pleas would cease to be a budgetary necessity and would become a means of settling easy cases, which is their proper role.

Changing the conduct of local prosecutors is a more difficult task. There are two large obstacles to a more transparent style of criminal justice. The first is prosecution by pretext: charging defendants with crimes other than the ones that prompted their prosecution. Martha Stewart's conviction for obstruction of justice, after an investigation that focused on insider trading, is a classic example.[44] Another is the nearly three hundred cases the Bush Justice Department claimed as terrorism prosecutions, the large majority of which led to convictions for immigration fraud and similar non-terrorism-related offenses.[45] The problem in such cases is not that defendants like Stewart or the terrorism defendants are treated unfairly. Immigration fraud and obstruction of justice are crimes worth punishing. The bigger problem is that, with few exceptions, such crimes are punished only as means of punishing other, more serious crimes that the government cannot prove. Voters and, for that matter, other government officials aren't told about those more serious crimes—one reason why the Bush administration's claims regarding terrorism cases attracted skepticism on Capitol Hill. So there is no way of knowing how good or bad a job the government is doing of investigating insider trading or terrorism, or whatever other crimes prompt pretextual prosecutions. Pretext cases render criminal prosecution opaque, hence unaccountable.[46]

Perhaps that is why prosecutors like them so much. Then–Attorney General John Ashcroft defended the practice, citing the means Robert Kennedy used to fight the Mafia when *he* headed the Justice Department:

> Attorney General [Robert] Kennedy made no apologies for using all of the available resources in the law to disrupt and dismantle organized crime networks. Very often, prosecutors were aggressive, using obscure statutes to arrest and detain suspected mobsters. One racketeer and his father were indicted for lying on a federal home loan application. A former gunman for the Capone mob was brought to court on a violation of the Migratory Bird Act. Agents found 563 game birds in his freezer—a mere 539 birds over the limit . . .
>
> [Kennedy's] Justice Department, it is said, would arrest mobsters for "spitting on the sidewalk" if it would help in the battle against organized crime. It has been and will be the policy of this Department of Justice to use the same aggressive arrest and detention tactics in the war on terror.[47]

Such prosecutions send different messages than prosecutors intend: if you belong to the relevant kind of criminal enterprise, be sure not to spit on the sidewalk—and take care when hunting migratory birds. Those are not promising messages if the goal is to take down Mafia families and terrorist networks.

The problem is not easily solved. It is hard to imagine a judicial ruling barring prosecutions for drug crimes when the defendant is suspected of having committed violent felonies—that would make defendants who committed many serious crimes better off than those who committed few. But the rule-of-law and antidiscrimination doctrines suggested above would help matters. Unless the government could point to other obstruction cases with facts like Stewart's (meaning the facts that gave rise to the obstruction charge, not facts related to insider trading), it could not proceed—at least, not if prosecutors wanted significant jail or prison time. If prosecutors could not identify drug cases from other parts of the state with sentences like those imposed on drug defendants from high-crime neighborhoods, those sentences would have to be reduced. That would reduce the government's gain from pretextual charges, and so would make such charges less common.

The second and larger obstacle to transparency is the nation's guilty plea rate. Guilty pleas, especially ones that happen early in the process, are largely invisible. So is the bargaining that lies behind them. That is a modest problem or no problem at all when the number of criminal trials is high: the public can see how the system functions in a large fraction of its cases, and prosecutors and defense attorneys alike must strike plea bargains with an eye toward likely trial outcomes. When trials are rare events, as is the case today, the public sees little. And when prosecutors can dictate trial outcomes, trials do not constrain the one-sided bargains the parties strike.[48] Plea bargains are no longer a means of settling easy cases, which is their proper role. Rather, guilty pleas and the quick bargains that precede them have become the system's primary means of judging criminal defendants' guilt or innocence. Given the quick-and-dirty character of the bargains, the judging is bound to be done badly.

The surest road to fewer pleas and more trials is to make trials cheaper and pleas more expensive from the prosecutors' point of view. Reducing the cost of criminal trials would require radical change in both the amount and content of criminal procedure doctrine: the undoing of the vast network of procedural rules the Supreme Court has crafted since the early 1960s. Unfortunately, that will not happen. The late twentieth century's counterproductive revolution in the law of criminal procedure may be trimmed around the edges, but it will not be undone. And today there is little sign even of trimming around the edges. The right to confront opposing witnesses, a right limited by the common law of evidence until recently, has burst its bounds to become a hugely important part of criminal litigation.[49] The right to trial by jury is still more so, thanks to the Supreme Court's series of decisions on the right to have juries, not judges, decide many of the facts on which criminal sentences rest.[50] The criminal procedure revolution is not in retreat. More than forty years after Earl Warren retired, it is still advancing.

Thankfully, raising the cost of guilty pleas is a simple matter. Military courts (along with a few state appellate courts) offer a useful model: they review the factual basis of guilty pleas with great care, and with little deference to the pleas themselves.[51] That should be the norm everywhere.[52] Stringent appellate review, with reversal in cases of what the military calls improvident pleas, would amount to a procedural tax on pleas. Tax anything and one is likely to see less of it. Plus, military-style review of guilty pleas would make the pleas that remain more accurate—a large social gain. Such review would also shift power from prosecutors to judges, another social gain.

Reducing the number of guilty pleas also may require changing the character of criminal law. A half-century ago, criminal law was still (mostly) a common-law field—crimes were nominally defined by statute, but courts exercised enormous power over their scope and definition. That was especially true of intent terms, but not only those. And—again especially with respect to intent, but not only there—the boundaries of criminal liability were usually fuzzy, leaving room for judges and juries to exercise judgment when applying those boundaries to individual cases. Today, criminal law is statutory not just in name but in practice, and the relevant statutes are far more detailed and precise than in the past. Outside of a few pockets like the law of homicide, criminal intent has become almost wholly mechanical. The change has more than a little to do with today's massive prison population. Highly specified criminal law makes for easily resolved cases, and easily resolved cases make for easily induced guilty pleas. And without the sharp rise in the guilty plea rate during the last generation, America's prison population could not be what it is today.

Vaguely defined crimes have one other critical virtue: they are democracy's friend. Reintroducing a measure of vagueness to American criminal law would trigger more jury trials, and would invite the kinds of jury verdicts Paul Butler encouraged—without the stigma of nullification. Any of three less-than-radical changes would advance those goals. First, courts could reestablish the older concept of *mens rea:* requiring that, save when legislators expressly impose strict liability, proof of a "guilty mind" or "criminal intent"—the kind of intent that Justice Jackson found lacking in *Morissette*—is present in every case.[53] Second, judges might apply generally a legal principle at the core of racketeering doctrine: when the culpability of defendants charged with a given set of crimes varies widely, the least culpable members of the group should be excused from liability for the most serious offenses.[54] Third, courts might import into American law the German legal doctrine that permits any defendant to claim that, though his conduct fits the definition of the relevant offense, it was not sufficiently "wrongful" to merit punishment.[55]

Any of those changes would make criminal liability more legally uncertain—yet also, paradoxically, more predictable. A century ago, American criminal law was filled with standards of the sort described in the preceding paragraph. Prison populations were more stable and punishment less discriminatory than in our own time. The explanation for that surprising truth is simple: when prosecutors have enormous discretionary power, giving other decisionmakers discretion promotes consistency, not arbitrariness. Vague legal lines give more discretion to juries and trial judges. Discretion limits discretion; institutional competition curbs excess and abuse. Vague criminal prohibitions once were, and might be again, part of a well-functioning system of checks and balances.[56]

For those checks and balances to work as they should, one more legal change is needed: a change in the manner in which juries are selected. Current law encourages, even requires, juries that represent the jurisdiction from which jurors are drawn,[57] usually the relevant county. If the goal is to protect the interests of residents of high-crime city neighborhoods, that is the wrong pool. Jury selection in large cities should be neighborhood based, and the number of peremptory challenges should be substantially reduced.[58] The former change would empower the black jurors whom Paul Butler rightly argues need more power over the fate of the young men in their communities. The latter change would remove the need for the expensive, elaborate, and largely ineffective body of law barring the discriminatory use of peremptory challenges.[59] Eliminating that body of law would make criminal trials cheaper, a large collateral benefit.

Fewer peremptories and more localized jury selection might make convictions harder to obtain. That is no bad thing in a system as stacked in the government's favor as ours is. If a prosecutor cannot convince a dozen residents of a high-crime neighborhood that one of their neighbors should be punished, punishment is probably unwise and could well be unjust. Current jury selection rules facilitate conviction in such cases instead of obstructing it.

These changes would serve to encourage another, deeper change: the growing trend in urban prosecutors' offices to form relationships with residents of high-crime city neighborhoods. Gradually, something akin to the community policing movement has begun in the realm of prosecution. "Community prosecution" has not transformed the work of prosecutors' offices, as community policing has done for many urban police forces. But the core idea—more neighborhood democracy, and a more politically responsive style of law enforcement—is the same.[60] Forcing prosecutors to prove their cases to neighborhood-based juries would reinforce that idea, and would go some distance toward undermining the southern-style democracy—some neighborhoods govern others—that dominates American criminal justice today.

Federalism

America's criminal justice system has long had a federalism problem, but the problem is not the one most readers will suspect. The usual concern is that an overlarge federal government will crowd out state and local agencies: a common fear during Prohibition, when federal agents and federal prosecutors were chiefly responsible for a large share of street-level law enforcement. But Prohibition is history, and whatever the dangers of a federal Leviathan in other settings, no such danger exists here. Twelve thousand FBI agents will not soon displace 600,000 local police officers. The small size of the federal law enforcement bureaucracy creates a different problem. Because federal criminal law has such small consequences for the federal budget, Congress makes too much of it. Senators and Representatives use criminal law and sentencing doctrine to send symbolic messages—we're tough on crime and criminals—not to define prohibited conduct and its consequences. So Congress criminalizes too much and sentences too harshly. It also devotes far too much legislative energy to making law for the occasional federal prosecution, and far too little to aiding the local officials who do the real work of catching and punishing criminals. In this area at least, the federal government makes too much law and spends too little money.

These tendencies are self-reinforcing. As Congress gives federal agents and prosecutors more room to pick and choose among potential targets, any one federal criminal prohibition or sentencing rule matters less. The less the rules matter, the more eager Congress is to add to them. So both the federal criminal code and the federal law of sentencing metastasize. That affects more than federal cases. Local district attorneys can threaten to send drug or gun crime defendants to the nearest U.S. Attorney's office. If plea bargaining works like other markets, those threats affect the bargains local prosecutors and defense attorneys strike. Defendants agree to harsher sentences in *state* court for fear of what might happen to them in *federal* court. Federal law acts as an unfunded mandate, raising state sentencing levels without paying for the increase.

The doctrines that purport to protect state and local officials' prerogatives—chiefly, the law of federal criminal jurisdiction, enforced through jurisdictional elements that attach to individual crimes—make the situation worse. Federalism-based doctrines in criminal law cut across crimes, not between them: instead of, say, assigning bribery to federal officials and arson to the locals, federal law covers some bribery and some arson, leaving local police and prosecutors the rest—with a fuzzy and constantly changing line between the two. A large fraction of federal criminal litigation is devoted to issues like whether robbery victims or torched buildings were sufficiently "commercial" to support federal charges.[61] This generates lines of cases devoted to such questions as whether arsons of churches that order Sunday School materials from out of state are within the scope of federal authority.[62] That kind of judicially mandated federalism obscures accountability and wastes the time of litigants and courts alike.

The pattern recurs throughout the federal criminal code. Voters cannot know whom to credit when the system functions well and whom to blame when it doesn't. That encourages irresponsible legislation. Better to draw some plausible lines between crimes that should be exclusively federal and crimes that should be exclusively enforced by state and local officials. Courts are poorly positioned to draw those lines, and Congress has no incentive to do so itself. Some mechanism is needed to encourage Congress to make federal law where federal law will count and not elsewhere.

There are several possibilities. The simplest and probably the best is a broad rule of preemption for criminal sentencing. Let federal sentences apply if, and only if, federal criminal law is exclusive: think immigration law,[63] or bribery of federal officials. If a given federal crime is regularly enforced by local prosecutors, let federal sentences be fixed by state law. Harsh federal sentences for drug crimes would disappear unless Congress decided to take over responsibility for enforcing drug laws nationwide, in which case federal sentences would grow less harsh. Giving federal law greater sentencing consequences would produce more moderate federal legislation.

If a given crime is *not* regularly enforced by local prosecutors or if Congress decides to act preemptively, federal jurisdiction should be judged crime by crime, not case by case. Fraud either falls within the scope of federal power or not; extortion either gives rise to federal jurisdiction or doesn't. Distinguishing among different types of extortion and fraud for jurisdictional purposes should go by the boards. A more categorical approach would lead to clearer lines of responsibility, and (one hopes) to a more politically accountable criminal justice system. More broadly, attaching a bigger price tag to federal criminal legislation might encourage different *kinds* of legislation—fewer criminal liability rules and sentencing regulations, and better funding for local agencies. A more fiscal federalism would better fit the federal government's two great advantages in criminal justice policymaking: its ability to spend when state and local budgets are tight,[64] and its concomitant ability to bribe local agencies to raise standards. The model should be Bill Clinton's proposal to put another 100,000 cops on city streets—and also to require police forces that accepted federal money to adopt some form of community policing.[65]

Could all these changes happen? Yes. Will they happen? Probably not. The disaster that is contemporary American criminal justice does not look so disastrous in most places, which is why there has been no sustained political demand for large-scale reform of the justice system. Major changes in the system's structure—and while the potential changes sketched above are not radical, they *are* major—require a critical mass of voters (also legislators and appellate judges) to support a program that carries little benefit for them.

The justice system has seen that reforming spirit take hold three times before. The first came during Reconstruction, when northern white voters backed a Fourteenth Amendment that promised ex-slaves the "equal protection of the laws." The second and third happened during the early decades of the twentieth century, when voters in already-dry jurisdictions first voted to impose Prohibition on wet cities, then voted for Repeal when the experiment failed. Notice that, all three times, this spirit of democratic reform yielded changes in the Constitution's text. Since the early 1930s, that spirit has not come easily to the sad world of criminal justice. It needs reviving.

The law, constitutional and otherwise, is one of the largest obstacles to that kind of reform. The last century's changes in criminal law and in the law of criminal procedure have been mostly destructive: they have made the law a barrier to reform rather than a facilitator of it. Worse, important parts of that barrier consist of constitutional decisions by the Supreme Court, which are far easier to make than to change once made. Political change is hard enough to bring about. Legal change is usually harder. Reforming American criminal justice requires both.

There is something odd about that picture. One of the law's central roles is to rein in politicians' tendency to go too far when political winds blow too strong.[66] Appellate judges ought to be the agents of reform, not obstacles to it. Too often, those judges—especially federal ones, and especially the nine who sit on the nation's highest court—have been obstacles. The pattern goes back a long way, and extends to the present: from the *Cruikshank* Court that put an end to the ideal of equal protection to Earl Warren's colleagues and their successors, who took on themselves the task of redefining the character of the criminal process and botched the redefinition.

Neither those errors nor their consequences are easily undone. If it happens, successful criminal justice reform will come mostly from politics, and mostly from below: from police chiefs and city councils, local judges and state legislators. Federal judges and members of Congress can play useful roles, but if productive change happens, they will not be its primary authors. Voters will, along with the state and local officials those voters elect.

So the source of the criminal justice system's key problem is also the biggest obstacle to its solution. When and where criminal justice was an exercise in local self-government, the system worked reasonably well: it controlled crime without today's massive prison populations or equally massive racial disparities in criminal punishment. The justice system stopped working when a particular kind of local democracy—the kind in which residents of high-crime neighborhoods shape the law enforcement that operates on their streets—ceased to govern the ways police officers, prosecutors, and trial judges do their jobs. A more distant and more detached democracy governs today's system. The voters with the most power—those who live in safe neighborhoods, not dangerous ones—have little stake in how that power is exercised. For genuine reform to happen, it is not enough that those who live with crime and punishment demand it. Some of the demand must also come from those who see both crime and punishment at a distance and who decide, at long last, that they don't like what they see. That attentive and altruistic style of voting is not unknown, but it is not the historical norm either, certainly not in this context. Hope seems justified. Optimism, not so much.

Epilogue:
Taming the Wolf

The quality of mercy is not strain'd,
It droppeth as the gentle rain from heaven
Upon the place beneath. It is twice blest;
It blesseth him that gives and him that takes.
—William Shakespeare, *The Merchant of Venice* (1596)

HOPE CAN BE A POWERFUL FORCE. The justice system of the last generation has given us a lot of bad news, but along with it has come some very good news. If backed up with enough personnel, the softer forms of policing work: they tame urban crime to a degree no one thought possible only a short time ago. At the same time, those policing strategies may also tame the other threat that looms over contemporary American criminal justice: the state's seemingly insatiable desire to punish young black men. Crime becomes less attractive when relationships between cops and would-be criminals make it so. Punishment becomes less attractive to the state when those relationships humanize the people the state targets. There are vicious circles in criminal justice, and for most of the past sixty years, America's justice system has been caught in one or another of them. But there are virtuous circles as well, and we may have stumbled into one unawares. If so, thank God for the stumbling. There is a chance—not a certainty, not even a probability, but a possibility—that, a few decades from now, this will look to be the time when the justice system turned, because the human beings who operate that system and those on whom it operates did so. Those who enforce the law and those most tempted to break it turned, if only slightly, toward each other—toward relationship rather than enmity.

We must remember that Thomas Jefferson was utterly wrong about slaves and slavery. Black slaves were not wolves ready to devour their white oppressors at the first opportunity. On the contrary, they were human beings victimized by a mind-bogglingly unjust social and legal order. The oppression could stop whenever their oppressors chose to make it stop. The massive number of young black men (and the increasingly large number of young black women) who live in prison cells are not victims in the same sense: their conduct has more than a little to do with their condition. But they *are* human beings—creatures entitled to "life, liberty, and the pursuit of happiness" as long as they permit their fellow human beings to seek those same ends. Their humanity entitles them to something else: a measure of understanding, and the mercy that flows from a justice system whose rulers remember that they too are tempted to do wrong, and often yield to the temptation. That understanding and that mercy, in turn, flow from an idea that once was so well understood that it needed never be expressed, yet now is all but forgotten: the idea that legal condemnation is a necessary but terrible thing—to be used sparingly, not promiscuously.

That idea is at once conservative (it represents the best of our legal tradition) and liberal (it offers the promise of genuine reform); the idea carries with it the possibility of a system that is both more effective and much more humane. It sets a standard that today's justice system and the justice system of the recent past have signally failed to meet, in both directions. A generation ago, Americans seemingly understood that criminal punishment was terrible but forgot that it was also necessary. Today, we understand punishment's necessity but have forgotten its destructive power. Americans need to remember both halves of the formula, and to build a justice system founded on the tension between them.

The notion that condemnation and punishment are essential but also dangerous comes most naturally to those whose lives most resemble the lives of the criminal defendants who are subject to the justice system's justice. This is why the style of local democracy that governed much of America's criminal justice system for much of the nation's past worked reasonably well, at least by comparison with the different kind of democracy that reigns over that system today. That earlier style of democracy was easier to pull off in a nation a large fraction of which lived in poverty, and another large fraction of which was only one misfortune away from such a life. One reason black criminals from poor city neighborhoods have been treated with so much more severity than criminals from white immigrant communities in America's past is that the former are more easily categorized as The Other, as a people whose lives are separate from the lives of those who judge them. The ease of that response to urban crime means that re-creating the right kinds of democracy is no simple task. But simple or not, it remains the good and just thing to do. And it is the essential thing to do, if we are ever to break the cycle of mass violence and mass incarceration.

The criminals we incarcerate are not some alien enemy. Nor, for that matter, are the police officers and prosecutors who seek to fight crime in those criminals' neighborhoods. Neither side of this divide is "them." Both sides are us. Democracy and justice alike depend on getting that most basic principle of human relations right.

Note on Sources and Citation Form

The endnotes frequently cite a set of sources for data—some current, some historical—on crime, policing, and punishment. For convenience, I use an abbreviated citation format to refer to several of those sources. The late Eric Monkkonen gathered data on homicide rates, especially those in New York City, to which I refer throughout the book. Monkkonen's data can be found at http://sociology.osu.edu/cjrc/researchprojects/hvd/usa/nyc/; the relevant data are also on file with Harvard University Press. In the endnotes, I refer to these sources as "Monkkonen's data."

The FBI publishes an annual volume titled *Crime in the United States.* For most of the Bureau's history, those annual volumes were called *Uniform Crime Reports,* and they date back to the mid-1930s. Those volumes contain reasonably reliable data on the year-to-year number of homicides in various cities; they also include information about the size of various cities' police forces. Recent volumes are available online at www.fbi.gov/about-us/cjis/ucr/ucr#ucr_cius. In the endnotes, these volumes are referred to as *Uniform Crime Reports: [year]* or *Crime in the United States: [year].*

The Census Bureau annually publishes the *Statistical Abstract of the United States,* which contains, among many other things, population data and the number of prisoners held in federal and state penitentiaries. Those volumes are available online at www.census .gov/compendia/statab/past_years.html. In the endnotes, they are referred to as *[year] Statistical Abstract.*

On occasion, when several volumes of the FBI or Census works are referenced, I cite "the relevant volumes of" the source.

Last but not least, many of the endnotes refer to a source of data on American criminal justice called the *Sourcebook of Criminal Justice Statistics.* The *Sourcebook* is published annually by the Bureau of Justice Statistics, an agency of the Justice Department. In addition to the *Sourcebook*'s annual volumes, an online version of the *Sourcebook* is maintained and regularly updated; it appears at www.albany.edu/sourcebook/. When referring to a printed volume of the *Sourcebook,* I refer to the volume as [*year*] *Sourcebook.* When referring to the online version, which contains the most current data, I use the form *Online Sourcebook.*

Notes

1. In Boston, the murder rate was 1 per 100,000 in 1950, and 10 per 100,000 in 2008. In Chicago, the analogous figures are 7 and 18; in Detroit, 6 and 34; and in Los Angeles, 3 and 10, respectively. See Uniform Crime Reports: 1950, at 94–101, table 35, and Crime in the United States: 2008, table 8; Campbell Gibson and Kay Jung, Historical Census Statistics on Population Totals by Race, 1790 to 1990, and by Hispanic Origin, 1970 to 1990, for Large Cities and Other Urban Places in the United States (Washington, DC: U.S. Census Bureau, Working Paper No. 76, February 2005).

2. See "250 Exonerated, Too Many Wrongfully Convicted: An Innocence Project Report on the First 250 Exonerations in the U.S.," available online at http://www .innocenceproject.org/docs/InnocenceProject_250.pdf. Were DNA testing more common, the number of exonerated prisoners would no doubt be a good deal higher. See D. Michael Risinger, Innocents Convicted: An Empirically Justified Wrongful Conviction Rate, Journal of Criminal Law and Criminology, vol. 97, 761–804 (2007) (finding a likely error rate of between 3 percent and 5 percent in capital rape-murder cases). If the same error rate exists in noncapital cases as in the cases Risinger studied, the justice system wrongfully convicts somewhere between 30,000 and 60,000 "felons" per year. The number of wrongfully convicted misdemeanants must be much higher, as misdemeanor prosecutions vastly outnumber felony cases. And the error rate in noncapital cases is probably higher than those numbers suggest because capital cases are investigated and litigated with more care and at greater expense than noncapital cases.

3. As of 2006, the imprisonment rate for drug offenses among non-Hispanic blacks stood at 321 per 100,000; among non-Hispanic whites, the figure was 36. Among

Hispanics, the analogous figure was 126. See Online Sourcebook, table 6.0001.2006; 2008 Statistical Abstract at 9, table 6.

4. A tactic that is perfectly legal. See Whren v. United States, 517 U.S. 806 (1996).

5. For the classic study on the racial mix of traffic stops, see John Lamberth, Revised Statistical Analysis of the Incidence of Police Stops and Arrests of Black Drivers/ Travelers on the New Jersey Turnpike between Exits or Interchanges 1 and 3 from the Years 1988 through 1991 (1994) (on file with author). The study's results are discussed in detail in David A. Harris, The Stories, the Statistics, and the Law: Why "Driving While Black" Matters, Minnesota Law Review, vol. 84, 265–326, at 277–80 (1999).

6. See, for example, United States v. Farrar, 281 U.S. 624 (1930).

7. Stewart was indicted and convicted of obstruction of justice for lying to federal agents about her alleged insider trading. See Constance L. Hays, Martha Stewart Indicted by U.S. on Obstruction, New York Times, June 5, 2003, at A1; David Carr and Claudia H. Deutsch, The Stewart Verdict—The Company: A Harsh Blow to a Company Based on Image, New York Times, March 6, 2004, at A1.

8. See Steve Friess, O. J. Simpson Found Guilty in Robbery Trial, New York Times, October 4, 2008; Steve Friess, After Apologies, Simpson Is Sentenced to at Least Nine Years for Armed Robbery, New York Times, December 6, 2008, at A9.

9. See Daniel C. Richman and William J. Stuntz, Al Capone's Revenge: An Essay on the Political Economy of Pretextual Prosecution, Columbia Law Review, vol. 105, 583–639, at 620–22 (2005).

10. For the data on illegal drug use, see Substance Abuse and Mental Health Services Administration, Results from the 2009 National Survey on Drug Use and Health: Volume I. Summary of National Findings 23 (Rockville, MD: Office of Applied Studies, 2010). For the drug imprisonment rates, see Online Sourcebook, table 6.0001.2006; 2008 Statistical Abstract at 9, table 6. As of 2006, the imprisonment rate for drug offenses among non-Hispanic blacks stood at 321 per 100,000; among non-Hispanic whites, the figure was 36; among Hispanics, the figure was 126, respectively. The ratio was still more extreme a few years earlier: in 2003, the black imprisonment rate for drug offenses was 359, and the white rate was a mere 28, respectively.

11. The demographic makeup of the dealer population is unknown, but dealers are almost certainly disproportionately black relative to the user population. Still, given that (1) most illegal markets are segregated, (2) there are thriving drug markets everywhere in the United States, and (3) there are several times more white drug users than black ones, it seems extraordinarily unlikely that the racial disproportion in drug prisoners reflects the racial disproportion in drug dealers.

12. FBI, U.S. Department of Justice, Crime in the United States: 2008, table 25.

13. As of 2002, 51.5 percent of America's black population lived in central cities, while 36 percent lived in metropolitan areas outside central cities, and a mere 12.5 percent lived outside metropolitan areas. Among non-Hispanic whites, the comparable figures were 21 percent, 57 percent, and 22 percent. Jesse McKinnon, The Black Population in the United States: March 2002, at 2, figure 2 (Washington, DC: U.S. Census Bureau, April 2003). On the link between concentrated black populations and

concentrated poverty, see Alemayehu Bishaw, Areas with Concentrated Poverty: 1999, at 8, figure 4 (Washington, DC: U.S. Census Bureau, July 2005). For evidence that race but not poverty is a strong negative predictor of clearance rates, see Janice L. Puckett and Richard J. Lundman, Factors Affecting Homicide Clearances: Multivariate Analysis of a More Complete Conceptual Framework, Journal of Research on Crime and Delinquency, vol. 40, 171–93 (2003).

14. On the imprisonment rate, see Online Sourcebook, table 6.28.2008. On the murder rate, I use the late Eric Monkkonen's data.

15. For the murder rates, see Uniform Crime Reports: 1950, at 94–101, table 35; Uniform Crime Reports: 1972, at 218, table 76; Gibson and Jung, Historical Census Statistics. For the imprisonment rates for these states, see 1952 Statistical Abstract at 14, no. 11, and 146, no. 175; 1991 Sourcebook, at 637, table 6.72.

16. For the imprisonment rate after the early 1970s, see Online Sourcebook, table 6.28.2009. On the nation's murder rate in the early 1970s, see Monkkonen's data. On the murder rate in 2000, see Crime in the United States: 2000, table 1.

17. On the huge rise in the nation's inmate population, see Online Sourcebook, tables 6.28.2009, 6.13.2009. That rise was not evenly distributed: even as the inmate population exploded, the black share of that population rose. See Margaret Werner Cahalan, Historical Corrections Statistics in the United States, 1850–1984, at 65, table 3-31 (Rockville, MD: Bureau of Justice Statistics, 1986); Michael Tonry, Obsolescence and Immanence in Penal Theory and Policy, Columbia Law Review, vol. 105, 1233–75, at 1255, table 3 (2005). By the beginning of the twenty-first century, the black imprisonment rate topped 1,800 per 100,000 population. (By comparison, the white imprisonment rate stood at 244.) See 2001 Sourcebook, 498, table 6.28; 2001 Statistical Abstract, 13, no. 10.

18. That was the theory that undergirded the successful Ku Klux Klan prosecutions of the early 1870s (see chapter 4 in Lou Falkner Williams, The Great South Carolina Ku Klux Klan Trials, 1871–1872 (Athens: University of Georgia Press, 1996). For the best account of those prosecutions, see Williams, ibid.

19. The key court decision was United States v. Cruikshank, 92 U.S. 542 (1876). For an excellent version of the basic story, see Charles Lane, The Day Freedom Died: The Colfax Massacre, the Supreme Court, and the Betrayal of Reconstruction, 18–19 (New York: Henry Holt, 2008).

20. The great majority of local prosecutors' offices are headed by elected officials. Steven W. Perry, Prosecutors in State Courts: 2005, at 2 (Washington, DC: Bureau of Justice Statistics, July 2006). Similarly, the large majority of trial judges either are elected or are appointed but subject to retention elections. See Jed Handelsman Shugerman, The People's Courts, introduction, appendix A, and ch. 3, "The Calm before the Storm" (Cambridge, MA: Harvard University Press, forthcoming 2011).

21. On the urban concentration of crime, see, for example, Joan E. Jacoby, The American Prosecutor: A Search for Identity, at 61 (Lexington, MA: D. C. Heath, 1980). On the concentration within poor city neighborhoods, see, for example, David A. Weiner, Byron F. Lutz, and Jens Ludwig, The Effects of School Desegregation on Crime, at 1 (NBER Working Paper No. 1530, September 2009).

22. See Eric H. Monkkonen, Murder in New York City, at 9, figure 1.1 (Berkeley and Los Angeles: University of California Press, 2001).

23. See Online Sourcebook, table 5.57.2006.

24. Exceptional, but not nonexistent. See Jeffrey Adler, First in Violence, Deepest in Dirt: Homicide in Chicago, 1875–1920, at 126–27 (Cambridge, MA: Harvard University Press, 2006); Lawrence Friedman and Robert V. Percival, The Roots of Justice: Crime and Punishment in Alameda County, California, 1870–1910 (Chapel Hill: University of North Carolina Press, 1981); Roger Lane, Murder in America: A History, at 266 (Columbus: Ohio State University Press, 1997); Monkkonen, Murder in New York City; Randolph Roth, American Homicide (Cambridge, MA: Harvard University Press, 2009). Notice that most of these books concern the history of American crime, not of American criminal justice.

25. The reference is to the famous joke about the man looking for his lost car keys on a portion of city sidewalk lit by a streetlight. When asked whether his car keys were lost near the streetlight, he answers, "No—I'm not looking where the keys are; I'm looking where the light is."

1. TWO MIGRATIONS

1. Compare Philip Taylor, The Distant Magnet: European Emigration to the U.S.A., at xiii (London: Eyre and Spottiswoode, 1971), who estimated 35 million immigrants came to the United States between 1830 and 1930, with John Higham, Send These to Me: Immigrants in Urban America, at 20–28 (Baltimore: Johns Hopkins University Press, 1984), who estimated 50 million European immigrants between the 1820s and 1924.

2. For a good discussion of the campaign that produced this lopsided result, see Tyler Anbinder, Nativism and Slavery: The Northern Know Nothings and the Politics of the 1850s, at 87–95 (New York: Oxford University Press, 1992).

3. On Curley, see Jack Beatty, The Rascal King: The Life and Times of James Michael Curley, 1874–1958 (Cambridge, MA: Da Capo Press, 1992). On the mayors, see Joseph Fahey, ed., Boston's Forty-five Mayors, from John Phillips to Kevin H. White (Boston: City Record, 1975).

4. See Nicholas Lemann, The Promised Land: The Great Black Migration and How It Changed America, at 6 (New York: Vintage Books, 1992): 6.5 million southern blacks moved north between 1910 and 1970.

5. The black percentages of city population are taken from Campbell Gibson and Kay Jung, Historical Census Statistics on Population Totals by Race, 1790 to 1990, and by Hispanic Origin, 1970 to 1990, for Large Cities and Other Urban Places in the United States (Washington, DC: U.S. Census Bureau, Working Paper No. 76, February 2005).

6. For some examples, see Reginald Stuart, New York Times, September 29, 1976, at 20, col. 3 (William Hart in Detroit); Chicago's Mayor Fills Two Top Jobs, August 24, 1983, at A20, col. 1 (Fred Rice in Chicago); Leonard Buder, Ward Sworn In, and Top Police Critic Is Guest, New York Times, January 6, 1984, at A1, col. 2 (Benja-

min Ward in New York); Paul W. Valentine, First Black Will Head Baltimore Police Force, Washington Post, June 20, 1984, at C3 (Bishop Robinson—a name, not a title— in Baltimore); New Police Commissioner, Washington Post, June 4, 1988, at A16 (Willie Williams in Philadelphia); Richard A. Serrano and James Rainey, Williams Sworn In as Chief, Calls for Healing; LAPD: He Says We Must "Make Peace with Ourselves and with Each Other," Unveils Plan to Recruit Minorities, Los Angeles Times, July 1, 1992, at A1, col. 2 (Williams again, this time in Los Angeles).

7. See Randolph Roth, American Homicide, at 197–98 (Cambridge, MA: Harvard University Press, 2009).

8. Ibid., 198. See also 392–93, noting the same phenomenon with respect to Italian immigrants in the late nineteenth century.

9. Roth notes that the end of the nineteenth century saw southern homicide rates surpass those in the Southwest, and saw a sharp rise in black homicide. See Roth, American Homicide, 387. The latter phenomenon happened in the North as well (ibid., 194–96, 387). Before the last years of the nineteenth century, whites were the more homicidal group. See, for example, the lower black homicide rate pre-1890 (ibid., 398).

10. See FBI, Crime in the United States: 2008, Expanded Homicide Data, table 3; 2010 Statistical Abstract, table 10.

11. See Roger Lane, On the Social Meaning of Homicide Trends in America, in Ted Robert Gurr, ed., Violence in America (Newbury Park, CA: Sage, 1989), 55–79, at 64–68.

12. Compare Elina Treyger, Soviet Roots of Post-Soviet Order (forthcoming 2011) (PhD diss., Harvard University), which studies crime and ethnic conflict in the former Soviet Union. Treyger's data suggest that change in the ethnic balance of power, not ethnic division itself, triggers heightened criminal violence. Similarly, Niall Ferguson suggests that economic volatility plays a larger role in promoting disorder and violence than poverty or economic downturns. Niall Ferguson, War of the World: Twentieth-Century Conflict and the Descent of the West, at lix–lxii (New York: Penguin Press, 2006). If these claims are correct, late nineteenth-century and early twentieth-century American cities were astonishingly peaceful, given the ethnic change and economic volatility seen in those years. Elina Treyger, Soviet Roots of Post-Soviet Order (PhD diss., Harvard University, forthcoming 2011).

13. See, for example, Lane, Homicide Trends, 70–74. In some places, the steep rise in black homicide rates happened sooner. See, for example, Jeffrey Adler, First in Violence, Deepest in Dirt: Homicide in Chicago, 1875–1920, at 126–27 (Cambridge, MA: Harvard University Press, 2006); Roth, American Homicide, 395–403.

14. These data appear in David A. Weiner, Byron F. Lutz, and Jens Ludwig, The Effects of School Desegregation on Crime, at 1 (NBER Working Paper No. 1530, September 2009).

15. See Joan E. Jacoby, The American Prosecutor: A Search for Identity, 61 (Lexington, MA: D.C. Heath, 1980): "Crime is an urban phenomenon."

16. See Crime in the United States: 2007, table 8.

17. See, for example, Michael W. Flamm, Law and Order: Street Crime, Civil Unrest, and the Crisis of Liberalism in the 1960s, at 1–22 (New York: Columbia University

Press, 2005); Tali Mendelberg, The Race Card: Campaign Strategy, Implicit Messages, and the Norm of Equality (Princeton, NJ: Princeton University Press, 2001). For an interesting study of the point, see Melissa Hickman Barlow, Race and the Problem of Crime in *Time* and *Newsweek* Cover Stories, 1946–1995, Social Justice, vol. 25, 149–83.

18. See then-candidate Obama's reference to his white grandmother in his Philadelphia race speech. Barack Obama, "A More Perfect Union," Philadelphia, PA (March 18, 2008): "[A] woman who loves me as much as she loves anything in this world, but a woman who once confessed her fear of black men who passed her on the street . . ."

19. The clearance rate data in Crime in the United States: 2008, table 25, confirms this point.

20. Randall Kennedy, Race, Crime, and the Law, at 158–60 (New York: Pantheon Books, 1997).

21. Vesla Weaver might call them "frontlashes." See Vesla M. Weaver, Frontlash: Race and the Development of Punitive Crime Police, Studies in American Political Development, vol. 21, 230–65 (2007).

22. See, for example, Mark Thomas Connelly, The Response to Prostitution in the Progressive Era, at 48–64 (Chapel Hill: University of North Carolina Press, 1980). In different parts of the country, different ethnic groups were stigmatized by this crusade. See, for example, Anne M. Butler, Daughters of Joy, Sisters of Misery: Prostitutes in the American West, 1865–1890, at 4 (Urbana: University of Illinois Press, 1985): In San Antonio, "the Mexican [prostitutes] occupied the lowest rung on the ladder of social acceptance."

23. Mann Act, ch. 395, §2, 36 Stat. 825 (1910).

24. John Higham, Strangers in the Land: Patterns of American Nativism, 1860–1925, at 318–24 (New York: Atheneum, 1965).

25. The Democratic losses were the three presidential elections held in the 1920s; the victories ran from 1932 through 1948. See Presidential Elections, 1789–2008, at 149–56 (Washington, DC: CQ Press, 2010).

26. In the 1920s, contemporaneous observers attributed the disproportionate targeting to the disproportionate Italian presence in the liquor trade. See, for example, Martha Bensley Bruère, Does Prohibition Work? at 57–60, 89, 139–40, 170–71, 186, 225, 258–59 (New York: Harper and Brothers, 1927). The South saw a similar pattern, with blacks as the targeted group (ibid., 112–13, 293–95). For drug imprisonment rates by race, see Online Sourcebook, table 6.0001.2006; 2008 Statistical Abstract at 9, table 6. See also David Cole, No Equal Justice: Race and Class in the American Criminal Justice System, at 34–52, 141–46 (New York: New Press, 1999).

27. For the best account of the federal legislation and the crusade against crack, see David A. Sklansky, Cocaine, Race, and Equal Protection, Stanford Law Review, vol. 47, 1283–322 (1995).

28. For the best account of the 1988 presidential campaign, see Richard Ben Cramer, What It Takes: The Way to the White House (New York: Random House, 1992). Cramer's discussion of the Horton issue appears at 996–1001, 1017–18.

29. Nationally, crime peaked in 1991; between that year and 2000, violent crime declined 33 percent. See Uniform Crime Reports: 1991, 10; Crime in the United States: 2000, 11.

30. According to Monkkonen's estimates, the nation's murder rate fell from just under 10 per 100,000 population in 1933 to 5 in 1944. See also Roger Lane, Murder in America: A History, at 308 (Columbus: Ohio State University Press, 1997).

31. Walsh won a fifth senatorial election: in 1926, he was elected to serve the two years that remained in the first Lodge's term (Lodge died in November 1924). Walsh won his four complete terms in 1918, 1928, 1934, and 1940; he was defeated for reelection in 1924 and 1946—the latter time by Henry Cabot Lodge Jr.

32. With respect to the politicians mentioned in this paragraph, see Dorothy G. Wayman, David I. Walsh: Citizen-Patriot, at 1–3, 45–52, 66–68, 98–102, 159, 172, 217–20, 285–88, 338–40 (Milwaukee: Bruce Publishing, 1952); J. Joseph Huthmacher, Senator Robert F. Wagner and the Rise of Urban Liberalism, at 12–15, 50–53, 104–06, 179, 218–20, 251–55, 308–10 (New York: Atheneum, 1968); Robert A. Slayton, Empire Statesman: The Rise and Redemption of Al Smith, at ix, 11–15, 35–41 (New York: Free Press, 2001); Charles J. Masters, Governor Henry Horner, Chicago Politics, and the Great Depression, at 2–9, 80–89 (Carbondale: Southern Illinois University Press, 2007); Allan Nevins, Herbert H. Lehman and His Era, at 3–4, 124–31 (New York: Charles Scribner's Sons, 1963); Brien McMahon, Late a Senator from Connecticut: Memorial Addresses Delivered in Congress, at 5, 31–102 (Washington, DC: U.S. Government Printing Office, 1953).

33. Tom Bradley, Ed Koch, and Andrew Young, respectively. Bradley lost in both the 1982 and 1986 general elections to California Governor George Deukmejian. Koch lost to Mario Cuomo in the 1982 Democratic primary in New York. Young lost to Zell Miller in the 1990 Democratic primary in Georgia. It is worth noting that Doug Wilder served as mayor of Richmond *after* his term as governor, not before.

34. For a good account of Jackson's 1984 and 1988 campaigns, see Marshall Frady, Jesse: The Life and Pilgrimage of Jesse Jackson, at 14–16, 303–401 (New York: Simon & Schuster Paperbacks, 2006). Frady reports that Jackson received 4 percent of the white vote in the 1984 Democratic primaries and 12 percent of the white vote in the 1988 primaries (ibid., 14–15, 391–92).

35. Roger Lane tells this story in Lane, Homicide Trends, 71, 74; Lane, Murder in America, 266.

36. See William Julius Wilson, The Truly Disadvantaged: The Inner City, the Underclass, and Public Policy (Chicago: University of Chicago Press, 1993); William Julius Wilson, When Work Disappears: The World of the New Urban Poor (New York: Vintage Books, 1997).

37. Through the 1970s, I use Monkkonen's data on the nation's murder rates. After that, I use the data in the annual volumes of the FBI's Uniform Crime Reports (later titled Crime in the United States).

38. Bruce Western has done a more fine-grained analysis of unemployment among unskilled young men and incarceration rates (not crime rates); there is a statistically significant relationship between the two, but the relationship is "quite modest." Bruce Western, Punishment and Inequality in America, at 72 (New York: Russell Sage Foundation, 2006).

39. In 1950, New York State's imprisonment rate stood at 102 per 100,000; New York City's murder rate was less than 4. By 1972, the analogous numbers were 64 and 22,

respectively. Illinois's imprisonment rate fell from 90 in 1950 to 50 in 1972; Chicago's murder rate rose from 7 in 1950 to 22 in 1972. In Michigan, imprisonment fell from 134 in 1950 to 94 in 1972, while Detroit's murder rate exploded, rising from 6 per 100,000 in 1950 to 42 in 1972. California's imprisonment rate stood at 98 in 1950, rising to 149 in 1963 before falling to 84 in 1972. Los Angeles's murder rate was 3 in 1950 and 18 in 1972. Last but not least, Massachusetts's imprisonment rate dropped from 54 in 1950 to 32 in 1972; Boston's murder rate rose from 1.4 in 1950 to 17 in 1972. The imprisonment rates for these states are taken from 1991 Sourcebook at 637, table 6.72; 1952 Statistical Abstract, at 14, no. 11, and 146, no. 175. The number of murders in each of the previously mentioned cities is taken from Uniform Crime Reports: 1950, 94–101, table 35; Uniform Crime Reports: 1972, 218, table 76. City populations, used to calculate murder rates, are taken from Gibson and Jung, Historical Census Statistics.

40. For a good summary, now a bit dated, see Daniel S. Nagin, Criminal Deterrence Research at the Outset of the Twenty-First Century, Crime and Justice, vol. 23, 1–37 (1999).

41. Using Monkkonen's data, New York's murder rate fell from 5.5 in 1882 to 2.4 a decade later, rising to 5.7 in 1914. Roth maintains that this pattern was general (American Homicide, 387–88). Chicago's story was different: there, the murder rate rose steadily throughout the relevant period (see Adler, First in Violence, 274, figure 14)—though the rise was much smaller than during the twentieth century's second half.

42. For murder rates in individual cities, see Uniform Crime Reports: 1972, 218, table 76; Uniform Crime Reports: 1990, 71–118, table 6. For the fluctuation in the nation's murder rate, see Monkkonen's data on the early 1970s and the early 1980s, plus Uniform Crime Reports: 1990, 8. For imprisonment rates, see 1991 Sourcebook, 637, table 6.72.

43. Roth, American Homicide, 16–26, 469–74.

44. See Tom R. Tyler, Why People Obey the Law (New Haven, CT: Yale University Press, 1990), and the large literature it has spawned.

45. On police jobs as political patronage, see Robert M. Fogelson, Big-City Police, at 17–22 (Cambridge, MA: Harvard University Press, 1977); Mark Haller, Historical Roots of Police Behavior: Chicago, 1890–1925, in Eric H. Monkkonen, ed., Crime and Justice in American History: Policing and Crime Control, vol. 5, part 1, at 244–64 (New York: K.G. Saur, 1992); Eugene J. Watts, The Police in Atlanta, 1890–1905, in Crime and Justice in American History: Policing and Crime Control, vol. 5, part 3, at 908–25. Compare with Roger Lane, Policing the City: Boston, 1822–1885, at 213 (Cambridge, MA: Harvard University Press, 1967); note the difficulty that upper-class Republicans in Boston had in controlling the local police force even when they won local elections. On immigrant voters' control of urban political machines, see, for example, M. Craig Brown and Barbara D. Warner, Immigrants, Urban Politics, and Policing in 1900, American Sociological Review, vol. 57, 293–305 (1992), which showed the strong negative correlation between machine control of city politics and the level of arrests for alcohol-related offenses. The one major city

with both a high level of machine control and a high level of alcohol arrests was Philadelphia, in which the political machine was Republican and relied on native-born voters for its support (ibid., 301, table 2). Elsewhere, the reigning machines—Republican and Democratic alike—depended on immigrant votes, and generally avoided strict enforcement of alcohol regulations.

46. The definition of the pool from which juries were selected is surprisingly hard to pin down, because records of jury selection practices in the past are thin. For a rare discussion of the scope of the community from which urban juries were actually drawn in generations past, see People v. Jones, 8 Cal.3d 546, 510 P.2d 705 (1973) (discussing jury selection under Los Angeles system of judicial districts). That said, the limited evidence available suggests that juries in the Gilded Age *were* locally selected—that, in large cities, selection was by district rather than by county. (Countywide selection is the norm today. See Steven A. Engel, The Public's Vicinage Right: A Constitutional Argument, New York University Law Review, vol. 75, 1658–719, at 1705n242 [2000].) For the standard historical discussion, see William Wirt Blume, The Place of Trial of Criminal Cases: Constitutional Vicinage and Venue, Michigan Law Review, vol. 43, 59–94 (1944). Custom, not law, determined the size of the community from which the jury was drawn. In England, locally selected juries were "a functional necessity," since local knowledge informed jury decision making (Engel, Vicinage Right, 1674). Local knowledge was still an important part of jury decisions in the late nineteenth and early twentieth centuries. The limits of urban transportation and the necessities of urban machine politics pushed in the same direction. But these forces shaped the practice of jury selection, not its legal form. Consequently, evidence of particular selection practices is hard to come by.

47. See Lawrence M. Friedman and Robert V. Percival, The Roots of Justice: Crime and Punishment in Alameda County, California, 1870–1910, at 166 table 5.8 (Chapel Hill: University of North Carolina Press, 1981). George Fisher finds a higher guilty plea rate in Middlesex County, Massachusetts—though not dramatically higher, at least not consistently. See George Fisher, Plea Bargaining's Triumph, at 93, figure 4.1 (Stanford, CA: Stanford University Press, 2003).

48. For cases embodying the earlier standard, see, for example, Masters v. United States, 42 App. D.C. 350 (D.C. Ct. App. 1914); State v. O'Neil, 126 N.W. 454 (Iowa 1910); State v. Moore, 14 S.W. 182 (Mo. 1890); State v. Blue, 53 P. 978 (Utah 1898). See also William Blackstone, Commentaries on the Laws of England, 4th ed., vol. 4, at *21 (Oxford: Clarendon Press, 1769): "an unwarrantable act without a vicious will is no crime at all."

49. Adler, First in Violence, 115–16.

50. In such cases, "vague, generic self-defense arguments . . . nearly always persuaded jurors." Ibid., 116.

51. Compare Margaret Werner Cahalan, Historical Corrections Statistics in the United States, 1850–1984, at 30, table 3-3 (Rockville, MD: Bureau of Justice Statistics, 1986), with Online Sourcebook, table 6.29.2008.

52. See Fogelson, Big-City Police, 15–30; Alexander von Hoffman, An Officer of the Neighborhood: A Boston Patrolman on the Beat in 1895, Journal of Social History,

Winter 1992, 309–30. "[M]any patrolmen belonged to the political clubs that dominated the wards [and] numbered district leaders among their friends and relatives"
(Fogelson, Big-City Police, 26). On the overlap between the relevant communities,
see, for example, Joel Best, Keeping the Peace in St. Paul: Crime, Vice, and Police
Work, 1869–1874, in Monkkonen, ed., Crime and Justice in American History, vol. 5,
part 1, 60–79, at 62, 69–70.

53. For the two sides of the coin, see von Hoffman, Officer of the Neighborhood (emphasizing the service orientation of the police); Fogelson, Big-City Police, 3–10,
148–49 (discussing police corruption); Marilynn S. Johnson, Street Justice: A History of Police Violence in New York City, at 12–113 (Boston: Beacon Press, 2003)
(discussing police violence in the late nineteenth and early twentieth centuries). On
some officers' resistance to walking their respective beats, see Fogelson, Big-City
Police, 31–32. For the view of urban police officers as licensors and regulators, see
ibid., 32–33.

54. On the role constrained resources played in the lenient justice system of the past,
see Eric H. Monkkonen, The American State from the Bottom Up: Of Homicides
and Courts, Law and Society Review, vol. 24, 521–31 (1990). On early twentieth-
century juries' composition, see Gustave F. Fischer, The Juries, in Felony Cases, in
Cook County, Illinois Crime Survey: 1929, ed. John Henry Wigmore, 225–43, at
232, table 1 (Chicago: Illinois Association for Criminal Justice, 1929). On class conflict and the police, see Sidney L. Harring, Policing a Class Society: The Experience of American Cities, 1865–1915 (New Brunswick, NJ: Rutgers University Press,
1983), which argues a bit polemically that the late nineteenth- and early twentieth-
century police served chiefly as capitalists' means of keeping workers in line.

55. This is a function of the twentieth-century movement to professionalize urban police forces. On that subject, see Robert M. Fogelson, Big-City Police, 141–92; David
Alan Sklansky, Democracy and the Police, at 33–38 (Stanford, CA: Stanford University Press, 2007).

56. In 2006, the plea rate in felony cases stood at 96 percent, counting those cases that
proceeded to final adjudication (including those that pled down to misdemeanors).
Online Sourcebook, table 5.57.2006. In 1962, a sample of 28 counties found a guilty
plea rate of 74 percent for defendants with court-appointed counsel and 48 percent
for defendants with retained counsel. See Lee Silverstein, Defense of the Poor in
Criminal Cases in American State Courts: A Field Study and Report, at 22–23 (Chicago: American Bar Foundation, 1965). Court-appointed counsel were used in
43 percent of all criminal cases (ibid., 7–8).

57. In 2006, the conviction rate in tried murder cases was 89 percent. See Online
Sourcebook, table 5.57.2006.

58. On the rise and character of rule-based sentencing in federal cases, see, for example,
Kate Stith and Jose A. Cabranes, Fear of Judging: Sentencing Guidelines in the
Federal Courts (Chicago: University of Chicago Press, 1998); Frank O. Bowman III,
The Failure of the Federal Sentencing Guidelines: A Structural Analysis, Columbia
Law Review, vol. 105, 1315–50 (2005). On its rise and character in state cases, see, for
example, Richard Frase, State Sentencing Guidelines: Diversity, Consensus, and

Unresolved Policy Issues, Columbia Law Review, vol. 105, 1190–232 (2005); Kevin Reitz, The New Sentencing Conundrum: Policy and Constitutional Law at Cross-Purposes, Columbia Law Review, vol. 105, 1082–123 (2005).

59. Ministry of Justice, Research and Documentation Centre (WODC), European Sourcebook of Crime and Criminal Justice Statistics—2010, 4th ed., at 295–96 tables 4.2.1.1, 4.2.1.2 (The Hague: Boom Juridische uitgevers, 2010). To make a comparison with American imprisonment rates appropriate, European imprisonment rates are calculated by subtracting the number of inmates detained pretrial from the rest of the incarcerated population—in the United States, pretrial detainees are housed in local jails, and so do not appear in the imprisonment figures. Where the number of pretrial detainees was not available for 2007, I used the nearest year with available data.

60. This statistic relies on the annual volumes of the Sourcebook of Criminal Justice Statistics for imprisonment rates and on the annual volumes of the FBI's Uniform Crime Reports/Crime in the United States for the relevant homicide data. UCR crime data are viewed with some suspicion by scholars—but not homicide data. And homicide is the one class of crime for which we have reasonably good historical data. It thus serves as a useful stand-in for crime rates more generally.

61. Russia's imprisonment rate is slightly higher than the United States', but its overall incarceration rate—counting American jail inmates, and counting Russian pretrial detainees—is substantially lower. Compare European Sourcebook 2010, 295, table 4.2.1.1 (showing an overall Russian incarceration rate of 625 in 2007), with Online Sourcebook, table 6.13.2009 (showing an American incarceration rate of 756 for the same year). These incarceration rates understate the gap between the two justice systems. According to the European Sourcebook, Russia's murder rate in 2007 stood at 16 per 100,000—nearly three times the rate in the United States. See European Sourcebook 2010, 40, table 1.2.1.6. Judged by punishment per unit crime, America's justice system is probably a good deal harsher than Russia's.

62. In the Northeast, imprisonment rates fell from 88 in 1950 to 82 in 1960 to 70 in 1970. In the Midwest, the analogous figures are 121, 114, and 86. In the South and West, imprisonment rose significantly in the 1950s, falling only after 1960. The figures appear in Margaret Werner Cahalan, Historical Corrections Statistics in the United States, 1850–1984, at 30, table 3-3 (Rockville, MD: Bureau of Justice Statistics, 1986).

63. See Cahalan, Historical Corrections Statistics, 65, table 3-31; Michael Tonry, Obsolescence and Immanence in Penal Theory and Policy, Columbia Law Review, vol. 105, 1233–75, at 1255, table 3 (2005).

64. Online Sourcebook, table 6.33.2008.

65. These figures come from Western, Punishment and Inequality, 26–28 and figure 1.4.

66. See 1991 Sourcebook, at 637, table 6.72.

67. See, for example, Wendy Kaminer, It's All the Rage: Crime and Culture (New York: Perseus Books, 1995), discussing the link between capital punishment and popular rage at crime and criminals.

68. See Western, Punishment and Inequality, 85–198.

69. The FBI's rate of index crimes—violent felonies and felony thefts—fell 30 percent between 1991 and 2000. The rate of violent crime fell 33 percent, while the murder rate fell 44 percent. During the same years, homicides fell 65 percent in Boston, 67 percent in Houston, and 69 percent in New York. See Uniform Crime Reports: 1991, at 5, 10, 13, 126, 139, 150; Crime in the United States: 2000, at 5, 11, 14, 129, 141, 151.

70. Using Monkkonen's data, the average murder rate in New York for 1900–1904 was 3.5 per 100,000 population. Using the FBI's data as recorded in the annual volumes of Crime in the United States, the city's average murder rate for 2004–2008 stands at 6.3. New York state's imprisonment rate for 1904—the nearest year to 1900 for which good data exist—was 71 per 100,000; today the figure is 307. See Cahalan, Historical Corrections Statistics, 30, table 3-3; Online Sourcebook, table 6.29.2008.

71. See, for example, David Garland, The Culture of Control: Crime and Social Order in Contemporary Society, at 95–96 (Chicago: University of Chicago Press, 2001). Vice President Hubert Humphrey captured the mind-set in the course of the 1968 presidential campaign: "You're not going to make this a better America just because you build more jails. What this country needs are more decent neighborhoods, more educated people, better homes . . . I do not believe repression alone can bring a better society." Quoted in Rick Perlstein, Nixonland: The Rise of a President and the Fracturing of America, at 343 (New York: Scribner, 2008).

72. On the link between Warren-era criminal procedure doctrine and class discrimination, see Lucas A. Powe Jr., The Warren Court and American Politics, at 379–86, 445–46 (Cambridge, MA: Harvard University Press, 2000); Michael J. Klarman, Rethinking the Civil Rights and Civil Liberties Revolutions, Virginia Law Review, vol. 82, 1–67, at 62–66 (1996). On the relationship between that doctrine's origins and race discrimination, see Michael J. Klarman, The Racial Origins of Modern Criminal Procedure, Michigan Law Review, vol. 99, 48–97 (2000).

73. The harshest drug law of them all—the federal statute mandating that possession of a single gram of crack be punished as severely as possession of 100 grams of cocaine powder—won the support of half the Congressional Black Caucus. See Kennedy, Race, Crime, and the Law, 301.

74. Adolf Berle and Gardiner Means, The Modern Corporation and Private Property (New York: Macmillan, 1932).

75. This has been the conventional academic wisdom for the past generation. For a recent articulation of the position, see, for example, Lucian A. Bebchuk, The Case for Increasing Shareholder Power, Harvard Law Review, vol. 118, at 833–914 (2005).

2. "THE WOLF BY THE EAR"

1. The text of the letter is taken from the Library of Congress website: www.loc.gov/exhibits/jefferson/159.html.

2. On the material in this paragraph, see William W. Freehling, The Road to Disunion: Secessionists at Bay, 1776–1854, at 144–49 (New York: Oxford University Press, 1990).

3. The Missouri Compromise would not have passed—actually, would have lost by a dozen or more votes—but for the Constitution's three-fifths clause, which gave House seats to slave states based on their white populations plus three-fifths of their slaves (ibid., 153).
4. For the facts in this paragraph and the preceding one, see ibid., 150–55.
5. Which is not to say that Jefferson disbelieved his argument: Jefferson appears to have believed that "diffusing" slavery was the key to abolishing it. A considerable number of Southerners, both at the time of the Missouri Compromise and afterward, agreed with him (ibid., 150–52).
6. Memoirs of John Quincy Adams, Comprising Portions of His Diary from 1795 to 1848, vol. 5, at 210 (Philadelphia: J.B. Lippincott, 1874).
7. The absence of large-scale slave insurrections during the Civil War would have surprised Jefferson—and Adams, too: in his diary entry at the time of the Missouri debate, Adams predicted that civil war, when it did come, would trigger "a servile war in the slave-holding States" (ibid.).
8. On the Fort Pillow massacre, see James M. McPherson, Battle Cry of Freedom: The Civil War Era, at 748 and note 48 (New York: Oxford University Press, 1988), and sources cited therein. The Battle of the Crater was fought after engineers in Grant's army dug a tunnel under the southern trenches and set off a bomb that left a large crater where a section of trenches had been. Northern soldiers, including an all-black unit, marched into the crater rather than around it. Confederate soldiers lined the crater's edge and fired into it, killing black soldiers even after those soldiers tried to surrender. Ibid., 758–60.
9. It is impossible to prove definitively that Caddo Parish was the nation's most murderous jurisdiction, but Caddo *was* the most violent parish in the nation's most violent state. Gilles Vandal, "Bloody Caddo": White Violence Against Blacks in a Louisiana Parish, 1865–1876, Journal of Social History, vol. 25, 373–88 (1991).
10. According to the 1860 census, the United States in 1860 held 3.95 million slaves, 488,000 free blacks, and 26.96 million whites. U.S. Census Bureau, Population of the United States in 1860, Compiled from the Original Returns of the Eighth Census 598–99 (Washington, DC: U.S. Government Printing Office, 1864).
11. For the inmate population, see Online Sourcebook, table 6.13.2008. For the general population, see 2009 Statistical Abstract, 7, table 2.
12. Generally, prison inmates are convicted felons sentenced to terms of incarceration of one year or more. Jail inmates include those detained prior to trial—but pretrial detention is usually the consequence of having committed serious crimes in the past. See, for example, the federal Bail Reform Act, codified at 18 U.S.C. §§ 3141–3147, which authorizes pretrial detention for dangerousness, with that term defined chiefly in terms of the defendant's criminal record.
13. U.S. Constitution, Amendment XIII (emphasis added).
14. See Sharon Dolovich, State Punishment and Private Prisons, Duke Law Journal, vol. 55, 437–546, at 455–62 (2005); Bruce Western, Punishment and Inequality in America, at 55–57 (New York: Russell Sage Foundation, 2006). The degree of the concentration is illustrated by the high percentage of criminal defendants—more

than 80 percent of felony defendants—who are poor enough to qualify for state-paid counsel. See Caroline Wolf Harlow, Bureau of Justice Statistics, Defense Counsel in Criminal Cases 1 (NCJ 179023, November 2000).

15. The three-fifths rule was established by U.S. Constitution, Article 1, Section 2, Paragraph 3. On the effects of felon disenfranchisement, see generally Developments in the Law: The Law of Prisons, Harvard Law Review, vol. 115, at 1939–63 (2002).

16. For the black percentage of the inmate population, see Online Sourcebook, tables 6.33.2008 (state prison population), 6.0022.2009 (federal prison population), 6.17.2008 (local jail population). For the black share of the general population, see 2009 Statistical Abstract, 9, table 6.

17. Because of that older view, the original Constitution never uses the word "slavery." With respect to the status of that older view on the eve of the Civil War, see William W. Freehling, The Road to Disunion: Secessionists Triumphant, 1854–1861 (New York: Oxford University Press, 2007).

18. John C. Calhoun, "Speech on Slavery," U.S. Senate, Congressional Globe, 24th Congress, 2nd Sess. (February 6, 1837), 157–59.

19. Imprisonment rates in the late nineteenth century were, in some jurisdictions in the Northeast and Midwest, one-tenth their levels today. See Margaret Werner Cahalan, Historical Corrections Statistics in the United States, 1850–1984, at 30, table 3-3 (Rockville, MD: Bureau of Justice Statistics, 1986); Online Sourcebook, table 6.28.2008. If imprisonment *wasn't* seen as a necessary evil, these figures are inexplicable.

20. Between 1939 and 1946, the nation's imprisonment rate fell from 137 to 99 per 100,000. Between 1944 and 1946, the nation's murder rate rose from 5.0 to 6.4 per 100,000. (Notice that the rise in murders came only after young men began to return home after fighting World War II—which is when the *effective* imprisonment rate, the rate at which crime-prone young men were removed from American city streets, began to fall rapidly.) Between 1961 and 1972, the nation's imprisonment rate fell from 119 to 93; the murder rate rose from 4.7 to 9.4. For the imprisonment rates cited above, see Online Sourcebook, table 6.28.2008. For the murder rates, see Monkkonen's data.

21. For imprisonment rates since 1925, see Online Sourcebook, table 6.28.2008. For earlier imprisonment rates, see Cahalan, Historical Corrections Statistics, 30, table 3-3.

22. Ibid.; Online Sourcebook, table 6.29.2008.

23. For the Texas 1950 imprisonment rate, see 1952 Statistical Abstract, at 14, no. 11, and 146, no. 175. For Massachusetts's imprisonment rate in 1972 and Mississippi's imprisonment rate in 1973, see 1991 Sourcebook, 637, table 6.72. For more recent imprisonment rates, see Online Sourcebook, table 6.29.2008.

24. Cahalan, Historical Corrections Statistics, 52, table 3-23; 2003 Sourcebook, 511, table 6.44.

25. As late as 1974, the drug imprisonment rate stood at 9 per 100,000. See 1976 Sourcebook, 689, table 6.46, and 694, table 6.50. By 2002, that figure was 91. See Online Sourcebook, tables 6.0001.2002, 6.29.2008. On the 20 percent figure, see ibid., table 6.0001.2006.

26. On the population of the Gulag in 1950, see Anne Applebaum, Gulag: A History, at 579 (New York: Random House, 2003); the estimated figure is 2.6 million. Applebaum estimates that, during Stalin's rule, some 18 million people were incarcerated in the camps. On the population of the Soviet Union in 1950, see Michael K. Roof, The Russian Population Enigma Reconsidered, Population Studies, vol. 14, no. 1, 3–16 (June 1960), which estimates that year's Soviet population at 181 million.

27. For marriage rates of black men and women, see Joy Jones, Marriage Is for White People, Washington Post, March 26, 2006, at B1; U.S. Census Bureau, table 56, Marital Status of the Population by Sex, Race, and Hispanic Origin, 1990–2009, Statistical Abstract of the United States (2011). For out-of-wedlock births by race, see Joyce Martin et al., Births: Final Data for 2008, National Vital Statistics Reports, vol. 59, at 15–16, table C, table 15 (December 2010).

28. See Western, Punishment and Inequality, 139–57.

29. Ibid., 89–90.

30. Ibid., chapter 4.

31. Ibid., chapter 5.

32. There is some disagreement as to *how* low. According to Steven D. Levitt and Sudhir Alladi Venkatesh, An Economic Analysis of a Drug-Selling Gang's Finances, Quarterly Journal of Economics, vol. 115, 755–89 (2000), drug-dealing gang members may make less than the minimum wage. According to Peter Reuter, Robert MacCoun, and Patrick Murphy, Money from Crime: A Study of the Economics of Drug Dealing in Washington, DC, at vii–x (Pittsburgh, PA: RAND Corporation, 1990), the wages are significantly better than wages available from legal jobs in inner-city neighborhoods. According to both studies, the typical inner-city drug dealer makes a modest income.

33. Roger Lane's and William Julius Wilson's work strikes this note. See Roger Lane, On the Social Meaning of Homicide Trends in America, in Ted Robert Gurr, ed., Violence in America, 55–79, at 71, 74 (Newbury Park, CA: Sage, 1989); Roger Lane, Murder in America: A History, at 266 (Columbus: Ohio State University Press, 1997); William Julius Wilson, The Truly Disadvantaged: The Inner City, the Underclass, and Public Policy (Chicago: University of Chicago Press, 1993); William Julius Wilson, When Work Disappears: The World of the New Urban Poor (New York: Vintage Books, 1997).

34. A total of 143,548 Americans died in the Spanish flu pandemic: 7.3 percent of the nation's population. See Alfred W. Crosby, America's Forgotten Pandemic: The Influenza of 1918, 2nd ed., at 209 (Cambridge, UK: Cambridge University Press, 2003); U.S. Census Bureau, Population of Continental United States and Specified Noncontiguous Territory: Estimates as of July 1, 1900, to July 1, 1921, Statistical Abstract of the United States, table 32 (1920). If current trends continue, more than one-fifth of black men will spend some time in prison (Western, Punishment and Inequality, 24–26).

35. In 1970, American prisons held 80,742 black inmates (1974 Sourcebook, 462 table 6.37). By 2000, that number was 587,300 (2003 Sourcebook, 505, table 6.34). The increase would be more extreme still if the same classifications were used in both figures. In 1970, the number of Latino prisoners was much smaller, partly because

many inmates who would today be classified as Latino were then classified as black.

36. On the rise in imprisonment in the 1920s and 1930s, see Cahalan, Historical Corrections Statistics, 30, table 3-3; Online Sourcebook, table 6.28.2008. On the state-by-state rise in imprisonment that began in the early 1970s, see 1991 Sourcebook, 637, table 6.72; Online Sourcebook, table 6.29.2008. According to Cahalan's data, North Carolina's imprisonment rate rose from 39 in 1923 to 120 in 1940; between 1973 and 2003, Mississippi's imprisonment rate rose from 76 to 768.

37. On the large gap between black and white crime rates, see, for example, Robert J. Sampson and Janet L. Lauritsen, Racial and Ethnic Disparities in Crime and Criminal Justice in the United States, Crime and Justice, vol. 21, 311–74 (1997); Robert J. Sampson and William Julius Wilson, Toward a Theory of Race, Crime, and Urban Inequality, in Shaun L. Gabbidon and Helen Taylor Greene, eds., Race, Crime, and Justice: A Reader, 177–89, at 177–78 (New York: Routledge, 2005). On the relationship between black crime and black imprisonment, see Western, Punishment and Inequality, 34–51. Western notes that, while high crime rates among young African American men seem to be correlated with high rates of imprisonment among members of the same group (see, for example, ibid., 37–38), the rise in imprisonment rates of the 1980s and 1990s does not track crime trends during that same period.

38. For the European figures, see Ministry of Justice, Research and Documentation Centre (WODC), European Sourcebook of Crime and Criminal Justice Statistics—2010, 4th ed., at 295–96, tables 4.2.1.1, 4.2.1.2 (The Hague: Boom Juridische uitgevers, 2010). Pretrial detainees are subtracted from those figures to make comparison with American imprisonment rates more apt. For the American figure, see Online Sourcebook, table 6.29.2008.

39. See European Sourcebook 2010, 49, table 1.2.1.16; 51, table 1.2.1.18; 53, table 1.2.1.20; Crime in the United States: 2009, table 1; Crime in the United States: 2007, table 1. Save for auto theft, the statements in the text are accurate whether one uses 2007 data for U.S. crime rates or the more current data from 2009. In 2007, France's rate of auto theft was the same as the U.S. rate, while Britain's rate of auto theft was modestly lower.

40. So long as punishment is appropriate, and so long as it is not vengeful. Compare Martha Minow, Between Vengeance and Forgiveness: Facing History after Genocide and Mass Violence (Boston: Beacon Press, 1998). On the appropriateness of criminalizing different kinds of conduct, see, for example, Jeffrie G. Murphy, Retribution Reconsidered: More Essays on the Philosophy of Law, at 1–13 (Dordrecht, the Netherlands: Kluwer Academic, 1992).

41. With respect to crime, the nation's murder rate fell from 10 per 100,000 in 1933 to 5 in 1944; the murder rate fell from 10 in 1991 to less than 6 in 2000. See Monkkonen's data; Lane, Murder in America, 308; Crime in the United States: 2000, 14. During the earlier of those two crime drops, the imprisonment rate peaked at 137 per 100,000 in 1939; during the later crime drop, the imprisonment rate hit 478 in 2000. See Online Sourcebook, table 6.28.2009.

42. Crime in the United States: 2008, table 2.

43. Bureau of Justice Statistics, U.S. Department of Justice, Criminal Victimization in the United States, 2007—Statistical Tables, table 1.

44. The total prison population stood at 1.5 million in 2008; drug prisoners occupied 20 percent of that population. See Online Sourcebook tables 6.13.2008, 6.0001.2006.

45. Ibid., tables 5.44.2004, 6.0009.2008.

46. Ibid., table 1.4.2006.

47. Daniel S. Nagin, Criminal Deterrence Research at the Outset of the Twenty-First Century, Crime and Justice, vol. 23, 1–37, at 4–5 (1999).

48. On the Reagan-era debate about Laffer and what was commonly called "supply-side economics," see Sean Wilentz, The Age of Reagan: A History, 1974–2008, at 121, 140–50 (New York: HarperCollins, 2008).

49. On the number of robberies, see Crime in the United States: 2008, table 7, which shows 441,855 reported robberies in 2008. On the number of robbery convictions, see Online Sourcebook, table 5.44.2004, which shows 38,850 such convictions in 2004.

50. For the best explanation of this point, at a time when the point was poorly understood, see Louis Michael Seidman, Soldiers, Martyrs, and Criminals: Utilitarian Theory and the Problem of Crime Control, Yale Law Journal, vol. 94, 315–49 (1984).

51. For extended discussions of the differences between urban and suburban drug markets, including the difference in the cost of policing, see William J. Stuntz, Race, Class, and Drugs, Columbia Law Review, vol. 98, 1795–842, at 1808–12, 1819–24 (1998).

52. For news stories noting this pattern in three metropolitan areas, see Kiljoong Kim, Where Do Chicago's Poor White People Live?, The Beachwood Reporter, September 11, 2006 (Chicago); Christopher Tidmore, Public Housing Redevelopment Sparks Multi-City Protest and Lawsuit, Louisiana Weekly, July 3, 2006 (New Orleans); Margery Austin Turner, Segregation by the Numbers, Washington Post, May 18, 1997, at C3 (Washington, DC). For a brief discussion of the more general pattern, see, for example, David R. Williams, Poverty, Racism, and Migration: The Health of the African American Population, in C. Michael Henry, ed., Race, Poverty, and Domestic Policy, 311–335, at 311, 320–23 (New Haven, CT: Yale University Press, 2004). For evidence of the high level of concentrated poverty in the African American population, see Alemayehu Bishaw, Areas with Concentrated Poverty: 1999, at 8, figure 4 (Washington, DC: U.S. Census Bureau, July 2005).

53. See Crime in the United States: 2008, table 25.

54. See Online Sourcebook, table 6.33.2008.

55. Between 1972 and 2001, spending on police rose 148 percent, spending on lawyers and courts rose 298 percent, and spending on prisons and jails rose a whopping 456 percent—all in inflation-adjusted dollars. See 1974 Sourcebook, 33, table 1.2; 2003 Sourcebook, 5, table 1.4. The inflation adjustment is taken from 2004–2005 Statistical Abstract, 461, no. 697. The number of local police officers per 100,000 population rose from 207 in 1971 to 210 in 1989. See Uniform Crime Reports: 1971, 159, table 52; Crime in the United States—1989, 236. The general population rose 19 percent during those years (1991 Statistical Abstract, 7, no. 2). The number of local prosecutors rose from 17,000 in 1974 to 20,000 in 1990; see Bureau of Justice Statistics, U.S. Department of Justice, Prosecutors in State Courts, 1990, at 1–2 (1992).

56. Chicago's number of police officers per 100,000 population fell from 423 in 1973 to 396 in 1989. During the same years, Los Angeles's policing rate fell from 260 to 229. Boston's policing rate was 430 in 1970, and dropped to 332 in 1988. New York's fell from 410 in 1974 to 354 in 1989. These data are taken from the relevant volumes of the Uniform Crime Reports. Los Angeles excepted, these cities saw substantial population declines during the relevant period. See Campbell Gibson and Kay Jung, U.S. Census Bureau, Historical Census Statistics on Population Totals by Race, 1790 to 1990, and by Hispanic Origin, 1970 to 1990, for Large Cities and Other Urban Places in the United States (Working Paper No. 76, February 2005).

57. With respect to per-case spending for indigent defense, see William J. Stuntz, The Uneasy Relationship between Criminal Procedure and Criminal Justice, Yale Law Journal, vol. 107, 1–76, at 9–10, notes 15–19 (1997), and sources cited therein. With respect to the number of felony prosecutions, compare State Court Caseload Statistics: Annual Report 1984, at 189–90, table 35 (Williamsburg, VA: National Center for State Courts, 1986), which shows a 36 percent increase in felony filings from 1978 to 1984, with State Court Caseload Statistics: Annual Report 1991, at 37, table 1.25 (Williamsburg, VA: National Center for State Courts, 1993), which shows a 51 percent increase in felony filings from 1985 to 1991. If filings were constant from 1984 to 1985, this would mean a 105 percent increase from 1978 to 1991. The increase was probably greater, as the number of filings was growing rapidly in the mid-1980s. See 1991 Caseload Statistics, 37, table 1.25, showing a 10 percent increase from 1985 to 1986. Keep in mind that these data begin in 1978; prison populations had been rising since 1973. It seems likely that the number of felony prosecutions rose by at least 20 to 25 percent in those five years; the prison population rose 38 percent in those same years (see 1991 Sourcebook, 637, table 6.72). If so, the number of felony prosecutions multiplied at least 2.5 times between 1973 and 1991. If the number of felony prosecutions rose by a third in those five years, as it may well have, that number tripled between 1973 and 1991.

58. See Milton Heumann, Plea Bargaining: The Experiences of Prosecutors, Judges, and Defense Attorneys (Chicago: University of Chicago Press, 1981). One of the themes of Heumann's excellent book is the tendency to reach plea bargains early in the process, before extensive trial preparation or pretrial litigation. If that tendency was strong in the 1970s, when Heumann gathered his data, it is all the stronger today, because docket pressure is much more extreme now than then.

59. For evidence of this sad proposition, see the data reported in Michael McConville and Chester L. Mirsky, Criminal Defense of the Poor in New York City, New York Review of Law and Social Change, vol. 15, 581–964, at 767 (1986–1987). And docket pressure has grown in the quarter century since McConville's and Mirsky's study.

60. For a detailed and opinionated review of the case, see Stuart Taylor and K. C. Johnson, Until Proven Innocent: Political Correctness and the Shameful Injustices of the Duke Lacrosse Rape Case (New York: Thomas Dunne Books, 2007).

61. See Peter Neufeld and Barry C. Scheck, Commentary, in Edward Connors et al., Convicted by Juries, Exonerated by Science: Case Studies in the Use of DNA Evidence to Establish Innocence after Trial (NCJ 161258, June 1996). Neufeld and Scheck describe the data as follows:

Every year since 1989, in about 25 percent of the sexual assault cases referred to the FBI where results could be obtained (primarily by State and local law enforcement), the primary suspect has been excluded by forensic DNA testing. Specifically, FBI officials report that out of roughly 10,000 sexual assault cases since 1989, about 2,000 tests have been inconclusive (usually insufficient high molecular weight DNA to do testing), about 2,000 tests have excluded the primary suspect, and about 6,000 have "matched" or included the primary suspect. The fact that these percentages have remained constant for 7 years, and that the National Institute of Justice's informal survey of private laboratories reveals a strikingly similar 26-percent exclusion rate, strongly suggests that postarrest and postconviction DNA exonerations are tied to some strong, underlying systemic problems that generate erroneous accusations and convictions.

3. IDEALS AND INSTITUTIONS

1. County sheriffs are usually elected by the counties they serve. Local police chiefs are usually appointed and supervised by the elected officials who run the cities *they* serve.

2. The large majority of judges in the United States, both trial and appellate, are elected, though a sizeable fraction are first appointed and then must defend their seats in retention elections in which voters choose either to retain or reject them. See Jed Handelsman Shugerman, The People's Courts, introduction and appendix A (Cambridge, MA: Harvard University Press, forthcoming 2011).

3. On the number of arrests, see Online Sourcebook, tables 4.1.2009, 4.33.2004, which shows just over 14 million arrests annually nationwide, of which some 140,000 are made by federal law enforcement officials. On the number of felony prosecutions, see ibid., table 5.44.2004, which shows 1.1 million felony convictions per year. Of felony cases that proceed to final adjudication, the conviction rate is 96 percent (ibid., table 5.57.2006).

4. On felonies, see ibid., tables 5.17.2004, 5.44.2004. With respect to misdemeanors, see ibid., tables 4.1.2004, 5.17.2004. The former table shows that there are several million misdemeanor charges filed each year; the latter shows that federal misdemeanor charges number some 10,000 per year.

5. Ibid., table 1.72.2004.

6. Ibid., table 1.27.2004.

7. On the number of local prosecutors, see ibid., table 1.85.2005; on the number of federal prosecutors, see ibid., table 1.79.2008.

8. For a good discussion of the U.S. Attorney firings in the Bush administration and the political firestorm they provoked, see Daniel Richman, Political Control of Federal Prosecutions: Looking Back and Looking Forward, Duke Law Journal, vol. 58, 2087–124, at 2099–107 (2009).

9. U.S. Constitution, Amendment IV.

10. The leading case is Fong Foo v. United States, 369 U.S. 141 (1962).

11. U.S. Constitution, Amendment V.

12. U.S. Constitution, Amendment VI.

13. U.S. Constitution, Amendment VIII.

14. U.S. Constitution, Amendment I. The amendment did not apply outside federal court until the late 1920s. See Whitney v. California, 274 U.S. 357 (1927); ibid., at 372–80 (Brandeis, J., concurring in the judgment).

15. Remedial limits were crucial. Before the 1950s, nearly all state court systems offered only money damages as a remedy for illegal searches. Because such searches rarely cause the kind of harm that is readily monetized, a damages remedy proved to be no remedy at all.

16. See Chapter 8 of this book.

17. For an extended discussion of this problem, see William J. Stuntz, The Pathological Politics of Criminal Law, Michigan Law Review, vol. 100, 505–600 (2001).

18. On the Lilburne story, see Leonard W. Levy, Origins of the Fifth Amendment, 2nd ed., at 271–313 (New York: Macmillan, 1986). On the privilege's pre-Lilburne roots, see 43–204 (discussing late sixteenth- and early seventeenth-century heresy investigations in which accused heretics were asked how and with whom they worshipped).

19. On Entick, see Entick v. Carrington, 19 Howell's State Trials 1029 (C.P. 1765). On Wilkes, see Wilkes v. Wood, 19 Howell's State Trials 1153 (C.P. 1763); Akhil Reed Amar, The Bill of Rights: Creation and Reconstruction, at 65–77 (New Haven, CT: Yale University Press, 1998).

20. On Zenger's case, see Albert W. Alschuler and Andrew G. Deiss, A Brief History of the Criminal Jury Trial in the United States, University of Chicago Law Review, vol. 61, 867–928, at 871–74 (1994); Matthew P. Harrington, The Law-Finding Function of the American Jury, Wisconsin Law Review, vol. 1999, 377–440, at 393–94 (1999). A closely related proposition—no juror may be compelled to vote to convict, nor punished for failing to do so—derives from Bushell's Case, 6 Howell's State Trials 999 (1670). Bushell was a juror who had refused to vote to convict in a case brought against two Quakers for unlawful religious assembly. The judge ordered Bushell locked up for disobeying the court's instruction. Bushell brought suit and won, thereby establishing that jurors' power was supreme within its sphere. Zenger's case showed how large that sphere was.

21. Not counting rebellions in the colonies. Near the end of the sixteenth century, the Earl of Essex raised an army to challenge the rule of Queen Elizabeth's counselors, and perhaps of the Queen herself. J. P. G. Hammer, The Polarisation of Elizabethan Politics: The Political Career of Robert Devereux, 2nd Earl of Essex 1585–1597 (Cambridge, UK: Cambridge University Press, 1999). The English Civil Wars of the mid-seventeenth century include three distinct military conflicts. See Michael Braddick, God's Fury, England's Fire: A New History of the English Civil Wars (London: Allen Lane, 2008). The Glorious Revolution of 1688–1689 was the political aftermath of a military victory by an invading army led by William of Orange. See Edward Vallance, The Glorious Revolution: 1688—Britain's Fight for Liberty (London: Pegasus Books, 2007). The unsuccessful Jacobite rebellions of 1715 and 1745 are the final two examples. See Michael Barthorp, The Jacobite Rebellions:

1689–1745 (London: Osprey Publishing, 1982). Both Oliver Cromwell's and King William's armies succeeded in overturning what had been lawful governments.

22. On the Boston Massacre generally, see Hiller B. Zobel, The Boston Massacre (New York: W.W. Norton, 1970); on the source of the initial violence, see ibid., 186–87. On the crisis in English criminal justice, see James Q. Whitman, The Origins of Reasonable Doubt: Theological Roots of the Criminal Trial, at 186–200 (New Haven, CT: Yale University Press, 2008). According to Whitman, the crisis's source was Christian jurors' unwillingness to convict if there was any doubt about the justice of punishing the defendant. The beyond-a-reasonable-doubt standard of proof, he argues convincingly, was established to make convictions easier to obtain, not more difficult.

23. A point John Langbein makes clear in his description of eighteenth-century criminal justice as an "accused speaks" system. See John H. Langbein, The Origins of Adversary Criminal Trial, at 48–61 (New York: Oxford University Press, 2003).

24. See Nicholas Parrillo's chapter on prosecution in Against the Profit Motive: The Transformation of American Government, 1780–1840, at 66–67 (forthcoming, Yale University Press; partial manuscript on file with author); Allen Steinberg, From Private Prosecution to Plea Bargaining: Criminal Prosecution, the District Attorney, and American Legal History, Crime and Delinquency, vol. 30, 568–92 (1984). But compare Joan A. Jacoby, The American Prosecutor: A Search for Identity, at 11–19 (Lexington, MA: D.C. Heath, 1980).

25. See, for example, George Fisher, Plea Bargaining's Triumph: A History of Plea Bargaining in America, at 35, table 1.2 (Stanford, CA: Stanford University Press, 2003).

26. On state debt and default, see Jed Handelsman Shugerman, Economic Crisis and the Rise of Judicial Elections and Judicial Review, Harvard Law Review, vol. 123, 1061–150, at 1076–80 (2010). On the rise of judicial elections that followed, see ibid., 1080–97. On the simultaneous rise of elected district attorneys, see Jacoby, American Prosecutor, 22–28.

27. See Simon Schama, Citizens: A Chronicle of the French Revolution, at 442–43 (New York: Alfred A. Knopf, 1989).

28. U.S. Constitution, Amendments IV, V, VI, and VIII.

29. In the order they appear in the text, the procedural guarantees are: (1) the right to be free of "unreasonable searches and seizures," (2) the requirement that search warrants be based on probable cause, (3) the requirement that warrants be supported by witnesses' oaths or affirmations, (4) the requirement that warrants specifically describe the targets of the relevant searches, (5) the right to indictment by grand jury, (6) the ban on double jeopardy, (7) the privilege against self-incrimination, (8) the guarantee of "due process of law," (9) the right to a speedy trial, (10) the right to a public trial, (11) the right to be tried by an impartial jury, (12) the requirement that the jury be selected from within "the State and district [wherein] the crime shall have been committed," (13) the right to be informed of the relevant charges, (14) the right to confront the state's witnesses, (15) the right to use "compulsory process," if need be, to call defense witnesses, and (16) the right to have the assistance of counsel.

30. Frank Maloy Anderson, The Constitutions and Other Select Documents Illustrative of the History of France, 1789–1907, at 15, 59–60 (New York: Russell & Russell, 1967).

31. In American law, the presumption of innocence is enforced through the requirement that the government prove guilt beyond a reasonable doubt in order to convict. See In re Winship, 397 U.S. 358 (1970). *Winship* is based on the Fourteenth Amendment's due process clause, and the beyond-a-reasonable-doubt standard arose from the common law, not from any constitutional provision. See Whitman, Origins of Reasonable Doubt. As for the ban on police torture, one might suppose that arises from the privilege against self-incrimination. But before Miranda v. Arizona, 384 U.S. 436 (1966), the privilege did not apply to police interrogation. Instead, the law barred admission of involuntary confessions, which effectively limited the gains from torture without prohibiting the practice—and that legal doctrine developed long after the Bill of Rights was written and ratified. See Henry E. Smith, The Modern Privilege: Its Nineteenth-Century Origins, in R. H. Helmholz et al., The Privilege against Self-Incrimination: Its Origins and Development, 145–180, at 146–47, 153–56 (Chicago: University of Chicago Press, 1997).

32. John Stuart Mill, On Liberty (annotations by Steven M. Cahn) (Lanham, MD: Rowman & Littlefield, 2005). Mill's book was first published in 1859.

33. See Declaration of the Rights of Man and of the Citizen of 1793, Constitution of the Year I, in Anderson, Constitutions and Other Select Documents, at 171–74.

34. The literature on this subject is large. For a recent example focusing on Central and South America, see Maximo Langer, Revolution in Latin American Criminal Procedure: Diffusion of Legal Ideas from the Periphery, American Journal of Comparative Law, vol. 55, 617–76 (2007).

35. The statement in the text is correct, but there remain large differences in the scope of substantive criminal law, which is broader and deeper in the United States than, say, in continental Europe. See James Q. Whitman, Equality in Criminal Law: The Two Divergent Western Roads, Journal of Legal Analysis, vol. 1, 119–65, at 129 (2009).

36. Online Sourcebook, table 6.0001.2006.

37. William Blackstone, Commentaries on the Laws of England, 4th ed., vol. 4, at 157–58 (cheating, a form of fraud), 190–201 (murder and manslaughter), 205–08 (mayhem, a rough equivalent of felony assault), 210–15 (rape), 216–18 (assault and battery), 219 (kidnapping), 220–23 (arson), 223–28 (burglary), 229–34 (larceny), 241–43 (robbery) (Oxford: Clarendon Press, 1769).

38. For the standard definition, see Wayne R. LaFave, Substantive Criminal Law, 2nd ed., vol. 3, §20.3 (St. Paul, MN: West Publishing, 2003).

39. For example, one might deem the threat-of-force element satisfied if the jury finds that the defendant *would have* used force had anyone tried to stop him. Under this standard, which applies in some jurisdictions, the thief is guilty of robbery rather than the lesser crime of larceny as long as he didn't plan on giving the stolen property back when asked. See, for example, State v. Keeton, 710 N.W.2d 531 (Iowa 2006).

40. By the author's count, as of the beginning of this century, the criminal code of Massachusetts included 169 distinct property crimes.

41. This rule dates to Blockburger v. United States, 284 U.S. 299 (1932).

42. See, for example, United States v. Pollard, 959 F.2d 1011 (D.C. Cir. 1992).

43. This is one reason why the number of life-without-parole sentences has risen dramatically since the early 1990s. See Note [unsigned], A Matter of Life and Death: The Effect of Life-Without-Parole Statutes on Capital Punishment, Harvard Law Review, vol. 119, 1838–54, at 1851–52 (2006).

44. This proposition appears to be true but is surprisingly hard to nail down. See Parrillo, Against the Profit Motive, 66–67; Steinberg, Private Prosecution. But compare Jacoby, American Prosecutor, 11–19.

45. See Harrington, Law-Finding Function; William E. Nelson, Americanization of the Common Law: The Impact of Legal Changes on Massachusetts Society, 1760–1830, at 18–35 (Cambridge, MA: Harvard University Press, 1975).

46. I borrow this apt phrase from George Fisher. See George Fisher, The Jury's Rise as Lie Detector, Yale Law Journal, vol. 107, 575–638.

47. See the discussion in Michael G. Kammen, A Machine That Would Go of Itself: The Constitution in American Culture, at 125 (New York: Alfred A. Knopf, 1986).

48. The overwhelming majority of local prosecutors' offices are headed by elected officials. Steven W. Perry, Prosecutors in State Courts: 2005, at 2 (Washington, DC: Bureau of Justice Statistics, July 2006). Outside New England, Virginia, South Carolina, and Hawaii, trial judges either are elected or are appointed but subject to retention elections. See Shugerman, People's Courts, introduction and appendix A.

49. On the means of appointment, see Jacoby, American Prosecutor, 19. On the clerical nature of the office, see Steinberg, Private Prosecution.

50. Contemporary judges define the law in their courtrooms; juries were responsible for that task—at least with respect to substantive law—in the late eighteenth century. See Nelson, Americanization of the Common Law, 18–35.

51. Jacoby, American Prosecutor, 11–19; Parrillo, Against the Profit Motive, 69–83.

52. Berger v. United States, 295 U.S. 78, 88 (1935) (Sutherland, J.).

53. Javert was a character in Victor Hugo's Les Misérables: the police officer who pursued Jean Valjean after the latter escaped from custody.

54. Parrillo, Against the Profit Motive, 84–102. As Parrillo notes, prosecutors were sometimes paid more for prosecuting crimes that were difficult to enforce because public sentiment often favored defendants. Post–Civil War Tennessee paid five times as much for the successful prosecution of a Klan case as for a successful capital murder prosecution (ibid., 99).

55. Parrillo's central claim concerns the abandonment of piecework pay and its replacement by government salaries. The older practice was abandoned slowly; the process lasted for much of the nineteenth century (ibid., 140–41).

56. See Jacoby, American Prosecutor, 22–28.

57. See Shugerman, People's Courts, introduction and appendix A.

58. On the rise of elected judges, see Shugerman, Economic Crisis, 1080–97. On the rise of elected district attorneys, see Jacoby, American Prosecutor, 22–28.

59. See Walter Stahr, John Jay: Founding Father, at 362–65 (New York: Hambledon & London, 2005). Jay told Adams the rigors of the job were too great for him, given his poor health. Jay was 55 years old when he turned down his reappointment; he lived another 28 years (ibid., 366, 383–84).

60. See Shugerman, Economic Crisis, 1147, appendix B.

61. Lance E. Davis and John Legler, The Government in the American Economy, 1815–1902: A Quantitative Study, Journal of Economic History, vol. 26, at 532–35, table 3 (1966).

62. Davis and Legler, Government in the American Economy, 529, 532–37, tables 1, 3, 8.

63. See James F. Richardson, The New York Police, Colonial Times to 1901, at 32, 49 (New York: Oxford University Press, 1970).

64. For the establishment of the Baltimore police force, see De Francias Folsom, ed., Our Police: A History of the Baltimore Force from the First Watchman to the Latest Appointee, at 23 (Baltimore: J. D. Ehlers, 1988); for Philadelphia, see Howard O. Sprogle, The Philadelphia Police, Past and Present at 86 (Philadelphia, 1887); for Boston, see A Brief History of the B.P.D., https://www.cityofboston.gov/police/about/history.asp (listing 1854 as the year the Boston police force was established); compare Roger Lane, Policing the City: Boston, 1822–1885, at 100 (Cambridge, MA: Harvard University Press, 1967) (listing formal date of establishment of the force by ordinance as 1855).

65. See Robert M. Fogelson, Big-City Police, at 14–15 (Cambridge, MA: Harvard University Press, 1977).

66. See Parrillo, Against the Profit Motive, 36–37.

67. Shugerman, People's Courts, at ch. 4, "Panic and Trigger."

68. On the material in this paragraph, see David Donald, Lincoln, at 58–62, 75–78, 95, 113–15, 132–33 (New York: Simon & Schuster, 1996). Lincoln's congressional district was the only one the Whigs held throughout the 1840s, until 1848—the election immediately following Lincoln's term in office.

69. This is a key theme of Daniel Walker Howe, What Hath God Wrought: The Transformation of America, 1815–1848 (New York: Oxford University Press, 2007).

70. See, for example, Fogelson, Big-City Police, 123–24. In St. Paul, Minnesota, Irish and Scandinavian officers decided which Irish and Scandinavian suspects to arrest. See Joel Best, Keeping the Peace in St. Paul: Crime, Vice, and Police Work, 1869–1874, in Eric H. Monkkonen, ed., Crime and Justice in American History, vol. 5, part 1, 60–79, at 62, 69–70 (New York: K.G. Saur, 1992).

71. With respect to contemporary search and seizure law, see Payton v. New York, 445 U.S. 573 (1979); Steagald v. United States, 451 U.S. 204 (1981). With respect to antebellum Virginia law, see Wells v. Jackson, 17 Va. 458 (1811).

72. Heath v. Alabama, 474 U.S. 82 (1985), defines current law on the subject. Alabama's rule is stated in State v. Adams, 14 Ala. 486 (1848). See Jason Mazzone, The Bill of Rights in the Early State Courts, Minnesota Law Review, vol. 92, 1–82 (2007), for these and other examples.

73. William W. Freehling, The Road to Disunion: Secessionists at Bay, 1776–1854, at 108 (New York: Oxford University Press, 1990).

74. On what is today called "transferred intent" and the traditional definition of murder, see, for example, Bratton v. State, 29 Tenn. 103, 105 (1849). On the result in the case described in the text, see Bob v. State, 29 Ala. 20 (1856).

75. Spence v. State, 17 Ala. 192 (1850).

76. See, for example, Smith, Modern Privilege, 146–53.

77. Freehling offers a portion of the quoted passage from Elijah v. State, 20 Tenn. 102 (1839), in Secessionists at Bay, 108. He takes Reese's language at face value, mistakenly in my view.
78. On Davis's plantation rules, see Freehling, Secessionists at Bay, 498–99.
79. Ibid., 502: "Davis considered juries a necessary check on nonowning overseers." In part, the check was paternalist: Freehling emphasizes Davis's desire to protect his slaves from "impersonal overseers who lashed family servants" (ibid.).
80. See William W. Freehling, The Road to Disunion: Secessionists Triumphant, 1854–1861, at 331–33 (New York: Oxford University Press, 2007).
81. On the staffing of slave patrols, see Sally E. Hadden, Slave Patrols: Law and Violence in Virginia and the Carolinas, at 63–65, 72–77 (Cambridge, MA: Harvard University Press, 2001). As Hadden notes, patrollers included well-off slaveowners, but membership in slave patrols extended well beyond them, and there were a number of ways the wealthy might avoid service. On the uncertain number of lynchings, see Philip Dray, At the Hands of Persons Unknown: The Lynching of Black America, at 22–30 (New York: Modern Library, 2002); Freehling, Secessionists at Bay, 98–113.
82. With respect to Fee, see Freehling, Secessionists Triumphant, 222–35. On McKinney, Blunt, and the Mississippi carpenters, see ibid., 332, 459. On the number of lynchings of southern whites, see Freehling, Secessionists at Bay, 103–06.
83. Randolph Roth, American Homicide, at 220–24 (Cambridge, MA: Harvard University Press, 2009).
84. See Crime in the United States: 2008, table 8.
85. See, for example, Edward L. Ayers, Vengeance and Justice: Crime and Punishment in the 19th-Century American South, at 9–33 (New York: Oxford University Press, 1984).
86. Fitzhugh's two books were titled Sociology of the South (1854) and Cannibals All! Or Slaves without Masters (1857).
87. Helper published The Impending Crisis of the South in 1857, and republished the book in shorter form in 1859. John Sherman, then a Congressman from Ohio, lost the 1859 House Speakership because he had signed an endorsement of the book, and thereby forfeited the support of the Upper South Whigs whose votes were the key to victory. Freehling, Secessionists Triumphant, 265–66.
88. For these data, see ibid., 16 (Western Virginia), 195 (Baltimore), 499 (Delaware, Maryland, and Missouri).
89. On Clay and the Missouri Compromise, see Glyndon G. Van Deusen, The Life of Henry Clay, at 134–48 (Boston: Little, Brown, 1937). On Johnson, Tyler, and Mason, see Freehling, Secessionists at Bay, 346–49, 440–52, 500–04. On Atchison and Taney, see Freehling, Secessionists Triumphant, 61–73, 109–22.

4. THE FOURTEENTH AMENDMENT'S FAILED PROMISE

1. U.S. Constitution, Article I, Section 8.
2. See Online Sourcebook, tables 5.44.2004 (showing 1.1 million state-court felony convictions), 5.17.2004 (showing just under 75,000 felony convictions in federal court).

3. See Eric Foner, Reconstruction: America's Unfinished Revolution, 1863–1877, at 457–59 (New York: Harper & Row, 1989), and sources cited therein. See also Lou Falkner Williams, The Great South Carolina Ku Klux Klan Trials, 1871–1872, at 45–50, 113, 122 (Athens: University of Georgia Press, 1996).

4. On the drop in alcohol consumption, see David E. Kyvig, Repealing National Prohibition, 2nd ed., at 23–25 (Kent, OH: Kent State University Press, 2000); Clark Warburton, The Economic Results of Prohibition, at 107, table 47 (New York: Columbia University Press, 1932). On the drop in alcohol-related misconduct, see Martha Bensley Bruère, Does Prohibition Work? at 297–304 (New York: Harper, 1927).

5. 92 U.S. 542 (1876).

6. So named because, when campaigning for a Senate seat in 1894, he promised to go to Washington with a pitchfork and prod President Grover Cleveland's "old fat ribs." See Frances Butler Simkins, Pitchfork Ben Tillman, South Carolinian, at 315–16 (1944; repr., Gloucester, MA: Peter Smith, 1964).

7. Ibid., 393–96, 404–07.

8. Foner, Reconstruction, 261–62.

9. Ibid., 262–63; James G. Hollandsworth Jr., An Absolute Massacre: The New Orleans Race Riot of July 30, 1866, at 140–41 (Baton Rouge: Louisiana State University Press, 2001); Joe Gray Taylor, Louisiana Reconstructed, 1863–1877, at 110 (Baton Rouge: Louisiana State University Press, 1974).

10. U.S. Constitution, Amendment XIV.

11. On the link between the Act and the Fourteenth Amendment, see, for example, Foner, Reconstruction, 257 ("Clearly, Republicans proposed to abrogate the Black Codes and eliminate any doubts as to the constitutionality of the Civil Rights Act"); Williams, Ku Klux Klan Trials, 41. On the character of the Black Codes, see Foner, Reconstruction, 199–201. For the timing of Johnson's veto and the congressional override, see Eric L. McKitrick, Andrew Johnson and Reconstruction, at 314–25, 427n18 (Chicago: University of Chicago Press, 1960). For the Act's content, see, for example, Foner, Reconstruction, 243–45.

12. The *Dred Scott* decision appears at 60 U.S. 393 (1857). On the Fourteenth Amendment's redefinition of citizenship, see, for example, Akhil Reed Amar, The Bill of Rights: Creation and Reconstruction, at 170–71 (New Haven, CT: Yale University Press, 1998); Richard A. Primus, The Riddle of Hiram Revels, Harvard Law Review, vol. 119, 1680–734, at 1685–98 (2006).

13. The Amendment refers to "States" rather than to counties or cities, but the conventional legal understanding of local governments, in the nineteenth century as today, sees those governments as creatures of the states in which they reside. Thus, federal constitutional rules that operate against state officials operate against local officials as well.

14. That is the canonical reading of *Barron*. For an argument that *Barron* applied only to enforcement by federal courts—meaning, the federal Bill of Rights was still enforceable by *state* courts against state and local governments, see Jason Mazzone, The Bill of Rights in the Early State Courts, Minnesota Law Review, vol. 92, at 1–81 (2007). Mazzone may well be right. Nevertheless, because nothing in the text turns on the question, I follow the traditional understanding.

15. See, for example, Akhil Reed Amar, The Bill of Rights: Creation and Reconstruction, at 164–69 (New Haven, CT: Yale University Press, 1998).

16. Among other things, the Act decreed that the commissioner charged with resolving disputed cases would be paid more if he resolved mistaken identity claims in slaveholders' favor than if he ruled for the alleged slaves in such cases. See, for example, ibid., 270–71n*.

17. The leading work on slave patrols, Sally E. Hadden, Slave Patrols: Law and Violence in Virginia and the Carolinas (Cambridge, MA: Harvard University Press, 2001), treats them as the functional equivalent of law enforcement agencies.

18. The Freedmen's Bureau was established by Congress in the last days of the Civil War as a means of aiding in the transition of ex-slaves from bondage to freedom. On the Bureau's creation and operation, see, for example, Foner, Reconstruction, 68–70, 148–70.

19. William Blackstone, Commentaries on the Law of England, 4th ed., vol. 1, at *124 (Oxford: Clarendon Press, 1769).

20. Earl M. Maltz, The Concept of Equal Protection of the Laws—A Historical Inquiry, San Diego Law Review, vol. 22, 499–540, at 507 (1985); Earl M. Maltz, Fourteenth Amendment Concepts in the Antebellum Era, American Journal of Legal History, vol. 32, 305–46 (1988).

21. On the rise of Republican governments in the post-Confederate South (and the role black officeholders played in those governments), see Foner, Reconstruction, 346–64.

22. For the number—1,081—and timing of the killings, see Charles Lane, The Day Freedom Died: The Colfax Massacre, the Supreme Court, and the Betrayal of Reconstruction, at 18–19 (New York: Henry Holt, 2008). My calculation of Louisiana's murder rate uses the 1870 census figures for that state's population. See 1878 Statistical Abstract, 143, no. 140. According to Monkkonen's figures, the nation's peak twentieth-century murder rate was 11 in 1980. The U.S. murder rate in 2008 stood at 5.4 per 100,000. Crime in the United States: 2008, table 1.

23. Lane, Day Freedom Died, 42–43.

24. Ibid., 63–66, 69–89.

25. Ibid., 90–109.

26. For a picture of the marker, see ibid., after page 170.

27. In Colfax, the killers belonged to the Knights of the White Camelia or the White League rather than the Klan (ibid., 217). The effect was the same.

28. U.S. Constitution, Amendment XV. On the politics of the Amendment's passage, see William Gillette, The Right to Vote, at 46–78 (Baltimore: Johns Hopkins University Press, 1965).

29. Enforcement Act of 1870, §§4–6, 16 Stat. 140 (1870).

30. Ku Klux Klan Act of 1871, §4, 17 Stat. 13 (1871).

31. See Williams, Ku Klux Klan Trials, 61–62.

32. See, generally, ibid., 60–88. There were variants on the voting theory used in different cases. For a discussion of one such variant, which rested not on the Fifteenth Amendment but on the authority of Congress to regulate federal elections, see Lane, Day Freedom Died, 115–17.

33. U.S. Constitution, Amendments XIV, XV.

34. 29 Fed. Cas. 79, 81 (Circuit Court, S.D. Ala. 1871).

35. Lane, Day Freedom Died, 139.

36. See Foner, Reconstruction, 458–59; Lane, Day Freedom Died, 122; Williams, Ku Klux Klan Trials, 45–50, 113, 122.

37. The Statistical History of the United States: From Colonial Times to the Present, prepared by the United States Bureau of the Census, at 1083 (New York: Basic Books, 1976).

38. See Foner, Reconstruction, 343.

39. Ibid., 340; Iver Bernstein, The New York City Draft Riots: Their Significance for American Society and Politics in the Age of the Civil War, at 1–25 (New York: Oxford University Press, 1990); James McCague, The Second Rebellion: The Story of the New York City Draft Riots of 1863, at 116 (New York: Dial Press, 1968).

40. Presidential Elections, 1789–2008, at 136–37 (Washington, DC: CQ Press, 2010).

41. See, for example, David Herbert Donald, Lincoln, at 380–84, 454–59, 529–32 (New York: Simon & Schuster, 1996).

42. See, for example, Samuel Rezneck, Distress, Relief, and Discontent in the United States during the Depression of 1873–78, Journal of Political Economy, vol. 58, 494–512, at 494–96 (1950).

43. Statistical History of the United States, 1083.

44. On Tilden, see, for example, Sean Dennis Cashman, America in the Gilded Age: From the Death of Lincoln to the Rise of Theodore Roosevelt, at 231 (New York: New York University Press, 1984); Foner, Reconstruction, 568. On Hayes, see, for example, Ari Hoogenboom, Rutherford B. Hayes: Warrior and President, at 356–57 (Lawrence: University Press of Kansas, 1995); Gretchen Ritter, Goldbugs and Greenbacks: The Antimonopoly Tradition and the Politics of Finance in America, 1865–1896, at 37–38, 77 (Cambridge, UK: Cambridge University Press, 1997).

45. See, for example, Foner, Reconstruction, 554–55, which details the reaction to the use of troops to sustain the Republican government of Louisiana in early 1875.

46. Ibid., 568.

47. For a detailed description of the indictments, see Lane, Day Freedom Died, 124–26. On the arrests, see 144–53, 159. For the results of the two trials, see 186 and 203, respectively.

48. Ibid., 210–11.

49. Ibid., 204–10. At the relevant time, appeals to the Supreme Court were allowed in cases in which two Circuit Judges—here, Bradley and Woods—disagreed, leaving the relevant case undecided absent appellate review. Today, the Courts of Appeals of the nation's thirteen circuits sit in panels of three, so equal division is impossible. And Supreme Court Justices no longer ride circuit.

50. United States v. Cruikshank, 92 U.S. 542, 554–55 (1876).

51. United States v. Reese, 92 U.S. 214 (1876).

52. See Lane, Day Freedom Died, 222–23.

53. Reese, 92 U.S. at 217–22.

54. See Lane, Day Freedom Died, 233–34.

55. Quoted in Lane, Day Freedom Died, 236, 237.

56. Ibid., 117–18.

57. Ibid., 119; Foner, Reconstruction, 530.

58. The Slaughter-House Cases, 83 U.S. 36 (1873).

59. The reference is to the Civil Rights Act of 1875, passed by the lame-duck 43rd Congress that had just been shattered in the 1874 elections. Charles Sumner—long a hero to those who sought to protect blacks' rights—had first introduced the legislation that became the Act several years earlier. Sumner died in the spring of 1874; the 1875 Act was, in part, a memorial to him. For the best account of the Act and its background, see Michael W. McConnell, Originalism and the Desegregation Decisions, Virginia Law Review, vol. 81, 947–1140 (1995).

60. 18 Stat. 335 (1875).

61. The Civil Rights Cases, 109 U.S. 3 (1883). Presumably Harlan would have dissented in *Cruikshank* as well had he been on the Court. He was appointed by President Hayes in 1877, a year after *Cruikshank* was decided.

62. Buck v. Bell, 274 U.S. 200, 205 (1927). Holmes wrote those words in a case that permitted the state-mandated sterilization of mentally retarded adults. The most famous line from Holmes's opinion is not the expression of contempt for equal protection claims, but an expression of contempt for the plaintiffs: "Three generations of imbeciles are enough."

63. For a rare exception, see Yick Wo v. Hopkins, 118 U.S. 356 (1886).

64. On the role self-defense doctrine played in Jim Crow criminal justice, see Michael J. Klarman, From Jim Crow to Civil Rights: The Supreme Court and the Struggle for Racial Equality, at 275–86 (New York: Oxford University Press, 2004).

65. 163 U.S. 537 (1896). The statutory language—"equal but separate"—is quoted at page 547.

66. For a good discussion of the NAACP's campaign against segregated graduate education, and of the Supreme Court's response to it, see Klarman, From Jim Crow to Civil Rights, 204–12.

67. McLaurin v. Oklahoma State Regents for Higher Education, 339 U.S. 637 (1950); Sweatt v. Painter, 339 U.S. 629 (1950).

68. Brown v. Board of Education of Topeka, 347 U.S. 483, 495 (1954).

69. For the most part, *Cruikshank* remains good law today. For a recent argument that the portion of the decision rejecting the victims' right to bear arms should be overturned, see McDonald v. Chicago, 130 S. Ct. 3020, 3060, 3084–88 (2010) (Thomas, J., concurring in part and concurring in the judgment). With rare exceptions, the Fourteenth Amendment did not and does not reach the conduct of private citizens: the core holding of *Cruikshank*. As for *Reese,* members of the Court continue to cite and quote that case favorably. See, for example, Skilling v. United States, 130 S. Ct. 2896, 2930, 2940–41 (2010) (Scalia, J., concurring in part and concurring in the judgment).

70. See Katzenbach v. McClung, 379 U.S. 294 (1964); Heart of Atlanta Motel 379 U.S. 241 (1964).

71. McCleskey v. Kemp, 481 U.S. 279 (1987); United States v. Armstrong, 517 U.S. 456 (1996); Castle Rock v. Gonzales, 545 U.S. 748 (2005).

72. *McCleskey,* 481 U.S. at 291–99.

73. *Armstrong,* 517 U.S. at 458–61, 463–71.

74. *Castle Rock,* 545 U.S. at 750–54, 758–68. See also DeShaney v. Winnebago County Dep't of Social Services, 489 U.S. 189 (1989).

75. That proposition is so legally uncontroversial that no one in *Castle Rock*—neither the plaintiff nor any of the judges who heard the case—claimed that the police violated the equal protection clause. Instead, Jessica Gonzales argued that her due process rights were violated; the equal protection claim was thought to be outside the bounds of plausible argument.

76. For a good, succinct account, see Amar, Bill of Rights, 181–87.

77. People v. Hurtado, 63 Cal. 288, 290–91 (1883); Hurtado v. California, 110 U.S. 516, 519–20 (1884).

78. U.S. Constitution, Amendment V. Indictments and informations are the charging documents with which criminal cases begin—the rough equivalent of a complaint in a civil case. The difference between them is that grand juries vote indictments; informations are issued solely on the authority of the local prosecutor. The issue in *Hurtado* was whether prosecutors could charge by information—or whether they must instead seek indictments—in capital cases.

79. U.S. Constitution, Amendments V, XIV.

80. *Hurtado,* 110 U.S. at 534–35.

81. Ibid., 535–36.

82. *Caldwell,* 137 U.S. 692 (1891); *Leeper,* 139 U.S. 462 (1891).

83. Ibid., 468.

84. *O'Neil,* 144 U.S. 323, 325–31 (1892).

85. Ibid., 336.

86. Ibid., 337–41 (Field, J., dissenting), 370–71 (Harlan, J., dissenting).

87. 153 U.S. 684 (1894).

88. See American Experience, People and Events: John Y. McKane, available at www .pbs.org/wgbh/amex/coney/peopleevents/pande03.html; Coney Island's Brutal Boss: American Citizens Beaten by M'Kane's Ruffians, New York Times, November 8, 1893; Professor Solomon, Coney Island, at 21–34 (Baltimore: Top Hat Press, 1999).

89. *McKane,* 153 U.S. at 687–89.

90. 211 U.S. 78 (1908).

91. For the facts of the case, see ibid., 78–89; State v. Twining, 64 A. 1073, 1076 (N.J. 1906); ibid., 1076 (Swayze, J., dissenting).

92. 211 U.S. at 102.

93. Borden was alleged to have killed her father and stepmother with an ax. The case was the O. J. Simpson prosecution of its day—and like O.J., Lizzie Borden won an acquittal. No one else was ever charged with the crime. See, generally, David Kent, Forty Whacks: New Evidence in the Life and Legend of Lizzie Borden (Emmaus, PA: Yankee Books, 1992).

94. Griffin v. California, 380 U.S. 609 (1965). The Justices had deemed the privilege incorporated in the Fourteenth Amendment's due process clause the year before, in Malloy v. Hogan, 378 U.S. 1 (1964).

5. CRIMINAL JUSTICE IN THE GILDED AGE

1. For the classic view, see Jack Beatty, Age of Betrayal: The Triumph of Money in America, 1865–1900 (New York: Vintage Books, 2008). For more nuanced views of the era, see Sean Dennis Cashman, America in the Gilded Age (New York and London: New York University Press, 1984); Rebecca Edwards, New Spirits: Americans in the Gilded Age, 1865–1905 (New York: Oxford University Press, 2006).

2. The sentence in the text probably still captures the conventional wisdom, but it describes the reality a bit too starkly. For a more balanced discussion of Gilded Age constitutional law, see Howard Gillman, The Constitution Besieged: The Rise and Demise of *Lochner* Era Police Powers Jurisprudence (Durham, NC: Duke University Press, 1993).

3. The classic treatment is the one from which the phrase in the text is borrowed. See C. Vann Woodward, The Strange Career of Jim Crow (New York: Oxford University Press, 1955).

4. See Gillman, Constitution Besieged.

5. Ibid.

6. The relevant phenomenon extended beyond the United States. See James W. Garner, Criminal Procedure in France, Yale Law Journal, vol. 4, 255–84 (1916), noting both low conviction rates and low crime rates in early twentieth-century Paris—lower than in France as a whole.

7. This piece of legal jargon is misleading: it isn't the classes that are suspect, but the way those classes are treated. The law uses this label to identify groups who are often the targets of discrimination and so should receive more legal protection than other groups.

8. On the rise of battered woman's syndrome evidence, see Elizabeth M. Schneider, Battered Women and Feminist Lawmaking, at 123–37 (New Haven and London: Yale University Press, 2000).

9. Although the right of husbands to beat their wives (the right of "marital chastisement") was formally repudiated by the American legal system by the end of the Civil War, this development was misleading, because during the postwar era, "jurists and lawmakers vehemently condemned chastisement doctrine, yet routinely condoned violence in marriage." Reva B. Siegel, "The Rule of Love": Wife Beating as Prerogative and Privacy, Yale Law Journal, vol. 105, 2117–207, at 2130 (1996). On the even more robust right of husbands to have forcible intercourse with their wives, see Jill Elaine Hasday, Contest and Consent: A Legal History of Marital Rape, California Law Review, vol. 88, 1373–1505 (2000).

10. The Nineteenth Amendment, which guaranteed women the vote, was ratified in 1920. Before that, eastern states were slow to adopt votes for women. See Anne F. Scott and Andrew M. Scott, One Half the People: The Fight for Woman Suffrage, at 166–68 (Philadelphia: Lippincott, 1975). Illinois granted women the vote in 1913 (ibid., 166). On the "unwritten law," see Jeffrey Adler, First in Violence, Deepest in Dirt: Homicide in Chicago, 1875–1920, at 112–13 (Cambridge, MA: Harvard University Press, 2006). Even if one counts only white women who were arrested for homicide,

a mere 11 percent were convicted (ibid., 329n141). On the character and power of this "law," see ibid., 108–17.

11. On the earlier pattern, see Roger Lane, Murder in America: A History, at 197 (Columbus: Ohio State University Press, 1997); see also Roger Lane, Roots of Violence in Black Philadelphia, 1860–1900, at 87–94 (Cambridge, MA: Harvard University Press, 1986). On the later pattern, see Lane, Murder in America, 198–99, 230.

12. Adler, First in Violence, chapter 4.

13. In the first trial, all eleven defendants were tried; in the second trial, Ossian's brother Henry Sweet—believed to be the shooter—was tried alone. Kevin Boyle, Arc of Justice: A Saga of Race, Civil Rights, and Murder in the Jazz Age, at 292–99, 331–36 (New York: Henry Holt, 2004).

14. Murphy later lost an election due to his stance on crime, but it was not black crime that prompted his defeat. In 1938, Murphy was running for reelection as Michigan's governor; his lenient treatment of sit-down strikers in automobile factories was a major issue, and Murphy lost in a close race. Richard D. Lunt, The High Ministry of Government: The Political Career of Frank Murphy, at 151–60 (Detroit: Wayne State University Press, 1965). In late 1930s America outside the South, being seen as soft on industrial labor unions carried a higher political price tag than being seen as soft on black violence.

15. Boyle, Arc of Justice, 142. For a discussion of the Klan's role in Detroit politics at the time, see 24, 140–43.

16. Adler, First in Violence, 116.

17. John Higham, Strangers in the Land: Patterns of American Nativism, 1860–1925, at 64–67, 285–86, 290–94 (New York: Atheneum, 1965). Politicians and some scholars argued that southern and eastern Europeans belonged to a different race than immigrants of the past; fears of inundation by immigrants of inferior racial "stock" were common (ibid., 131–57).

18. With respect to the Kentucky figures, see Malcolm Gladwell, Outliers: The Story of Success, at 165 (New York: Little, Brown, 2008). Some Appalachian counties had murder rates as high as 250 per 100,000. See Randolph Roth, American Homicide, at 336–39 (Cambridge, MA: Harvard University Press, 2009). The New York figures in the text are taken from Monkkonen's data.

19. Gladwell, Outliers, 165–66.

20. See Steven D. Levitt, Understanding Why Crime Fell in the 1990s: Four Factors that Explain the Decline and Six That Do Not, Journal of Economic Perspectives, vol. 18, 163–90, at 176–77 (2004). Steven D. Levitt and Stephen J. Dubner are the authors of Freakonomics: A Rogue Economist Explores the Hidden Side of Everything (New York: William Morrow, 2005).

21. For the Alameda County figures, see Lawrence Friedman and Robert V. Percival, The Roots of Justice: Crime and Punishment in Alameda County, California, 1870–1910, at 166, table 5.8 (Chapel Hill: University of North Carolina Press, 1981). Today, more than 80 percent of murder charges lead to conviction. Online Sourcebook, table 5.57.2006. In felony cases that go to trial in metropolitan counties, the conviction rate is 68 percent (ibid.).

22. See Online Sourcebook, table 5.57.2006.

23. Friedman and Percival, Roots of Justice, 166, table 5.8.

24. California's imprisonment rate was double the rate in the Northeast, meaning that Californians saw substantially more criminal prosecutions than their northeastern cousins. More prosecutions meant more docket pressure for prosecutors, which in turn likely meant more guilty pleas and fewer trials.

25. The quoted phrase is from People v. Bedell, 127 N.W. 33, 36 (Mich. 1910) (Ostrander, J., concurring); see also People v. Peterson, 120 N.W. 570 (Mich. 1909).

26. See People v. Yund, 163 Mich. 504, 508–09, 128 N.W. 742, 744 (1910). For a decision rejecting the doctrine, see People v. Sherman, 14 Mich. App. 720, 166 N.W.2d 22 (1968).

27. On the resistance rule in rape cases, see Susan Estrich, Rape, Yale Law Journal, vol. 95, 1087–1184, at 1105–21 (1986), which discusses the misogyny of the common law of rape more generally.

28. Another historical theme is nicely captured by Anne M. Coughlin, Sex and Guilt, Virginia Law Review, vol. 84, 1–46 (1998). Coughlin notes that, at the time the force and resistance requirements evolved, a good deal of *consensual* sex was criminalized. Requiring proof of defendant force and victim resistance was the equivalent of requiring proof that the victim had engaged in sex under duress—and therefore could not be held responsible for what might otherwise be deemed the crimes of adultery or fornication.

29. Chief Justice Taft's opinion in United States v. Balint, 258 U.S. 250 (1922)—a case in which proof of moral fault was not required—makes the point. Balint was charged with violating the Harrison Act; his only possible defense was that he did not know either the character of the drugs he was charged with selling or the legal conditions the Act placed on drug sales. Taft reasoned that Congress "weighed the possible injustice of subjecting an innocent seller to a penalty against the evil of exposing innocent purchasers to danger from the drug, and concluded that the latter was the result preferably to be avoided" (ibid., at 254). His opinion makes sense only on the assumption that moral blameworthiness was a prerequisite for criminal liability: that, save for a few unusual cases, the government must prove the defendant knew enough about the relevant facts and law to render his behavior culpable.

30. On the limits of late twentieth-century self-defense doctrine in domestic violence cases, see, for example, Kit Kinports, Defending Battered Women's Self-Defense Claims, Oregon Law Review, vol. 67, 393–465 (1988). On the more generous treatment given women who killed abusive husbands in early twentieth-century Chicago, see Adler, First in Violence, chapter 3.

31. Compare the more modern role of juries, as judges of witness credibility. See George Fisher, The Jury's Rise as Lie Detector, Yale Law Journal, vol. 107, 575–638 (1997).

32. See M. Craig Brown and Barbara D. Warner, Immigrants, Urban Politics, and Policing in 1900, American Sociological Review, vol. 57, 293–305, at 301, table 2 (1992).

33. See Gustave F. Fischer, The Juries, in Felony Cases, in Cook County, in Illinois Crime Survey: 1929, ed. John Henry Wigmore, 225–243 at 232, Table 1 (Chicago: Illinois Association for Criminal Justice, 1929).

34. On police corruption, see Robert M. Fogelson, Big-City Police, 3–10, 148–49 (Cambridge, MA: Harvard University Press, 1977). On the different levels of violence inside and outside Irish neighborhoods, see Marilynn S. Johnson, Street Justice: A History of Violence in New York City, at 28, table 1.9 (Boston: Beacon Press, 2003).

35. See W. Marvin Dulaney, Black Police in America, at 11–14 (Bloomington: Indiana University Press, 1996); Fogelson, Big-City Police, 14–15.

36. As long ago as 1855, Boston's policing rate stood at 153 per 100,000. Roger Lane, Policing the City: Boston, 1822–1885, at 238 (Cambridge, MA: Harvard University Press, 1967). A century later, Houston's policing rate was barely half as high—77 per 100,000. 1961 Statistical Abstract, 16, no. 10; Uniform Crime Reports: 1956, 29, table 13. Today, the wealth gap between North and South has narrowed considerably— and so have the gaps in murder and policing rates. In 2005, Atlanta had a higher policing rate than either Boston or Detroit, and a significantly lower homicide rate than Detroit. Crime in the United States: 2005, 78, table 8.

37. See Hortense Powdermaker, After Freedom: A Cultural Study in the Deep South (New York: Viking Press, 1939).

38. In 1950, South Carolina's population was nearly 40 percent black, yet more than two-thirds of the state's imprisoned felons were white. Federal Bureau of Prisons, National Prisoner Statistics: Prisoners in State and Federal Institutions: 1950, 55, table 21 (Washington, DC: Government Printing Office, 1954). According to the same source, in the eleven states of the old Confederacy minus Georgia (for which data are missing), 44 percent of imprisoned felons were black, compared with 24 percent of the general population. By comparison, in the Northeast, 29 percent of prisoners were black, compared with only 5 percent of the general population.

39. Data on sentences broken down by demographic group are nearly nonexistent for the early twentieth century, but data from midcentury support the picture painted in the text. In general, black prisoners served more time than white ones, but the differences were modest. The same was true even in the South, with the important exceptions of homicide and rape—as to those offenses, blacks served considerably longer sentences than did whites. Bureau of the Census, U.S. Department of Commerce, Prisoners in State and Federal Prisons and Reformatories: 1938, 74–75, tables 45–46 (Washington, DC: United States Government Printing Office, 1941). The chief difference between the races—and also between the different regions—was one that recorded data do not capture: the selection of cases for prosecution. Many more black-on-black crimes were prosecuted and punished in the North than in the South, as the demographics of the two regions' prison populations show. See National Prisoner Statistics: 1950, 55, table 21.

40. See Matthew J. Mancini, One Dies, Get Another: Convict Leasing in the American South, 1866–1928 (Columbia: University of South Carolina Press, 1996).

41. On the latter point, see Stewart E. Tolnay and E. M. Beck, A Festival of Violence: An Analysis of Southern Lynchings, 1882–1930, at 30 (Urbana: University of Illinois Press, 1995).

42. See Philip Dray, Capitol Men: The Epic Story of Reconstruction through the Lives of the First Black Congressmen, at 344–46, 380 (New York: Houghton Mifflin, 2008).

43. Presidential Elections, 1789–2008, at 140 (Washington, DC: CQ Press, 2010).

44. Thomas Adams Upchurch, Legislating Racism: The Billion Dollar Congress and the Birth of Jim Crow, at 2 (Lexington: University Press of Kentucky, 2004).

45. That is the traditional account. See Fred Wellborn, The Influence of the Silver-Republican Senators, 1889–1891, Mississippi Valley Historical Review, vol. 14, 462–80 (1928); Vincent P. DeSantis, Republicans Face the Southern Question: The New Departure Years, 1877–1897, at 209–13 (Baltimore: Johns Hopkins University Press, 1959). A recent book on the subject argues that the pro-silver Republicans opposed voting rights legislation on principle: they believed Congress should focus not on civil rights but on the stagnant rural economy. See Upchurch, Legislating Racism, 167–76.

46. Tolnay and Beck, Festival of Violence, 29–31. According to Dray, the number of lynchings peaked at 160 in 1892. Philip Dray, At the Hands of Persons Unknown: The Lynching of Black America, at viii (New York: Modern Library, 2002). According to Klarman, the number of lynchings averaged 188 during the 1890s, gradually falling to 17 in the late 1920s. Michael J. Klarman, From Jim Crow to Civil Rights: The Supreme Court and the Struggle for Racial Equality, at 119 (New York: Oxford University Press, 2004).

47. On the number of lynchings, see Klarman, Jim Crow to Civil Rights, 119. The annual number of executions in the contemporary United States peaked at 98 in 1999; the number declined to 37 in 2008. Online Sourcebook, table 6.79.2008.

48. See Dray, Capitol Men.

49. See Morgan Kousser, The Shaping of Southern Politics: Suffrage Restriction and the Establishment of the One-Party South, 1880–1910 (New Haven, CT: Yale University Press, 1974). On suffrage restrictions—and their effect on white voters—in particular states, see ibid., 49 (Louisiana), 58–62 (Louisiana and Mississippi), 208 (Texas), 240–41 (South Carolina and Virginia). "When asked whether Christ could register under the good character clause, a leader of the Alabama [constitutional] convention replied, 'That would depend entirely on which way he was going to vote.'" Ibid., 59.

50. See, for example, Tolnay and Beck, Festival of Violence, 86: "[A]verage white Southerners would have described lynching as an exercise in popular justice." Tolnay and Beck argue persuasively that lynchings were not a means of limiting black political power—after 1890, that power was basically nonexistent. See ibid., 183–90. At the same time, it seems fair to say that lynchings of blacks were, at least in part, a response to the limited political power poor whites exercised over the formal justice system.

51. See Dray, Hands of Persons Unknown, 5–14; Klarman, Jim Crow to Civil Rights, 119.

52. After holding a small House majority in the Congress elected in 1888, Republicans held fewer than 30 percent of House seats in the next Congress, and fewer than 40 percent in the one after that. See The Statistical History of the United States: From Colonial Times to the Present, Prepared by the United States Bureau of the Census, at 1083 (New York: Basic Books, 1976). On Grover Cleveland's 1892 margin of victory as compared with the margins of his predecessors, see Presidential Elections, 137–42.

53. See Presidential Elections, 142–46; Statistical History, 1083.

54. See Dray, Hands of Persons Unknown, 122–27 (Wilmington), 162–67 (Atlanta).

55. Klarman, Jim Crow to Civil Rights, 68.

56. The three Justices were Edward Douglass White, Horace Lurton, and Joseph Lamar. White was already on the Court; Taft named him Chief Justice in 1910. Lurton and Lamar were appointed Associate Justice in 1910 and 1911, respectively. The two ex-Confederate soldiers were White and Lurton. See Clare Cushman, ed., The Supreme Court Justices: Illustrated Biographies, 1789–1993, at 271–75, 301–05, 316–20 (Washington, DC: Congressional Quarterly, 1993).

57. Phillip Langsdon, Tennessee: A Political History, at 265–67, 299–302 (Franklin, TN: Hillsboro Press, 2000).

58. See V. O. Key Jr., Southern Politics in State and Nation: A New Edition, at 318–19 (Knoxville: University of Tennessee Press, 1984). Though the parties did not divide on race, southern whites who lived in black belts were much more likely to support Smith than whites who lived in areas with few blacks. Ibid., 318–29.

59. For another example of this point, see the confirmation battle of John J. Parker, a Virginia federal judge whom Herbert Hoover nominated for the Supreme Court—and whom the Senate rejected, partly because of his history of racism. Parker was a Republican. For a good general discussion, see Ernesto J. Sanchez, John J. Parker and the Beginning of the Modern Confirmation Process, Journal of Supreme Court History, vol. 32, 22–45 (2007).

60. See Leonard Dinnerstein, The Leo Frank Case, rev. ed. (Athens: University of Georgia Press, 2008); Klarman, Jim Crow to Civil Rights, 120–21; Steve Oney, And the Dead Shall Rise: The Murder of Mary Phagan and the Lynching of Leo Frank (New York: Pantheon Books, 2003).

61. On the quite real threat of lynching Slaton faced, see Oney, And the Dead Shall Rise, 503–11.

62. C. Vann Woodward, Tom Watson: Agrarian Rebel, at 381 (Savannah, GA: The Beehive Press, 1938). Watson's Senate opponent was none other than Hugh Dorsey, the prosecutor in the Leo Frank case. Dorsey had served two terms as governor of Georgia, and had taken a public stand against lynching. Watson made him pay. See Klarman, Jim Crow to Civil Rights, 262; Woodward, Tom Watson, 407–10.

63. See Political Notes: Ritchie Out, Time Magazine (November 19, 1934).

64. For the facts in this paragraph, see Allen Barra, Inventing Wyatt Earp: His Life and Many Legends, at 29–30, 97, 115, 118, 126 (New York: Carroll & Graff, 1999); Richard E. Erwin, The Truth about Wyatt Earp, at 23, 149, 166 (Carpinteria, CA: O.K. Press, 1992); Casey Tefertiller, Wyatt Earp: The Life behind the Legend, at 4–5 (New York: John Wiley & Sons, 1997). The town marshal was Fred White; the man who (accidentally) shot him was "Curly Bill" Brocius. Strangely, Wyatt Earp testified in Brocius's favor at his preliminary hearing. Erwin, Truth about Wyatt Earp, 174; Tefertiller, Wyatt Earp, 59. Allen Barra nevertheless points to the incident as one of the sources of friction between the Earps and the Clantons. Barra, Inventing Wyatt Earp, 180. It was not the only such source. In the weeks leading up to the shootout at the OK Corral, Ike Clanton repeatedly threatened to kill the Earps,

partly in order to prevent them from spreading the word that Clanton had fingered a trio of other local thieves. Erwin, Truth about Wyatt Earp, 258; Tefertiller, Wyatt Earp, 115.

65. See Barra, Inventing Wyatt Earp, 188–89; Erwin, Truth about Wyatt Earp, 261; Tefertiller, Wyatt Earp, 119–23.

66. At the same time, some local residents hailed the Earps as vindicators of law and order. See Tefertiller, Wyatt Earp, 125.

67. Ibid., 115–17.

68. Roth lists this figure for post–Civil War Arizona; New Mexico's peak murder rate was roughly 250 per 100,000 adults, while Colorado's was 140. See Roth, American Homicide, 354. By comparison, in 2008, the U.S. homicide rate per 100,000 adults stood at 7.6. See Crime in the United States: 2008, table 4; 2010 Statistical Abstract, table 7. Notice that the rate is per 100,000 *adults;* the rate per 100,000 population is significantly lower.

69. See Roth, American Homicide, 404–05, 408–10.

70. See Arthur Quinn, The Rivals: William Gwin, David Broderick, and the Birth of California, at 260–70 (New York: Crown, 1994); Alexander E. Wagstaff, Life of David S. Terry: Presenting an Authentic, Impartial, and Vivid History of His Eventful Life and Tragic Death, at 217 (San Francisco: Continental, 1892).

71. On the long feud between Terry and Field, see Carl Brent Swisher, Stephen J. Field, Craftsman of the Law, at 73–74, 346–49 (Washington, DC: Brookings Institution, 1930).

72. On the number of prisoners and the territory's population, see Margaret Werner Cahalan, Historical Corrections Statistics in the United States, 1850–1984, at 29–30 (Rockville, MD: Bureau of Justice Statistics, 1986). We lack data on the New Mexico territory's prison population in 1880—but a decade later, the share of New Mexicans who were incarcerated was nearly identical to the share of Arizonans in 1880. Ibid., 30, table 3-3. According to Roth, the murder rate in late nineteenth-century New Mexico was 250 per 100,000 adults. See Roth, American Homicide, 354.

73. In 2008, New York's imprisonment rate stood at 307 per 100,000. Online Sourcebook, table 6.29.2008. That same year, the state's homicide rate was 4 per 100,000. Crime in the United States: 2008, table 4.

74. Lawrence Friedman, Crime and Punishment in American History, at 179–87 (New York: Basic Books, 1993); Robert M. Senkewicz, Vigilantes in Gold Rush San Francisco, at 8–9, 84–85, 160 (Stanford, CA: Stanford University Press, 1985).

75. Friedman, Crime and Punishment, 181; Senkewicz, Vigilantes, 85.

76. Regarding Broderick and the second committee, see Friedman, Crime and Punishment, 182; Senkewicz, Vigilantes, 188. Regarding the quasi-trials given "defendants" before the San Francisco vigilance committee, see Friedman, Crime and Punishment, 180–81.

77. On Oakland's murder rate, see Friedman and Percival, Roots of Justice, 27. In 1890, Oakland employed a mere thirty-eight police officers to patrol a population of nearly 50,000. By 1910, the number of police officers had grown to 109—but the city's

population had mushroomed to 150,000 (ibid., 77, table 4.1). Boston had twice that ratio of police to local population *in the years before the Civil War.* See Roger Lane, Policing the City, 238; see also Friedman and Percival, Roots of Justice, 76–78 (showing that Oakland's police force was small compared with the forces in other cities across the nation). As for prison populations, in the late nineteenth and early twentieth centuries, California imprisoned twice the percentage of its population as states in the Northeast. See Cahalan, Historical Corrections Statistics, 30, table 3-3.

78. The data on imprisonment rates are organized by state, not by city; nevertheless, there is good reason to suppose that the share of city residents who lived behind bars was (and is) positively correlated with state imprisonment rates.

79. See Dan M. Kahan, The Secret Ambition of Deterrence, Harvard Law Review, vol. 113, 413–500, at 432–33; see also Garrett Epps, Any Which Way but Loose: Interpretive Strategies and Attitudes toward Violence in the Evolution of the Anglo-American Retreat Rule, Law and Contemporary Problems, vol. 55, 303–31, at 311–14 (1992).

80. State v. Bartlett, 71 S.W. 148, 151–52 (Mo. 1902), quoted in Kahan, Secret Ambition, 429.

81. See Lynn v. People, 48 N.W. 964 (Ill. 1897). *Lynn* held that the retreat obligation does not apply to police officers; the discussion assumes that the obligation applies to the citizenry as a whole.

82. See Klarman, Jim Crow to Civil Rights, 275–86.

6. A CULTURE WAR AND ITS AFTERMATH

1. For a good exposition of the localist position, see Michael W. McConnell, Federalism: Evaluating the Founders' Design, University of Chicago Law Review, vol. 54, 1484–512 (1987).

2. Lincoln and Douglas were battling for the latter's Senate seat in 1858. Republican legislators allied with Lincoln won more votes than pro-Douglas Democrats. But the votes of Democratic legislators not up for reelection gave Douglas a narrow victory. Michael Burlingame, Abraham Lincoln: A Life, vol. 1, at 545–57 (Baltimore: Johns Hopkins University Press, 2008).

3. Typically, those battles arise at the beginning of new administrations. See Neil A. Lewis, Abortions Abroad Are New Focus of Widening Battle over Reagan's Policy, New York Times (June 1, 1987); Steven A. Holmes, U.S. Set to Change Abortion Policies, New York Times (May 12, 1993); Brian Knowlton, Funds for Overseas Abortion Advice to End: In First Policy Moves, Bush Team Focuses on Role Abroad, New York Times (January 23, 2001); Obama Ends Ban on U.S. Funds to Aid Abortions, New York Times (February 3, 2009).

4. On Lincoln's "don't care" formula, see, for example, Abraham Lincoln, Speech at Hartford, Connecticut on March 5, 1860, Evening Press Version, in Roy P. Basler, ed., The Collected Works of Abraham Lincoln, vol. 4, at 10 (New Brunswick, NJ:

Rutgers University Press, 1953); see also Harold Holzer, Lincoln at Cooper Union: The Speech That Made Abraham Lincoln President, at 185–87 (New York: Simon & Schuster Paperbacks, 2004). On Lincoln's "ultimate extinction" formula, see Abraham Lincoln, Speech at Springfield, Illinois, on June 16, 1858, in Basler, Collected Works, vol. 2, 461.

5. In the gay rights context, consider the Defense of Marriage Act (DOMA) (defining marriage as a legal union between one man and one woman and authorizing states to deny recognition to same-sex marriages from other states), Public Law No. 104-199, 110 Stat. 2419, on one side; and on the other, the Matthew Shepard and James Byrd Jr. Hate Crimes Prevention Act (extending federal hate crime laws to cover crimes motivated by the victim's actual or perceived sexual orientation, gender, gender identity, or disability), Public Law No. 111-84, and the proposed Employment Non-Discrimination Act (ENDA) (extending federal prohibitions on employment discrimination to sexual orientation and gender identity), S. 1584/H.R. 3017. With respect to abortion, compare the Hyde Amendment (a legislative provision routinely attached to appropriations bills that bars the use of certain federal funds to pay for abortions) and Executive Order 13535 (reaffirming the principles of the Hyde Amendment following passage of The Patient Protection and Affordable Care Act, Public Law No. 111-148, and the Health Care and Education Reconciliation Act of 2010, Public Law No. 111-152) with the Freedom of Access to Clinic Entrances Act (forbidding with criminal and civil penalties the use of "force, threat of force or physical obstruction" to prevent someone from providing or receiving reproductive health services), Public Law No. 103-259. With respect to both sets of issues, groups on both sides have worked hard to cement their policy preferences at the national level.

6. For a copy of the platform, see Independence Hall Association, "Republican Philadelphia: Republican Platform of 1956," at www.ushistory.org/gop/convention _1856republicanplatform.htm.

7. See Sarah Barringer Gordon, The Mormon Question: Polygamy and Constitutional Conflict in Nineteenth Century America, at 92–99, 102–07, 196 (Chapel Hill: University of North Carolina Press, 2002). The battle began in the 1850s, even as the national debate about slavery was reaching its peak. In 1857, then-President James Buchanan sent an army detachment to Utah to bring the territory into compliance. The "war" was limited to shadow boxing, as the army and the territorial militia never came into direct contact (ibid., 58–62).

8. On the role sexual coercion played in antislavery politics, see, for example, William W. Freehling, The Road to Disunion: Secessionists Triumphant, 1854–1861 (New York: Oxford University Press, 2007), which also stresses the indignation of white Southerners facing such accusations—even when the accusations were plainly true. For the similar role the same issue played in anti-polygamy politics, see Gordon, Mormon Question, 14, 47–48, 167–71. The so-called three-fifths clause in Article I provided that, when apportioning seats in the House of Representatives and Electoral College, the local population include both the free population and three-fifths of all slaves. This arrangement ensured that portions of the South with large slave

populations enjoyed disproportionate political influence in the national government. The arrangement had large political consequences: without it, Thomas Jefferson would have lost the election of 1800 to John Adams. See Garry Wills, "Negro President": Jefferson and the Slave Power, at 2 (Boston: Houghton Mifflin, 2003).

9. See Gordon, Mormon Question, 81. The Act's author was Justin Morrill, then a member of the House of Representatives (and later a Senator for thirty years) from Vermont. Morrill is better known as the author of the Land Grant Colleges Act of 1862, which is responsible for the establishment of MIT, Cornell, and the great state universities of the Midwest. In both that Act and this one, Morrill showed a willingness to use federal power to advance classically local agendas: the promotion of higher education on the one hand, the enforcement of the law of domestic relations on the other.

10. U.S. Constitution, Article IV, section 3.

11. Add to that the fact that the Supreme Court had held that Congress had decidedly limited power to regulate slavery in the territories in the *Dred Scott* case. If slavery were too local an enterprise to support federal regulation, surely marriage was.

12. U.S. Constitution Amendment I.

13. 98 U.S. 145 (1879).

14. Reynolds's first conviction was overturned on appeal; at his second trial, his second wife did not take the witness stand, but the government was permitted to read into the record her testimony from the first trial, which again led to Reynolds's conviction. See Gordon, Mormon Question, 114–16, 154.

15. To be sure, Congress plainly had greater legislative authority over territories, which were creatures of the federal government, than over states—a proposition that distinguished *Cruikshank* from *Reynolds*. But in the battle against polygamy, the stakes plainly went beyond territorial law: part of the purpose of Congress was to induce the church to abandon plural marriage as a condition of statehood. Thus, Congress was, in effect, striving to govern a traditionally state-law field—and striving to do so with respect to a (soon-to-be) state, not just a territory.

16. *Reynolds,* 98 U.S., at 166–67.

17. The Edmunds Act appears at 22 Stat. 30 (1882) and was codified at 48 U.S.C. § 1461; it was repealed in 1983. The sponsors of the Morrill and Edmunds Acts, Justin Morrill and George F. Edmunds, were two longtime Vermont Senators from the more aggressively antislavery wing of the Republican party. On the number of prosecutions, see Gordon, Mormon Question, 155. On the territory's population, see 1951 Statistical Abstract, 31. On Clawson's prosecution, see Gordon, Mormon Question, 157, and regarding the prosecution of Mormon women, see 166, 181. Some readers may wonder how the federal government had the authority to prosecute classic common-law crimes like fornication in federal territories; it had been seventy years since John Marshall's Supreme Court had held that there was no such thing as a federal common law of crimes. See United States v. Hudson, 11 U.S. 32 (1812). The answer is that, as with the law of marriage, the federal government had more extensive legal authority when governing the residents of federal territories than when governing state residents.

18. Gordon, Mormon Question, 211–13, 219–20.

19. See Henry Chafetz, Play the Devil: A History of Gambling in the United States from 1492 to 1955, at 299–300 (New York: C. N. Potter, 1960); Richard McGowan, State Lotteries and Legalized Gambling, at 14–15 (Westport, CT: Praeger, 1994); Ronald J. Rychlak, Lotteries, Revenues and Social Costs: A Historical Examination of State-Sponsored Gambling, Boston College Law Review, vol. 34, 11–81, at 38–44 (1992).

20. For the legislation, see Act of August 11, 1868, 1868 La. Acts 24. On the corruption that attended it, see Ellan Lonn, Reconstruction in Louisiana: After 1868, at 523 (New York: G. P. Putnam's Sons, 1918). On the corruption of Louisiana's Reconstruction-era government more generally, see Eric Foner, Reconstruction: America's Unfinished Revolution, 1863–1877, at 385, 388, 550–51 (New York: Harper & Row, 1989).

21. A Lottery Bribe Refused: Gov. Nichols Returns a Check for $100,000; But Mayor Shakespeare Accepts for the City of New Orleans; Break in the Levee at East Carroll, New York Times (March 16, 1890).

22. For the two federal statutes, see the Anti-Lottery Act of 1890, ch. 908, 26 Stat. 465; the Lottery Act of 1895, ch. 191, 28 Stat. 963. On Dauphin's finances, see Succession of Dauphin, 36 So. 287 (La. 1904).

23. 188 U.S. 321 (1903).

24. 188 U.S. at 364–65 (Fuller, C.J., dissenting).

25. 18 U.S.C. §§ 2422–2423 (the current version of the Mann Act), 1952 (the Travel Act), 922(g) (the felon-in-possession statute). For the jurisdictional rule governing the felon-in-possession statute, see Scarborough v. United States, 431 U.S. 563 (1977).

26. Or, sometimes, that the transaction itself crossed state lines. See, for example, United States v. Jackson, 196 F.3d 383 (2d Cir. 1999).

27. The same is true of drug laws, where federal offenses require no proof of border crossing or interstate commercial effects in order to establish federal jurisdiction. See Gonzales v. Raich, 545 U.S. 1 (2005).

28. For the classic discussion, see Morton Grozdins, The American System: A New View of Government in the United States (Chicago: Rand McNally, 1966).

29. 188 U.S., at 356–57.

30. See Timothy J. Gilfoyle, City of Eros: New York City, Prostitution, and the Commercialization of Sex, 1790–1920, at 29, 253–54 (New York: W. W. Norton, 1992).

31. Sometimes, enforcement was privatized, as the vigilante-style private organizations that sought to attack prostitution networks in New York illustrate. Gilfoyle, City of Eros, 187–89; Jennifer Fronc, New York Undercover, at 34, 62 (Chicago: University of Chicago Press, 1974). On the durability of prostitution markets, see, for example, Lawrence Friedman's characterization of the "army of customers" who kept prostitution markets thriving. Lawrence Friedman, Crime and Punishment in American History, at 331 (New York: Basic Books, 1993).

32. With respect to Chicago, see Mark Haller, Historical Roots of Police Behavior: Chicago, 1890–1925, in Eric H. Monkkonen, ed., Crime and Justice in American History: Policing and Crime Control, vol. 5, part 1, 244–64, at 257 (New York: K. G. Saur, 1992). On the tolerance of more discreet prostitution markets, see Friedman, Crime and Punishment, 226–28, 328–32; Sidney L. Harring, Policing a Class Society: The

Experience of American Cities, 1865–1915, at 191–95 (New Brunswick, NJ: Rutgers University Press, 1983). On Atlanta, see Eugene J. Watts, The Police in Atlanta, 1890–1905, in Crime and Justice in American History: Policing and Crime Control, vol. 5, part 3, 908–25, at 917. On St. Paul, see Joel Best, Keeping the Peace in St. Paul: Crime, Vice, and Police Work, 1869–1874, in Crime and Justice in American History, vol. 5, part 1, 60–79, at 73. On other western cities, see Gene Simmons, Ladies of the Night: A Historical and Personal Perspective on the Oldest Profession in the World, at 136 (Beverly Hills, CA: Phoenix Books, 2008).

33. On the number of prostitutes in Manhattan, see H. W. Brands, T.R.: The Last Romantic, at 7 (New York: Basic Books, 1997). On the number in Storyville and the profits made from their labor, see Al Rose, Storyville, New Orleans: Being an Authentic, Illustrated Account of the Notorious Red Light District, at 96 (Tuscaloosa: University of Alabama Press, 1974). On Storyville and New Orleans music, see Alecia P. Long, The Great Southern Babylon, at 105, 196–97 (Baton Rouge: Louisiana State University Press, 1966). On Storyville's end, see Long, Southern Babylon, 226–27.

34. On the Raines Law, see Fronc, New York Undercover, 40, 67; Gilfoyle, City of Eros, 243–48.

35. See David J. Langum, Crossing Over the Line: Legislating Morality and the Mann Act, at 38–41 (Chicago: University of Chicago Press, 1994).

36. Mann Act, ch. 395, § 2, 36 Stat. 825 (1910) (emphasis added).

37. Langum, Crossing the Line, 1–3.

38. Ibid., 182–85. Johnson was later prosecuted and convicted for traveling and sleeping with a white prostitute.

39. 242 U.S. 470, 482 (1917).

40. Ibid., 496–502 (McKenna, J., dissenting). Chief Justice White and Justice Clarke joined McKenna's dissent.

41. Compare Exxon Mobile Corp. v. Allapattah Services, Inc., 545 U.S. 546, 568 (2005) ("[T]he authoritative statement is the statutory text, not the legislative history or any other extrinsic material") with Church of Holy Trinity v. United States, 143 U.S. 457, 459 (1892) ("It is a familiar rule, that a thing may be within the letter of the statute and yet not within the statute, because not within its spirit, nor within the intention of its makers").

42. For the best discussion, see David A. Sklansky, Cocaine, Race, and Equal Protection, Stanford Law Review, vol. 47, 1283–322 (1993).

43. See chapter 1 of George Fisher, The Euphoria Taboo: Alcohol Monogamy, Narcotic Temptation (unpublished manuscript), which discusses the risk of users becoming "slaves to pleasure."

44. Concerning both alleged cocaine use by southern blacks and the falsity of the claim that such use was widespread, see David F. Musto, The American Disease: Origins of Narcotic Control, at 7–8 (New York: Oxford University Press, 1999).

45. Again, see Musto for this story, which he tells in elaborate detail (ibid., 25–63).

46. That changed beginning in the 1930s and 1940s. Today's federal drug prohibitions require no proof of interstate movement—simple possession and distribution of

drugs are federal crimes, without regard for their effects on interstate commerce. See Gonzales v. Raich, 545 U.S. 1 (2005).

47. Harrison Act, ch. 1, §2, 38 Stat. 785 (1914).

48. United States v. Doremus, 249 U.S. 86 (1919).

49. United States v. Balint, 258 U.S. 250 (1922).

50. United States v. Behrman, 258 U.S. 280 (1922).

51. *Balint,* 258 U.S., at 251–54; the quote appears at 251.

52. *Behrman,* 258 U.S. at 290 (Justice Holmes, joined by Justices McReynolds and Brandeis, dissenting).

53. *Balint,* 258 U.S., at 251–52.

54. Ibid., 252.

55. Compare United States v. Hurwitz, 495 F.3d 463 (4th Cir. 2006), a contemporary case in which a misnamed "good faith" defense was allowed—but only if the defendant could show he had behaved reasonably.

56. Famous, but not quite accurate—Hoover really said, "Our country has undertaken a great social and economic experiment, noble in motive and far-reaching in purpose." Fred R. Shapiro ed., The Yale Book of Quotations, at 369 (New Haven, CT: Yale University Press, 2006).

57. For a contemporaneous account, see Martha Bensley Bruère, Does Prohibition Work? at 278–79, 297 (New York: Harper & Brothers, 1927). See also Mark Keller, Alcohol Problems and Policies in Historical Perspective, in David E. Kyvig, ed., Law, Alcohol, and Order: Perspectives on National Prohibition, at 163 (Westport, CT: Greenwood Press, 1985) ("Prohibition manifested immediate benefits. Those wicked saloons closed . . . the effect was seen in diminished rates of arrests for drunkenness and of alcohol-related admissions to hospitals"); David M. McDowell and Henry Spitz, Substance Abuse: From Principles to Practice, at 250 (Philadelphia: Taylor & Francis, 1999) ("[Prohibition] did have some unintended positive effects: Alcohol consumption did plummet, as did complications of alcohol abuse; rates of domestic violence decreased, and for years after, the rates of cirrhosis greatly diminished"). It seems churlish to dismiss these benefits as "unintended."

58. David E. Kyvig, Repealing National Prohibition, 2nd ed., at 25 (Kent, OH: Kent State University Press, 2000), which cites a 1928 study of alcohol prices.

59. See Bruère, Does Prohibition Work?, 299–300, for one example.

60. The figures come from Edward Rubin, A Statistical Study of Federal Criminal Prosecutions, Law and Contemporary Problems, vol. 1, 494–508, at 497, table 1 (1933–34). Today, drug cases occupy a bit more than one-fifth of federal criminal cases, and more than one-third of criminal cases in state courts. See Online Sourcebook, tables 5.10.2009, 5.52.2006.

61. U.S. Constitution, Amendment XVIII.

62. United States v. Farrar, 281 U.S. 624 (1930).

63. National Prohibition Act, ch. 85, §§ 6, 33, Public Law No. 66–66, 41 Stat. 305 (1919).

64. See United States v. Behrman, 258 U.S. 280 (1922).

65. See Gonzales v. Raich, 545 U.S. 1 (2005).

66. National Prohibition Act § 1.

67. Baltimore Mayor Supports Legalization of Illicit Drugs, New York Times, September 30, 1988, at B4.

68. Concerning Smith, see Michael A. Lerner, Dry Manhattan: Prohibition in New York City, at 239–54 (Cambridge, MA: Harvard University Press, 2007). Concerning Ritchie, see, for example, Effects of a Groundswell, Time, September 29, 1930, at 16–18; From Anne Arundel Town, Time, May 24, 1926, at 8–9.

69. Two states, Connecticut and Rhode Island, rejected the Amendment. As for the length of the national debate, by the time the Eighteenth Amendment was ratified, the movement for state-level prohibition had been going on for three decades. See Robert Post, Prohibition in the Taft Court Era, William and Mary Law Review, vol. 48, 1–182, at 5–6 and notes 5–6 (2006).

70. The ten states that declined to ratify Repeal were Georgia, Kansas, Louisiana, Mississippi, Nebraska, North Carolina, North Dakota, Oklahoma, South Carolina, and South Dakota. Kyvig, Repealing Prohibition, 178–79. Ratification was by state conventions and not by state legislatures, a departure from the norm for constitutional amendments (ibid., 170–75).

71. Lerner, Dry Manhattan, 77–78.

72. On the jail numbers, see Margaret Werner Cahalan, Historical Corrections Statistics in the United States, 1850–1984, at 86–87, tables 4–10, 4–11 (Rockville, MD: Bureau of Justice Statistics, 1986). On the prison numbers, see Bureau of the Census, U.S. Department of Commerce, Prisoners in State and Federal Prisons and Reformatories: 1926, at 11, table 6 (Washington, DC: Government Printing Office, 1929); Bureau of the Census, U.S. Department of Commerce, Prisoners in State and Federal Prisons and Reformatories: 1931 and 1932, at 6, table 6 (Washington, DC: Government Printing Office, 1934).

73. See Lerner, Dry Manhattan, 93–95.

74. National Commission on Law Observance and Enforcement, Report on the Enforcement of the Prohibition Laws of the United States, at 54–55 (Washington, DC: U.S. Government Printing Office, 1931).

75. See Kyvig, Repealing Prohibition, 23–25. Kyvig's data show that consumption fell by more than half between the mid-1910s (just before Prohibition) and 1934 (just after Repeal). The drop must have been considerably larger if measured *before* Repeal. Clark Warburton's study found beer consumption down by two-thirds, and also found liquor consumption increased relative to pre-Prohibition levels. Clark Warburton, The Economic Results of Prohibition, at 107, table 47 (New York: Columbia University Press, 1932). The latter conclusion is implausible given the sharp rise in liquor prices, which must have suppressed demand to some extent. It seems likely that liquor consumption was down at least modestly, and that beer consumption was down by more than two-thirds.

76. For an elaboration of these points, see William J. Stuntz, Race, Class, and Drugs, Columbia Law Review, vol. 98, 1795–842 (1998).

77. A Georgia newspaper captures the point: "the drink habit is not going by enforcement until more people believe it is wrong to drink." Quoted in Post, Prohibition and the Taft Court, 6n6.

78. The figures are reviewed in William J. Stuntz, The Political Constitution of Criminal Justice, Harvard Law Review, vol. 119, 780–851, at 814 and notes 190–191 (2006).

79. See Rubin, Statistical Study, 497, table 1; 499, table 2. The actual percentage was almost certainly lower; the data lump all "postal" cases together, and while fraud was the largest portion of that category, it was not the entire category.

80. See Steve Neal, Happy Days Are Here Again: The 1932 Democratic Convention, the Emergence of FDR—and How America Was Changed Forever, at 236–49 (New York: HarperCollins, 2004).

81. East of Ohio and North of the Potomac River, Roosevelt won 50 percent of the popular vote to Hoover's 46 percent. In the Midwest and West, Roosevelt won by a two-to-one margin; in the South, the margin was greater still. If one adjusts for the different national percentages, the distribution of Roosevelt's and Hoover's vote totals in 1932 parallel the distribution of the vote totals of William Jennings Bryan and William McKinley in 1896 and 1900. Presidential Elections, 1789–2008, at 143–44, 152 (Washington, DC: CQ Press, 2010). In his first presidential election, FDR represented Bryan's once-dry Democratic Party, not Al Smith's wet party.

82. See Bruère, Does Prohibition Work?, 108, 111, 114; Thomas A. Guglielmo, White on Arrival: Italians, Race, Color, and Power in Chicago, 1890–1945, at 83 (New York: Oxford University Press, 2003).

83. 410 U.S. 113 (1973).

84. See Richard D. Lunt, The High Ministry of Government: The Political Career of Frank Murphy, at 154–60 (Detroit: Wayne State University Press, 1965). Though, as Lunt notes, the sit-down strikes were widely blamed for Murphy's defeat, Lunt argues that Murphy was simply caught up in a Republican tide.

85. The Ten Most Wanted list didn't appear until the early 1950s. Before that, Hoover used a variant of the same strategy, hyping the search for high-profile offenders like John Dillinger. Dillinger's capture and death in 1934, at the hands of FBI agents, helped to make the Bureau's reputation—and Hoover's. See Bryan Burrough, Public Enemies: America's Greatest Crime Wave and the Birth of the FBI, 1933–34, at 402–16 (New York: Penguin Books, 2004). On Hoover's use of battles against high-profile criminals to raise his own political profile, see Richard Gid Powers, Secrecy and Power: The Life of J. Edgar Hoover, at 189–93, 196–209 (New York: Free Press, 1987).

86. On the Whitney and Luciano convictions, see Richard Norton Smith, Thomas E. Dewey and His Times, at 189–206, 249–50 (New York: Simon & Schuster, 1982). Dewey convicted Luciano of multiple counts of conspiracy to commit prostitution (ibid., 205–06). The prostitution charges seem an obvious law enforcement tactic today, but the tactic was at least somewhat novel then: most prosecutors probably assumed that voters would attach no value to such convictions. Dewey saw that the political payoff from criminal prosecution depended more on the identity of the defendant than on the law that formed the basis of the conviction. For the *Time* cover story, see Fight against Fear, Time, February 1, 1937, at 14–16. For the polls, see Smith, Dewey and His Times, 285 (reporting Gallup Poll results showing Dewey as

the choice of 50 percent of Republicans for his party's presidential nomination, and giving Dewey 58 percent in a head-to-head matchup with FDR). Dewey won most of the primaries in 1940 and led on the first three ballots of the Republican convention, before losing to Wendell Willkie on the sixth ballot. Ibid., 294–314; Charles Peters, Five Days in Philadelphia, at 57–108 (New York: PublicAffairs, 2005).

87. Smith, Dewey and His Times, 352–539, 553–604.

88. See Bruce Allen Murphy, Wild Bill: The Legend and Life of William O. Douglas, at 124–54 (New York: Random House, 2003).

89. On the genesis of the Kefauver Committee, see Joseph Bruce Gorman, Kefauver: A Political Biography, at 74–102 (New York: Oxford University Press, 1971); William Howard Moore, The Kefauver Committee and the Politics of Crime: 1950–1952 (Columbia: University of Missouri Press, 1974). On the Committee's enormous viewership, see Moore, Kefauver Committee, 169.

90. The literature on McCarthyism is massive. For a good general discussion of the Wisconsin Senator's work and legacy, see James T. Patterson, Grand Expectations: The United States, 1945–1974, at 196–205, 264–70 (New York: Oxford University Press, 1996). For more extended treatments, see Richard Fried, Nightmare in Red: The McCarthy Era in Perspective (New York: Oxford University Press, 1990); David Oshinsky, A Conspiracy So Immense: The World of Joe McCarthy (New York: Oxford University Press, 2005). On the February 1950 speech at Wheeling, West Virginia, and its aftermath, see Fried, Nightmare in Red, 124–31.

91. For a critical view of Kennedy's work on the Rackets Committee, see Paul Jacobs, Extracurricular Activities of the McClellan Committee, California Law Review, vol. 51, 296–310 (1963).

92. On Douglas's Supreme Court appointment, see Murphy, Wild Bill, 165–75. On the 1944 vice-presidential nomination, see 211–30. The man who *was* chosen to run with FDR, Harry Truman, became president upon Roosevelt's death in April 1945. It could easily have been Douglas.

93. Obviously, his service as his brother's campaign manager didn't hurt. But the appointment would have been politically impossible without Kennedy's role in the Rackets Committee hearings.

94. See Moore, Kefauver Committee, 97–98.

95. Ibid., 151–52, 155–57.

96. William Manchester, The Glory and the Dream: A Narrative History of America, 1932–1972, at 734 (Boston: Little, Brown, 1974).

97. See Moore, Kefauver Committee, 184, 190.

98. Ibid., 174, 196–97.

99. Federal Kidnapping Act, Public Law No. 72–189, 47 Stat. 326 (1932); Anti-Racketeering Act, Public Law No. 73–376, 48 Stat. 979 (1934); National Firearms Act, Public Law No. 73–474, 48 Stat. 1236 (1934).

100. Johnson Act, ch. 1194, 64 Stat. 1134 (1951); Travel Act, Public Law No. 87–228, 75 Stat. 498 (1961).

101. See William J. Stuntz, The Pathological Politics of Criminal Law, Michigan Law Review, vol. 100, 505–600, at 531–32 (2001).

102. See James A. Strazella, The Federalization of Criminal Law, at 20–21 (Washington, DC: American Bar Association, Criminal Justice Section, 1998).

103. The focus was on Mafia-style organized crime. See Nancy E. Marion, A History of Federal Crime Control Initiatives, 1960–1993, at 28–30 (Westport, CT: Praeger, 1994).

104. On the historical relationship between New York's homicide rate and the nation's, see Eric H. Monkkonen, Murder in New York City, at 9, figure 1.1 (Berkeley: University of California Press, 2001). According to Monkkonen's figures, the nation's murder rate in 1980 was 11 per 100,000; New York's murder rate was 26. On the rise of violent crime in blue-collar suburbs: in the Boston area, Brockton has a murder rate of 9 per 100,000; Lawrence's murder rate is 12. Both are higher than Boston's murder rate. In the New York area, Mount Vernon's homicide rate is 15 per 100,000, nearly three times New York City's rate. All figures are taken from Crime in the United States: 2009, table 8. Randolph Roth states that, between 1955 and 1962, the African American homicide rate stood at 23 per 100,000; the white rate stood at a historically low 2 per 100,000. Randolph Roth, American Homicide, at 452 (Cambridge, MA: Harvard University Press, 2009).

105. These figures are taken from 1951 Statistical Abstract, tables 55, 56; 1961 Statistical Abstract, 15, table 10; 1981 Statistical Abstract, tables 23, 24. The Abstracts do not have running totals of metropolitan *county* populations; cities' share of the metropolitan *area* populations are the best proxy available.

106. Today, Chicago's population stands at 2.8 million; the population of Cook County, Illinois—the county in which Chicago resides—is 5.3 million. Detroit has 871,000 residents; Wayne County, Michigan, has 1.9 million. Los Angeles is home to 3.8 million people; Los Angeles County's population is just under 10 million. See U.S. Census Bureau, State and County QuickFacts, available at http://quickfacts.census.gov.

107. See Cahalan, Historical Corrections Statistics, 65, table 3-31. The black share of the prison population was 23 percent in 1923, rising to 37 percent in 1960. The percentage increases in the black and white imprisonment rates are the author's calculation, based on the percentages in the preceding note, the imprisonment rates found in Cahalan (Historical Corrections Statistics, 30, table 3-3), and the black and white shares of the general population as listed in the annual volumes of the Statistical Abstract.

108. Robert M. Fogelson, Big-City Police, at 141–92 (Cambridge, MA: Harvard University Press, 1977); David Alan Sklansky, Democracy and the Police, at 33–38 (Stanford, CA: Stanford University Press, 2007).

109. See David Garland, The Culture of Control: Crime and Social Order in Contemporary Society, at 89–96 (Chicago: University of Chicago Press, 2001).

7. CONSTITUTIONAL LAW'S RISE

1. In Wolf v. Colorado, 338 U.S. 25 (1949), the Court declared the states bound by the Fourth Amendment's restrictions on searches and seizures—but declined to enforce

those restrictions with a federal remedy. The real application of Fourth Amendment law to state and local officials came in 1961, when Mapp v. Ohio, 367 U.S. 643 (1961), imposed the exclusionary rule (which bars the use of illegally seized evidence in criminal trials) on state courts.

2. 116 U.S. 616 (1886).

3. For the facts in this paragraph, see *Boyd,* 116 U.S. at 617–20, 630 (quote); Brief for Plaintiffs, Boyd v. United States, 116 U.S. 616 (1886) (No. 983), reprinted in Philip B. Kurland and Gerhard Casper, eds., Landmark Briefs and Arguments of the Supreme Court of the United States: Constitutional Law, vol. 8, at 479, 480–85 (Washington, DC: University Publications of America, 1975); Brief for the United States, Boyd v. United States, 116 U.S. 616 (No. 983), reprinted in Kurland and Casper, Landmark Briefs, 505, 506–09.

4. 201 U.S. 43 (1906).

5. 275 U.S. 192 (1927).

6. 335 U.S. 1 (1948).

7. 277 U.S. 438 (1928).

8. For Holmes's dissent, see 277 U.S., at 469–71. For Brandeis's dissent, see ibid., 471–85. For an interesting and insightful account of the case, see Robert Post, Prohibition in the Taft Court Era, William and Mary Law Review, vol. 48, 1–182, at 137–59 (2006). Regarding Brandeis's dissent, see ibid., 154–59. For reasons explained in the text, I believe Post overstates *Olmstead*'s importance. Finally, on the (belatedly) changed legal status of wiretapping, see Berger v. New York, 388 U.S. 41 (1967); Katz v. United States, 389 U.S. 347 (1967).

9. See William J. Stuntz, The Substantive Origins of Criminal Procedure, Yale Law Journal, vol. 105, 393–447, at 428–35 (1995).

10. Especially so after Prohibition. See Kenneth M. Murchison, Federal Criminal Law Doctrines: The Forgotten Influence of National Prohibition, at 74–103 (Durham, NC: Duke University Press, 1994), which notes that during Prohibition's latter years, the Supreme Court issued a series of rights-protective decisions that made enforcing the alcohol ban difficult.

11. *Weeks,* 232 U.S. 383 (1914).

12. 255 U.S. 298, 310 (1921): "The Government could desire . . . possession [of the relevant document] only to use it as evidence against the defendant and to search for and seize it for such purpose was unlawful." The Court did not use the phrase "mere evidence" in *Gouled;* that phrase was later used to capture the case's holding. See Warden v. Hayden, 387 U.S. 294 (1967) (overruling *Gouled*).

13. This was the position William O. Douglas later took in Berger v. New York, 388 U.S. 41, 64–67 (1967) (Douglas, J., concurring).

14. For the standard exposition of the point, see Telford Taylor, Two Studies in Constitutional Interpretation, at 27–29 (Columbus: Ohio State University Press, 1969).

15. *Lefkowitz,* 285 U.S. 452 (1932). In cases in which the suspect was arrested at home, the historical norm was to permit a search of the entire house or apartment. See Taylor, Two Studies, 27–29.

16. 287 U.S. 124, 127–28 (1932).

17. Compare Grau v. United States, 56 F.2d 779, 781 (6th Cir. 1932) ("One does not manufacture liquor for his own use in such quantities as to require wholesale deliveries of corn sugar or the other ingredients of mash") with *Grau,* 287 U.S., 128–29 ("While a dwelling used as a manufactory or headquarters for merchandising may well be and doubtless often is the place of sale, its use for those purposes is not alone probable cause for believing that actual sales are there made"). The Supreme Court's decision conflicts with the spirit, if not the letter, of contemporary drug cases that punish possession with intent to distribute the drugs. In those cases, the charge is usually proved by the quantity of drugs possessed—evidence that the Supreme Court found inadequate to show distribution in *Grau.*

18. *Sgro,* 287 U.S. 206 (1932).

19. The quoted term is used in Post, Prohibition and the Taft Court, 172: "A sumptuary law that was out of touch with the conscience of the community, and that was obeyed only because of an escalating spiral of repressive enforcement, was simply not sustainable."

20. *Olmstead,* 277 U.S., 456; *Grau,* 287 U.S., 127–28.

21. Kenneth Murchison argues that this fact is key, that the Court turned against Prohibition toward the end of its thirteen-year reign. See Murchison, Federal Criminal Law Doctrines, 74–103.

22. Michael J. Klarman, From Jim Crow to Civil Rights: The Supreme Court and the Struggle for Racial Equality, at 98 (New York: Oxford University Press, 2004).

23. From white Southerners' point of view, that thin veneer was a sign of racial *progress:* it was the means by which the court system prevented a lynching of the more customary kind. Ibid., 119–20.

24. Moore v. Dempsey, 261 U.S. 86, 91 (1923). Eight years earlier, the same claim had been raised and rejected—over Holmes's dissent—in Leo Frank's case. See Frank v. Mangum, 237 U.S. 309 (1915). Such claims had been granted by a number of southern state appellate courts, going back to the 1890s. See cases cited in Klarman, From Jim Crow to Civil Rights, 505n84.

25. 261 U.S., 89–90.

26. On southern cases, see Neil R. McMillen, Dark Journey: Black Mississippians in the Age of Jim Crow, at 206–15 (Urbana: University of Illinois Press, 1989). For a representative northern case, see United States ex rel. Darcy v. Handy, 203 F.2d 407 (3d Cir. 1953), in which the *Moore* claim prevailed. Compare *Darcy* with State v. Newsome, 143 S.E. 187 (N.C. 1928), in which the defendant was attacked during the course of the trial by men who proposed to drag him from the courtroom and lynch him. Order was restored; the defendant's trial continued and led to a conviction. The North Carolina Supreme Court held that these events were not sufficient cause for reversal. 143 S.E. at 194. (The court did reverse the conviction on other grounds: the trial judge had mistakenly declined to instruct the jury on second-degree murder.) As Klarman notes, if mob-dominated trials grew less common, the reason was the decline of actual and threatened lynchings, something over which the Supreme Court had no control. See Klarman, From Jim Crow to Civil Rights, 153.

27. For the facts in this paragraph, see Powell v. Alabama, 287 U.S. 45 (1932); Dan T. Carter, Scottsboro: A Tragedy of the American South, rev. ed., at 3–49 (Baton Rouge: Louisiana State University Press, 2007); James Goodman, Stories of Scottsboro, at xi, 1–26 (New York: Pantheon Books, 1994); Klarman, From Jim Crow to Civil Rights, 123–25.

28. 287 U.S. 45 (1932).

29. 294 U.S. 587 (1935).

30. Klarman, From Jim Crow to Civil Rights, 125.

31. See Goodman, Stories of Scottsboro, 396–97.

32. Ibid., 118–35, 209–14, 254–59.

33. Klarman notes that integrated jury pools became more common in the border South in the wake of *Norris* (From Jim Crow to Civil Rights, 127). All-white juries in places with large black populations became uncommon only after the Supreme Court's decision in Batson v. Kentucky, 476 U.S. 79 (1986), outlawing race-based use of peremptory challenges.

34. On the first proposition, note that the law of rape seems to have been designed to *prevent* convictions based solely on the victim's accusation. See Susan Estrich, Rape, Yale Law Journal, vol. 95, 1087–184, at 1094–132 (1986). On the second, see, for example, Carol S. Steiker, Remembering Race, Rape, and Capital Punishment, Virginia Law Review, vol. 83, 693–712, at 701–2, 706–7 (1997).

35. In the 1960s and after, both decisions were superseded by Sixth Amendment law. In place of *Powell*'s requirement of appointed counsel in capital cases, Gideon v. Wainwright, 372 U.S. 335 (1963), held that the Sixth Amendment required appointment of counsel in all felony cases. In place of *Norris*'s ban on discriminatory jury selection, Taylor v. Louisiana, 419 U.S. 522 (1975), and Duren v. Missouri, 439 U.S. 357 (1979), held that the Sixth Amendment required that the pool from which juries are chosen must represent a "fair cross section" of the community.

36. 297 U.S. 278 (1936).

37. See *Brown,* 297 U.S., 285–87; Brown v. State, 158 So. 339 (Miss. 1935); Klarman, From Jim Crow to Civil Rights, 117, 129 (quote), 131–33.

38. Twining v. New Jersey, 211 U.S. 78 (1908). With respect to the privilege's inapplicability to police interrogation, Eben Moglen has shown that, at the time of the Founding, there was a long tradition of pretrial examination of defendants by justices of the peace, without regard for the privilege against self-incrimination. Eben Moglen, Taking the Fifth: Reconsidering the Origins of the Constitutional Privilege against Self-Incrimination, Michigan Law Review, vol. 92, 1086–130, at 1094–111 (1994).

39. For a sampling of Supreme Court voluntariness cases, see Chambers v. Florida, 309 U.S. 227 (1940); Ashcraft v. Tennessee, 322 U.S. 143 (1944); Malinski v. New York, 324 U.S. 401 (1945); Watts v. Indiana, 338 U.S. 49 (1949); Fikes v. Alabama, 352 U.S. 191 (1957); Payne v. Arkansas, 356 U.S. 560 (1958); Spano v. New York, 360 U.S. 315 (1959); Blackburn v. Alabama, 361 U.S. 199 (1960); Rogers v. Richmond, 365 U.S. 534 (1961); Culombe v. Connecticut, 367 U.S. 568 (1961); and Davis v. North Carolina, 384 U.S. 737 (1966). In all the cases just cited, the Court found the defendant's confession involuntary.

40. See, for example, Spano v. New York, 360 U.S. 315 (1959), where a police officer's decision to pose as the suspect's friend rather than his interrogator was enough to render the confession involuntary.

41. The best source on the Till murder, and the primary source for the next few paragraphs, is Stephen J. Whitfield, A Death in the Delta: The Story of Emmett Till (New York: Free Press, 1988).

42. Ibid., 16–21.

43. Ibid., 22–23.

44. Ibid., 23–55. The ban on double jeopardy bars any further criminal proceedings in cases that end in an acquittal. See Fong Foo v. United States, 369 U.S. 141 (1962).

45. Whitfield, Death in the Delta, 20, 38–39.

46. For the classic statement, see Inmates of Attica Correctional Facility v. Rockefeller, 477 F.2d 375 (2d Cir. 1973).

47. The number of appellate cases was fewer in the 1950s than today, partly because the scope of the right to state-paid counsel on appeal was smaller. Today, that right applies not only to defendants who appeal trial convictions (see Douglas v. California, 372 U.S. 353 [1963]), but also to some defendants who plead guilty (see Halbert v. Michigan, 545 U.S. 605 [2005]).

48. See Klarman, From Jim Crow to Civil Rights, 271–73.

49. See Swain v. Alabama, 380 U.S. 202 (1965), which declined to put an end to race-based peremptory challenges, and Batson v. Kentucky, 476 U.S. 79 (1986), which belatedly did so.

50. See Robert M. Fogelson, Big-City Police, at 246 (Cambridge, MA: Harvard University Press, 1977).

51. See William O. Douglas, Vagrancy and Arrest on Suspicion, Yale Law Journal, vol. 70, 1–14 (1960); Caleb Foote, Vagrancy-Type Law and Its Administration, University of Pennsylvania Law Review, vol. 104, 603–50 (1956).

52. See Griffin v. Illinois, 351 U.S. 12 (1956).

53. 355 U.S. 225 (1957).

54. 370 U.S. 660 (1962).

55. 381 U.S. 479 (1965).

56. See Roe v. Wade, 410 U.S. 113 (1973); Lawrence v. Texas, 539 U.S. 558 (2003). On the limits of these rights, see, for example, Gonzales v. Carhart, 550 U.S. 124 (2007) (upholding statute banning "partial birth" abortion); *Lawrence,* 539 U.S. 578 (noting that the case's holding does not apply either to prostitution or to the legal definition of marriage).

57. *Robinson* also might have abolished strict liability, still an important concept in the law of statutory rape and regulatory crimes.

58. On *Lambert*'s failure, see, for example, United States v. Wilson, 159 F.3d 280 (7th Cir. 1998) (rejecting a *Lambert*-style fair notice argument). *Robinson* was all but undone by Powell v. Texas, 392 U.S. 514 (1968), a case in which an alcoholic was convicted of public drunkenness; the Court affirmed the conviction. And *Griswold* followed a path largely independent of criminal law once abortion rights took hold.

See Roe v. Wade, 410 U.S. 113 (1973); Planned Parenthood of Southeastern Pennsylvania v. Casey, 505 U.S. 833 (1992).

59. 351 U.S. 12 (1956).

60. 372 U.S. 353 (1963).

61. See, for example, Rachel King, Bush Justice: The Intersection of Alaska Natives and the Criminal Justice System in Rural Alaska, Oregon Law Review, vol. 77, 1–57, at 25–27 (1998). As King notes, detained defendants have higher conviction rates partly because they can often shorten their time of incarceration by pleading guilty.

62. 380 U.S. 202 (1965). Goldberg's dissent, joined by Warren and Fortas, appears at ibid., 228–47. For the facts of the case, see Swain v. State, 156 So.2d 368, 369–70 (Ala. 1963). Swain was charged with capital rape—a charge that was almost never brought, in Alabama or elsewhere, against anyone save black defendants accused of raping white women. That too was deemed no equal protection violation.

63. For the latest example, see McDonald v. Chicago, 130 S. Ct. 3020 (2010), which held that the Second Amendment applies to state and local governments through the Fourteenth Amendment's due process clause.

64. 384 U.S. 436 (1966).

65. Criminal procedure aficionados may take issue with this sentence, but it remains true. An important part of that truth lies in the proposition that, in this area, the law's standards often turn out to be rules in disguise. Consent searches must be voluntary, see Schneckloth v. Bustamonte, 412 U.S. 218 (1973), which sounds like the same open-ended standard used in Brown v. Mississippi, 297 U.S. 278 (1936). But voluntariness turns out to be automatic if the police put their command to search in the form of a question—even though most people take such questions as commands. Another piece of Fourth Amendment doctrine grants police officers the power to conduct street stops and frisks if they have reasonable grounds to suspect that the search target possesses a weapon. See Terry v. Ohio, 392 U.S. 1 (1968). That sounds like another open-ended standard, but it reduces to a rule: suspicion of crimes associated with violence—including drug crimes—automatically translates into reasonable suspicion of the presence of a weapon. Similarly, the complicated and seemingly standard-like law of search warrants boils down to the rule-like proposition that warrants are needed to search homes and offices, but—with rare exceptions—nowhere else.

66. 391 U.S. 145 (1968).

67. The best account of Duncan's story, from which the following paragraphs are drawn, is Nancy J. King, *Duncan v. Louisiana:* How Bigotry in the Bayou Led to the Federal Regulation of State Juries, in Carol S. Steiker, ed., Criminal Procedure Stories, at 261–93 (New York: Foundation Press, 2006). On the alleged slap, see Duncan v. Perez, 445 F.2d 557, 558–59 (5th Cir. 1971).

68. Ibid., 265–66.

69. Quoted in *Duncan,* 391 U.S., 146n1.

70. Quoted in State v. Poe, 38 So.2d 359, 364 (1948).

71. *Duncan,* 391 U.S., 146–47.

72. On Duncan's jury right, see *Duncan,* 391 U.S., 149–50, 159. On Louisiana's evasion of that right, see King, Bigotry in the Bayou, 281 and note 139. In the end, Duncan

prevailed—but not through his lawyer's jury argument. When local district attorney Leander Perez Jr.—son and namesake of Plaquemines Parish's longtime segregationist boss—tried to reprosecute Duncan, the federal district court enjoined the prosecution on the ground that the government had no legitimate interest in prosecuting such a trivial "crime." See Duncan v. Perez, 445 F.2d 557 (5th Cir. 1971). It was a one-off ruling: good for Duncan but for no one else—no body of law arose from the decision.

8. EARL WARREN'S ERRORS

1. See Kevin Starr, Golden Dreams: California in an Age of Abundance, 1950–1963, at 193 (New York: Oxford University Press, 2009).
2. Fred Graham makes this point. See Fred P. Graham, The Self-Inflicted Wound, at 4 (New York: Macmillan, 1970).
3. See Henry J. Friendly, The Bill of Rights as a Code of Criminal Procedure, California Law Review, vol. 53, 929–56 (1965).
4. See Miranda v. Arizona, 384 U.S. 436 (1966) (police station); Gideon v. Wainwright, 372 U.S. 335 (1963) (at trial); Douglas v. California, 372 U.S. 353 (1963) (on appeal).
5. For example, the right of the defense to see any material exculpatory evidence in the government's possession. See Brady v. Maryland, 373 U.S. 83 (1963).
6. *Mapp,* 367 U.S. 643 (1961).
7. *Miranda,* 384 U.S. 436 (1966).
8. U.S. Constitution, Amendments IV, V, and VI.
9. For the facts in this paragraph, see Yale Kamisar, *Mapp v. Ohio:* The First Shot Fired in the Warren Court's Criminal Procedure "Revolution," in Carol S. Steiker ed., Criminal Procedure Stories, 45–99, at 47–48 (New York: Foundation Press, 2006).
10. Ibid. The decision that adopted Mapp's First Amendment argument was Stanley v. Georgia, 394 U.S. 557 (1969).
11. The key evidence for a drop in the number of prosecutions is a modest drop in the number of arrests, and a larger drop in the number of prison inmates. On the arrests, see the "city arrests" table in the annual volumes of the Uniform Crime Reports. On prison inmates, see Online Sourcebook, table 6.28.2009.
12. Regarding school desegregation litigation, see, for example, Swann v. Charlotte-Mecklenburg Board of Education, 402 U.S. 1 (1971). Regarding prison conditions litigation, see Hutto v. Finney, 437 U.S. 678 (1978). On the rise of institutional injunction litigation more generally, see Abram Chayes, The Role of the Judge in Public Law Litigation, Harvard Law Review, vol. 89, 1281–316 (1976).
13. 379 U.S. 89 (1964).
14. 389 U.S. 347 (1967). See also Kyllo v. United States, 533 U.S. 27 (2001) (same conclusion where thermal imaging device was used to detect presence of marijuana plants in part of a private home).
15. 392 U.S. 1 (1968).
16. *Terry* was widely seen at the time and is widely seen today as a victory for criminal defendants because the Court did not require probable cause to arrest when officers

conducted street stops and frisks. But until a few years before *Terry,* those stops and frisks were, as a practical matter, wholly unregulated. Officers could justify most street seizures, brief or otherwise, on the ground that the suspect appeared to be loitering or was a vagrant. See William O. Douglas, Vagrancy and Arrest on Suspicion, Yale Law Journal, vol. 70, 1–14 (1960). Beginning in the mid-1960s, the Supreme Court began invalidating loitering and vagrancy laws; that trend reached its full fruition shortly after *Terry,* in Papachristou v. Jacksonville, 405 U.S. 156 (1972). Taken together, *Terry* and *Papachristou* required that officers have reasonable suspicion of a real crime in order to justify brief street seizures, instead of requiring that officers have probable cause of a phony crime defined so broadly that it permitted just about any street stop officers might wish to make. The standard that *Terry* and *Papachristou* established was demanding. The one that preceded those cases wasn't.

17. *Gideon,* 372 U.S. 335 (1963). On *Gideon*'s expansion, see Alabama v. Shelton, 535 U.S. 654 (2002); Argersinger v. Hamlin, 407 U.S. 25 (1972).

18. 372 U.S. 353 (1963). The *Douglas* right applied only to the first round of appeals. See Ross v. Moffitt, 417 U.S. 600 (1974).

19. 377 U.S. 201 (1964).

20. 378 U.S. 478 (1964).

21. *Miranda,* 384 U.S. 436, 479 (1966).

22. 384 U.S. at 473–75; see also Edwards v. Arizona, 451 U.S. 477 (1981); Minnick v. Mississippi, 498 U.S. 146 (1990). Or, the Court held still later, after a delay of at least two weeks. See Maryland v. Shatzer, 130 S. Ct. 1213 (2010).

23. This is why the ACLU's brief argued that no waiver could be valid without counsel's presence. See Brief for the American Civil Liberties Union as Amicus Curiae, at 22–25, Miranda v. Arizona, 384 U.S. 436 (1966).

24. The police can make offers, but the offers are not binding. See United States v. Flemmi, 225 F.3d 78 (1st Cir. 2000).

25. On the percentage of suspects who invoke their *Miranda* rights, see Richard A. Leo, The Impact of *Miranda* Revisited, Journal of Criminal Law and Criminology, vol. 86, 621–92, at 653 (1996). On the lax standard for *Miranda* waivers, see Berghuis v. Thompkins, 130 S. Ct. 2250 (2010). In that case, the Court found a valid waiver where the defendant remained silent in the face of questioning for nearly three hours. Apparently, as long as the defendant talks *sometime,* he has waived his *Miranda* rights. The language quoted in the text comes from the *Miranda* majority, 384 U.S. at 455. The three verbs were meant to capture what the police could not do, not what they could do.

26. Yale Kamisar, Equal Justice in the Gatehouses and Mansions of American Criminal Procedure, in A. E. Dick Howard, ed., Criminal Justice in Our Time, at 1–95 (Charlottesville: University Press of Virginia, 1965).

27. Recidivists disproportionately invoke their *Miranda* rights (see Leo, *Miranda* Revisited, 654–55), while the police do not bother to interrogate most white-collar suspects on the assumption that they would always invoke their rights.

28. Virginian James Madison was the Bill's primary author; several of its provisions were modeled on the Virginia Declaration of Rights authored by George Mason.

29. On the one-sidedness of the warrant process, see William J. Stuntz, Warrants and Fourth Amendment Remedies, Virginia Law Review, vol. 77, 881–942, at 881 (1991). On the low rate at which warrant applications are denied, see Richard Van Duizend et al., The Search Warrant Process: Preconceptions, Perceptions, and Practices (Williamsburg: National Center for State Courts, 1985).

30. David Sklansky notes that a great deal of criminal procedure doctrine rests on the proposition that adversarial justice systems are superior to inquisitorial systems— but with no clear rationale explaining why that proposition is true. See David Alan Sklansky, Anti-Inquisitorialism, Harvard Law Review, vol. 122, 1634–704, at 1636– 39 (2009).

31. See Mapp v. Ohio, 367 U.S. 643 (1961). Wolf v. Colorado, 338 U.S. 25 (1949), had already held that state and local police were bound by the Fourth Amendment, but *Wolf* provided no remedy for Fourth Amendment violations. *Mapp* marks the moment when Fourth Amendment rules began to affect local policing.

32. See Malloy v. Hogan, 378 U.S. 1 (1964), and Benton v. Maryland, 395 U.S. 784 (1969), respectively.

33. Gideon v. Wainwright, 372 U.S. 335 (1963).

34. Duncan v. Louisiana, 391 U.S. 145 (1968).

35. Pointer v. Texas, 380 U.S. 400 (1965).

36. Washington v. Texas, 388 U.S. 14 (1967).

37. That right, in turn, has become a part of the law of capital punishment, not criminal procedure more generally: with few exceptions, only capital murder defendants prevail on their ineffective assistance claims (sometimes). See Nancy J. King et al., Habeas Litigation in U.S. District Courts: An Empirical Study of *Habeas Corpus* Cases Filed by State Prisoners under the Antiterrorism and Effective Death Penalty Act of 1996, at 51–52 (Washington, DC: U.S. Department of Justice, 2007). Of the 368 capital cases that King and her coauthors studied, a mere 33 (9 percent) led to a grant of relief for habeas petitioners. Of the 2384 noncapital cases the authors studied, only seven habeas petitioners won relief: less than one-third of 1 percent of the total.

38. On the Sixth Amendment and jury selection, see Duren v. Missouri, 439 U.S. 357 (1979); Batson v. Kentucky, 476 U.S. 79 (1986). Formally, *Batson* and the many cases that follow it are based on the Fourteenth Amendment's equal protection clause, not on the Sixth Amendment's jury right. Functionally, *Batson*'s doctrine is best seen as a means of applying *Duren*'s fair cross-section principle—the idea that the pool or "venire" from which juries are chosen must represent a fair cross section of the local population—to the selection of individual jurors. On the body of Sixth Amendment law that defines the relationship between juries and sentencing, see Apprendi v. New Jersey, 530 U.S. 466 (2000); Blakely v. Washington, 542 U.S. 296 (2004); Oregon v. Ice, 129 S. Ct. 711 (2009).

39. 380 U.S. 400 (1965).

40. 554 U.S. 353 (2008).

41. 129 S. Ct. 2527 (2009).

42. Sklansky, Anti-Inquisitorialism, 1655, makes this point.

43. See Corinna Barrett Lain, Countermajoritarian Hero or Zero? Rethinking the Warren Court's Role in the Criminal Procedure Revolution, University of Pennsylvania Law Review, vol. 152, 1361–452, at 1379–82, 1389–99 (2004).

44. Michael McConville and Chester L. Mirsky, Criminal Defense of the Poor in New York City, New York Review of Law and Social Change, vol. 15, 581–964, at 767 (1986–1987).

45. Richard Klein and Robert Spangenberg, The Indigent Defense Crisis, at 8 (prepared for the American Bar Association Section of Criminal Justice Ad Hoc Committee on Indigent Defense Crisis, 1993).

46. For the content of those rights, see Strickland v. Washington, 466 U.S. 668 (1984), and Kyles v. Whitley, 514 U.S. 419 (1995), respectively.

47. Plaquemines Parish was an example: the local political boss, Leander Perez Sr.—father of the district attorney who prosecuted Duncan—established what amounted to a concentration camp for civil rights protesters; the camp was filled by the relevant local authorities, not by mobs. Nancy J. King, *Duncan v. Louisiana:* How Bigotry in the Bayou Led to the Federal Regulation of State Juries, in Carol S. Steiker, ed., Criminal Procedure Stories, 261–93, at 264 (New York: Foundation Press, 2006).

48. Margaret Werner Cahalan, Historical Corrections Statistics in the United States, 1850–1984, at 30, table 3-3 (Rockville, MD: Bureau of Justice Statistics, 1986).

49. For the prisoner data, see Bureau of the Census, U.S. Department of Commerce, Prisoners in State and Federal Prisons and Reformatories: 1937, at 28, table 22; Federal Bureau of Prisons, National Prisoner Statistics: State Prisoners: Admissions and Releases, 1964, at 23, table A8 (Washington, DC: Government Printing Office, 1964). For the population data, see 1965 Statistical Abstract, at 26, no. 23.

50. Hortense Powdermaker's study of homicides in Depression-era Mississippi, a time and place where white-on-black crime was appallingly common, still shows that most homicides were committed by persons of the same race as their victims. It also shows how rarely blacks killed whites in the Jim Crow South. Hortense Powdermaker, After Freedom: A Cultural Study in the Deep South, at 395–96 (New York: Viking Press, 1939).

51. Both numbers of prisoners and the state populations used to calculate imprisonment rates are taken from 1952 Statistical Abstract, 11, no. 10; 146, no. 175; and 1965 Statistical Abstract, 11, no. 7; 158, no. 220. The figures on homicides in the listed cities are taken from Uniform Crime Reports: 1950, part 2, 94–101, table 35; and Uniform Crime Reports: 1963, 155–70, table 49. The city populations used to calculate homicide rates appear in Campbell Gibson and Kay Jung, U.S. Census Bureau, Historical Census Statistics on Population Totals by Race, 1790 to 1990, and by Hispanic Origin, 1970 to 1990, for Large Cities and Other Urban Places in the United States (Washington, DC: U.S. Census Bureau, Working Paper No. 76, February 2005).

52. The data on arrests (including the total population of the cities reporting) are taken from the "city arrest" and "city arrest by race" tables in the 1960 and 1968 volumes of the Uniform Crime Reports. The racial composition of the urban population is taken from data in the annual volumes of the Statistical Abstract.

53. Nationwide, both black and white imprisonment fell in the 1960s: see Cahalan, Historical Corrections Statistics, 65, table 3-31, and 193, table 8-2. These tables show that while the U.S. population rose between 1960 and 1970, the rate of imprisonment for both blacks and whites fell, although the black share of the (smaller) imprisoned population rose from 37 percent to 41 percent. Given southern punishment trends, that meant substantial drops in black imprisonment in the Northeast, Midwest, and West.

54. Hidden from appellate courts—but not from black communities, which saw police neglect and police brutality as comparably serious problems. Michael W. Flamm, Law and Order: Street Crime, Civil Unrest, and the Crisis of Liberalism in the 1960s, at 137 (New York: Columbia University Press, 2005).

55. Ibid., 58 (Los Angeles), 87 (Newark), 92 (Detroit).

56. See Presidential Elections, 1789–2008, at 160–61 (Washington, DC: CQ Press, 2010).

57. Nationwide, the homicide rate rose from 5 per 100,000 in 1961 to 10 in 1973; the imprisonment rate fell from 119 per 100,000 to 96 during the same years. Homicide data are taken from Monkkonen; for the imprisonment data, see Online Sourcebook, table 6.28.2009.

58. For a similar account that is more sympathetic to the Warren Court's decisions, see Carol S. Steiker, Counter-Revolution in Criminal Procedure? Two Audiences, Two Answers, Michigan Law Review, vol. 94, 2466–551 (1996). Steiker notes, rightly, that the generous waiver doctrines of the 1970s and after had the effect of undermining the Warren Court's decisions, yet left those decisions intact as targets of political attack.

59. For a study showing that most people do think that—even people who are unusually well-informed about their legal rights—see David K. Kessler, Free to Leave? An Empirical Look at the Court's Seizure Standard, Journal of Criminal Law and Criminology, vol. 99, 51–88 (2009). On the ease of showing consent, see Ohio v. Robinette, 517 U.S. 33 (1996); Schneckloth v. Bustamonte, 412 U.S. 218 (1973); Janice Nadler, No Need to Shout: Bus Sweeps and the Psychology of Coercion, Supreme Court Review, vol. 2002, 153–222.

60. On the meaning of *Miranda*'s waiver standard, see, for example, Moran v. Burbine, 475 U.S. 412, 420–28 (1986). On the ease of obtaining waivers, see Leo, *Miranda* Revisited, 653.

61. See, for example, Miles v. Dorsey, 61 F.3d 1459 (10th Cir. 1995), in which prosecutors threatened to charge the defendant's parents if the defendant refused to plead guilty; the plea was held to be voluntary; United States v. Pollard, 959 F.2d 1011 (D.C. Cir. 1992), in which prosecutors threatened to charge the defendant's wife if the defendant refused to plead guilty; the plea was held to be voluntary.

62. Louis Michael Seidman, *Brown* and *Miranda,* California Law Review, vol. 80, 673–753, at 742–47 (1992).

63. See Nadler, No Need to Shout, 208–10.

64. In a 1962 study of criminal litigation in 28 counties, the author found a plea rate of 74 percent for defendants with court-appointed lawyers and 48 percent for defendants

with retained counsel. Lee Silverstein, Defense of the Poor in Criminal Cases in American State Courts: A Field Study and Report, at 22–23 (Chicago: American Bar Foundation, 1965). (The latter category was a good deal larger then than it is now.) Forty-four years later, a study of criminal litigation in seventy-five metropolitan counties found that more than 95 percent of felony convictions were by guilty plea. Online Sourcebook, table 5.57.2006.

65. On the elder Taft's opposition to Prohibition, see Robert Post, Federalism in the Taft Court Era: Can It Be "Revived"? Duke Law Journal, vol. 51, 1513–639, at 1540–41n109 (2002). On then-Senator Taft's criticism of the Nuremberg trials on rule-of-law grounds, see James T. Patterson, Mr. Republican: A Biography of Robert A. Taft, at 326–29 (Boston: Houghton Mifflin, 1972). The younger Taft's libertarianism ran deep: while serving in the Ohio legislature, he opposed Klan-sponsored legislation banning dancing on Sundays and mandating Bible readings in public schools (ibid., 96–97, 100–02). On his relationship with Senator McCarthy, see ibid., 445–49.

66. Interestingly, neither Wallace nor Reagan had deep roots in American conservatism. Wallace grew to political maturity as a liberal populist and ally of "Big Jim" Folsom, one of the South's most liberal midcentury politicians. See Stephan Lesher, George Wallace: American Populist, at 81–83, 99–101 (New York: Addison-Wesley, 1994). Before his ideological conversion, Reagan was a pro–New Deal Democrat. Matthew Dallek, The Right Moment, at 1, 29–32 (New York: Free Press, 2000).

67. Two generations of southern members of Congress fought to prevent federal anti-lynching legislation; Lyndon Johnson's first speech in the Senate was an argument against such legislation. See Robert A. Caro, The Years of Lyndon Johnson: Master of the Senate, at 187–202, 212–18 (New York: Alfred A. Knopf, 2002). During his Dixiecrat campaign for the White House, Strom Thurmond told New Yorkers that federal civil rights legislation would be as much an affront to his state as a federal ban on gangland murders would be to theirs. Zachary Karabell, The Last Campaign: How Harry Truman Won the 1948 Election, at 224 (New York: Alfred A. Knopf, 2000).

68. The first quote appears in Lucas A. Powe Jr., The Warren Court and American Politics, at 410 (Cambridge, MA: Harvard University Press, 2000). The second appears in Dan T. Carter, Legacy of Rage: George Wallace and the Transformation of American Politics, Journal of Southern History, vol. 62, 3–26, at 11 (1996). On Wallace's electoral performance in 1964 and 1968, see Lesher, George Wallace, 284–85, 295, 303–04; Michael Barone, Our Country: The Shaping of America from Roosevelt to Reagan, at 434–36, 449–51 (New York: Free Press, 1990).

69. The quote appears in Dallek, Right Moment, 195. Reagan's opponent, Pat Brown—the two-term Democratic governor and father of Reagan's successor (and the current California governor), Jerry Brown—was known as "the giant killer" because of his two previous gubernatorial victories (ibid., 13–16, 20–23). Brown won the office in 1958 by beating then-Senator William Knowland, a leading presidential contender before his defeat. Four years later, Brown won reelection by beating former Vice President Richard Nixon, who had narrowly missed winning the presidency in 1960.

70. Ibid., 185–89, 195–96, for discussion of Reagan's use of campus disorder in his first gubernatorial campaign; Lou Cannon, Governor Reagan: His Rise to Power, at 122, 132–33, 139–40 (New York: PublicAffairs, 2003), for discussion of Reagan's opposition to the Civil Rights Act of 1964; ibid., 263–68, for details on Reagan's efforts to appeal to Wallace supporters during his 1968 campaign for the Republican presidential nomination.

71. On Eisenhower's vote, see Doug McAdam, Political Process and the Development of Black Insurgency, 1930–1970, at 158 (Chicago: University of Chicago Press, 1982); on Nixon's, see Barone, Our Country, 557.

72. See Caro, Master of the Senate, 841–1012.

73. Democrats won the large congressional majority they held throughout the 1960s in the off-year election of 1958, in which Republican candidates throughout the country campaigned for anti-union right-to-work laws. See Barone, Our Country, 301–04.

74. For the best discussions to date, see Flamm, Law and Order, 124–41; Jonathan Simon, Governing through Crime, at 75–110 (New York: Oxford University Press, 2007).

75. The focus of Estes Kefauver's Senate hearings in 1950–1951 was Mafia influence over big-city Democratic machines. Robert Kennedy first won fame as chief counsel to the Senate committee holding hearings on labor racketeering in the late 1950s, the same hearings that made Jimmy Hoffa a household name.

76. California's imprisonment rate fell from 146 in 1966 to 84 in 1972. 1968 Statistical Abstract, 12, table 11; 159, table 237; 1991 Sourcebook, 637, table 6.72. In the meantime, the state's murder rate doubled. Sean Wilentz, The Age of Reagan: A History, 1974–2008, at 133–34 (New York: HarperCollins, 2008). Between 1962 and 1976, Alabama's imprisonment rate fell from 166 to 83. See 1964 Statistical Abstract, 11, table 8; 159, table 216; 1991 Sourcebook, 637, table 6.72. Wallace and his wife Lurleen governed the state for eleven of those fourteen years, winning four consecutive gubernatorial elections between them.

77. Like Wallace and Reagan before him, Nixon was no lifelong conservative. In 1960, he sought the White House by running to the left, seeking and winning Rockefeller's support and angering Barry Goldwater and the Republican right in the process. See Barone, Our Country, 330. In 1968, Nixon switched sides, winning longtime segregationist Strom Thurmond's support at the cost of alienating the pro–civil rights Rockefeller wing of the party (ibid., 442). The "law and order" issue played a key role in that right turn, and in Nixon's subsequent victory. See Flamm, Law and Order, 162–78.

78. The Act seeking to overrule *Miranda* can be found at Pub. L. No. 90–351, 82 Stat. 197 (1968). For the story of Johnson's involvement with this legislation, see Flamm, Law and Order, 132–41. On the recent history of federal crime legislation, see Nancy E. Marion, A History of Federal Crime Control Initiatives, 1960–1993 (Westport, CT: Praeger, 1994).

79. On crime and Kennedy's campaign, see Flamm, Law and Order, 148–50. On Georgia and Alabama imprisonment rates in the early and mid-1970s, see 1991 Sourcebook,

637, table 6.72. On the Rockefeller laws, see Alan Chartock, Narcotics Addiction: The Politics of Frustration, Proceedings of the Academy of Political Science, vol. 31, 239–49, at 242–48 (1974). Those laws were signed in 1973. New York's imprisonment rate fell in at least ten of the preceding fifteen years (data concerning two of the remaining five years are missing). For the data, see the annual volumes of Statistical Abstract. The year of 1973 saw the first of twenty-seven consecutive increases in that rate. 2003 Sourcebook, 501, table 6.29; 1991 Sourcebook, 637, table 6.72.

80. Between 1972 and 1980, the nation's imprisonment rate rose by half, after falling by 22 percent in the preceding eleven years. Online Sourcebook, table 6.28.2006.

81. Compare Simon, Governing through Crime, 49–52, the discussion of Robert Kennedy's posture toward crime; 90–101, the discussion for Lyndon Johnson. For an argument that the punitive turn did come from the right, and that it was consciously chosen from the beginning, see Vesla M. Weaver, Frontlash: Race and the Development of Punitive Crime Police, Studies in American Political Development, vol. 21, 230–65 (2007).

82. For the best account of the passage of the federal legislation that mandated the 100:1 crack-powder sentencing ratio—meaning possession of one gram of crack cocaine was punished as severely as possession of one hundred grams of cocaine powder—see David A. Sklansky, Cocaine, Race, and Equal Protection, Stanford Law Review, vol. 47, 1283–322 (1995). In 1980, the year before Reagan took office, the federal imprisonment rate was 9 per 100,000. By 1989—the year Reagan left the White House—the federal imprisonment rate had risen to 19. Online Sourcebook, table 6.29.2008. During the same years, the state imprisonment rate rose from 130 to 253 (ibid.).

83. On the usual partisan pattern—with Republican governors correlated with higher incarceration rates—see Bruce Western, Punishment and Inequality in America, at 71 (New York: Russell Sage Foundation, 2006). For the data cited in the text, see Online Sourcebook, table 6.29.2008; 2003 Sourcebook, 501, table 6.29. With respect to George Allen's campaign to end parole in Virginia, see Donald P. Baker, Winner Talks Tough, Cites Mandate for Change, Washington Post, November 4, 1993, at A1. The figures in this paragraph were calculated using the imprisonment rates reported in the Online Sourcebook as of December 31 of the relevant years. Because governors usually begin their terms in early January, there is a nearly year-long time lag between the beginning of each new governor's term and the reported imprisonment rate which, in the text, I attribute to that governor's term in office. The time lag is consciously chosen; it ordinarily takes at least a year for state-level policy decisions to affect the relevant state's imprisonment rate.

84. See Christopher Lydon, Sex, War, and Death: Covering Clinton Became a Test of Character—For the Press, Columbia Journalism Review, May–June 1992, 57–60.

85. Even Atwater found it distasteful, after the fact. See John Brady, Bad Boy: The Life and Politics of Lee Atwater, at 315–16 (Reading, MA: Addison Wesley, 1997).

86. According to the Uniform Crime Reports' "city arrest" tables, the arrest rate actually rose 6 percent from 1964 to 1969. Uniform Crime Reports: 1964, at 119, table 26; Uniform Crime Reports: 1969, at 121, table 32. During those same years, the nation's imprisonment rate fell 13 percent. Online Sourcebook, table 6.28.2009.

87. Arkansas, Kentucky, New Hampshire, New Jersey, Rhode Island, Tennessee, and Wisconsin all saw increases in state imprisonment rates during the 1960s. See Cahalan, Historical Corrections Statistics, 30, table 3-3.
88. On the Court and the 1968 campaign, see Simon, Governing through Crime, 114–16. On crime as the top domestic issue, see George Gallup, The Gallup Poll: Public Opinion, 1935–1971, at 2107–08 (New York: Random House, 1972).
89. A single survey showed public support for *Miranda*. See Lain, Countermajoritarian, 1423–24. Other surveys showed substantial majorities opposed to *Miranda;* for Lain's discussion of those surveys, see ibid., 1421–24. The provision purporting to repeal *Miranda* was a part of the Omnibus Crime Control and Safe Streets Act of 1968, Pub. L. No. 90-351, 82 Stat. 197. The same legislation also established the Law Enforcement Assistance Administration—which, for the first time, put significant federal money into local law enforcement. For a history of the LEAA, see Malcolm M. Feeley and Austin D. Sarat, The Policy Dilemma: Federal Crime Policy and the Law Enforcement Assistance Administration, 1968–1978 (Minneapolis: University of Minnesota Press, 1980).
90. Dickerson v. United States, 530 U.S. 428 (2000).
91. Texas v. Johnson, 491 U.S. 397 (1989).
92. Miranda v. Arizona, 384 U.S. 436 (1966); Mapp v. Ohio, 367 U.S. 643 (1961). The vote on the result in *Mapp* was 6 to 3, but Potter Stewart voted to decide the case on different grounds than the other members of the *Mapp* majority. Only four of his colleagues joined Tom Clark's majority opinion.
93. On the politics of Brennan's appointment, see Seth Stern and Steven Wermeil, Justice Brennan: Liberal Champion, at 74–80 (New York: Houghton Mifflin Harcourt, 2010).
94. For a good discussion of Warren's days as the tough-on-crime district attorney of Alameda County, California, see Jed Handelsman Shugerman, The People's Courts, at ch. 9, "Earl Warren, Crime, and the Revival of Appointment" (Cambridge, MA: Harvard University Press, forthcoming 2011).
95. On Dewey's rejection of Eisenhower's offer, see Richard Norton Smith, Thomas E. Dewey and His Times, at 605 (New York: Simon & Schuster, 1982). On Warren's background, see John D. Weaver, Warren: The Man, The Court, The Era, at 45–50, 105–14 (Boston: Little, Brown, 1967). Dewey's quotes appear in Smith, Dewey and His Times, 607–08.
96. See Graham, Self-Inflicted Wound.

9. THE RISE AND FALL OF CRIME, THE FALL AND RISE OF CRIMINAL PUNISHMENT

1. With respect to the imprisonment figures, see Online Sourcebook, table 6.28.2009. With respect to the crime data, see Crime in the United States—2003, 11; Uniform Crime Reports: 1991, 10. Those data show a drop in violent crime of 37 percent.
2. For the national figures, I use Monkkonen's estimated national rate for homicides, and the Sourcebook's historical imprisonment table, see Online Sourcebook, table

6.28.2009, for imprisonment rates. For regional and local trends, I rely on the city homicide numbers in the annual volumes of the Uniform Crime Reports, and on the prison population data in the annual volumes of the Statistical Abstract. For state populations (used to calculate imprisonment rates), I again use the annual volumes of the Statistical Abstract. For city populations (used to calculate urban homicide rates), I rely on Campbell Gibson and Kay Jung, U.S. Census Bureau, Historical Census Statistics on Population Totals by Race, 1790 to 1990, and by Hispanic Origin, 1970 to 1990, for Large Cities and Other Urban Places in the United States (Washington, DC: U.S. Census Bureau, Working Paper No. 76, February 2005).

3. According to Monkkonen's data, the nation's homicide rate stood at 5 per 100,000 in 1950, rising to 10 by 1973. In New York, the analogous figures are 4 and 22; in Detroit, 6 and 48. See Uniform Crime Reports: 1950, 95–99, table 35; Uniform Crime Reports: 1973, 223–24, table 75; Gibson and Jung, Historical Census Statistics.

4. The nation's murder rate fell from 10 per 100,000 in 1973 to 8 in 1985, rising to 10 in 1991. See Monkkonen's data; Uniform Crime Reports: 1985, 7; Uniform Crime Reports: 1991, 13. Between 1973 and 1991, Detroit's murder rate rose from 48 to 59, Houston's rose from 20 to 37, Los Angeles' rose from 18 to 29, and New York's rose from 22 to 30. See Uniform Crime Reports: 1973, 223–24, table 75; Uniform Crime Reports: 1991, 108–56, table 8; Gibson and Jung, Historical Census Statistics.

5. See Daniel Patrick Moynihan, Defining Deviancy Down, The American Spectator, Winter 1993, at 17–30. The argument has a long pedigree. Émile Durkheim wrote in 1895 that the amount of deviant behavior that any society is willing to condemn is basically fixed. See Émile Durkheim, The Rules of Sociological Method, 8th ed., trans. Sarah A. Solovay and John H. Mueller, at 99 (orig. published 1895; New York: Free Press, 1964). Seventy years later, Kai Erikson found that Durkheim's insight appeared to fit the experience of the seventeenth-century Massachusetts Bay colony. Kai Erikson, Wayward Puritans (New York: Wiley, 1966). As noted in the text, Durkheim's argument does not fit the experience of the twentieth-century United States.

6. Federal Bureau of Prisons, National Prisoner Statistics: Prisoners in State and Federal Institutions: 1950, at 55, table 21 (Washington, DC: Government Printing Office, 1954).

7. See Robert M. Fogelson, Big-City Police, at 17–30, 123–24, 248 (Cambridge, MA: Harvard University Press, 1977).

8. Joan Jacoby's discussion of urban prosecutors' offices is telling. In the chapter that examines political constraints on local prosecutors, Jacoby treats urban prosecutors as constrained primarily by docket pressure and bureaucratic form. See Joan A. Jacoby, The American Prosecutor: A Search for Identity, at 64–71 (Lexington, MA: D. C. Heath, 1980).

9. See, for example, Carolyn B. Ramsey, The Discretionary Power of "Public" Prosecutors in Historical Perspective, American Criminal Law Review, vol. 39, 1309–93, at 1342–47, 1356–60 (2002). Compare Jeffrey S. Adler, "It Is His First Offense. We Might as Well Let Him Go": Homicide and Criminal Justice in Chicago, 1875–1920, Journal of Social History, Fall 2006, 5–24 (attributing low incidence of punishment for Chicago homicides to local juries, not to local prosecutors).

10. Ramsey, Discretionary Power of "Public" Prosecutors, has the best discussion of the politicized character of local prosecutors in the late nineteenth century, and of elite response to it. For the study of Cleveland prosecutions, see Roscoe Pound and Felix Frankfurter, eds., Criminal Justice in Cleveland, at 544–55 (Philadelphia: Wm. F. Fell, 1922).

11. See David Garland, The Culture of Control: Crime and Social Order in Contemporary Society, at 95–96 (Chicago: University of Chicago Press, 2001).

12. Quoted in Rick Perlstein, Nixonland: The Rise of a President and the Fracturing of America, at 343 (New York: Scribner, 2008).

13. See Ethan Brown, Snitch: Informants, Cooperators, and the Corruption of Justice, at 9–12 (New York: PublicAffairs, 2007).

14. Concerning the run-up in imprisonment that began in 1973, see Online Sourcebook, table 6.28.2009. Concerning the earlier run-up in imprisonment that took hold in the 1920s and 1930s, see ibid., and Margaret Werner Cahalan, Historical Corrections Statistics in the United States, 1850–1984, at 30, table 3-3 (Rockville, MD: Bureau of Justice Statistics, 1986) On the 49 percent drop in homicide rates that began in 1934, see Monkkonen's homicide data.

15. This point seems to run counter to Bruce Western's argument that changes in crime rates had little effect on the imprisonment rate. See Bruce Western, Punishment and Inequality in America, at 34–43, 180–83 (New York: Russell Sage Foundation, 2006). Actually, the two points are consistent. Western's argument applies to changes in crime *during* the run-up in imprisonment. My claim is more general: that the punitive turn was in large measure the product of a backlash, and that the backlash was prompted, again in large measure, by a generation-long crime wave that began in the 1950s—long before the run-up in imprisonment. In addition, that backlash was immeasurably strengthened by the fact that the first two decades of that crime wave corresponded with *falling* prison populations. Western acknowledges this link between crime and punishment trends (ibid., 48–49).

16. The state's subsidy of criminal punishment is a crucial fact was ignored in the legal literature until Robert Misner highlighted it. See Robert L. Misner, Recasting Prosecutorial Discretion, Journal of Criminal Law and Criminology, vol. 86, 717–77 (1996). On local governments' responsibility for the expense of local policing, see Online Sourcebook, table 1.4.2006.

17. The numbers of prison inmates and police officers per 100,000 population in 1970 were 96 and 204, respectively. Online Sourcebook, table 6.28.2009; Uniform Crime Reports: 1970, 163, table 51. In 1989, the analogous numbers were 276 and 210. Online Sourcebook, table 6.28.2009; Uniform Crime Reports: 1989, 238, table 66. In 2008, the imprisonment rate had risen to 504, while the number of police officers per 100,000 population had risen only to 232. Online Sourcebook, table 6.28.2009; Crime in the United States: 2008, table 71.

18. For different versions of that claim, see Garland, Culture of Control at 98–102, 196–97; Jonathan Simon, Governing through Crime, at 6–7 (New York: Oxford University Press, 2007); Vesla M. Weaver, Frontlash: Race and the Development of Punitive Crime Police, Studies in American Political Development, vol. 21, 230–65 (2007).

19. On state and local spending on prisons and jails, schools, health care, and high-ways, see Online Sourcebook, table 1.4.2005; 2009 Statistical Abstract, 266, table 4.18. With respect to federal spending, both totals and on federal prisons, see Online Sourcebook, table 1.4.2005; 2009 Statistical Abstract, 303, table 453.

20. In the 1990s, state and local revenues nearly doubled; those revenues rose 2.5 times between 1990 and 2005 (2009 Statistical Abstract, 265, table 417). Federal revenues quadrupled between 1980 and 2000 (ibid., 302, table 451).

21. See Uniform Crime Reports: 1976, 188, table 36; 225, table 59; Uniform Crime Reports: 1989, 193, table 39; 238, table 66. The increase in urban arrests per officer was just over 32 percent.

22. On the number of local prosecutors, see Carol J. DeFrances, Prosecutors in State Courts—1990, at 1–2 (Washington, DC: Bureau of Justice Statistics, 1992), which shows the rise in the number of local prosecutors from 17,000 in 1974 to 20,000 in 1990. On the number of felony prosecutions, compare National Center for State Courts, State Court Caseload Statistics: Annual Report 1984, at 189–90, table 35 (1986), which shows a 36 percent increase in felony filings from 1978 to 1984, with National Center for State Courts, State Court Caseload Statistics: Annual Report 1991, 37, table 1.25 (1993), which shows a 51 percent increase in felony filings from 1985 to 1991. If filings were constant from 1984 to 1985, this would mean a 105 percent increase from 1978 to 1991. Undoubtedly, filings did not hold constant for that year, and the growth in felony filings did not begin in 1978. Given those reasonable suppositions, it seems likely that filings grew by at least 135 percent or thereabouts between 1974 and 1990—in which case felony prosecutions per prosecutor doubled during those years.

23. Total spending on indigent defense rose slightly more than 60 percent in constant dollars between 1979 and 1990. See 1993 Sourcebook, 3, table 1.3; 1996 Statistical Abstract, 483. Meanwhile, the percentage of cases in which defendants were given appointed counsel was also rising, from just under half in the late 1970s and early 1980s to 80 percent by 1992. Bureau of Justice Statistics, U.S. Department of Justice, National Criminal Defense Systems Study, 33 (1986); Steven K. Smith and Carol J. DeFrances, Indigent Defense, Bureau of Justice Statistics Selected Findings, February 1996, at 1, 4. And the total number of criminal cases was rising as well: state court felony filings more than doubled between 1978 and 1990 (see the sources cited in the preceding note). Thus, notwithstanding nominal budget increases, spending on indigent defendants in constant dollars per case appears to have fallen by about half between the late 1970s and the early 1990s.

24. The number of local prosecutors rose from approximately 17,000 in 1974 to approximately 26,500 in 2005. See DeFrances, Prosecutors in State Courts—1990, 1–2; Stephen W. Perry, Prosecutors in State Courts—2005, at 2 (Washington, DC: Bureau of Justice Statistics, 2006). With respect to the number of state prison inmates, both in the early 1970s and in 2005, see Online Sourcebook, tables 6.28.2009, 6.29.2008.

25. 434 U.S. 357 (1978).

26. Ibid., 358–59.

27. See United States v. Pollard, 959 F.2d 1011 (D.C. Cir. 1992).

28. See Miles v. Dorsey, 61 F.3d 1459 (10th Cir. 1995).

29. See Albert W. Alschuler, Plea Bargaining and the Death Penalty, DePaul Law Review, vol. 58, 671–80 (2009).

30. A good example comes from the conventional definition of second-degree murder, which includes homicides committed with a "depraved heart." See, for example, State v. Robinson, 934 P.2d 38 (Kan. 1997).

31. 342 U.S. 246 (1952).

32. Ibid., 247–49.

33. Ibid., 276 (emphasis in original).

34. 31 Cal. Rptr. 2d 887 (Court of Appeals, Third Appellate District 1994).

35. Ibid., 887–88.

36. Ibid., 888–90.

37. The difference is not simply the consequence of the fact that Morissette's crime—theft—was traditionally classified as a specific intent crime, while Stark's required proof only of general intent. First, Jackson's opinion in *Morissette* did not rely on the categorization of the intent standard. Second, today's version of specific intent likewise requires no finding of wrongful intent, but only the intent to bring about a legally forbidden result, which Joe Morissette had.

38. On the law of intoxication and criminal intent, see, for example, People v. Hood, 462 P.2d 370 (Cal. 1969).

39. See, for example, State v. Keeton, 710 N.W.2d 531 (Iowa 2006).

40. See, for example, People v. Sparks, 47 P.3d 289 (Cal. 2002).

41. See, for example, People v. Perry, 864 N.E.2d 196 (Ill. 2007).

42. See 18 U.S.C. § 1346. Under a recent Supreme Court decision narrowing the scope of "honest services" fraud, the "intangible right of honest services" is infringed only by schemes involving bribes or kickbacks. Skilling v. United States, 130 S. Ct. 2896 (2010).

43. The proposition that false promises yield liability dates to Durland v. United States, 161 U.S. 306 (1896). As for the sufficiency of even passive deception, see, for example, Carpenter v. United States, 484 U.S. 19 (1987).

44. The rule cited in the text comes from Blockburger v. United States, 284 U.S. 299 (1932).

45. See Francis Wharton, A Treatise on Criminal Law, 3rd ed., rev. by Wm. Draper Lewis, at §§ 550, 576–78 (Philadelphia: Kay & Brother, 1896).

46. The most famous example of this phenomenon is State in the Interest of M.T.S., 609 A.2d 1266 (N.J. 1992). But the best evidence of the phenomenon is the growing body of law on what is called "post-penetration rape"—meaning rape that happens after intercourse has begun. For an example in the case law, see In re John Z., 60 P.3d 183 (Cal. 2003). Until recently, such cases would have been unimaginable: the level of force required to satisfy the law was nearly impossible in a case in which sex had begun voluntarily.

47. California Penal Code §§ 243.4, 261, 261.5.

48. See Susan Brownmiller, Against Our Will: Men, Women, and Rape (New York: Bantam Books, 1976); Susan Estrich, Real Rape (Cambridge, MA: Harvard University

Press, 1987); Catharine A. MacKinnon, Toward a Feminist Theory of the State (Cambridge, MA: Harvard University Press, 1989).

49. Though these changes are often deemed not to have gone far enough. See Stephen J. Schulhofer, Unwanted Sex: The Culture of Intimidation and the Failure of Law (Cambridge, MA: Harvard University Press, 1998).

50. By the "guilty plea rate," I mean the percentage of convictions obtained by guilty plea rather than by trial. That rate is 96 percent in felony cases. See Online Sourcebook, table 5.57.2006. On the prison population, see Online Sourcebook, table 6.13.2009.

51. See, for example, Simon, Governing through Crime, 75.

52. Antonin Scalia, The Rule of Law as a Law of Rules, University of Chicago Law Review, vol. 56, 1175–88 (1989).

53. 18 U.S.C. § 1001. Congress has altered the language of the false statements statute several times, but not in a way that affected the "exculpatory no" issue.

54. See, for example, Moser v. United States, 18 F.3d 469 (7th Cir. 1994); United States v. Tabor, 788 F.2d 714 (11th Cir. 1986); United States v. Chevoor, 526 F.2d 178 (1st Cir. 1975); Paternostro v. United States, 311 F.2d 298 (5th Cir. 1962).

55. 522 U.S. 398 (1998).

56. See ibid., 399–400, 402–08. The reason for the agents' behavior—their belief that the labor racketeering charge might not hold up—goes unstated in the Court's opinion; the account in the text is speculative, though the speculation is more than plausible. If agents *weren't* seeking a backstop criminal charge, their conduct makes no sense.

57. American Law Institute, Model Penal Code (1962). The official draft, with some modest revision from the 1962 version, was issued in 1980. For a good statement of Wechsler's goals for the MPC, see Herbert Wechsler, The Challenge of a Model Penal Code, Harvard Law Review, vol. 65, 1097–133 (1952).

58. Wechsler and coauthor Jerome Michael famously but incorrectly wrote of that standard: "'malice aforethought' [is] a term of art signifying neither malice nor forethought . . ." Herbert Wechsler and Jerome Michael, A Rationale of the Law of Homicide, Columbia Law Review, vol. 37, 701–61, at 707 (1938).

59. As of 1997, a mere eleven states had adopted the Code's key provision: the establishment of recklessness as the default intent standard for all crimes. See Dannye Holley, The Influence of the Model Penal Code's Culpability Provisions on State Legislatures: A Study of Lost Opportunities, Including Abolishing the Mistake of Fact Doctrine, Southwestern University Law Review, vol. 27, 229–62, at 243 and note 40 (1997). The numbers have changed little since that date; most of the MPC-influenced code revisions had happened by the late 1970s. See Holley, Influence of the Model Penal Code, at 236 note 21; Model Penal Code and Commentaries, at xi (Official Draft and Revised Comments, 1985).

60. 196 F.3d 687 (7th Cir. 1999).

61. Ibid., 689–92.

62. 48 P.3d 555 (Colo. 2002).

63. Ibid., 557–59 and note 1.

64. See Online Sourcebook, tables 6.0001.2006 (20 percent of state prisoners are incarcerated on drug charges); 6.0023.2009 (52 percent of federal prisoners are incarcer-

ated on drug charges); 6.29.2008 (showing state and federal imprisonment rates of 445 and 60, respectively); 6.28.2009 (total imprisonment rate in 1975 stood at 111).

65. Officials Say Vow Kept with Arrests—22 Gang Members Now in Custody, Boston Globe, May 25, 2007, at B4.

66. Tracey L. Meares, Neal Katyal, and Dan M. Kahan, Updating the Study of Punishment, Stanford Law Review, vol. 56, 1171–210, at 1178 and note 22 (2004).

67. See Nancy E. Marion, Rethinking Federal Criminal Law: Symbolic Policies in Clinton's Crime Control Agenda, Buffalo Criminal Law Review, vol. 1, 67–108, at 97 (1997); Daniel C. Richman and William J. Stuntz, Al Capone's Revenge: An Essay on the Political Economy of Pretextual Prosecution, Columbia Law Review, vol. 105, 583–639, at 598–99 (2005) (quoting speech by then–Attorney General John Ashcroft, noting and endorsing this policy). This approach has made the federal law of gun registration and possession a de facto federal law of violent crime. See Daniel C. Richman, The Past, Present, and Future of Violent Crime Federalism, Crime and Justice, vol. 34, 377–439 (2006).

68. More whites than blacks are convicted of drug felonies in state courts. See Online Sourcebook, table 5.45.2004. Yet the ratio of black to white drug prisoners in state penitentiaries is more than three to two (ibid., table 6.0001.2004).

69. See Roger Lane, Violent Death in the City: Suicide, Accident, and Murder in Nineteenth-Century Philadelphia, 2nd ed., at 81 (Columbus: Ohio State University Press, 1979), which notes that 91 percent of homicides were cleared in mid-twentieth-century Philadelphia, a figure "very close to that reported for other cities in the same period"; Roger Lane, Murder in America: A Historian's Perspective, Crime and Justice, vol. 25, 191–224, at 208–10 (1999).

70. See Paul G. Cassell and Richard Fowles, Handcuffing the Cops? A Thirty-Year Perspective on *Miranda*'s Harmful Effects on Law Enforcement, Stanford Law Review, vol. 50, 1055–145, at 1066–70 and figures 1 and 2 (1998).

71. See Miranda v. Arizona, 384 U.S. 436 (1966); Massiah v. United States, 377 U.S. 201 (1964). At the same time, silence became a more viable litigation strategy. See Griffin v. California, 380 U.S. 609 (1965) (barring comment on defendant's failure to testify).

72. For a telling example, see Sudhir Alladi Venkatesh, Off the Books: The Underground Economy of the Urban Poor, at 302–18 (Cambridge, MA: Harvard University Press, 2006). In these pages, Venkatesh tells the story of a gang murder; the victim's brother witnessed the killing and was left alive. Nevertheless, no one was ever prosecuted for the homicide. Not long afterward, Venkatesh asked a local minister whether "Big Cat," leader of the local gang, was responsible. The minister's answer was telling: "If I say yes, you'll ask me how do I know . . . *I* know, *we* know, the *community* knows." Quoted ibid., 318 (emphasis in original).

73. See Dickerson v. United States, 530 U.S. 428 (2000); Davis v. Washington, 547 U.S. 813 (2006); Crawford v. Washington, 541 U.S. 36 (2004).

74. See, for example, William J. Stuntz, Race, Class, and Drugs, Columbia Law Review, vol. 98, 1795–842, at 1813–15 (1998).

75. For the legal side of this equation, see David A. Sklansky, Cocaine, Race, and Equal Protection, Stanford Law Review, vol. 47, 1283–322 (1995). On the character of the relevant drug markets, see Stuntz, Race, Class, and Drugs, 1804–15.

76. The Mann Act banned illicit sex plus interstate travel; the point of the prohibition was to punish interstate prostitution.

77. In 1970, there were roughly 10 prisoners incarcerated for drug crimes per 100,000 population. See Cahalan, Historical Corrections Statistics, 30, table 3-3; 45, table 3-17. By 2002, that figure stood at 102. See Online Sourcebook, tables 6.0001.2002, 6.29.2006. On rates of drug punishment by race, see Online Sourcebook, table 6.0001.2006; 2008 Statistical Abstract, 9, table 6. On rates of drug crime by race, see Substance Abuse and Mental Health Services Administration, U.S. Department of Health and Human Services, Results from the 2008 National Survey on Drug Use and Health: National Findings, NSDUH Series H-36, HHS Publication No. SMA 09-4434, at 25 (Rockville, MD: Office of Applied Studies, 2009). The number of murders in 2006, by race of the offender, appears in Crime in the United States: 2006, Expanded Homicide Data, table 3. The general population for 2006, by race, appears in 2008 Statistical Abstract, table 6. The rates stated in the text assume that murders by offenders of unknown race were committed by whites and blacks in the same proportion as murders by offenders whose race is known.

78. See Caminetti v. United States, 242 U.S. 470, 483 (1917); Lawrence v. Texas, 539 U.S. 558 (2003).

79. See Robert Post, Federalism, Positive Law, and the Emergence of the American Administrative State: Prohibition in the Taft Court Era, William and Mary Law Review, vol. 48, 1–182, at 83–137 (2006).

80. See, for example, John DiIulio, Help Wanted: Economists, Crime, and Public Policy, Journal of Economic Perspectives, vol. 10, 3–24, at 8 (1996); James Q. Wilson, Crime and Public Policy, in James Q. Wilson and Joan Petersilia, eds., Crime, 489–510, at 507 (San Francisco: ICS Press, 1995).

81. Steven D. Levitt, Understanding Why Crime Fell in the 1990s: Four Factors That Explain the Decline and Six That Do Not, Journal of Economic Perspectives, vol. 18, 163–90 (2004).

82. Uniform Crime Reports: 1991, 13 (showing a murder rate of 9.8 per 100,000), 35 (showing felony property crime rate of 5,140); Crime in the United States: 2000, 14 (showing a murder rate that had fallen to 5.5), 38 (felony property crime rate had fallen to 3,618).

83. In 2008, New York's murder rate stood at 6.3 per 100,000; the city's murder rate in 1950 was 3.7. See Crime in the United States: 2008, tables 1 and 8; Monkkonen's data.

84. The figures are taken from Crime in the United States—2008, tables 1 and 8. The 2008 murder rates for the nine cities are as follows: Atlanta, 20; Boston, 10; Chicago, 18; Denver, 7; Detroit, 34; Houston, 13; Los Angeles, 10; New York, 6; Philadelphia, 23. Boston, Denver, Houston, and Philadelphia all saw their murder rates rise; the other five cities saw those rates fall. All rates are per 100,000 population.

85. See Fox Butterfield, Punitive Damages: Crime Keeps on Falling, but Prisons Keep on Filling, New York Times, September 28, 1997, section 4, at 1; Fox Butterfield,

Prison Population Growing although Crime Rate Drops, New York Times, August 9, 1998, section 1, at 18.

86. See, for example, Thomas Sowell, Criminal Counts, National Review Online, March 11, 2008, available at www.nationalreview.com/articles/223886/criminal -counts/thomas-sowell; George F. Will, More Prisoners, Less Crime, Washington Post, June 22, 2008, at B7.

87. See Phillip Pina, Drug War, Crime on Many Minds, USA Today, December 12, 1995, at 1D; Frank Newport, American Perceptions of Economic Conditions and Crime Reach New Highs of Optimism, Gallup News Service, November 22, 1997; Lydia Saad, Fear of Conventional Crime at Record Lows, Gallup News Service, October 22, 2001.

88. See Daniel Richman, The Right Fight, Boston Review, December 2004–January 2005, at 6.

89. The relevant provision is 42 U.S.C. § 14141. Section 14141 was part of the Violent Crime Control and Law Enforcement Act of 1994, Pub. L. No. 103–322, 108 Stat. 1796.

90. Ken Armstrong and Steve Mills, Ryan Suspends Death Penalty; Illinois First State to Impose Moratorium on Executions, Chicago Tribune, January 31, 2000, at 1.

91. On state anti-profiling laws, see Police Foundation, Racial Profiling: The State of the Law (March 2005). On some state legislatures' decisions to find ways to save money by reducing the size of their prison populations, see, for example, Rachel E. Barkow, Administering Crime, UCLA Law Review, vol. 52, 715–814 (2005).

92. Save for the last, all the arguments advanced in this paragraph are surveyed in Levitt, Understanding Why Crime Fell. The "cyclical forces" theory is advanced in Franklin E. Zimring, The Great American Crime Decline, at vi (New York: Oxford University Press, 2007).

93. See Levitt, Understanding Why Crime Fell, 170–71, 173–75.

94. For the original abortion theory, see John Donohue and Steven Levitt, The Impact of Legalized Abortion on Crime, Quarterly Journal of Economics, vol. 116, 379–420 (2001). For a detailed analysis of the relationship among abortion rates, teenage fertility, and crime rates, see Anindya Sen, Does Increased Abortion Lead to Lower Crime? Evaluating the Relationship between Crime, Abortion, and Fertility, B. E. Journal of Economic Analysis and Policy, vol. 7, 1–36 (2007).

95. Levitt, Understanding Why Crime Fell, 178–79; Western, Punishment and Inequality, 180–85.

96. See Online Sourcebook, table 6.28.2009.

97. Levitt, Understanding Why Crime Fell, 179; Bruce Western, Race, Crime, and Punishment, Cato Unbound, March 18, 2009, available online at www.cato-unbound. org/2009/03/18/bruce-western/race-crime-and-punishment/.

98. For Levitt's estimate, see Levitt, Understanding Why Crime Fell, 176–77. The rate of police officers per 100,000 population rose 10 percent from 1990 to 2000. Uniform Crime Reports: 1990, 239, table 66; Uniform Crime Reports: 2000, 293, table 71. The increase between 1989 and 1999 was 17 percent. Uniform Crime Reports: 1989, 238, table 66; Crime in the United States—1999, 293, table 71. If one uses the

higher of those two figures to calculate the policing cost associated with a 1 percent drop in crime (based on Levitt's estimated crime drop), the figure in the text rises to between $1.2 billion and $1.4 billion. On the 1990s increase in the imprisonment rate, see Online Sourcebook, table 6.28.2009.

99. The figures in the text use 2000 dollars and the budget numbers in 2003 Sourcebook, 4, table 1.3.

100. The relevant data are based on the figures compiled in the "city arrests" tables in the annual volumes of FBI, Crime in the United States. The year the arrest rate peaked was 1990; the drop in arrests hit its trough in 2003.

101. For a good discussion of the rise of community policing and the various meanings of the term, see David Alan Sklansky, Democracy and the Police, at 82–105, 114–24 (Stanford, CA: Stanford University Press, 2007). For the canonical works that preceded and, to some degree, precipitated that rise, see Herman Goldstein, Improving Policing: A Problem Oriented Approach, Crime and Delinquency, vol. 25, 236–58 (1979); Herman Goldstein, Problem Oriented Policing (New York: McGraw-Hill, 1990).

102. See Online Sourcebook, table 1.4.2006.

103. The rate of police officers per 100,000 population rose from 219 in 1990 to 240 in 2000; the rate peaked at 246 in 1999. See Uniform Crime Reports: 1990, 239, table 66; Crime in the United States—1999, 293, table 71; Crime in the United States—2000, 293, table 71. As of 2009, the rate stood at 231. Crime in the United States—2009, table 71. Since 2000, the nation's imprisonment rate has risen from 478 per 100,000 to 504. Online Sourcebook, table 6.28.2009.

10. FIXING A BROKEN SYSTEM

1. Paul Butler, Racially Based Jury Nullification: Black Power in the Criminal Justice System, Yale Law Journal, vol. 105, 677–725, at 680 (1995); Paul Butler, Black Jurors: Right to Acquit? Harper's Magazine, December 1995, at 11.

2. Editorial, When Jurors Ignore the Law, New York Times, May 27, 1997, at A16.

3. For a sample of the academic criticism, see Jeffrey Abramson, Two Ideals of Jury Deliberation, University of Chicago Legal Forum, vol. 1998, 125–60, at 145–52; Andrew D. Leipold, The Dangers of Race-Based Jury Nullification: A Response to Professor Butler, UCLA Law Review, vol. 44, 109–41 (1996); Nancy S. Marder, The Myth of the Nullifying Jury, Northwestern University Law Review, vol. 93, 877–959, at 937–47 (1999); Frank I. Michelman, "Racialism" and Reason, Michigan Law Review, vol. 95, 723–40, at 733–34 (1997).

4. As Darryl Brown has explained, those propositions are (to say the least) debatable. Darryl K. Brown, Jury Nullification within the Rule of Law, Minnesota Law Review, vol. 81, 1149–200 (1997). But they remain the conventional wisdom. For an aggressive defense of that conventional wisdom, see Andrew D. Leipold, Rethinking Jury Nullification, Virginia Law Review, vol. 82, 253–324 (1996).

5. In 2008, the number of local police officers and prison inmates per 100,000 population stood at 232 and 504, respectively. Online Sourcebook, table 6.28.2009; Uni-

form Crime Reports: 1989, at 238, table 66. In 1880, the average number of police officers per 100,000 population in the nation's ten largest cities was 152. See Lawrence Friedman and Robert V. Percival, The Roots of Justice: Crime and Punishment in Alameda County, California, 1870–1910, at 78, table 4.2 (Chapel Hill: University of North Carolina Press, 1981). Nationwide, the number of prisoners per 100,000 stood at 61. Margaret Werner Cahalan, Historical Corrections Statistics in the United States, 1850–1984, at 30, table 3-3 (Rockville, MD: Bureau of Justice Statistics, 1986). For the more nearly even ratios that were common in the South and West, see Figure 4 in Chapter 5.

6. New York City's policing rate rose from 367 officers per 100,000 population in 1990 to 508 in 1997. See Uniform Crime Reports: 1990, at 101, table 6; 278, table 72; Crime in the United States: 1997, at 146, table 8; 347, table 78. On the city's crime drop, see Franklin E. Zimring, The Great American Crime Decline, at 136–41 (New York: Oxford University Press, 2007). New York State's imprisonment rate stood at 304 in 1990, rising to 400 in 1999, then falling to 307 in 2008. Online Sourcebook, table 6.29.2008.

7. The percentages are calculated based on data in Uniform Crime Reports: 1991, at 68–78, table 5; Crime in the United States: 2000, at 76–84, table 5; and Online Sourcebook, table 6.29.2008.

8. Regarding the rise in New York's policing rate, see the figures in the preceding note, which show a 38 percent increase between 1990 and 1997. During the same years, the ratio of nondrug felony arrests to index crimes (violent felonies plus felony thefts) improved dramatically—from 14 percent to 25 percent—and felony drug arrests fell 13 percent. See Jeffrey Fagan et al., Neighborhood, Crime, and Incarceration in New York City, Columbia Human Rights Law Review, vol. 36, 71–107, at 76, table 1 (2004).

9. See Robert L. Misner, Recasting Prosecutorial Discretion, Journal of Criminal Law and Criminology, vol. 86, 717–77 (1996).

10. See Online Sourcebook, table 1.4.2006.

11. On the limited benefit of bigger school budgets, see, for example, Eric A. Hanushek, Assessing the Effects of School Resources on Student Performance: An Update, Educational Evaluation and Policy Analysis, vol. 19, no. 2, 141–64 (1997). On the effects of hiring more police officers, see, for example, Steven D. Levitt, Understanding Why Crime Fell in the 1990s: Four Factors That Explain the Decline and Six That Do Not, Journal of Economic Perspectives, vol. 18, 163–90, at 176–77 (2004).

12. See David A. Sklansky, The Private Police, UCLA Law Review, vol. 46, 1165–287, at 1171–77 (1999); see also David Alan Sklansky, Private Police and Democracy, American Criminal Law Review, vol. 43, 89–105 (2006).

13. The stimulus bill authorized $4 billion for local police forces. See David A. Harris, What Criminal Law and Procedure Can Learn from Criminology: How Accountability-Based Policing Can Reinforce—or Replace—the Fourth Amendment Exclusionary Rule, Ohio State Journal of Criminal Law, vol. 7, 149–213, at 186 (2009).

14. The second time, the investment in more local police also helped to spur falling crime and helped to slow the rise of imprisonment. In 1994, when the legislation was

enacted, the nation's homicide rate stood at 9 per 100,000. By 2000, that rate had fallen to 5.5 (Crime in the United States: 2001, table 1), the steepest decline in homicides in sixty years. The late 1990s also saw the nation's imprisonment rate rise 21 percent: at that point, the smallest six-year increase since prison populations began their upward climb in 1973 (Online Sourcebook, table 6.28.2009).

15. The 1994 legislation appropriated $8.8 billion over six years for aid to local police forces. For this and other details of the Act, see Harry A. Chernoff et al., The Politics of Crime, Harvard Journal on Legislation, vol. 33, 527–79 (1996). Using 2000 budget figures, that amount paid for just under 18,000 local police officers per year during those six years. See 2003 Sourcebook, 4, table 1.3; 37, table 1.26.

16. As of 2004—the most recent year for which the Sourcebook of Criminal Justice Statistics offers complete data—there were 731,903 full-time state and local police officers in the United States, plus an additional 86,627 federal officers (not counting federal prison guards). See Online Sourcebook, tables 1.27.2004, 1.72.2004. That total amounted to 279 officers per 100,000 population. See 2007 Statistical Abstract, 7, table 2. Adding 100,000 officers would have increased the nation's policing rate to 313 (ibid.). On the European policing rate in 2004, see European Sourcebook of Crime and Criminal Justice Statistics: 2010, 113, table 1.2.4.1, for the median policing rate of 351 officers per 100,000 population.

17. See Online Sourcebook, tables 1.4.2006, 1.27.2004.

18. 92 U.S. 542 (1876).

19. *McCleskey,* 481 U.S. 279 (1987); *Castle Rock,* 545 U.S. 748 (2005).

20. For a chilling example of a violent raid gone wrong—the mayor of a town in Prince George's County, Maryland, was mistakenly targeted in a drug raid—see April Witt, "Deadly Force; What a SWAT Team Did to Cheye Calvo's Family May Seem Extreme, but Decades into America's War on Drugs, It's Business as Usual," Washington Post Magazine, February 1, 2009, at 8. With respect to stop-and-frisks, a late 1990s study of police stops in New York found that only one-ninth of such stops led to arrests. State of New York, Office of the Attorney General, Civil Rights Bureau, The New York City Police Department's "Stop & Frisk" Practices: A Report to the People of the State of New York from the Office of the Attorney General, at 111 (1999).

21. Herman Goldstein, Improving Policing: A Problem Oriented Approach, Crime and Delinquency, vol. 25, 236–58 (1979); Herman Goldstein, Problem Oriented Policing (New York: McGraw-Hill, 1990).

22. James Q. Wilson and George Kelling, Broken Windows, Atlantic Monthly, March 1982, at 29–38; see also George Kelling and Catherine Coles, Fixing Broken Windows (New York: Free Press, 1996). For a more skeptical take on the thesis, see Bernard E. Harcourt, Illusion of Order: The False Promise of Broken Windows Policing (Cambridge, MA: Harvard University Press, 2005).

23. Damien Cave, Troops Cut Death, but Not Fear, in Baghdad Zone, New York Times, September 4, 2006, at A1.

24. On the equation between the two, see Ganesh Sitaraman, The Counterinsurgent's Constitution: Law in the Age of Small Wars, at ch. 6, "The Organic Rule of Law" (Cambridge, MA: Harvard University Press, forthcoming 2011). The literature on

community policing is massive; even a fair sampling would be too much for a single footnote. For insightful discussions from two different perspectives, the first celebratory and the second mildly skeptical, see Tracey L. Meares, Praying for Community Policing, California Law Review, vol. 90, 1593–634 (2002); David Alan Sklansky, Democracy and the Police, at 82–105, 114–24 (Stanford, CA: Stanford University Press, 2007).

25. On Chicago, see Meares, Praying for Community Policing, 1594–95. On the mix of carrots and sticks used to send signals to gang members, see Anthony A. Braga and David M. Kennedy, Reducing Gang Violence in Boston, in Winifred L. Reed and Scott H. Decker, eds., Responding to Gangs: Evaluation and Research, at 265–88 (Washington, DC: National Institute of Justice, 2002).

26. On the breadth of the idea of community policing, see Sklansky, Democracy and the Police, 114–24.

27. As of 2009, 38 percent of black respondents reported having "a great deal" or "quite a lot" of confidence in the police, compared to 58 percent who had "some" or "very little" (Online Sourcebook, table 2.12.2009). In 1970, blacks rated the police unfavorably by a margin of 50 to 43 percent (1974 Sourcebook at 189 table 2.48). The black imprisonment rate stood at 361 per 100,000 in 1970. See Cahalan, Historical Corrections Statistics, 65, table 3-31; 1972 Statistical Abstract, at 16, no. 15. In 2008, the imprisonment rate among non-Hispanic blacks was roughly 1,600 per 100,000 (Online Sourcebook, table 6.33.2008).

28. Jim Whitman reports that average time served for French prisoners stood at 8 months in 1999; in 1975 the figure had been a little over 4 months. James Q. Whitman, Harsh Justice: Criminal Punishment and the Widening Divide between America and Europe, at 70 (New York: Oxford University Press, 2003). Average time served in American state prisons was 53 months in 1999 (2003 Sourcebook, 510, table 6.43). The analogous figure was 28 months in 1960 (Cahalan, Historical Corrections Statistics, 52, table 3-23).

29. On the racial breakdown of the inmate population, see Online Sourcebook, table 6.33.2008. On the racial breakdown of the general population, see 2010 Statistical Abstract, table 10.

30. On initiatives to cut down the number of inmates who are ex-parolees or ex-probationers, see Jeffrey Rosen, Prisoners of Parole, New York Times Magazine, January 10, 2010, at 36. For a discussion of California's use of anti-gang injunctions, see Kim Strosnider, Anti-Gang Ordinances after *Chicago v. Morales:* The Intersection of Race, Vagueness Doctrine, and Equal Protection in the Criminal Law, American Criminal Law Review, vol. 39, 101–44 (2002).

31. Frank O. Bowman III, Beyond Band-Aids: A Proposal for Reconfiguring Federal Sentencing after *Booker,* University of Chicago Legal Forum, vol. 2005, 149–216, at 157. Bowman notes that this is a far greater number of sentencing categories than in any state's system of sentencing law.

32. 543 U.S. 220 (2005).

33. *Booker* produced two majority opinions. The first, by Justice Stevens, held that prior practice under the Guidelines was unconstitutional; the second, authored

by Justice Breyer, rendered the Guidelines advisory. Ibid., 226–44 (majority opinion authored by Justice Stevens), 244–71 (majority opinion authored by Justice Breyer).

34. See Gall v. United States, 552 U.S. 38 (2007). The consequence is that vastly more defendants are sentenced below the specified guideline range than are sentenced above that range. See, for example, Paul J. Hofer, How Well Do Sentencing Commission Statistics Help in Understanding the Post-*Booker* System?, Federal Sentencing Reporter, vol. 22, no. 2, 89–95, at 91, table 1 (December 2009).

35. According to the FBI's most current data on homicides, the homicide rate among blacks is seven times the homicide rate for the rest of the population. See Crime in the United States: 2009, Expanded Homicide Data, table 3; for population data, see 2010 Statistical Abstract, table 10.

36. According to the government's data, 9.6 percent of blacks, 8.8 percent of whites, and 7.9 percent of Latinos use illegal drugs on a regular basis. Substance Abuse and Mental Health Services Administration, Results from the 2009 National Survey on Drug Use and Health: Volume I. Summary of National Findings 23 (Rockville, MD: Office of Applied Studies, 2010).

37. For an early example of the academic argument for this change, see David A. Sklansky, Cocaine, Race, and Equal Protection, Stanford Law Review, vol. 47, 1283–322 (1995). Federal law has changed on this issue; the ratio is now 18 to 1 rather than 100 to 1. See Fair Sentencing Act of 2010, Pub. L. No. 111–220, 124 Stat. 2372 (August 3, 2010). It should be closer to 1 to 1.

38. *McCleskey*, 481 U.S. 279 (1987); *Armstrong*, 517 U.S. 456 (1996).

39. 130 S. Ct. 2011 (2010).

40. Ibid., 2024.

41. See Rachel E. Barkow, Administering Crime, UCLA Law Review, vol. 52, 715–814 (2005); Rachel E. Barkow, Federalism and the Politics of Sentencing, Columbia Law Review, vol. 105, 1276–314 (2005).

42. With respect to the number of prosecutors, see Bureau of Justice Statistics, U.S. Department of Justice, Prosecutors in State Courts, 1990, at 1–2 (1992); Online Sourcebook, table 1.85.2005. For the guilty plea rate in the mid-1970s and in the mid-2000s, see David A. Jones, Crime Without Punishment, 44, table 4-1 (1979); Online Sourcebook, table 5.57.2006. With respect to the number of felony prosecutions, the 300,000 figure is extrapolated from several other figures. Between 1978 and 1991, the number of felony prosecutions rose by something in excess of 105 percent; 120 to 125 percent is a reasonable estimate. See National Center for State Courts, State Court Caseload Statistics: Annual Report 1984, 189–90, table 35 (1986); National Center for State Courts, State Court Caseload Statistics: Annual Report 1991, 37, table 1.25 (1993). In the early 1990s, that number stood at between 800,000 and 900,000 per year. See 1993 Sourcebook, 535, table 5.55. It seems reasonable to suppose that felony prosecutions rose at least 20 to 25 percent during the period between 1974 and 1978; the prison population rose more than that, and average sentences were not rising substantially during those years. Put these facts together, and something in the neighborhood of 300,000 prosecutions per year in the mid-1970s is a reasonable estimate.

43. Initially, it did not seem so. In Powell v. Alabama, 287 U.S. 45 (1932), the Supreme Court overturned criminal convictions of defendants who were assigned counsel on the day of trial; the heart of the constitutional error was that defendants did not receive the *amount* of representation the Sixth Amendment requires. A line of cases beginning with United States v. Cronic, 466 U.S. 648 (1984), aims to protect that right, but the protection is illusory. See Bell v. Cone, 535 U.S. 685 (2002).

44. See Constance L. Hays, Martha Stewart Indicted by U.S. on Obstruction, New York Times, June 5, 2003, at A1; David Carr and Claudia H. Deutsch, The Stewart Verdict—The Company: A Harsh Blow to a Company Based on Image, New York Times, March 6, 2004, at A1.

45. See Daniel C. Richman and William J. Stuntz, Al Capone's Revenge: An Essay on the Political Economy of Pretextual Prosecution, Columbia Law Review, vol. 105, 583–639, at 620–21 (2005).

46. For a more extended version of this argument, see ibid., 618–24.

47. Attorney General John Ashcroft, Prepared Remarks for the U.S. Mayors' Conference, October 25, 2001 (available at www.justice.gov/archive/ag/speeches/2001/agcrisisremarks10_25.htm).

48. The phrase is borrowed from Stephanos Bibas, Plea Bargaining outside the Shadow of Trial. For the classic discussion of (federal) plea bargaining as an autonomous system of adjudication, see Gerard Lynch, Our Administrative System of Criminal Justice, Fordham Law Review, vol. 66, 2117–51 (1998).

49. The leading cases are Crawford v. Washington, 541 U.S. 36 (2004); Davis v. Washington, 547 U.S. 813 (2006); and Melendez-Diaz v. Massachusetts, 129 S. Ct. 2527 (2009).

50. See Apprendi v. New Jersey, 530 U.S. 466 (2000); Blakely v. Washington, 542 U.S. 296 (2004); United States v. Booker, 543 U.S. 220 (2005).

51. For representative examples, see United States v. Coffman, 62 M.J. 677 (N.-M. Ct. Crim. App. 2006); United States v. Oglivie, 29 M.J. 1069 (A.C.M.R. 1990). For a state-court case applying a similar standard to the review of a guilty plea, see State v. Schminkey, 597 N.W.2d 785 (Iowa 1999).

52. The Supreme Court took a step in this direction with its decision in Halbert v. Michigan, 545 U.S. 605 (2005). *Halbert* holds that indigent defendants who plead guilty are constitutionally entitled to state-paid counsel on direct appeal—a necessary condition of the kind of review the military employs.

53. No doubt legislators would impose strict liability more often. But expressly legislated strict liability would be more transparent than the current regime, which has the functional character of strict liability but retains formal intent standards. Plus, at least sometimes, legislators would permit the older intent standard to stand—which would be a large gain for the cause of justice.

54. The leading case is United States v. Viola, 35 F.3d 37, 43 (2d Cir. 1994), where the court held that an errand-boy for a Mob boss could not be found to have "participate[d], directly or indirectly, in the conduct of the affairs" of the boss's criminal enterprise under 18 U.S.C. § 1962(c).

55. See George P. Fletcher, Rethinking Criminal Law, at 779–98 (1978; repr., New York: Oxford University Press, 2000).

56. That proposition probably applies as much to sentencing rules as it does to liability rules. Especially federal sentencing rules: bright-line, severe sentencing rules make for more effective threats in plea negotiations and, over the past generation, federal sentencing law has been famously rulelike and severe. See, for example, Kate Stith and José A. Cabranes, Fear of Judging: Sentencing Guidelines in the Federal Courts (Chicago: University of Chicago Press, 1998). Recent changes in federal sentencing doctrine increase district judges' power over federal sentences. See Gall v. United States, 552 U.S. 38 (2007); Kimbrough v. United States, 552 U.S. 85 (2007); United States v. Booker, 543 U.S. 220 (2005). Over time, that should reduce federal law's effect on state-court plea bargains: a step toward both lenity and equality.

57. The Sixth Amendment's fair cross-section doctrine requires that jury venires represent the general population of the relevant jurisdiction. See Duren v. Missouri, 439 U.S. 357 (1979). Current equal protection law forbids the use of peremptory strikes against jurors because of their race or sex. See Miller-El v. Dretke, 545 U.S. 231 (2005); J.E.B. v. Alabama ex rel. T.B., 511 U.S. 127 (1994); Batson v. Kentucky, 476 U.S. 79 (1986).

58. More radical changes in jury selection might be needed. If jurors are chosen based on voter rolls and driver's licenses and if the urban poor appear more rarely on those lists, different means of selection might be a useful means of increasing jury representation among the urban poor.

59. On the law's ineffectiveness, see Miller-El v. Dretke, 545 U.S. 231, 266–73 (2005) (Breyer, J., concurring).

60. On the still-nascent community prosecution movement, see, for example, Brian Forst, Prosecutors Discover the Community, Judicature, vol. 84, 135–41 (November–December 2000); Kelley Bowden Gray, Community Prosecution: After Two Decades, Still New Frontiers, Journal of the Legal Profession, vol. 32, 199–214; Kay Levine, The New Prosecution, Wake Forest Law Review, vol. 40, 1125–214 (2005).

61. On the torched buildings, see Jones v. United States, 529 U.S. 848 (2000). On the robberies, see Craig M. Bradley, Federalism and the Federal Criminal Law, Hastings Law Journal, vol. 55, 573–611, at 592–98 (2004).

62. As Dave Barry is wont to say, I am not making this up. See United States v. Terry, 257 F.3d 366, 369–70 (4th Cir. 2001) (finding federal jurisdiction because the burned church ran a not-for-profit daycare center); ibid., at 373 (King, J., concurring in the judgment), agreeing, in part because the church ordered Sunday School materials from out of state; United States v. Rayborn, 312 F.3d 229, 234–35 (6th Cir. 2002), finding federal jurisdiction because the burned church broadcast its services on the radio, because some churchgoers may have crossed state lines on Sunday mornings, and—best of all—because the church owned a recreational vehicle; compare United States v. Lamont, 330 F.3d 1249, 1255 (9th Cir. 2003), concluding that most church arsons would not give rise to federal jurisdiction but arsons of "mega-churches" might.

63. Though immigration law is less exclusive than first appears. See Cristina M. Rodriguez, The Significance of the Local in Immigration Regulation, Michigan Law Review, vol. 106, 567–642 (2008).

64. See David A. Super, Rethinking Fiscal Federalism, Harvard Law Review, vol. 118, 2544–652 (2005). The major theme of Super's article is state and local governments' sensitivity to the business cycle. Federal spending is also sensitive to economic peaks and troughs, but in the opposite direction: when the economy tanks, federal spending rises. The consequence, as Super notes, is that other levels of government tend to undermine the federal fiscal stimulus (ibid., 2607–15). To put the point more positively, when state and local government spending falls, federal spending can cushion the blow.

65. The proposal was enacted—though with much less funding than Clinton sought—as the Violent Crime Control and Law Enforcement Act of 1994, Public Law No. 103–322, 108 Stat. 1796. Strangely, the proposed bill became known chiefly for its funding of so-called "midnight basketball" leagues in urban areas. For a good discussion of the bill and the politics surrounding it, see Chernoff et al., Politics of Crime.

66. For classic works taking this tack, see Vincent Blasi, The Pathological Perspective and the First Amendment, Columbia Law Review, vol. 85, 449–514 (1985); John Hart Ely, Democracy and Distrust: A Theory of Judicial Review (Cambridge, MA: Harvard University Press, 1980).

Acknowledgments

Bill turned in the final manuscript for this book in January 2011, about the time he went onto hospice care. He was able to confer with the Press editors and designers until a week or two before his death on March 15. His colleagues have seen the book through to publication. We are glad to be able to thank them, and everyone else who helped Bill with this book, from the beginning to the end.

In conversations, co-teaching, encouragement, support, careful reading, and constructive criticism, many colleagues over many years, from many disciplines, helped Bill clarify his ideas. He spent more than a decade each at the University of Virginia School of Law and Harvard Law School; he also visited at Yale and Columbia Law Schools. The colleagues at these schools, as well as the students, deans, and staff, were an integral part of his life and the life of his ideas. Bill also took his ideas on the road, when he was able to travel, and participated in numerous workshops, roundtables, and symposia. It is impossible to list everyone Bill would want to thank, so we will not try. We hope you know who you are.

Three people deserve special mention, however. Carol Steiker, Danny Richman, and Mike Klarman were loyal friends and intellectual sparring partners throughout Bill's career. His gratitude for their generosity in shepherding his manuscript through the final publication process is reflected in the book's dedication. The book is better for their help, but Bill would have taken responsibility for any errors.

Although Bill learned from his many students as well as from his colleagues, he would want to single out the Harvard Law School research assistants who worked on this book. He appreciated the intelligence, hard work, and dedication of Alan Cliff, Jennifer Dein, Mariana Jackson, Matthew Kelly, Joshua Matz, Caitlan McLoon, Rajiv Mohan, Jacob Robinson, Lindsay See, Shaud Tavakoli, Tim Taylor, and Connie Wu. Also at Harvard, Bill relied on the expert assistance of Janet C. Katz, senior research librarian, and was extremely grateful for both the assistance and the friendship of his extraordinarily able Harvard faculty assistant of the past three years, Lauren Chitwood Schauf.

The editorial staff at Harvard University Press was also tremendously supportive of Bill as he worked to complete this manuscript during his long illness. He appreciated the helpful comments of the four anonymous reviewers of his manuscript. He was especially grateful for the work of Elizabeth Knoll, senior editor for the behavioral sciences and law at HUP.

Over the course of his years of cancer treatment, Bill was tremendously grateful for the expertise and compassion of the doctors, nurses, technicians, and staff of his medical support team at the Cancer Center at Massachusetts General Hospital and the Hospice of the North Shore. Their goal of helping him do as well as possible for as long as possible enabled him to devote his last year to completing this project.

Bill also drew great strength from his church community, first at Christ the King Presbyterian Church in Cambridge, and more recently at the Park Street Church in Boston. The prayers and encouragement of pastors and other members of this fellowship meant a great deal to him, and to all our family.

Bill had an extraordinary number of friends, more than he realized. He was amazed and grateful for their love and support. As he wrote in 2008 in the blog he shared with David Skeel, "Less than the Least," he discovered in his illness "a host of friends, including more than a few I didn't know I had, coming out of the woodwork—offering blessing and support, assistance and encouragement, precisely as those things have been needed, all without my lifting a finger to ask for them."

We, along with his parents and siblings, were the recipients of those good things as well, and we are very grateful. We were doubly blessed to be Bill's inner circle and witness the way he devoted himself to this project, to teaching, and to us. We cared for him physically, but he continued to serve, comfort, and encourage us even in the face of difficult medical news. He always gave us his best. We are so thankful for the time we had with him and for this opportunity to celebrate his life's work.

Ruth Stuntz
Sarah Stuntz
Samuel and Elizabeth Cook-Stuntz
Andrew Stuntz

Index

Quantity favored over quality of criminal justice, 59, 299

Race riots: of mid- and late-1960s, 35, 233–234; after Civil War, 43
Racial profiling, 3, 22, 277
Racism, 21–22, 25, 136
Racketeering, 303
Rape cases. *See* Sexual assault cases
Reagan, Ronald, 216, 217, 236, 237–238, 239, 253, 374n66, 376n82
Reconstruction: fall of, 6, 43, 111–117; federal government role as criminal law enforcer during, 100; massacres during early years of, 101–107; as law enforcement success, 110. *See also* Fourteenth Amendment
Reconstruction Finance Corporation, 189
Recordkeeping of criminal cases, 214
Rector, Ricky Ray, 240
Reese; United States v. (1876), 114, 116–117
Regional differences. *See* North, the; South, the; The West in Gilded Age
Regulatory agencies, role of, 132
Rehnquist, William, 242
Reles, Abe, 189
Religions of migrants, 18, 25, 137–138
Resistance by victim, 263–264
Retreat rule, 155–156
Retributive justice, 55
Reynolds, George, 162–163
Reynolds v. United States (1879), 162–165, 172, 196, 356n14
Richards, Ann, 240
Richards, Joseph, 268
Rigged criminal process, 80–81
Riots. *See* Race riots
Ritchie, Albert, 149, 181
Rite of passage, imprisonment considered as, 54
Robberies, 50, 53, 262
Robinson v. California (1962), 210, 211
Rockefeller, Nelson, 239, 253
Roe v. Wade (1973), 185
Roosevelt, Franklin D., 185, 187, 361n81
Roosevelt, Theodore, 170
Roth, Randolph, 29, 321n9

Rule of law: collapse of, 2, 286; adherence to, in criminal sentencing, 298
Russia, imprisonment rates in, 50, 327n61. *See also* Soviet Union
Rust Belt decline, effect of, 27

Samuelson, Robert, 244
San Francisco and vigilance committees, 153
Scalia, Anton, 266, 267
Schmoke, Kurt, 181
School desegregation, 118–119, 221
Scottsboro Boys cases, 203–204
Scott v. Sandford. See Dred Scott (1857)
Search and seizure, 67, 72, 218–221, 368n65. *See also* Fourth Amendment
Search warrants, 67, 200, 224–225
Seditious libel, 70, 71, 72
Seidman, Louis Michael, 235
Self-defense, 118, 135–136, 140, 156
Self-help in law enforcement, 151
Self-incrimination, 67, 68, 70, 72, 126, 197, 205, 219, 366n38
Self-preservation, 56–59
Sentencing: mandatory minimums and guidelines, 32, 47, 259, 268, 295, 392n56; legislators deciding rules for, 65, 82; discretionary, 259, 296; Hawaii's experiment with probation violations, 295; preemption doctrine for, 306–307; by demographic groups, 350n39. *See also* Lenity; Prison population; Severity of punishment
Severity of punishment: move from leniency to, 2–3, 5, 31–32, 34, 248; and budget authority, 253, 254–257; and guilty pleas, 253; duration of, 253–254; reasons for, 253–267; future changes of, 294–295; equal imposition of, 298
Sex for profit and pleasure, 169–174
Sexual assault cases, 58, 140, 263–264, 335n61, 349n28, 381n46
Seymour, Horatio, 110
Sgro v. United States (1932), 200, 221
Shah of Iran, 29
Shakespeare, William, 29, 310
Shapiro v. United States (1948), 198